AFTER AMERICA

AFTER AMERICA

GET READY FOR ARMAGEDDON

★ ★ ★ ★ ★

MARK STEYN

Since 1947
REGNERY
PUBLISHING, INC.
An Eagle Publishing Company • Washington, DC

Library of Congress Cataloging-in-Publication Data

Steyn, Mark.
  After America / by Mark Steyn.
    p. cm.
  ISBN 978-1-59698-100-3
  1. United States--Politics and government--2009- 2. United States--Economic policy--2009- 3. United States--Economic conditions--21st century. 4. Obama, Barack. I. Title.
  E907.S72 2011
  973.932--dc23
                    2011023444

Published in the United States by
Regnery Publishing, Inc.
One Massachusetts Avenue, NW
Washington, DC 20001
www.regnery.com

Manufactured in the United States of America

10 9 8 7 6 5 4 3 2 1

Books are available in quantity for promotional or premium use. Write to Director of Special Sales, Regnery Publishing, Inc., One Massachusetts Avenue NW, Washington, DC 20001, for information on discounts and terms or call (202) 216-0600.

Distributed to the trade by:
Perseus Distribution
387 Park Avenue South
New York, NY 10016

CONTENTS

Prologue   The Stupidity of Broke...................................... 1

Chapter One   The New Rome.................................... 25

Chapter Two   Undreaming America............................. 45

Chapter Three   The New Athens 103

Chapter Four   Decline.. 127

Chapter Five   The New Britannia 189

Chapter Six   Fall.. 211

Chapter Seven   The New Jerusalem 269

Chapter Eight   After 279

Epilogue   The Hope of Audacity........................... 325

                    Acknowledgments.............................. 351

                    Notes 353

                    Index 405

THE STUPIDITY OF BROKE

There is the moral of all human tales;
'Tis but the same rehearsal of the past,
First Freedom, and then Glory—when that fails,
Wealth, vice, corruption—barbarism at last.
—**Lord Byron,** ***Childe Harold's Pilgrimage*** **(1812–1818)**

The sun'll come out tomorrow
Bet your bottom dollar
That tomorrow there'll be sun
—**Charles Strouse and Martin Charnin,** ***Annie*** **(1977)**

reviously on *Apocalypse Soon* …

It was the worst of times, it was the not quite so worst of times. The predecessor to this book was called *America Alone: The End of the World as We Know It*, and, given the title, you may be tempted to respond, "C'mon, man. You told us last time it was the end of the world. Well, where the hell is it? I want my money back. Instead, you come breezing in with this season's Armageddonouttahere routine. It's like Barbra Streisand farewell tours—there'll be another along next summer."

Well, now: *America Alone: The End of the World as We Know It* was about the impending collapse of all of the western world *except* America.

The good news is that the end of the rest of the West is still on schedule.

The bad news is that America shows alarming signs of embracing the same fate, and then some.

Nobody writes a doomsday tome because they want it to come true. From an author's point of view, the apocalypse is not helpful: the bookstores get looted and the collapse of the banking system makes it harder to cash the royalty check. But Cassandra's warnings were cursed to go unheeded, and so it seems are mine. Last time 'round, I wrote that Europe was facing a largely self-inflicted perfect storm that threatened the very existence of some of the oldest nation-states in the world. My warning proved so influential that America decided to sign up for the same program but supersized. Heigh-ho.

It starts with the money. In "The Run Upon the Bankers" (1720), Jonathan Swift wrote:

> A baited banker thus desponds,
> From his own hand foresees his fall,
> They have his soul, who have his bonds;
> 'Tis like the writing on the wall.

A lot of writing on the wall these days. Who has the bonds of a "developed world" developed to the point that it's institutionally conditioned to living beyond its means? Foreigners with money. So who's available and flush enough? The Chinese Politburo; Saudi sheikhs lubricated with oil but with lavish worldwide ideological proselytizing to fund; Russian "businessmen."… These are not the fellows one might choose to have one's bonds, never mind one's soul, but there aren't a lot of other options.

So it starts with the money—dry stuff about numbers and percentage of GDP. As Senator Michael Bennet of Colorado fumed to a room of voters in 2010, "We have managed to acquire $13 trillion of debt on our balance sheet. In my view, we have nothing to show for it."[1]

He's right—and $13 trillion is the lowest of lowball estimates. But why then did Senator Bennet vote for the "stimulus" and ObamaCare and all the other trillion-dollar binges his party blew through? Why did Senator Bennet string along and let the 111th Congress (2009–2011) run up more debt than the first one hundred Congresses (1789–1989) combined?[2] Panicked by pre-election polls into repudiating everything he'd been doing for the previous two years, the senator left it mighty late to rediscover his virtue. You would think that Colorado voters might have remembered that, like Groucho Marx apropos Doris Day, they knew Michael Bennet before he was a virgin. Alas, an indulgent electorate permitted the suddenly abstemious spendaholic to squeak back into office.

And, contra Senator Bennet, eventually you *do* have something to show for it. It starts with the money, but it doesn't stop there. It ends with a ruined and reprimitivized planet, in fewer easy stages than you might expect.

Let's take a thought by the economist Herbert Stein:

If something cannot go on forever, it will stop.[3]

This is a simple but profound observation. Dr. Stein first used it in the context of the long-ago debts and deficits of the Reagan era. "The Federal debt cannot rise forever relative to the GNP. Our foreign debt cannot rise forever relative to the GNP," he said. "But, of course, if they can't, they will stop." It was, as he later wrote, "a response to those who think that if something cannot go on forever, steps must be taken to stop it—even to stop it at once."[4] And he has a point: if something can't go on, you don't have to figure out a way to stop it, because it's going to stop anyway.

Eventually.

As you might have noticed, since he first made the observation, the debt has gone on rising, very dramatically. But the truth is unarguable. If you're careening along a road toward a collapsed bridge, you'll certainly stop, one way or the other. But it makes a difference, at least to you, whether you skid to a halt four yards before the cliff edge or whether you come to rest at the bottom of the ravine.

In 2010, Douglas Elmendorf, director of the Congressional Budget Office (CBO), described current U.S. deficits as "unsustainable."[5] On that everyone's agreed. So let's make them even more so! On assuming office, President Obama assured us, with a straight face, that his grossly irresponsible wastrel of a predecessor had taken the federal budget on an eight-year joyride. So the only way his sober, fiscally prudent successor could get things under control was to grab the throttle and crank it up to what Mel Brooks in *Spaceballs* (which seems the appropriate comparison) called "Ludicrous Speed." Let's head for the washed-out bridge, but at Obamacrous Speed!

The *Spendballs* plans of the Obama administration took the average Bush deficit for the years 2001–2008 and doubled it, all the way to 2020.[6] "We've got a big hole that we're digging ourselves out of," the president declared in 2011.[7] Usually, when you're in a hole, it's a good idea to stop digging. But, seemingly, to get out of the Bush hole, we needed to dig a hole twice as deep for one-and-a-half times as long. And that's according to the official projections of the president's economics czar, Ms. Rose Colored-Glasses. By 2020, the actual hole will be so deep that even if you toss every Obama speech down it on double-spaced paper you still won't be able to fill it up. In the spendthrift Bush days, federal spending as a proportion of GDP averaged 19.6 percent.[8] That's crazy. Obama's solution was to attempt to crank it up to 25 to 30 percent as a permanent feature of life. That's load up the suicide-bomber underpants and pass me the matches.

The CBO doesn't put it quite like that. Musing on the likelihood of a sudden fiscal crisis, it murmurs blandly, "The exact point at which such a crisis might occur for the United States is unknown, in part because the ratio of federal debt to GDP is climbing into unfamiliar territory."[9]

But it'll get real familiar real soon. A lot of the debate about America's date with destiny has an airy-fairy beyond-the-blue-horizon mid-century quality, all to do with long-term trends and other remote indicators. In fact, we'll be lucky to make it through the short-term in sufficient shape to get finished off by the long-term. According to CBO projections, by 2055 interest payments on the debt will exceed federal revenues.[10] But I don't think we'll need to worry about a "Government of the United States" at that stage. By 1788, Louis XVI's government in France was spending a mere 60 percent of revenues on debt service, and we know how that worked out for the House of Bourbon shortly thereafter.[11]

So take your eye off the far prospect, and instead look about fourteen inches in front of your toecap. Within a decade, the United States will be spending more of the federal budget on its interest payments than on its military. You read that right: more on debt service than on the armed services. According to the CBO's 2010 long-term budget outlook, by 2020 the government will be paying between 15 and 20 percent of its revenues in debt interest.[12] Whereas defense spending will be down to between 14 and 16 percent.

Just to clarify: we're not talking about paying down the federal debt, just keeping up with the annual interest charges on it. Yet within a decade the United States will be paying more in interest payments than it pays for the military—and that's not because the Pentagon is such a great bargain. In 2009, the United States accounted for over 43 percent of the world's military expenditures.[13] So America will be spending more on debt interest than China, Britain, France, Russia, Japan, Germany, Saudi Arabia, India, Italy, South Korea, Brazil, Canada, Australia, Spain, Turkey, and Israel spend on their militaries *combined*. The superpower will have evolved from a nation of aircraft carriers to a nation of debt carriers. The CBO numbers foresee net interest payments rising from 9 percent of revenue to 36 percent in 2030, then to 58 percent in 2040, and up to 85 percent in 2050.[14] If that trajectory holds, we'll be spending more than the planet's entire military budget on debt interest.

But forget mid-century—because, unless something changes, whatever goes by the name of "America" under those conditions isn't worth talking about.

By 2010, about half our debt was owned by foreigners, and somewhere over a quarter of that was held by the Chinese (officially).[15]

What does that mean? In 2010, the U.S. spent about $663 billion on its military, China about $78 billion.[16] If the People's Republic carries on buying

American debt at the rate it has in recent times, then within a few years U.S. interest payments on that debt will be covering the entire cost of the Chinese armed forces. In 2010, the Pentagon issued an alarming report to Congress on Beijing's massive military build-up, including new missiles, upgraded bombers, and an aircraft carrier research and development program intended to challenge U.S. dominance in the Pacific. What the report didn't mention is who's paying for it.[17]

Answer: Mr. and Mrs. America.

To return to the president's declared strategy: "We've got a big hole that we're digging ourselves out of." Every politician's First Rule of Holes used to be: When you're in one, stop digging. If you don't, as every child knows, eventually you dig so deep you come out on the other side of the world—someplace like, oh, China. By 2015 or so, the People's Liberation Army, which is the largest employer on the planet, bigger even than the U.S. Department of Community-Organizer Grant Applications, will be entirely funded by U.S. taxpayers.[18] As Bugs Bunny is wont to say when his tunnel comes out somewhere unexpected: "I musta took a wrong turn at Albuquerque." Indeed. When the Commies take Taiwan, suburban families in Albuquerque and small businesses in Pocatello will have paid for it.

And even that startling scenario is premised on the most optimistic assumptions—of resumed economic growth but continued low interest rates. If interest rates were to return to, say, 5.7 percent (the average for the period 1990–2010), the debt service projections for 2015 would increase from $290 billion to $847 billion.[19] China would be in a position to quadruple its military budget and stick U.S. taxpayers with the bill.

The existential questions for America loom not decades hence, but right now. It is not that we are on a luge ride to oblivion but that the prevailing political realities of the United States do not allow for any meaningful course correction. And, without meaningful course correction, America is doomed.

It starts with the money. It always does. P. G. Wodehouse fans will recall the passage in *Right Ho, Jeeves* in which Bertie Wooster's uncle, like many Americans today, is much preoccupied by the Exchequer's claim upon him:

"Is he still upset about that income-tax money?" asks Bertie.

"Upset is right," replies Aunt Dahlia. "He says that Civilization is in the melting-pot and that all thinking men can read the writing on the wall."

"What wall?"

"Old Testament, ass," snaps Aunt Dahlia. "Belshazzar's feast."

"Oh, that, yes," says Bertie. "I've often wondered how that gag was worked. With mirrors, I expect."

The gag with mirrors comes from the Book of Daniel: Babylon's king throws a wild party and, in the midst of his drunkenness, toasts the gods of gold, silver, and various other commodities. No sooner has he done so than the writing appears on the wall, spelling out with disembodied fingers "mene mene, tekel, upharsin." They're currency units: half-dollar, half-dollar, penny, and two bits. But what does it mean? None of the A-list seers Belshazzar keeps on the payroll has a clue what it portends, so the King calls in Daniel the Jew to explain things, which he does, very bluntly:

Mene: "God hath numbered thy kingdom, and finished it."

Tekel: "Thou art weighed in the balances, and art found wanting."

Upharsin: "Thy kingdom is divided, and given to the Medes and Persians."

Within twenty-four hours, Belshazzar is slain and Darius the Mede is king.

Today, the units are larger than in Babylon: "Mene mene, tekel, upharsin" is now trillion trillion, billion, half-trillion. But the upshot's the same. We've spent too much of tomorrow today—to the point where we've run out of tomorrow: fiscally, our days are numbered; structurally, we've been weighed in the balances and found wanting; and geopolitically, the Medes are thin on the ground but the Persians have gone nuclear.

★ ★ ★ ★ ★

MENE MENE...

So, if the deficits are "unsustainable," then what happens when they can no longer be sustained? A failure of bond auctions? A downgraded government debt rating? Reduced GDP growth? Total societal collapse? Mad Max on the New Jersey Turnpike?

Testifying to the House Budget Committee in 2010, CBO chief Douglas Elmendorf attempted to pull back from the wilder shores of "unsustainable": "I think most observers expect that the government will act, that the unsustainability will be resolved through action, not through witnessing some collapse down the road," he told the political grandees. "If literally nothing is done, then eventually something very, very bad happens. But I think the widespread view is that you and your colleagues will take action."[20]

Dream on, you kinky fantasist. If that's your *deus ex machina*, bet on Mad Max. As an example of the "action" being contemplated, Obama's Debt Commission produced a report melodramatically titled "The Moment of Truth"—and then proposed such "actions" as raising the age of Social Security eligibility to sixty-nine.[21]

By the year 2075.

As that "solution" suggests, the real problem is that over the last three-quarters of a century the United States has adopted a form of government all but impervious to reality. Come alternate Novembers, the American people have a choice between a fellow running on fluffy abstract nouns— "hope," "change," "generic gaseous uplift"—and a fellow promising small government. That's a best case scenario, by the way. Sometimes, as in 2008, you find yourself choosing between a candidate promising to guarantee the mortgages of people who "bought" houses they and their banks knew they couldn't afford, and a candidate promising to give "tax cuts" to millions of people who pay no taxes. But, assuming you did get a genuine choice, what is the net result of these two starkly different platforms?

None. In America, federal spending (in inflation-adjusted 2007 dollars) went from $600 billion in 1965 to $3 trillion in 2008.[22] Regardless.

The Heritage Foundation put it in a handy cut-out'n'weep graph: until the Democrats accelerated up to Obamacrous Speed in 2009, it's a near perfect straight line across four decades, up, up, up.[23] Doesn't make any difference who controls Congress, who's in the White House—Democrat,

Republican, bit of both. The government just grows and grows, remorselessly. A president of one party and a Congress of the other? Up and up it goes. So much for those sophists who hymn the virtues of "gridlock." Every two years, the voters walk out of their town halls and school gyms and tell the exit pollsters that three-quarters of them are "moderates" or "conservatives" (a clear center-right majority) and barely 20 percent are "liberals."[24] Sometimes, as in 1980, 1994, and 2010, they explicitly vote for small government. And then, on the Wednesday morning after the Tuesday night before, Big Government resumes its inexorable growth. Newt Gingrich and his dragon-slayers? According to a 2000 report by the Cato Institute, "the "combined budgets of the 95 major programs that the Contract with America promised to eliminate have increased by 13 percent."[25]

That's what's happened since the Sixties. What of the future? The CBO ran the longer-term numbers: The "alternative fiscal scenario," which factors in likely changes in policy, calculates that public debt will rise from 44 percent of GDP in 2008 to 716 percent by 2080.[26] Then again, the CBO's "extended-baseline scenario," which assumes there will be no changes to current policy, says public debt will only rise to 280 percent by 2080.

It doesn't matter which of these figures is correct, and it was a complete waste of time running the numbers. The worst case is 716 percent? And the best is 280 percent? That's a choice between dead and deader. Who cares? If either number is right, there isn't going to be a 2080, not for America.

You can spend a month ploughing through the CBO statistics, but the numbers don't matter because they all make the same point: under no likely scenario does America's debt burden do anything but go up. Whether it's Cloud-Cuckoo Land up or Planet Zongo up is mere details. Nothing is certain but debt and taxes. And then more debt. If the government of the United States had to use GAAP (the "Generally Accepted Accounting Practices" that your company and mine and the publishers of this book have to use), Uncle Sam would be under an SEC investigation and his nephews and nieces would have taken away the keys and cut up his credit cards. By 2010, the federal government was issuing about $100 billion of Treasury bonds every month—or, to put it another way, Washington is dependent on the bond markets being willing to absorb an increase in federal debt equivalent to the GDP of Canada or India—every year.[27] While India's growing its economy, we're growing our debt to match. We're asking the world to dump the equivalent of a G7 nation into U.S. Treasury debt every Christmas.

So let's take it to the next stage: we know American government has outspent America. What happens if it outspends the entire planet?

John Kitchen of the U.S. Treasury and Menzie Chinn of the University of Wisconsin published a study in 2010 entitled:

Financing U.S. Debt: Is There Enough Money in the World— and At What Cost?[28]

The fact that sane men are even asking this question ought to be deeply disturbing. As to the answer, foreign official holdings of U.S. Treasury securities have usually been less than 5 percent of the rest of the world's GDP. By 2009, they were up to 7 percent. By 2020, Kitchen and Chinn project them to rise to about 19 percent of the rest of the world's GDP, which they say is ... *do-able*.

Whether the rest of the world will want to do it is another matter. A future that presumes the rest of the planet will sink a fifth of its GDP into U.S. Treasuries is no future at all. But on Big Government's streetcar named Desire we have come to depend on the kindness of strangers.

If something cannot go on forever, it can still go on long enough—especially if you enjoy bookkeeping advantages the government denies to the private sector. And the idea that "you and your colleagues will take action" to reverse it, or at least end it, or maybe just slow it down a wee bit, flies in the face of that Heritage graph. The one thing that can be said for certain is that the political class, whether led by Barack Obama, Harry Reid, and Nancy Pelosi, or the usual reach-across-the-aisle Republican accommodationists, or even the Gingrichite revolutionaries of 1994, will not take meaningful, transformative action.

That leaves Director Elmendorf's alternative scenario. What was it again? Oh, yeah:

Some collapse down the road.

And you'll be surprised how short that road is.

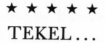

TEKEL...

Two propositions. First, Adam Smith, after the Battle of Saratoga, in reply to a friend despondent that the revolting colonials were going to be the ruin of Britain:

There is a great deal of ruin in a nation.[29]

Alternatively, Samuel Huntington in his final book, *Who Are We?*

A nation is a fragile thing.[30]

Who's right?

Smith's view is correct for a lot of European countries: The "deal of ruin"—incremental decay—is seductive. In some ways, the most pleasant place to live is a colossus in gradual decline. Great powers aren't Sudan or the Congo, where you're sliding from the Dump category to the Even Crummier Dump category. Genteel decline from the heights can be eminently civilized, especially to those of a leftish bent. Francophile Americans passing through bucolic Provençal villages with their charmingly state-regulated charcuteries and gnarled old peasants wholly subsidized by the European Union's Common Agricultural Policy can be forgiven for wondering if global hegemony is all it's cracked up to be. Okay, the empire busted up, but the capital still has magnificent architecture, handsome palaces, treasure houses of great art, a world-class orchestra, fabulous restaurants, stylish women.... You still have the opera house, but it's easier to get a parking space. Who wouldn't enjoy such "decline"? To be sure, everything new—or, anyway, everything new that works—is invented and made elsewhere. But still: you benefit from all the cultural inheritance of greatness without being troubled by any of its tedious responsibilities. Much of Europe feels like that: a sidewalk café, chestnuts in blossom, have another coffee and a pastry, and watch the world go by. Life is good, work is undemanding, vacation's coming up, war has been abolished. Somewhere beyond the horizon is a seething Muslim ghetto of 50 percent youth unemployment, whence the men swagger forth at sundown to torch the Renaults and Citroëns of the infidels.[31] But not in your *arrondissement*. And not even on the Friday afternoon drive to your country place. What's to worry about?

There may be a deal of it, but in the end ruin is the natural condition of the nation-state: three of the five permanent members of the Security Council have endured revolutionary upheaval and/or constitutional collapse since their "permanency" was established by the United Nations in 1945. Four of the G7 major economic powers have constitutions dating back barely half a century.

And, even if you escape (as most nations do not) coups, invasions, civil wars, and/or occupations, there arrives the moment when ruin comes to close the deal. Whether decline will seem quite so bucolic viewed from a Jersey strip mall rather than the Auvergne remains to be seen. But, either way, gradual decay is not the way it will go. American ruin will not be like France's or Austria's.

The exception to the Smith rule, and something closer to Huntington, is this: for dominant powers, ruin comes by the express lane. Unlike AIG, Fannie Mae, Detroit, and Greece, the United States *is* big enough to fail, spectacularly—and big enough to drag much of the world down with it. Most citizens of advanced western democracies haven't read Gibbon's *Decline and Fall of the Roman Empire*, but they figure they get the general idea. The "decline" bit of the title suggests you've got a bit of time before you get to the "fall," and actually, given that he took six volumes and covered a millennium and a half, that may be all the time you need. In fact, once the key elements were in place, the fall was very swift. By the time Odoacer took Rome in 476, the city's population had fallen by 75 percent in barely half a century—or the equivalent of the Beatles to now. Within a few years, a prototype "globalization" of European commerce had reverted to a subsistence economy of local agriculture.

The question to ask is: What's holding the joint up? A second- or third-tier nation—Iceland, for example—is generally resting on modest assumptions about its resources and economic outlook. There is a deal of it in a nation, but a superpower relies on subtler stocks, like image and credibility. If you're on a train going uphill and you're out of fuel, you'll still move forward—for a bit. By the time you notice you're slowing down, the coal's already gone. What comes next? You roll backwards, downhill, fast.

It starts with the money. For dominant powers, it always does—from the Roman Empire to the British Empire. "Declinism" is in the air these days, but we full-time apocalyptics are already well past that stage. In the space of one generation, a nation of savers became the world's largest debtors, and a nation of makers and doers became a cheap service economy. Everything that can be outsourced has been—manufacturing to by no means friendly nations overseas; and much of what's left in agriculture and construction to the armies of the "undocumented." At the lower end, Americans are educated at a higher cost per capita than any nation except Luxembourg in order to do minimal-skill checkout-line jobs about to be rendered obsolete by technology.[32] At the upper end, America's elite goes to school till early middle age in order to be credentialed for pseudo-employment as $350 grand-a-year diversity consultants (Michelle Obama) or in one of the many other make-work schemes deriving from government micro-regulation of virtually every aspect of endeavor.

So we're not facing "decline." We're already in it. What comes next is the "fall"—fast, sudden, off the cliff, if only because the Obama spending binge made what was vague and distant explicit and immediate. America has squandered its supposedly unipolar moment on the world's most expensive suicide. What is happening to the United States is not "cyclical," but structural. Like Belshazzar's Babylon, when you weigh us in the balances, we're seriously wanting. Under a ruling class comprehensively inept but comfortably insulated, America has been thoroughly unbalanced: thanks largely to distortions driven by government, we have too much college, too much housing, too much financial sector, too much "professional servicing"—accounting, lawyering, and other activities necessary to keep the fine print in compliance with the regulatory state. All of these are huge obstacles to making productive use of even our non-borrowed money and to keeping America competitive with the rest of the world.

Even in its glory days, the Age of Abundance wasn't exactly a Belshazzaresque party for most folks: since 1973, the wages of 90 percent of Americans have grown by only 10 percent in real terms, and consumption even of cheap Chinese goods was fueled by borrowing.[33] But eventually even that mirage fades and you see the writing on the Wal-Mart.

When government spends on the scale Washington's got used to, that's not a spending crisis, it's a moral one. The Irish have a useful word for the times—*flaithiúlacht*—which translates to ruinous generosity, invariably with someone else's money. There's nothing virtuous about "caring" "compassionate" "progressives" demonstrating how caring and compassionate and progressive they are by spending money yet to be earned by generations yet to be born. That's what "fiscal conservatives" often miss: this isn't a green-eye-shade issue. Increasing dependency, disincentivizing self-reliance, absolving the citizenry from responsibility for their actions: the multitrillion-dollar debt catastrophe is not the problem but merely the symptom. It's not just about balancing the books, but about balancing the most basic impulses of society. These are structural and, ultimately, moral questions. Credit depends on trust, and trust pre-supposes responsibility. So, if you have a credit boom in an age that has all but abolished personal responsibility, it's not hard to figure how it's going to end.

The U.S. Bureau of the Public Debt (and no, that's not a satirist's fancy but an all too real government body) uses as its motto the words of Alexander Hamilton:

> The United States debt, foreign and domestic, was the price of liberty.[34]

But in the early twenty-first century, foreign and domestic debt piles up to the cost of liberty. As I wrote in *America Alone*, it's not the "deficit": these programs would be wrong if Bill Gates wrote a check to cover them every month. They're wrong because they represent a transfer from the citizen to the state not of money but of power. And over time, as we see in the urge to expunge words like "default" and "foreclosure" and indeed any form of consequence from life, they have a debilitating effect. A society can cope with corroded infrastructure and a devalued currency more easily than with corroded liberty and a devalued citizenry.

King Belshazzar's wild party began with an act of desecration:

> Then they brought the golden vessels that were taken out of the temple of the house of God which was at Jerusalem; and the king, and his princes, his wives, and his concubines, drank in them. They drank wine, and praised the gods of gold, and of silver, of brass, of iron, of wood, and of stone.

Similarly, the statists took the vessels of the American republic and filled them up with Big Government happy juice. The United States joined the rest of a cosseted western world in voting itself a lifestyle it was not willing to pay for. The bad news is our children will not enjoy the American Dream. The good news is that under the next "stimulus" bill they'll be eligible to apply for a position as a federally funded American Dream Awareness Assistance Coordination Program Grantwriter. If the political class plus their dependents in the underclass and their cheerleaders in the media and academy have disconnected themselves from the animating principles of the American idea, what then is the point of America? Like President Obama, the progressive elite doesn't believe in American exceptionalism, yet somehow assumes that the very exceptional peace and prosperity Americans have enjoyed since 1945 are eternal—as permanent a fact of life as the sky and the oceans.

The "bubble" is not the property market or cheap credit. The bubble is twenty-first-century America itself, from the financial sector to a wretched education system culminating in languorous, undemanding "college" courses whose absurd soaraway prices were affected not a jot by the economic downturn. When you weigh America in the balances, it's not just wanting, it's wanting a sugar daddy—urgently: if Europe's somewhat agreeable post-war decline was cushioned by America, who's volunteering to do the cushioning for America?

There is no good answer to that question.

★ ★ ★ ★ ★

UPHARSIN . . .

By September 2010, America's public debt was up to 94 percent of GDP. Hey, relax, says *New York Times* columnist and Nobel Prize-winning economist Paul Krugman. Back in 1945, it was 113 percent.[35]

That was also the year that America made Hiroshima and Nagasaki the first and to date only recipients of the world's newest and most devastating technology. That's a helluva bang for the buck. The America sliding ever faster to that 1945 debt burden and way past it has no such credibility—and, as every two-bit nationalist provocateur in any old dusty colonial backwater will tell you, for a superpower, credibility is essential. America hit 113 percent after a world war in which it vanquished mighty enemies of global reach and established itself as the dominant power on the planet.

What do Americans have to show for the debt this time 'round? Cash-for-clunkers? Stimulus funding for a stimulus-funding application-coordinator in Idaho? Take Your Child Bride to Work Day in Afghanistan?

As to worshipping false gods, even avowed secularists have their moments of evangelical fervor. There have been two competing theories at play in the twenty-first century. The first and better known is "globalization"—which is less a theory and more a religion with universalist claims. To its worshippers, globalization is some kind of mysterious metaphysical force that's out there remaking our assumptions about the planet. May the Force be with you—because, if it's not, you're just a squaresville daddy-o receding in the rear view mirror of history. The high priest of this cult is the *New York Times*' in-house thinker and beloved comic figure Thomas L. Friedman. Hardly a week goes by without the *Times*' most frequent flyer filing from a state-of-the-art departure lounge on the other side of the planet and marveling at its complimentary wi fi, light-rail link, and the way his luggage was brought in by cheery native bearers in traditional dress playing some raucous Abkhazi-Nauruan hybrid of Gamelan gangsta rap on an affordable new xPod-iBox you can wear under your sarong made at a state-of-the-art plant by a small Uighur start-up backed by a Herzogovine hedge fund. All of which makes a forlorn contrast with the scene that greets him when he lands back at Newark.

The United States has two roles in a "globalized" world: it funds the transnational bodies, it keeps the sea lanes open, it's there when an earthquake or tsunami strikes—at least until the debt and politically untouchable social programs necessitate sweeping cuts in military capability. Which, for great powers in decline, they always do.

That's America's first role. Its second is just as important: the burgeoning middle classes of China, India, and elsewhere improve their lives by making stuff to sell to us. America's government is the guarantor of global order; its people are the guarantors of global prosperity. That's the United States the world needs: in security terms, the order maker; in economic terms, the order placer.

Unfortunately, neither role is sustainable. America is on course to be the first great power in history literally to shop till we drop. And the way to bet is one hell of a drop, and sooner than you think.

"Globalization" has the appeal of all inevitablist theories: it's gonna happen. Why? It just is. Don't sweat it. Likewise, Francis Fukuyama and *The End of History*: No nation can resist the pull of western liberal democracy, and so one day the entire planet will be Sweden and there will be no more wars. These days, even Sweden isn't Sweden. Ask a Jew in Malmö, if you can find one.

Against this globaloney is the thesis put forward by the late Samuel Huntington in *The Clash of Civilizations*. Huntington's view is less appealing because it's less sedating. Globalization asks nothing of us, whereas the clash of civilizations puts a cold hard question mark over the future. Huntington posits that cultural identifiers count for more than economic ones. A man in a factory on the other side of the world may make parts for an electronic gizmo Thomas Friedman plays with while waiting for the VIP lounge to call his flight, but that does not mean they share anything like the same worldview. It seems sad to have to point out something so obvious. Which, after all, is more central to a man's identity? The fact that he makes trinkets for Thomas Friedman? Or the fact that he's an Indonesian Muslim? In 1996, Huntington identified ten world civilizations, including three major ones—western, Muslim, and Sinic.[36] A decade and a half on, China— the Sinic power—is on the rise economically but is demographically weak, while Islam is surging demographically but is economically irrelevant, except for that portion of the Muslim world that sits on oil it needs foreigners to extract. Meanwhile, the West is in steep decline both economically and demographically. And as western civilization was the indispensable component in the construction of the modern world, that raises a question: What comes next?

Which brings us to the third line of the warning to Belshazzar, the geopolitical writing on the wall. Not a lot of Medes around these days, but the Persians are still in business, and the nuclear mullahs are eager to advance the finishing of the Great Satan and divide up what's supposed to be a "unipolar" world. North Korea is assisting the Iranians with their delivery systems, and the Iranians are promising to share their nukes with

Sudan. Far from Obama's plea for "a world without nuclear weapons," we face the prospect of a planet in which the wealthiest societies in history, from Norway to New Zealand, are incapable of defending their borders, while impoverished Third World basket cases go nuclear.

How long do you think that arrangement will last? As the Medes and Persians did to Belshazzar, the Russians, the Chinese, the new Caliphate, and others are looking forward to carving up the western world.

When money drains, so does power. The British learned that the hard way, even as theirs drained to the friendliest of successor powers across the Atlantic in Washington. Today, money is draining across the Pacific. They have our soul who have our bonds. Just as America had Britain's money, so China has America's. How will it use it to advance its power and influence? What might prompt the threat of a little economic blackmail? American action against North Korea? Washington's support for Taiwan? China is dangerous not (as many argue) because of its strength but because of its weakness. As I wrote in *America Alone*, the People's Republic has a crude structural flaw: thanks to its disastrous one-child policy, it will get old before it gets rich, and, unless it's planning on becoming the first gay superpower since Sparta, the millions of surplus young men whom the government's One-Child Policy has deprived of female companionship is a recipe either for wrenching social convulsions at home—or for war abroad, the traditional surplus inventory-clearance method of great powers. That's actually worse news than if China was cruising to uncontested global hegemony—because it means that Beijing's calculations on how the Sino-American relationship evolves are even less likely to align with ours. China has to maximize its power before demographic decay sets in. In other words, it has strong incentives to be bold and to push, hard and fast. And, when it happens, Washington will be taken by surprise by something that was entirely inevitable.

Faced with a choice between unsustainable entitlements and maintaining armed forces of global reach, the United States, as Europe did, will abandon military capability and toss the savings into the great sucking maw of social spending. That, in turn, will make for not only a more dangerous world but a more vulnerable America that, to modify President Bush, will wind up having to fight them over here because we no longer have the capacity to fight them over there.

For Americans, the best-case scenario is that Washington's ruling kleptocracy sleepwalks its subjects into smaller homes, smaller cars, smaller lives, and soft despotism so beguilingly they don't notice it's over until late in the day. A more likely prospect is a catastrophically convulsed America that descends into Balkanized ruin and social collapse on a planet with no global order in which the former hyperpower still makes the most inviting target.

What? You wanted a happy ending? Well, you're going to have to make that happen—because, without fundamental course correction, there is only the certainty of disaster, and a step-by-step descent deeper into the abyss:

A is for ADDICTION
We spend too much, borrowing from the future to such an extent it's no longer clear we've got one.

R is for REDISTRIBUTION
Day by day, an unprecedented transfer of wealth from the productive class to the obstructive class is delivering a self-governing republic into rule by regulators, bureaucrats, and social engineers.

M is for MONOPOLY
Old ruling class: "We the People." New ruling class: "We the People who know better than you frightful people...." America is ruled not by a meritocracy but by a cartel of conformicrats imposing a sterile monopoly of outmoded ideas.

A is for ARTERIOSCLEROSIS
"Yes, we can"? No, we can't! By comparison with the past, America is already seizing up.

G is for GLOBAL RETREAT

As Britain and other great powers quickly learned, the price of Big Government at home is an ever smaller presence abroad. An America turned inward will make for a more dangerous world.

E is for ENGINEERING

"Celebrate Diversity"? The ideological homogeneity and social engineering of the nation's schools would be regarded as child abuse in any other age. Aside from its other defects, it diverts too many Americans into frivolous unproductive activity, while our competitors get on with the real work.

D is for DECAY

Mired in dependency and decline, much of the United States will be on a fast track to the Third World. And, no matter how refined the upscale communities the elites retrench to, it will prove increasingly impossible to insulate yourself from the pathologies a decadent liberalism has loosed to rampage Godzilla-sized across the land.

D is for DISINTEGRATION

We are becoming the highly singular United State of America. No advanced society has ever tried hyper-regulatory direct rule for 350 million people. Will it work? Or is it more likely that increasingly incompatible jurisdictions and social groups will conclude that the price for keeping fifty stars in the flag is too high? Without the American idea, there will be insufficient glue to hold the United States together.

O is for OPEN SEASON

Do you find it hard to imagine a world without America? The Russians, the Chinese, and the would-be New Caliphate don't.

And on a planet where rich passive nations are defenseless while every failed state from North Korea to Sudan is butching up, it's not hard to figure out what comes next.

N is for NUKES AWAY!

Addiction, Redistribution, Monopoly, Arteriosclerosis, Global retreat, social Engineering, Decay, Disintegration, Open season, Nukes away. Put them all together, they spell … ?

From Big Government to busted government, from federally regulated school bake sales to Armageddon—in nothing flat.

Look around you. From now on, it gets worse. In ten years' time, there will be no American Dream, any more than there's a Greek or Portuguese Dream. In twenty, you'll be living the American Nightmare, with large tracts of the country reduced to the *favelas* of Latin America, the rich fleeing for Bermuda or New Zealand or wherever on the planet they can buy a little time, and the rest trapped in the impoverished, violent, diseased ruins of utopian vanity.

"After America"? Yes. It will linger awhile in a twilight existence, arthritic and ineffectual, declining into a kind of societal dementia, unable to keep pace with what's happening and with an ever more tenuous grip on its own past. For a while, there may still be an entity called the "United States," but it will have fewer stars in the flag, there will be nothing to "unite" it, and it will bear no relation to the republic of limited government the first generation of Americans fought for. And life, liberty, and the pursuit of happiness will be conspicuous by their absence.

On the other hand:

The United States is still different. In the wake of the economic meltdown, the decadent youth of France rioted over the most modest of proposals to increase the retirement age. Elderly "students" in Britain attacked the heir to the throne's car over footling attempts to constrain bloated, wasteful, and pointless "university" costs. Everywhere from Iceland to Bulgaria angry mobs besieged their parliaments demanding the same thing: Why didn't you the government do more for me? America was the only nation in the developed world where millions of people took to the streets to tell the state: I can do just fine if you control-freak statists would shove your non-stimulating stimulus, your jobless jobs bill, and your multitrillion-dollar porkathons, and just stay the hell out of my life and my pocket.

That's the America that has a fighting chance—a nation that stands for economic dynamism, not the stagnant "managed capitalism" of France; for the First Amendment and the free-est, widest, rudest bruiting of ideas, not Canadian-style government regulation of approved opinion; for self-reliance and the Second Amendment, not the security state in which Britons are second only to North Koreans in the number of times they're photographed by government cameras in the course of going about their daily business. But when you hit the expressway to Declinistan there are few exit ramps. That America's animating principles should require a defense at all is a melancholy reflection on how far we've already gone. Live free—or die from a thousand soothing caresses of nanny-state sirens.

Like I said, if you want a happy ending, it's up to you.

Your call, America.

CHAPTER ONE

THE NEW ROME
The Decaying City

The form was still the same, but the animating
health and vigor were fled.
—Edward Gibbon, *The History of the Decline*
***and Fall of the Roman Empire* (1776–1789)**

Picture a man of the late nineteenth century, perhaps your own great-grandfather, sitting in an ordinary American home of 1890. And now pitch him forward in an H. G. Wells machine, not to our time but about halfway—to that same ordinary American home, circa 1950.

Why, the poor gentleman of 1890 would be astonished. His old home is full of mechanical contraptions. There is a huge machine in the corner of the kitchen, full of food and keeping the milk fresh and cold! There is another shiny device whirring away and seemingly washing milady's bloomers with no human assistance whatsoever! Even more amazingly, there is a full orchestra playing somewhere within his very house. No, wait, it's coming from a tiny box on the countertop!

The music is briefly disturbed by a low rumble from the front yard, and our time-traveler glances through the window: a metal conveyance is coming up the street at an incredible speed—with not a horse in sight. It's enclosed with doors and windows, like a house on wheels, and it turns into the yard, and the doors open all at once, and two grown-ups and four children all get out—just like that, as if it's the most natural thing in the world! He notices there is snow on the ground, and yet the house is toasty warm, even though no fire is lit and there appears to be no stove. A bell jingles from a small black instrument on the hall table. Good heavens! Is this a "telephone"? He'd heard about such things, and that the important people in the big cities had them. But to think one would be here in his very own home! He picks up the speaking tube. A voice at the other end says there is a call from across the country—and immediately there she is, a lady from California talking as if she were standing next to him, without having to shout, or even raise her voice! And she says she'll see him tomorrow!

Oh, very funny. They've got horseless carriages in the sky now, have they?

What marvels! In a mere sixty years!

But then he espies his Victorian time machine sitting invitingly in the corner of the parlor. Suppose he were to climb on and ride even farther into the future. After all, if this is what an ordinary American home looks like in 1950, imagine the wonders he will see if he pushes on another six decades!

So on he gets, and sets the dial for our own time.

And when he dismounts he wonders if he's made a mistake. Because, aside from a few design adjustments, everything looks pretty much as it did in 1950: the layout of the kitchen, the washer, the telephone.... Oh, wait. It's got buttons instead of a dial. And the station wagon in the front yard has dropped the woody look and seems boxier than it did. And the folks getting out seem ... larger, and dressed like overgrown children.

And the refrigerator has a magnet on it holding up an endless list from a municipal agency detailing what trash you have to put in which colored boxes on what collection days.

But other than that, and a few cosmetic changes, he might as well have stayed in 1950.

Let's pause and acknowledge the one exception to the above scenario: the computer. Instead of having to watch Milton Berle on that commode-like thing in the corner, as one would in 1950, you can now watch Uncle Miltie on YouTube clips from your iPhone. But be honest, aside from that, what's new? Your horseless carriage operates on the same principles it did a century ago. It's added a CD player and a few cup holders, but you can't go any faster than you could fifty years back. As for that great metal bird in the sky, commercial flight hasn't advanced since the introduction of the 707 in the 1950s. Air travel went from Wilbur and Orville to bi-planes to flying boats to jetliners in its first half-century, and then for the next half-century it just sat there, like a commuter twin-prop parked at Gate 27B at LaGuardia waiting for the mysteriously absent gate agent to turn up and unlock the jetway.

Other arenas aren't quite as static as the modern American airport, but nor do they move at the same clip they used to. When was the last big medical breakthrough? I mean "big" in the sense of something that takes a crippling worldwide disease man has accepted as a cruel fact of life and so clobbers it that a generation on nobody gives it a thought. That's what the polio vaccine did in 1955. Why haven't we done that for Alzheimer's? Today, we have endless "races for the cure," and colored ribbons advertising one's support for said races for the cure, and yet fewer cures. It's not just pink ribbons for breast cancer, and gray ribbons for brain cancer, and white for bone cancer, but also yellow ribbons for adenosarcoma, light blue for Addison's Disease, teal for agoraphobia, periwinkle for acid reflux, pink and blue ribbons for amniotic fluid embolisms, and pinstripe ribbons for amyotrophic lateral sclerosis. We have had phenomenal breakthroughs in hues of awareness-raising ribbons. Yet for all the raised awareness, very few people seem aware of how the whole disease-curing business has ground to a halt.

Compare the Twenties to the Nineties: in the former, the discovery of insulin and penicillin, plus the first vaccines for tuberculosis, diphtheria, tetanus, whooping cough, on and on. In the last decade of the twentieth century, what? A vaccine for Hepatitis A, and Viagra. Good for erectile dysfunction, but what about inventile dysfunction? In October 1920, a doctor in London, Ontario, Frederick Banting, had an idea as to how insulin might be isolated and purified and used to treat diabetes, which in those days killed you.[1] By August 1922, Elizabeth Hughes, the daughter of America's Secretary of State and a diabetic near death, was being given an experimental course of the new treatment. By January 1923, Eli Lilly & Company were selling insulin to American druggists. That's it: a little over two years from concept to patient. Not today: the U.S. Food and Drug Administration now adds half a decade to the process by which a treatment makes it to market, and they're getting slower. Between 1996 and 1999, the FDA approved 157 new drugs. Between 2006 and 2009, the approvals fell by half—to 74.[2] What happens during that half-decade? People die, nonstop—as young Elizabeth Hughes would have died under the "protection" of today's FDA. Because statism has no sense of proportion. You can still find interesting articles about new discoveries that might have implications for, say, Parkinson's disease. But that's all you'll find: articles, in periodicals, lying around your doctor's waiting room. The chances of the new discovery advancing from the magazine on the coffee table to your prescription are less and less. To begin the government-approval process is to enter what the cynics of the twenty-first-century research biz call the valley of death.

When *America Alone* came out, arguing that the current conflict is about demographic decline, globalized psychoses, and civilizational confidence, a lot of folks objected, as well they might: seeing off supple amorphous abstract nouns is not something advanced societies do well. You're looking at it the wrong way, I was told. Technocratic solutions, new inventions, the old can-do spirit: that's the American way, and that's what will see us through.

Well, okay, so where is it?

★ ★ ★ ★ ★

CRESCENT MOON

Half a century ago, the future felt different. Take 1969, quite a year in the aerospace biz: in one twelve-month period, we saw the test flight of the Boeing 747, the maiden voyage of the *Concorde*, the RAF's deployment of the Harrier "jump jet," and Neil Armstrong's "giant step for mankind."

Buzz Aldrin packed a portable tape player with him on Apollo 11, and so Sinatra's ring-a-ding-ding recording of "Fly Me to the Moon" became the first (human) music to be flown to the moon and played there.[3] Had any other nation beaten NASA to it, they'd have marked the occasion with the "Ode to Joy" or *Also Sprach Zarathustra*, something grand and formal. But there's something marvelously American about the first human being to place his feet on the surface of a heavenly sphere standing there with a cassette machine blasting out Frank and the Count Basie band in a swingin' Quincy Jones arrangement—the insouciant swagger of the American century breaking the bounds of the planet.

In 1961, before the eyes of the world, President Kennedy had set American ingenuity a very specific challenge—and put a clock on it:

> This nation should commit itself to achieving the goal, before this decade is out, of landing a man on the moon and returning him safely to the earth.[4]

That's it. No wiggle room. A monkey on the moon wouldn't count, nor an unmanned drone, nor a dune buggy that can't take off again but transmits grainy footage back to Houston as it rusts up in the crater it came to rest in. The only way to win the bet is with a real-live actual American standing on the surface of the moon planting the Stars and Stripes. Even as it happened, the White House was so cautious that William Safire wrote President Nixon a speech to be delivered in the event of disaster:

> Fate has ordained that the men who went to the moon to explore in peace will stay on the moon to rest in peace…[5]

Yet America did it. "Fly Me to the Moon/Let me sing forever more." What comes after American yearning and achievement? Democratization: "Everybody Gets to Go the Moon." That all but forgotten Jimmy Webb song from 1969 catches the spirit of the age:

Isn't it a miracle
That we're the generation
That will touch that shiny bauble with our own two hands?

Whatever happened to that?

Four decades later, Bruce Charlton, professor of Theoretical Medicine at the University of Buckingham in England, wrote that "that landing of men on the moon and bringing them back alive was the supreme achievement of human capability, the most difficult problem ever solved by humans."[6] That's a good way to look at it: the political class presented the boffins with a highly difficult and specific problem, and they solved it—in eight years. Charlton continued:

> Forty years ago, we could do it—repeatedly—but since then we have *not* been to the moon, and I suggest the real reason we have not been to the moon since 1972 is that we cannot any longer do it. Humans have lost the capability.
>
> Of course, the standard line is that humans stopped going to the moon only because we no longer *wanted* to go to the moon, or could not afford to, or something…. But I am suggesting that all this is BS…. I suspect that human capability reached its peak or plateau around 1965-75—at the time of the Apollo moon landings—and has been declining ever since.

Can that be true? Charlton is a controversialist gadfly in British academe, but, comparing 1950 to the early twenty-first century, our time traveler from 1890 might well agree with him. And, if you think about it, isn't it kind of hard even to *imagine* America pulling off a moon mission now? The countdown, the takeoff, a camera transmitting real-time footage of a young American standing in a dusty crater beyond our planet blasting out from his iPod Lady Gaga and the Black-Eyed Peas or whatever the twenty-first-century version of Sinatra and the Basie band is…. It half-lingers in collective consciousness as a memory of faded grandeur, the way a ninetheenth-century date farmer in Nasiriyah might be dimly aware that the Great Ziggurat of Ur used to be around here someplace.

So what happened? According to Professor Charlton, in the 1970s "the human spirit began to be overwhelmed by bureaucracy." The old can-do spirit? Oh, you can try to do it, but they'll toss every obstacle in your path. Go on, give it a go: invent a new medical device; start a company; go to the airport to fly to D.C. and file a patent. Everything's longer, slower, more soul-crushing. And the decline in "human capability" will only worsen in the years ahead, thanks not just to excess bureaucracy but insufficient cash.

"Yes, we can!" droned the dopey Obamatrons of 2008. No, we can't, says Charlton, not if you mean "land on the moon, swiftly win wars against weak opposition and then control the defeated nation, secure national borders, discover breakthrough medical treatments, prevent crime, design and build to a tight deadline, educate people so they are ready to work before the age of 22…."

Houston, we have a much bigger problem.

To be sure, there's still something called "NASA" and it still stands for the "National Aeronautics and Space Administration." But there's not a lot of either aeronautics or space in the in-box of the agency's head honcho. A few days after Charlton penned his elegy for human capability, NASA Administrator Charles Bolden appeared on al-Jazeera and explained the brief he'd been given by President Obama:

> One was he wanted me to help re-inspire children to want to get into science and math; he wanted me to expand our inter-national relationships; and third and perhaps foremost, he wanted me to find a way to reach out to the Muslim world and engage much more with dominantly Muslim nations to help them feel good about their historic contribution to science and math and engineering.[7]

Islam: The final frontier! To boldly go where no diversity outreach consultant has gone before! What's "foremost" for NASA is to make Muslims "feel good" about their contributions to science. Why, as recently as the early ninth century Muhammad al-Khwarizmi invented the first universal horary quadrant! Things have been a little quiet since then, or at least since Taqi-al-Din's observatory in Istanbul was razed to the ground by the Sultan's janissaries in 1580. If you hear a Muslim declaring "We have lift off!" it's likely to be a triumphant ad-lib after lighting up his crotch. As far as I recall, the most recent Islamic contribution to the subject of space exploration came from Britain's most prominent imam, Abu Hamza, who in 2003 declared that the fate of the space shuttle *Columbia* was God's punishment "because it carried Americans, an Israeli and a Hindu, a trinity of evil against Islam."[8]

It's easy to laugh at the likes of Abu Hamza, although not as easy as it should be, not in Europe and Canada, where the state is eager to haul you into court for "Islamophobia." But the laugh's on us. NASA is the government agency whose acronym was known around the planet, to every child who looked up at the stars and wondered what technological marvels the space age would have produced by the time he was out of short pants. Now the starry-eyed moppets are graying boomers, and the agency that symbolized man's reach for the skies has transformed itself into a self-esteem boosterism operation. Is there an accompanying book—*Muslims Are from Mars, Infidels Are from Venus*?

There's your American decline right there: from out-of-this-world to out-of-our-minds, an increasingly unmanned flight from real, historic, technological accomplishment to unreal, ahistorical, therapeutic, touchy-feely multiculti.

So we can't go to the moon. And, by the time you factor in getting to the airport to do the shoeless shuffle and the enhanced patdown, flying to London takes longer than it did in 1960. If they were trying to build the transcontinental railroad now, they'd be spending the first three decades on the environmental-impact study and hammering in the Golden Spike to celebrate the point at which the Feasibility Commission's expansion up from the fifth floor met the Zoning Board's expansion down from the twelfth floor.

Google and Apple and other latter day American success stories started in somebody's garage—the one place where innovation isn't immediately buried by bureaucracy, or at least in most states, not until some minor municipal functionary discovers you neglected to apply for a Not Sitting Around on My Ass All Day permit. What did Apple and company do in those garages? They invented and refined home computers—an entirely logical response to late twentieth-century America: when reality seizes up, freedom retreats and retrenches to virtual reality, to the internal. Where once space was the final frontier, now we frolic in the canyons of our mind. We're in the Wilbur & Orville era of the Internet right now, but at the Federal Communications Commission and other agencies they're already designing the TSA uniforms for the enhanced cyber-patdown.

And what do you have to show for all that government? It's amazing with a multi-trillion-dollar barrel how quickly you wind up scraping the bottom of it. In Obama's "American Recovery and Reinvestment Plan," two of the five objectives were to "computerize the health-care system" and "modernize classrooms."[9] That sound you hear is the computerized eye-rolling with which every modernized hack author now comes equipped. For its part, the Congressional Progressive Caucus wanted "green jobs creation" and "construction of libraries in rural communities to expand broadband access."[10] And in a postmodern touch, Mark Pinsky at the *New Republic* made the pitch for a new Federal Writers' Project, in which writers laid off by America's collapsing newspaper industry would be hired by the government to go around the country "documenting the ground-level impact of the Great Recession."[11] America has a money-no-object government with a lot of money but no great objects.

★ ★ ★ ★ ★

GOTTERDAMMERUNG

When the father of Big Government, Franklin Roosevelt, was brought before the Hoover Dam, he declared:

This morning I came, I saw, and I was conquered, as everyone would be who sees for the first time this great feat of mankind.[12]

But the bigger government gets, the less it actually *does*. You think a guy like Obama is going to put up a new Hoover Dam (built during the Depression and opened two years ahead of schedule)? No chance. Today's Big Government crowd is more likely to put up a new regulatory agency to tell the Hoover Dam it's non-wheelchair accessible and has to close. As Deanna Archuleta, Obama's Deputy Assistant Secretary of the Interior, assured an audience in Nevada: "You will never see another federal dam."[13] "Great feats of mankind" are an environmental hazard, for mankind has great feats of clay. But hang on, isn't hydropower "renewable" energy? It doesn't use coal or oil, it generates electricity from the natural water cycle. If that's not renewable, what is? Ah, but, according to environmental "dam-busters," reservoirs are responsible for some 4 percent of the earth's carbon dioxide emissions. Environmental devastation-wise, the Hoover Dam is the patio pool to Al Gore's mansion. Out, out, dammed spot!

So, just as the late Roman Empire was no longer an aqueduct-building culture, we are no longer a dam-building one. It's not just that we no longer invent, but that we are determined to disinvent everything our great-grandparents created to enable the self-indulgent lives we take for granted and that leave us free to chip away at the foundations of our own society. So-called "progressives" actively wage war on progress. They're opposed to dams, which spurred the growth of California. They're opposed to air-conditioning, which led to the development of the Southwest. They're opposed to light bulbs, which expanded man's day, and they're opposed to automobiles, which expanded man's reach. They're still nominally in favor of mass transit, so maybe we can go back to wood-fired steam trains? No, sorry, no can do. The progressives are opposed to logging; they want a ban on forestry work in environmentally sensitive areas such as forests. Ultimately, progressives are at war with mass prosperity.

In the old days, we didn't have these kinds of problems. But then Mr. and Mrs. Peasant start remodeling the hovel, adding a rec room and indoor plumbing, replacing the emaciated old nag with a Honda Civic and driving to the mall in it, and next thing you know, instead of just having an extra yard of mead every Boxing Day at the local tavern and adding a couple more pustules to the escutcheon with the local trollop, they begin taking vacations in Florida. When it was just medieval dukes swanking about like that, the planet worked fine: that was "sustainable" consumerism. But now the masses want in. And, once you do that, there goes the global neighborhood.

Human capital is the most important element in any society. The first requirement of the American Dream is Americans. Today we have American sclerosis, to which too many Americans are contributing. Capitalism is liberating: you're born a peasant but you don't have to die one. You can work hard and get a nice place in the suburbs. If you're a nineteenth-century Russian serf and you get to Ellis Island, you'll be living in a tenement on the Lower East Side, but your kids will get an education and move uptown, and your grandkids will be doctors and accountants in Westchester County.

And your great-grandchild will be a Harvard-educated dam-busting environmental activist demanding an end to all this electricity and indoor toilets.

To go back to 1950, once our friend from 1890 had got his bearings in mid-century, he'd be struck by how our entire conception of time had changed in a mere sixty years. If you live in my part of New Hampshire and you need to pick something up from a guy in the next town, you hop in the truck and you're back in little more than an hour. In a horse and buggy, that would have been most of your day gone. The first half of the twentieth century overhauled the pattern of our lives: the light bulb abolished night; the internal combustion engine tamed distance. They fundamentally reconceived the rhythms of life. That's why our young man propelled from 1890 to 1950 would be flummoxed at every turn. A young fellow catapulted from 1950 to today would, on the surface, feel instantly at home—and then notice a few cool electronic toys. And, after that, he might wonder about the defining down of "accomplishment": Wow, you've invented a more compact and portable delivery system for Justin Bieber!

Long before they slump into poverty, great powers succumb to a poverty of ambition. It could be that the Internet is a lone clipper of advancement on a sea of stasis because, as its proponents might argue, we're on the brink of a reconceptualization of space similar to the reconceptualization of time that our great-grandparents lived through with the development of electricity and automobiles. But you could as easily argue that for most of the citizenry the computer is, in the Roman context, a cyber-circus. In Aldous Huxley's *Brave New World*, written shortly after Hollywood introduced us to "the talkies," the masses are hooked on "the feelies":

"Take hold of those metal knobs on the arms of your chair," Lenina whispers to her date. "Otherwise you won't get any of the feely effects." He does so. The "scent organ" breathes musk; when the on-screen couple kiss with "stereoscopic lips," the audience tingles. When they make out on the rug, every moviegoer can feel every hair of the bearskin.

In our time, we don't even need to go to the theater. We can "feel" what it's like to drive a car on a thrilling chase through a desert or lead a commando raid on a jungle compound without leaving our own bedrooms. We can photoshop ourselves into pictures with celebrities. We can have any permutation of men, women, and pre-operative transsexuals engaging in every sexual practice known to man or beast just three inches from our eyes: a customized 24-hour virtual circus of diverting games, showbiz gossip, and downloadable porn, a refuge from reality, and a gaudy "feely" playground for the plebs at a time when the regulators have made non-virtual reality a playground for regulators and no one else.

In the end, the computer age may presage not a reconceptualization of space but an abandonment of the very concept of time. According to Mushtaq Yufzai, the Taliban have a saying:

Americans have all the watches, but we've got all the time.[14]

Cute. If it's not a Taliban proverb, it would make an excellent country song. It certainly distills the essence of the "clash of civilizations": Islam is playing for tomorrow, whereas much of the West has, by any traditional indicator, given up on the future. We do not save, we do not produce, we do not reproduce, not in Europe, Canada, Vermont, or San Francisco. Instead, we seek new, faster ways to live in an eternal present, in an unending whirl of sensory distraction. Tocqueville's prediction of the final stage of democracy prefigures the age of "social media":

> It hides his descendants and separates his contemporaries from him; it throws him back for ever upon himself alone, and threatens in the end to confine him entirely within the solitude of his own heart.

★ ★ ★ ★ ★

THE HOLE IS GREATER THAN THE SUM OF ITS PARTS

Almost anyone who's been exposed to western pop culture over the last half-century is familiar with the brutal image that closes *Planet of the Apes*: a loinclothed Charlton Heston falling to his knees as he comes face to face with a shattered Statue of Liberty poking out of the sand and realizes that the "planet of the apes" is, in fact, his own—or was. What more instantly recognizable shorthand for civilizational ruin? In the film *Independence Day*, Lady Liberty gets zapped by aliens. In *Cloverfield*, she's decapitated by a giant monster. If you're in the apocalyptic fantasy business, clobbering the statue in the harbor is *de rigueur*.

As far as I can ascertain, the earliest example of Liberty-toppling dates back to an edition of *Life*, and a story called "The Next Morning," illustrated by a pen-and-ink drawing of a headless statue with the smoldering rubble of the city behind her. That was in 1887. The poor old girl had barely got off the boat from France and they couldn't wait to blow her to kingdom come. Two years later, on the cover of J. A. Mitchell's story *The Last American*, she still stands but the city around her has sunk into a watery grave as a Persian sailing ship navigates the ruins of a once mighty nation called Mehrika in the year 2951.

But liberty is not a statue, and that is not how liberty falls. So what about a different kind of dystopian future? Picture a land where the Statue of Liberty remains in the harbor, yet liberty itself has withered away. The word is still in use. Indeed, we may have a bright shiny array of new "liberties," new freedoms—"free" health care, "free" college education. If you smash liberty in an instant—as the space aliens do in *Independence Day*—we can all have our Charlton Heston moment and fall to our knees wailing about the folly and stupidity of man. But when it happens incrementally, and apparently painlessly, free peoples who were once willing to give their lives for liberty can be persuaded very easily to relinquish their liberties for a quiet life. In the days when President Bush was going around promoting the notion of democracy in the Muslim world, there was a line he liked to fall back on:

Freedom is the desire of every human heart.[15]

If only that were true. It's doubtful whether that's actually the case in Gaza and Waziristan, but we know for absolute certain that it's not in Paris and Stockholm, London and Toronto, Buffalo and San Jose. The story of the western world since 1945 is that, invited to choose between freedom and government "security," large numbers of people vote to dump freedom every time—the freedom to make their own decisions about health care, education, property rights, the right to eat non-state-licensed homemade pie, and eventually (as we already see in Europe, Canada, the UN Human Rights Council, and U.S. college campuses) what you're permitted to say and think. An America running out of ideas eventually gives up on *the* American idea.

The pop-cultural detonation of national landmarks is a mostly American phenomenon. In the rest of the world, it happens for real. At the same time as *Amazing Stories* and *Astounding Science Fiction* were running those covers of the Statue of Liberty decapitated and toppled in one lurid fantasy after another, Buckingham Palace took nine direct hits during the Blitz. Reducing British landmarks to rubble wasn't *Fiction* and it wasn't that *Astounding*, and it didn't even require much *Science*. On one occasion, an enterprising lone German bomber flew low up the Mall and dropped his load directly above the Royal Family's living quarters. The King and Queen were in their drawing room and showered with shards of glass. When American audiences whoop and holler at the vaporizing of the White House in *Independence Day*, it's because such thrills are purely the stuff of weekend multiplex diversion.

Or at least they were until a Tuesday morning one September when a guy in a cave remade the Manhattan skyline.

Somewhere along the way, back home in Saudi, at summer school in Oxford, or on a VCR hooked up to the generator at Camp Jihad in Waziristan, Osama bin Laden must surely have seen some of those despised Hollywood blockbusters, because he evidently gave some thought to the iconography of the moment. Planning the operation, did he ever consider taking out the Statue of Liberty? Fewer dead, but what a statement! A couple of days after 9/11, the celebrated German composer Karlheinz Stockhausen told a radio interviewer that the destruction of the World Trade Center was "the greatest work of art ever."[16] I'm reminded of the late Sir Thomas Beecham's remark when asked if he'd ever conducted any Stockhausen: "No," he replied. "But I think I've trodden in some."[17] Stockhausen stepped in his own that week: in those first days after the assault, even the anti-American Left felt obliged to be somewhat circumspect. But at a certain level the composer understood what Osama was getting at.

Nevertheless, Stockhausen was wrong. The "greatest work of art" is not the morning of 9/11, with the planes slicing through the building, and the smoke and the screaming and the jumping, and the swift, eerily smooth collapse of the towers. No, the most eloquent statement about America in the early twenty-first century is Ground Zero in the years after. 9/11 was something America's enemies did to us. The hole in the ground a decade later is something we did to ourselves. By 2010, Michael Bloomberg, the take-charge get-it-done make-it-happen mayor of New York was reduced to promising that that big hole in Lower Manhattan isn't going to be there for another decade, no, sir. "I'm not going to leave this world with that hole in the ground ten years from now," he declared defiantly.[18] In the twenty-first century, that's what passes for action, for get-tough leadership, for riding herd. When the going gets tough, the tough boot the can another decade down the road. Sure, those jihad boys got lucky and took out a couple of skyscrapers, but the old can't-do spirit kicked in, and a mere ten years later we had a seven-storey hole on which seven billion dollars had been lavished. But, if we can't put up a replacement building within a decade, we can definitely do it within two. Probably. As a lonely steel skeleton began lethargically to rise from the 16-acre site, the unofficial estimated date of completion for the brand new "1 World Trade Center" was said to be 2018.[19] That date should shame every American.

What happened? Everyone knows the "amber waves of grain" and "purple mountain majesties" in "America the Beautiful," but Katharine Lee Bates' words are also a hymn to modernity:

> Oh beautiful for patriot dream
> That sees beyond the years
> Thine alabaster cities gleam
> Undimmed by human tears ...

"America the Beautiful" is not a nostalgic evocation of a pastoral landscape but a paean to its potential, including the gleaming metropolis. Miss Bates visited the Columbian Exposition in Chicago just before July 4, 1893, and she meant the word "alabaster" very literally: the centerpiece of the fair was the "White City" of the future, fourteen blocks of architectural marvels with marble facades painted white, and shining even whiter in the nightly glow of thousands of electric light bulbs, like a primitive prototype of Al Gore's carbon-offset palace in Tennessee. They were good times, but even in bad the United States could still build marvels. Much of the New York skyline dates from the worst of times. As Fred Astaire and Ginger Rogers sang in the Thirties: "They all laughed at Rockefeller Center, Now they're fighting to get in..."

The Empire State Building, then the tallest in the world, was put up in eighteen months during a depression—because the head of General Motors wanted to show the head of Chrysler that he could build something that went higher than the Chrysler Building. Three-quarters of a century later, the biggest thing either man's successor had created was a mountain of unsustainable losses—and both GM and Chrysler were now owned and controlled by government and unions.

In the months after 9/11, I used to get the same joke emailed to me every few days: the proposed design for the replacement World Trade Center. A new skyscraper towering over the city, with the top looking like a stylized hand—three towers cut off at the joint, and the "middle finger" rising above them, flipping the bird not only to Osama bin Laden but also to Karlheinz Stockhausen and the sneering Euro-lefties and all the rest who rejoiced that day at America getting it, pow, right in the kisser: they all laughed at the Twin Towers takedown. Soon they'll be fighting to get in to whatever reach-for-the-skies only-in-America edifice replaces it. The very word "skyscraper" is quintessentially American: it doesn't *literally* scrape the sky, but hell, as soon as we figure out how to build an even more express elevator, there's no reason why it shouldn't.

But the years go by, and they stopped emailing that joke, because it's not quite so funny after two, three, five, nine years of walking past Windows on the Hole every morning. It doesn't matter what the eventual replacement building is at Ground Zero. The ten-year hole is the memorial: a gaping, multi-story, multi-billion-dollar pit, profound and eloquent in its nullity.

As for the gleam of a brand new "White City," well, in the interests of saving the planet, Congress went and outlawed Edison's light bulb. And on the grounds of the White City hymned by Katherine Lee Bates stands Hyde Park, home to community organizer Barack Obama, terrorist educator

William Ayers, and Nation of Islam numerologist and Jeremiah Wright Award-winner Louis Farrakhan. That's one fruited plain all of its own.

In the decade after 9/11, China (which America still thinks of as a cheap assembly plant for your local KrappiMart) built the Three Gorges Dam, the largest electricity-generating plant in the world.[20] Dubai, a mere sub-jurisdiction of the United Arab Emirates, put up the world's tallest building and built a Busby Berkeley geometric kaleidoscope of offshore artificial islands.[21] Brazil, an emerging economic power, began diverting the Sao Francisco River to create some 400 miles of canals to irrigate its parched northeast.[22]

But the hyperpower can't put up a building.

Happily, there is one block in Lower Manhattan where ambitious redevelopment is in the air. In 2010, plans were announced to build a 15-story mosque at Ground Zero, on the site of an old Burlington Coat Factory damaged by airplane debris that Tuesday morning.

So, in the ruins of a building reduced to rubble in the name of Islam, a temple to Islam will arise.

A couple years after the events of that Tuesday morning, James Lileks, the bard of Minnesota, wrote:

> If 9/11 had really changed us, there'd be a 150-story building on the site of the World Trade Center today. It would have a classical memorial in the plaza with allegorical figures representing Sorrow and Resolve, and a fountain watched over by stern stone eagles. Instead there's a pit, and arguments over the usual muted dolorous abstraction approved by the National Association of Grief Counselors.[23]

The best response to 9/11 on the home front—if only to demonstrate that there is a "home front" (which is the nub of al-Qaeda's critique of a soft and decadent West)—would have been to rebuild the World Trade Center bigger, better, taller—not 150 stories, but 250, a marvel of the age. And, if there had to be "the usual muted dolorous abstraction," the National Healing Circle would have been on the penthouse floor with a clear view all the way to al-Qaeda's executive latrine in Waziristan.

Leslie Gelb, president emeritus of the Committee on Foreign Relations, is no right-winger but rather a sober, respected, judicious paragon of torpidly conventional wisdom. Nevertheless, musing on American decline, he writes, "The country's economy, infrastructure, public schools and political system have been allowed to deteriorate. The result has been diminished economic strength, a less-vital democracy, and a mediocrity of spirit."[24]

That last is the one to watch: a great power can survive a lot of things, but not "a mediocrity of spirit." A wealthy nation living on the accumulated cultural capital of a glorious past can dodge its rendezvous with fate, but only for so long. "Si monumentum requiris, circumspice"[25] reads the inscription on the tomb of Sir Christopher Wren in St. Paul's Cathedral: If you seek my monument, look around. After two-thirds of the City of London was destroyed in the Great Fire of 1666, Wren designed and rebuilt the capital's tallest building (St. Paul's), another fifty churches, and a new skyline for a devastated metropolis. Three centuries later, if you seek our monument, look in the hole.

It's not about al-Qaeda. It's about us.

UNDREAMING AMERICA
Serfing USA

*Nothing is more senseless than to base so many expectations
on the state, that is, to assume the existence of collective wisdom
and foresight after taking for granted the existence of individual
imbecility and improvidence.*
—Frédéric Bastiat, *Economic Sophisms* (1845)

There is a famous passage by Alexis de Tocqueville. Or, rather, it would be famous were he still widely read. For he knows us far better than we know him: "I would like to imagine with what new traits despotism could be produced in the world," he wrote two centuries ago. He and his family had been on the sharp end of France's violent convulsions and knew what forms despotism could take in Europe. But he considered that, to a democratic republic, there were slyer seductions:

> I see an innumerable crowd of like and equal men who revolve
> on themselves without repose, procuring the small and vulgar
> pleasures with which they fill their souls.

"Small and vulgar pleasures"? I've nothing against *Dancing with the Stars* (which I rather enjoy) or *American Idol* (not so much), but Tocqueville's right on the money there. "Revolving on themselves without repose"?

That's not a bad description of a populace preoccupied with "social media." But then he goes on:

> Over these is elevated an immense, tutelary power, which takes sole charge of assuring their enjoyment and of watching over their fate. It is absolute, attentive to detail, regular, provident, and gentle. It would resemble the paternal power if, like that power, it had as its object to prepare men for manhood, but it seeks, to the contrary, to keep them irrevocably fixed in childhood... it provides for their security, foresees and supplies their needs, guides them in their principal affairs....
>
> The sovereign extends its arms about the society as a whole; it covers its surface with a network of petty regulations—complicated, minute, and uniform—through which even the most original minds and the most vigorous souls know not how to make their way... it does not break wills; it softens them, bends them, and directs them; rarely does it force one to act, but it constantly opposes itself to one's acting on one's own... it does not tyrannize, it gets in the way: it curtails, it enervates, it extinguishes, it stupefies, and finally reduces each nation to being nothing more than a herd of timid and industrious animals, of which the government is the shepherd.

Welcome to the twenty-first century.

The all-pervasive state "does not tyrannize, it gets in the way." It "enervates," but nicely, gradually, so that after a while you don't even notice...

But once in a while even the mellowest hippie emerges from the stupor. In 1969, George Harrison of the Beatles, in the course of a wide-ranging ramble, briefly detoured out of the Hare Krishna chants into some remarks about the Monopolies Commission (the British equivalent of the U.S. government's Antitrust Division):

You know, this is the thing I don't like. It's the Monopolies Commission. Now if anybody, you know, Kodak, or somebody is cleaning up the market with film, the Monopolies Commission, the government send them in there, and say you know, you're not allowed to monopolize. Yet, when the government's monopolizing, who's gonna send in, you know, this Commission to sort that one out?[1]

Good question. There was an old joke in Britain: "Why is there only one Monopolies Commission?" In fact, it's an incisive observation on the nature of government. We wouldn't like it if there were only one automobile company or only one breakfast cereal, but by definition there can be only one government—which is why, "when the government's monopolizing," it should do so only in very limited areas. That's particularly true for national governments when the nation they govern has more than 300 million people dispersed over a continent and halfway across the Pacific.

These days America's government is doing a lot of monopolizing. If it were a private company such as Kodak (to use George Harrison's quaint example), it would be attracting anti-trust suits. By 2008, the government-sponsored Fannie Mae and Freddie Mac had a piece of over half the mortgages issued in the United States.[2] As a result, a government-mandated form of pseudo-ownership came close to collapsing the world economy. Which the politicians then, naturally, blamed on capitalist greed. Fresh from their success in undermining the property market, the government went on to seek a monopoly in college loans, plus control of the automobile industry and health care.

In his dissenting opinion on *United States* vs. *Columbia Steel Co.* (1948), Justice William Douglas wrote:

We have here the problem of bigness.... The Curse Of Bigness [Justice Louis Brandeis' essay] shows how size can become a menace—both industrial and social. It can be an industrial menace because it creates gross inequalities against existing or putative competitors. It can be a social menace—because of its control of prices....

Now who does that sound like? No, not Kodak. The fact that George Harrison's selection of an all-powerful monopoly rings so sweetly nostalgic just a few decades later is testament to the self-correcting mechanisms of a functioning market. Kodak, which actually invented some of the first digital camera technology in 1975, failed to foresee how fast things were changing, and eventually wound up laying off 60 percent of its workforce.[3] Had the statists been in charge of that sector as they now are of so many others, we'd still be snapping with Kodak Instamatics, and it would take you two weeks to get your holiday pics and cost you $800, because the government had intervened to protect the jobs of Instastatistmatic film developers in the unionized Kodacrony lab.

These days, the Number One example of the Curse of Bigness is government. It doesn't just create "gross inequalities" against existing or putative competitors, it passes laws and drives them out, as it's done to everything from genuinely private health-care arrangements to non-state-licensed kids' lemonade stands. In Justice Marshall's words, it's a "social menace" because of its "control of prices."

How does it control them? Michael Fleischer, the owner of a small company in New Jersey, explained to readers of the *Wall Street Journal* that in order to put $44,000 in his employee's pocket and give her an additional $12,000 worth of benefits he has to pay $74,000: Big Government imposes a 30 percent surcharge on the cost of providing employment to Sally.[4] It "controls the price" of hiring Sally, and it massively distorts it. Which is one reason the unemployment rate is stuck where it is.

How else does it control prices? In 2009, something called the State Council of Higher Education in Virginia decided that studios offering yoga teacher instruction had to be "certified."[5] So what else is new? Everything's certified these days. Why not yoga? It's just a $2,500 certification fee, plus annual charges of at least $500, plus state audits, plus a ton of paperwork. But don't worry, with a bit of practice, you can multitask and fill in all the forms in the lotus position. In the Fifties, one in twenty members of the workforce needed government permission in order to do his job.[6] Today, it's one in three. So Big Government "controls the price" of your yoga lesson. Look on it as a twofer: all the purifying benefits of yoga, now with the dead weights of Big Government.

Government today has a monopoly of monopoly. If you were to update the board game of the same name to reflect reality, every square you land on would require you to pay a fee to government before you can do any-thing—occupational license, commercial-use permit, processing fee for a license to permit you to collect sales tax. You'd go straight to jail without passing "Go" for putting up a yoga studio on Atlantic Avenue and being delinquent in your meditation-accreditation application, but the govern-ment would let you plea-bargain it down to a $3,000 fine. If you land on "Go," you'd have to pass a "Go" impact-study inspection before being allowed to go.

There's your Curse of Bigness, and the only one beyond the jurisdiction of the Antitrust Division.

Alas, the monopolizers don't see it as a curse. Before he became Treasury Secretary, Timothy Geithner (by his own admission) failed to pay the United States Treasury the taxes he owed because he couldn't follow the yes/no prompts of elementary TurboTax software. Undaunted, by early 2009, he and President Obama, two men with no business management experience whatsoever, who have never created a nickel of wealth between them, were "managing" more money than any individuals anywhere on the planet have ever done. Fans of Big Government take it for granted that Obama, Geithner, and a handful of other guys can "run" the financial sector, and the auto industry, and the insurance industry, and the property market, and health care, and even the very climate of the planet. The Barackracy assume that a few clever people in Washington can direct trillions of dollars more productively than the companies and individuals from whom they confiscated it. There are many people who can run businesses worth a million dollars. The ability to run a billion-dollar corporation is the province of very few individuals. The skill-set required to run a multi-trillion-dollar enterprise is unknown to human history.

In Justice Marshall's words:

> Industrial power should be decentralized. It should be scattered into many hands so that the fortunes of the people will not be dependent on the whim or caprice, the political prejudices, the emotional stability of a few self-appointed men. The fact that they are not vicious men but respectable and social minded is irrelevant.

In 1948 Marshall was worried about steel. But the dominant industrial power of our time is government. And it is because of the government monopoly that "the fortunes of the people" are dependent on "the whim or caprice" (not to mention "the emotional stability") of a small number of all too like-minded individuals.

You can see where power lies in the very landscape: go to a steel town six decades after Marshall's warning. The burg's shot to hell. The handsome Victorian homes on the tree-lined avenues are worn and crumbling, with cracked clapboards and sagging porches, and cheaply partitioned into low-rent apartments. The railroad halts that sent the products of American industry across the nation and around the world are dead, their depots converted into laundromats and pizza joints or, worse, "community centers," with the track removed and its weed-strewn path redesignated as a "heritage trail." Where do wealth and power gravitate today? In 2009 Reuters reported:

> Washington, D.C., has become the favorite area for wealthy young adults, with the nation's highest percentage of 25-34 year-olds making more than $100,000 a year.[7]

You don't say! Now I wonder why that would be. Of the fifty counties with the biggest percentage of young high earners, sixteen were in the D.C. area. Of the top ten, only two were not near either Washington or a state capital.[8] Reuters filed this revealing analysis in its "lifestyle" section. Which makes sense. The easiest way to a "lifestyle" is a government job. The following year, another survey (from *Newsweek*) found that seven of the ten wealthiest counties in the United States were in the Washington commuter belt.[9] What matters in the America of the twenty-first century is proximity not to industry or to wealth creation but to government.

As George Harrison warned, "the government's monopolizing": it has a monopoly of law, of licensing, of regulation, and when it abuses that monopoly then eventually you can't move without encountering government at every turn. Even before the Obama spendaholics got to work supersizing the state, all levels of government, federal to local, were already sucking up over 40 cents of every dollar American workers generate.[10] (European nations were able to go beyond even that dismal figure only because the United States has relieved them of the responsibility for their own defense.) The assumed rationale for an ever more intrusive superstate is that, thanks to technology and globalization, the world is far more complex and interconnected than in the days when hardscrabble farmers in New England townships could be trusted to run their own affairs. There is little objective evidence to support this argument, but it conveniently bolsters the political class's belief in its own indispensability. Willie Whitelaw, the genial old buffer who served as Margaret Thatcher's deputy for many years, once accused the Labour Party of going around Britain stirring up apathy. Viscount Whitelaw's apparent paradox is, in fact, a shrewd political insight, and all the sharper for being accidental. Big Government depends on going around the country stirring up apathy—creating the sense that problems are so big, so complex, so intractable that even attempting to think about them for yourself gives you such a splitting headache it's easier to shrug and accept as given the proposition that only government can deal with them.

Take health care. Through all the interminable health-care "debates" of Obama's first year, did you read any of the proposed plans? Of course not. They're huge and turgid and indigestible. Unless you're a health-care lobbyist, a health-care think-tanker, a health-care correspondent, or some other fellow who's paid directly or indirectly to plough through this stuff, why bother? None of the senators whose names are on the bills ever read 'em; why should you?

And you can understand why they drag on a bit. If you attempt to devise a health-care "plan" for over 300 million people, it's bound to get a bit complicated. But a health-care plan for you, Mabel Scroggins of 27 Elm Street, didn't used to be that complicated, did it? Let's say you carelessly drop the ObamaCare bill on your foot and it breaks your toe. In the old days, you'd go to your doctor (or, indeed, have him come to you—that's how insane it was back then), he'd patch you up, and you'd write him a check. That's the way it was in most of the developed world within living memory.

When did it get too complicated to leave to individuals? "Health" is potentially a big-ticket item, but so's a house and a car, and most folks manage to handle those without a Government Accommodation Plan or a Government Motor Vehicles System—or, at any rate, they did in pre-bailout America.

Ah, but government health care is not about health care, it's about government. That's why the Democrats spent the first year of a brutal recession trying to ram ObamaCare down the throats of a nation that didn't want it. Because the governmentalization of health care is the fastest way to a permanent left-of-center political culture. It redefines the relationship between the citizen and the state in fundamental ways that make small government all but impossible ever again. In most of the rest of the western world, it's led to a kind of two-party one-party state: right-of-center parties will once in a while be in office, but never in power, merely presiding over vast left-wing bureaucracies that cruise on regardless. All such "technocratic" societies slide left, into statism and stasis.

Many Americans are happy with the government monopoly. The monarchical urge persists even in a two-and-a-third-century-old republic.

So, when the distant Sovereign from Barackingham Palace graciously confers an audience on his unworthy subjects, they are eager to petition him to make all the bad stuff go away. "I have an urgent need," one lady beseeched King Barack at a "town hall meeting" in Fort Myers early in 2009. "We need a home, our own kitchen, our own bathroom."[11]

He took her name—Henrietta Hughes—and ordered his staff to meet with her. Hopefully, he didn't insult her by dispatching some no-name deputy assistant secretary of whatever instead of flying in one of the big-time tax-avoiding cabinet honchos to nationalize a Florida bank and convert one of its branches into a desirable family residence, with a swing set hanging where the drive-thru ATM used to be. The audience roared their gratitude. "Yes!" they yelped, and "Amen!" and even "Gracious God, thank you so much!"

As Bing Crosby said to Bob Hope in *The Road to Utopia*, "Leave your name with the girl, and we may get to you for some crowd noises." That's the citizen's role on America's road to Utopia: Leave your name with the girl and, after the background check, you may qualify for the crowd scenes.

Early in his term, President Obama called in some fellow smarties to test out some slogans. FDR had a "New Deal," so Obama thought he'd wrap up his domestic innovations under the umbrella title of "New Foundation." The historian Doris Kearns Goodwin cautioned against it. "New Foundation," she said, sounds like a lady's girdle.[12] Actually, it's more like a whalebone corset. When the American citizen climbs into the "New Foundation," the stays get cranked tighter and tighter, but incrementally—so you barely feel it, till you realize the bottom's dropped out, and you're coughing up blood, and they're still cranking.

★ ★ ★ ★ ★

THE STATIST QUO

FDR was the first American president to pass off Big Government as technocracy. He had a so-called "Brains Trust." As with so many pious liberal concepts, the term started as a throwaway joke. Back in the trust-busting days of the 1890s, a wag at *The Daily Star* of Marion, Ohio, mused: "Since everything else is tending to trusts, why not a brain trust … ? Our various and sundry supplies of gray matter may as well be controlled by a central syndicate."[13]

That's how America's ruling class now regards itself: a central syndicate of gray matter. Which brings us back to George Harrison and the Monopolies Commission. The Big Government "brains trust" is a trust like any other: it exists to monopolize, to prevent free trade, to rig the market. Specifically, it exists to enforce a monopoly of ideas, and squash all alternatives. You'll recall that, during the 2008 primary season, Barack Obama was revealed, at a private fundraiser in San Francisco, to have belittled his own party's voters in rural Pennsylvania as "bitter" people who "cling to guns or religion or antipathy to people who aren't like them."[14] He subsequently "apologized" by explaining that "I said something everybody knows is true."[15]

"*Everybody*"? Well, maybe at a swank Dem fundraiser in California—and, if that's not "everybody," who is? This was an even more revealing remark than the original bitter-clingers crack. It deserves to be as celebrated as the famous response to the 1972 election results by a bewildered Pauline Kael, doyenne of the *New Yorker*, that nobody she knew voted for Nixon. Just as "everybody" knows "we can't just keep driving our SUVs, eating whatever we want, keeping our homes at 72 degrees,"[16] so nobody we know voted for Nixon and everybody we know agrees that those crackers are embittered fundamentalist gun-nut bigots. Oh, c'mon, I said something *everybody* knows is true.

"Everybody" knows this stuff, especially if he reads the *New York Times* or listens to National Public Radio. "Everybody" knows that raising taxes is responsible, and "everybody" knows that cutting spending is just crazy talk. "Everybody" knows that the governmentalization of health care—the annexation of one-sixth of the economy, the equivalent of the U.S. taking over the entire British or French economy, or the Indian economy twice over—"everybody" knows that that's sober, prudent, technocratic, reasonable. And "everybody" knows that wanting to repeal ObamaCare is extremist, radical, dangerous. "Everybody" knows that serious proposals to address a looming shortfall in obligations of tens of trillions of dollars puts you in wide-eyed nut territory, just as "everybody" knows that massively increasing government spending is a moderate, centrist approach to stimulating the economy. Why, it's in the *Washington Post*! As the paper reported, after yet another anemic quarter:

> Another big rise in growth came from the federal government, which rose at a 9.2 percent annual rate, including a 13 percent pace of gain in nondefense spending. That reflects in part the fiscal stimulus action that was enacted last year.... [17]

So the establishment newspaper of the capital city of the so-called hyperpower thinks economic growth and government growth are the same thing? Maybe if we'd had a 20 or 30 percent "big rise in growth" of government, the economy would *really* be roaring along.

Who are these everybodies who know instinctively what's true and what isn't? The idea of a technocracy—a "central syndicate of gray matter"—is vital to Big Government's sense of itself. It's not about tired outmoded concepts of left or right, it's about "smart solutions" from smart guys— starting with the president. "He's probably the smartest guy ever to become president," said Michael Beschloss the day after Obama's election. [18]

Really? Other than demonstrate a remarkably focused talent for self-promotion, what has he ever *done*? Even as a legendary thinker, what original thought has he ever expressed in his entire life? And yet he's "probably the smartest guy ever to become president" says Beschloss—and he's a presidential historian so he should know, 'cause he's a smart guy, too.

Lending a hand, another smart guy, the *New York Times*' house conservative David Brooks, cooed over the credentialed-to-the-hilt smarts of the incoming administration: "If a foreign enemy attacks the United States during the Harvard-Yale game any time over the next four years, we're screwed."[19]

He's right. Over a quarter of Obama's political appointees had ties to Harvard; over 90 percent had "advanced degrees."[20] And yet we're screwed anyway, with or without the Harvard-Yale game. If the smart guys are so smart, how come we're broke? How come those Americans who aren't tenured *New York Times* columnists or ex-legislators parlaying their Rolodexes into lucrative but undemanding "consultancies" or cozy "private-sector" sinecures as Executive Vice-President for Government Relations, are going to end their days significantly poorer? And how come those European social democracies that blazed the trail to Big Government are already poorer, and in several cases insolvent?

Unlike less sophisticated creeds, the statist ideology denies it's any such thing. Why, they're way beyond that: just as the political class are merely technocrats, so our educators are not leftist ideologues but impartial scholars, and the media establishment are objective reporters who would never dream of imposing their own biases even if they had any. Because, if you accept the idea that your worldview is merely that—a view—it implicitly acknowledges there are other views, against which yours should be tested. Far easier to pronounce your side of the table the objective truth, and therefore any opposing argument is not a disagreement about policy or philosophy or economics, but merely evidence of Nazism, racism, or mental retardation. Contemplating a hostile electorate on the eve of the 2010 election, John Kerry bemoaned the ignorance of the voters: "Truth and facts and science don't seem to weigh in," he sighed.[21]

Senator Kerry is so wedded to "truth" and "facts" that, like his fellow Massachusetts patrician Ted Kennedy, he spent the Bush years disseminating a fake Thomas Jefferson quote ("Dissent is the highest form of patriotism").[22] Barack Obama is so smart he had a fake Martin Luther King quote sewn onto the Oval Office carpet ("The arc of the moral universe is long, but it bends toward justice").[23] Barbra Streisand is so smart she sonorously declaimed to a Democratic Party national gala a fake Shake-

speare quote she insisted was from *Julius Caesar* ("Beware the leader who
bangs the drums of war in order to whip the citizenry into a patriotic
fervor... "[24]—poor Will must have been having an off day). Hundreds of
leftie websites are so smart that, after the 2011 shootings in Tucson, they
all blamed it on Sarah Palin by using the same fake Sinclair Lewis quote
from *It Can't Happen Here* ("When fascism comes to America, it will be
wrapped in the flag and carrying a cross"—er, no, as it happens that's not
in *It Can't Happen Here* or any other Sinclair Lewis novel).[25] But why
quibble over the veracity of mere sentences? Liberals are so smart they
teach a fake book in college (*I, Rigoberta Menchu*).

In a culture so convinced of its truth, facts, science, and smarts, even
the Cliffs Notes are too much like hard work. As Shakespeare said to Sinclair Lewis at a Friars' Club roast for Thomas Jefferson, when conformity
comes to America, it will be wrapped in torpor and bent in the arc of
portentous banality. The United States has not just a ruling class, but a
ruling monoculture. Its "truth" and "facts" and "science" permeate not just
government but the culture, the media, the institutions in which we educate our children, the language of public discourse, the very societal air we
breathe. That's the problem, and just pulling the lever for a guy with an R
after his name every other November isn't going to fix it. If Hollywood's
liberal, if the newspapers are liberal, if the pop stars are liberal, if the grade
schools are liberal, if the very language is liberal to the point where all the
nice words have been co-opted as a painless liberal sedative, a Republican
legislature isn't going to be a shining city on a hill so much as one of those
atolls in the Maldives being incrementally swallowed by Al Gore's allegedly
rising sea levels.

In such a world, the Conformicrats think of themselves as a meritocracy,
a term coined by the sociologist Michael Young in 1958 for a satirical fantasy
contemplating the state of Britain in the year 2032.[26] And, as with "brains
trust," a droll jest got taken up by humorless lefties for real. By the time Tony
Blair started bandying the word ad nauseam as a description of the bright
new talents running the United Kingdom in the twenty-first century,

Lord Young felt obliged to object. Six decades earlier, he had written the party manifesto that swept the Labour Party to power in 1945, and he reminded the Blairite generation of two of the most powerful members of that government: Ernie Bevin, the Foreign Secretary, and Herbert Morrison, Lord President of the Council (and deputy prime minister). Morrison had left school at fourteen and become an errand boy, Bevin at eleven to work as a farmhand. Against considerable odds, they rose to become two of the most powerful men in the land. There were no such figures in Tony Blair's "meritocratic" cabinet—nor in Barack Obama's. But there used to be, even in the Oval Office.

Yet today, whene'er such a person heaves on the horizon, the so-called meritocrats recoil in horror. Remember the early sneers at Sarah Palin? Not for her policy positions or her track record as governor but for her life, where she came from, where she went to, her frightful no-name schools: My dear, who goes to North Idaho College? Or Matanuska-Susitna College, wherever and whatever that is. "Celebrate diversity"? Well, yes, but good grief, there are limits ...

Imagine what the new Condescendi would have made of candidates from Allegheny College (William McKinley, for one term), or, despite its name, Clinton Liberal Academy (Grover Cleveland, but he left to support his family). Why, Truman didn't even have a degree! And Van Buren left school at fourteen! And Lincoln only had eighteen months of formal education! And Zachary Taylor never went to school at all! Since the departure of Ronald Reagan (Eureka College, Illinois), America, for the first time in its history, has lived under continuous rule by Ivy League—less a two-party than a two-school system: Yale (Bush I), Yale Law (Clinton), Harvard Business (Bush II), Harvard Law (Obama). In an America ever less educated but ever more credentialed, who wants to take a flyer on autodidacts like Truman or Lincoln? And, even if you went to the right schools and got higher scores than John Kerry, as Bush Jr. did, the slightest departure from the assumptions of the conformocracy will earn you a zillion "SOMEWHERE IN TEXAS A VILLAGE IS MISSING ITS IDIOT" stickers.[27]

Our new elite have more refined sensibilities than the old aristocracy: just as dowager duchesses would sniff that so-and-so was "in trade," so today's rulers have an antipathy to doers in general. How could Sarah Palin's executive experience running a state, a town, and a commercial fishing operation compare to all that experience Barack Obama had in sitting around thinking great thoughts? In forming his war cabinet, Winston Churchill said that he didn't want to fill it up with "mere advisors at large with nothing to do but think and talk."[28] But Obama sent the Oval Office bust of Sir Winston back to the British, and now we have government by men who've done nothing but "think and talk."[29] There was less private-sector business experience in Obama's cabinet than in any administration going back a century.[30]

If you sit around "thinking and talking," the humdrum responsibilities of government are bound to seem drearily earthbound. Hence, the political class' preference for ersatz crises, and the now routine phenomenon of leaders of advanced, prosperous societies talking like gibbering madmen escaped from the padded cell, whether it's President Obama promising to end the rise of the oceans[31] or the Prince of Wales saying we only have ninety-six months left to save the planet.[32] *Time* magazine ran a fawning cover story on Arnold Schwarzenegger, Governor of California, and Michael Bloomberg, Mayor of New York: "The New Action Heroes."[33] So what action were they taking? Why, Bloomberg was "opening a climate summit" and "talking about saving the planet." All of it, including the bits west of the Holland Tunnel. And Schwarzenegger was "talking about eliminating disease." All of them. "I look forward to curing all these terrible illnesses," he announced.

As Madame Cornuel observed, no man is a hero to his valet. But fortunately it's a lot easier to be a hero to your typist, especially when it's *Time*'s Michael Grunwald. These action heroes are "doing big things." Bloomberg, cooed Grunwald, "enacted America's most draconian smoking ban and the first big-city trans-fat ban."

Wow!

Back in the real world, a couple days after Christmas 2010, a snow storm descended on New York, and the action-hero mayor, relentless in his pursuit of trans-fats, was unable, for more than three days, to fulfill as basic a municipal responsibility as clearing the streets.[34] His Big Nanny administration can regulate the salt out of your cheeseburger, but he can't regulate it on to Seventh Avenue. Perhaps, if New Yorkers had appeared to be enjoying the snow by engaging in unregulated sledding or snowballing without safety helmets, Nanny Bloomberg could have scraped the boulevards bare in nothing flat. But, lacking that incentive, he let it sit there.

In Governor Schwarzenegger's state, over one-third of the patients in Los Angeles County hospitals are illegal immigrants, and they've overwhelmed the system: dozens of emergency rooms in the state have closed after degenerating into a de facto Mexican health-care network.[35] If you're a legal resident of the state of California, your health system is worse than it was a decade ago and will be worse still in a decade's time. Fortunately, by then your now retired action-hero governor will have cured "all these terrible illnesses" and there will be no need for California's last seven hospitals.

The illegal immigration question is an interesting test of government in action, at least when it comes to core responsibilities like defense of the nation. Enforcing the southern border? Too porous. Can't be done, old boy. Cloud-cuckoo stuff. Pie-in-the-sky.

But changing the climate of the entire planet to some unspecified Edenic state? *That* we can do. Politicians incapable of clearing snow from city streets three days after a storm are nevertheless taken seriously when they claim to be able to change the very heavens—if only they can tax and regulate us enough.

On the eve of the 2010 Massachusetts election to fill what the Democrats insisted on referring to as "Ted Kennedy's seat," the president came to town to help out his candidate, a party hack named Martha Coakley. He had nothing to say, but he said it anyway. All those cool kids on his speechwriting team bogged him down in the usual leaden sludge. He went to the trouble of flying in to phone it in. The defining moment of his doomed attempt to prop up Ms. Coakley was his peculiar obsession with the emblem of Scott Brown's campaign—the Republican candidate's five-year-old pickup: "Forget the ads. Everybody can run slick ads," President Obama, standing alongside John Kerry, told an audience of out-of-state students at a private school. "Forget the truck. Everybody can buy a truck."[36]

How they laughed! But what was striking was the thinking behind Obama's line: that anyone can buy a truck for a slick ad, that Brown's pickup was a prop—like the herd of cows Al Gore rented for a pastoral backdrop when he launched his first presidential campaign. Or the "Iron Chef" TV episode featuring delicious healthy recipes made with produce direct from Michelle Obama's "kitchen garden": the cameras filmed the various chefs meeting the First Lady and wandering with her 'midst the beds picking out choice organic delicacies from the White House crop, and then for the actual cooking the show sent out for stunt-double vegetables from a grocery back in New York.[37] Viewed from Obama's perspective, why wouldn't you assume the truck's just part of the set? "In his world," wrote the *Weekly Standard*'s Stephen Hayes, "everything is political and everything is about appearances."[38]

Howard Fineman, the Chief Political Correspondent of *Newsweek*, took it a step further. The truck wasn't just any old prop but a very particular kind: "In some places, there are codes, there are images," he told MSNBC's Keith Olbermann. "You know, there are pickup trucks, you could say there was a racial aspect to it one way or another."[39]

Ah, yes. Scott Brown has over 200,000 miles on his odometer.[40] Man, he's racked up a lot of coded racism on that rig. But that's easy to do in notorious cross-burning KKK swamps like suburban Massachusetts.

Whenever aspiring authors ask me for advice, I usually tell 'em this: Don't just write there, *do* something. Learn how to shingle a roof, or cultivate orchids, or raise sled dogs. Because if you don't do anything, you wind up like Obama and Fineman—men for whom words are props and codes and metaphors but no longer expressive of anything real. America is becoming a bilingual society, divided between those who think a pickup is a rugged vehicle useful for transporting heavy-duty items from A to B, and those who think a pickup is coded racism. Unfortunately, the latter group forms most of the Democrat-media one-party state running the country. In perhaps the most explicit testament to the ever widening gulf between the metaphorical class and the simple-minded literalists they reign over, the liberal reaction to a murderous attack in Tucson by a deranged nut of no political affiliation was to blame it on the right's "extreme rhetoric"—all this talk of "targeting" marginal seats and having your opponent in the "crosshairs." Liberals can be expected to understand sophisticated concepts such as figures of speech, which is why they can safely name their Clinton campaign documentary *The War Room* and why Democratic Congressman Paul Kanjorski can recommend, re: the Republican Governor of Florida, "put him against the wall and shoot him."[41] Liberals exist in a world of metaphor, so it would be unlikely for them ever to rouse themselves to act on their rhetorical flourishes. But simple, embittered red-state types are too stupid to be entrusted with such potentially lethal weapons as literary devices.

Obama himself is not about "doing." Why would you expect him to be able to "do" anything? What has he ever "done" other than publish books about himself? That was the story of his life: Wow! Look at this guy! Wouldn't it be great to have him ... as *Harvard Law Review* editor, as community organizer, as state representative, as state senator, as United States senator. He was wafted ever upwards, staying just long enough in each "job" to get another notch on the escutcheon, but never long enough to leave any trace—until a freak combination of circumstances (war weariness, financial meltdown, divisive incumbent, inept opponent, the chance to cast a history-making vote) put Obama in line for the ultimate waft. If only Hogarth had been on hand to record a very contemporary *Fake's Progress*. No rail-splitting, like Lincoln. No farm work, like Coolidge. No swimming-pool lifeguard duty, like Reagan. Upward he wafted without breaking a sweat, except perhaps when briefly blocked on his whiney Valley Girl autobiography—as who wouldn't be blocked? It's tough to write an autobiography when you haven't done anything.

The new "meritocratic" elite, wrote Michael Young just before his death, "can be insufferably smug, much more so than the people who knew they had achieved advancement not on their own merit but because they were, as somebody's son or daughter, the beneficiaries of nepotism."[42] As Young had foreseen in his original essay, a cult of (pseudo-)meritocracy absolves the ruling class from guilt. They assume not, as princes of old did, that they were destined to rule, but that they *deserve* to. Which is wonderfully liberating. They "actually believe they have morality on their side," said Young of Britain's Blairites. The bigger government gets, the more transformative, the more intrusive, the louder it proclaims its moral purity/virtue. Thus, as Peter Berkowitz puts it, the ostensibly impartial concept of "fairness" is now no more or less than "the name progressives have given their chief policy goals."[43] This is politics as a form of narcissism: Mirror, mirror on the wall, who is the fairest of them all? In the name of "fairness," they grant privileges to preferred identity groups over others—that is, they treat certain people unfairly. Yet, if you oppose "fairness," you must be on the unfair side.

And who wants to find themselves hanging with that crowd? So, in government, in the dinosaur media, in the faculty lounge, in the community-organizing community, in the boardrooms of connected corporations, America's rulers are conformicrats. They have the same opinions, the same tastes, the same vocabulary. They think the same, and they expect you to do likewise. As Michael Tomasky, former editor of the lefty mag *The American Prospect*, explained it: "At bottom, today's Democrats from [Senator Max] Baucus to [Congresswoman Maxine] Waters are united in only two beliefs, and they demand that American citizens believe in only two things: diversity and rights."[44]

By "rights," they mean not "negative rights" as understood by the U.S. Constitution—the right to be left alone by the government in respect of your speech, your guns, etc—but "rights" *to* stuff, granted by the government, distributed by the government, licensed by the government, rationed by the government, but paid for by you. In the Orwellian language of Big Government, "rights" are no longer individual liberties that restrain the state but state power that restrains you. And by "diversity," they mean the state ideology of stultifying homogeneity. Hence, the peculiar spectacle of American "artists" from George Clooney to Stephen Sondheim to Green Day congratulating themselves on their truth-telling courage by producing films, plays, CDs, TV shows, and novels with which everyone they know is in full agreement. In such a world, to disagree with the liberal agenda is not so much an act of political dissent but, worse, a ghastly social faux pas. To take Mr. Tomasky's own profession, the average American newsroom ostentatiously recruits for diversity of race, sex, sexual orientation, and every other diversity except the only one that matters—diversity of ideas. To achieve its own propaganda goals, the Soviet politburo had to smash printing presses and jam radio signals. America's nomenklatura achieved the same level of dreary conformity just by leaving it to ABC, CBS, NBC, CNN, the *New York Times*, and the *Washington Post*. Which is why, as the first industry to prostrate itself before the deeply unAmerican idea of enforced uniformity, America's moribund monodailies are on life support and openly auditioning for a government bailout.

The advantage of life in the self-flattering conformicrat cocoon is that you never have to address anybody's arguments. All those tea parties and town halls with ordinary citizens protesting governmentalized health care? Oh, don't be so naïve. As the *New York Times* assured its readers, "The Rage Is Not About Health Care."[45] "It's merely a handy excuse," Frank Rich explained. "The real source of the over-the-top rage of 2010 is the same kind of national existential reordering that roiled America in 1964...."

Ah, in the Democratic Party it's always 1964 and Selma, Alabama. Except that now it's not the Democrats who are the redneck racists, it's you—yes, you. As Frank Rich explains:

> If Obama's first legislative priority had been immigration or financial reform or climate change, we would have seen the same trajectory. The conjunction of a black president and a female speaker of the House—topped off by a wise Latina on the

Supreme Court and a powerful gay Congressional committee chairman—would sow fears of disenfranchisement among a dwindling and threatened minority in the country no matter what policies were in play.... When you hear demonstrators chant the slogan "Take our country back!," these are the people they want to take the country back from.

So you may think you object to ObamaCare because you're very concerned about what you've heard about two-year wait times for MRIs in Canada, but it's really because you're itchin' to get your sheet on and string up that uppity Negro.

You may think you object to ObamaCare because it will lead to a massive shortage of primary care physicians as has already happened in Massachusetts,[46] but it's really because you'd like to slap around that Nancy Pelosi the way Bogey does Mary Astor in *The Maltese Falcon* 'cause that's the only language these lippy broads understand.

You may think you object to ObamaCare because the Federal Government forcing you to make health-care arrangements that meet the approval of the state commissars is unconstitutional, but it's really because you think that that wise Latina on the Supreme Court should be turning down your hotel bed and leaving a complimentary hazelnut truffle on your pillow.[47]

You may think you object to ObamaCare because its absurd bureaucratic insistence that you need a doctor's prescription in order to pay for your Tylenol from a health savings account will waste untold hours of doctors', patients', and pharmacists' time, but it's really because Barney Frank reminds you that you've always been slightly confused about your own sexuality and at the back of the desk drawer you've still got the phone number of that guy who wrote back when you put the "Bi-Curious Male Seeks Similar" ad in the classifieds, and to be honest when Congressman Frank gets butch and beats up on those bank executives it kinda turns you on.

I can't speak for the rest of you racists, sexists, and homophobes, but I've opposed government health care in Canada, the United Kingdom,

Bulgaria, and anywhere else I've been on the receiving end of it. And in Britain no blacks, women, or gays were involved in its introduction, just pasty-faced white blokes. In Canada, it was just pasty-faced white blokes with a pronounced hint of maple. In Bulgaria, it was swarthy Slavic blokes with impressively hirsute monobrows. Okay, that is racist, but only mildly so. And in any case when it comes to Slavic monobrows I prefer the women. Okay, that's racist and sexist, so I'll quit while I'm behind. But the point is, throughout most of the western world, government health care has been the creation of white males of drearily conventional orientation.

Yet, if you write for the *New York Times* or teach race and gender studies at American colleges for long enough, it seems entirely reasonable to conclude that a difference of opinion over health-care policy is being driven by nostalgia for segregated lunch counters. Invited by National Public Radio to expound on the use of "racial code words" in "the current opposition to health care reform," Melissa Harris-Lacewell, Professor of African-American Studies at Princeton, informed her listeners that "language of personal responsibility is often a code language used against poor and minority communities."[48]

"Personal responsibility" is racial code language? Phew, thank goodness America is belatedly joining Europe in all but abolishing the concept.

"Code language" is code language for "total bollocks." "Code word" is a code word for "I'm inventing what you really meant to say because the actual quote doesn't quite do the job for me." "Small government"? Racist code words! "Non-confiscatory taxes"? Likewise. "Individual liberty"? Don't even go there! With interpreters like Professor Harris-Lacewell on the prowl, I'm confident 95 percent of Webster's will eventually be ruled "code language."

Faced with public discontent about the statist agenda, the Condescendi look out the window at the unlovely mob in their "Don't tread on me" T-shirts and sneer, "The peasants are revolting." You oppose illegal immigration? You're a xenophobe. Gay marriage? Homophobe. The Ground Zero mosque? Islamophobe. If that's the choice, I'd rather be damned as racist and sexist. The evolution from -isms to phobias is part of the medicalization of dissent: the Conformicrats simply declare your position a form of mental illness. After firing commentator Juan Williams for some insufficiently politically correct observations about Muslims, NPR exec Vivian Schiller suggested her longtime colleague needed to see a psychiatrist.[49] That's the polite version of dismissing him as just another one of those "fucking Nascar retards," the elegant formulation Eric Alterman (Distinguished Professor of English and Journalism at Brooklyn College, and Professor of Journalism at the CUNY Graduate School of Journalism) used on the in-house "JournoList" to describe those Americans who disagree with him and his fellow media professionals.[50] Juan Williams seems an unlikely Nascar retard. He is not only liberal but black. Had a conservative hinted that an eminent African-American Democrat had mental health issues, he'd be the one headed for the funny farm. But, of course, in briefly wandering off liberalism's ideological plantation, Mr. Williams had behaved so irrationally that, as in the Soviet Union, only a medical condition could explain it. Don't worry about it, Juan. Just let the men in white coats get the straps around you, and shoot the needle into your arm, and you'll soon be feeling much better, and thinking just the same as everybody else.

On most of these issues, from illegal immigration to the Ground Zero mosque, the Conformicrats are losing the battle for public opinion by as much as 70/30. Yet even that isn't enough to persuade them to mount an argument. So much liberal debate boils down to Ring Lardner's great line: "'Shut up,' he explained."

Fewer people know the line that precedes it (in Lardner's story, *The Young Immigrunts*): a kid asking, "Are you lost, daddy?" The rulers think we're kids, they're the daddy, and it takes a village to raise a fuckin' Nascar retard child. The ruled think we're lost, and being driven farther and farther off the map.

But the disparagement of dissenters as racists, sexists, homophobes, and retards is not entirely an act of misdirection. It reflects the so-called technocracy's priorities: for Big Government bent on social micromanagement, ideological enforcement takes priority over any other activity. When Hurricane Katrina swept in and devastated Louisiana and Mississippi, volunteer firemen—whoops, "firefighters"—from across the map headed south to help with disaster relief. FEMA dispatched them to ...

New Orleans?

Gulfport?

No, to Atlanta—for diversity and sexual-harassment training.[51]

Which most of them had already undergone back home. But you can't be too careful: Heaven forbid that a waterlogged granny should be rescued by an insufficiently non-homophobic fireman.

FEMA is supposed to be the Federal Emergency Management Agency, not the Fairyland Equality Makework Agency. But so it goes. Government agencies created to demonstrate the laser-sharp problem-solving skills of the elite technocracy in the end mostly just enforce conformity with the state ideology. Thus, the "enhanced patdowns" of U.S. airport security are less about preventing terrorism than about preventing the acknowledgment of inconvenient truths at odds with the diversity cult. Contemporary Big Government is like a widget factory that no longer makes widgets but holds sensitivity training sessions all day long. And, if you're a nonagenarian spinster at LaGuardia with a TSA agent's paws roaming 'round your bloomers while the Yemeni madrassah alumnus sails through the express check-in, the involuntary sensitivity training isn't all that sensitive.

★ ★ ★ ★ ★

TWO SOLITUDES

If it were just Good King Barack and Henrietta Hughes, rulers and subjects, all would be well. But America still has a citizenry: the productive class—the ones whose labors have to fund both the swollen state bureaucracy and its dependents. It's tough if you happen to fall into this third category. Most of the time, such as at that town hall meeting in Fort Myers, you're not even part of the national conversation: you live in the Flownover Country. In 1945, Hugh MacLennan wrote a novel set in Montreal whose title came to sum up the relationship between the English and the French in Canada: *Two Solitudes*. They live in the same nation, sometimes in the same town, sometimes share the same workspace. But they inhabit different psychologies. In 2008, David Warren, a columnist with *The Ottawa Citizen*, argued that the concept has headed south:

> In the United States, especially in the present election, we get glimpses of two political solitudes that have been created not by any plausible socio-economic division within society, nor by any deep division between different ethnic tribes, but tauto-logically by the notion of "two solitudes" itself. The nation is divided, roughly half-and-half, between people who instinc-tively resent the Nanny State, and those who instinctively long for its ministrations.[52]

John Edwards, yesterday's coming man, had an oft retailed stump speech about "the two Americas," a Disraelian portrait of Dickensian gloom conjured in the mawkish drool of a Depression-era sob-sister: one Amer-ica was a wasteland of shuttered mills and shivering "coatless girls," while in the other America Dick Cheney and his Halliburton fat cats were sitting 'round the pool swigging crude straight from the well and toasting their war profits all day long.[53] Edwards was right about the "two Americas," but not about the division: in one America, those who subscribe to the ruling ideology can access a world of tenured security lubricated by government and without creating a dime of wealth for the overall economy; in the other America, millions of people go to work every day to try to support their families and build up businesses and improve themselves, and the harder they work the more they're penalized to support the government class in its privileges. Traditionally, he who paid the piper called the tune. But not anymore. Flownover Country pays the piper, very generously, in salaries, benefits, pensions, and perks. But Conformicrat America calls the tune, the same unending single-note dirge. David Warren regards these as

"two basically irreconcilable views of reality": "Only in America are they
so equally balanced. Elsewhere in the west, the true believers in the Nanny
State have long since prevailed."[54]

Increasingly, America's divide is about the nature of the state itself—
about the American idea. And in that case why go on sharing the same real
estate? As someone once said, "A house divided against itself cannot stand."
The Flownover Country's champion ought, in theory, to be the Republican
Party. But, even in less fractious times, this is a loveless marriage. Much of
the GOP establishment is either seduced by the Conformicrats or terrified
by them, to the point where they insist on allowing the liberals to set the
parameters of the debate—on health care, immigration, education, Social
Security—and then wonder why elections are always fought on the Democrats' terms. If you let the left make the rules, the right winds up being
represented by the likes of Bob Dole and John McCain, decent old sticks
who know how to give dignified concession speeches. If you want to get
rave reviews for losing gracefully, that's the way to go. If you want to prevent
Big Government driving America off a cliff, it's insufficient.

The Conformicrats need Flownover Country to fund them. It's less clear
why Flownover Country needs the Conformicrats—and a house divided
against itself cannot stand without the guy who keeps up the mortgage
payments.

According to the Tax Policy Center, for the year 2009, 47 percent of U.S.
households paid no federal income tax.[55] Obviously, many of them paid
other kinds of taxes—state tax, property tax, cigarette tax. But at a time of
massive increases in federal spending, half the country is effectively making
no contribution to it, whether it's national defense, or interest payments on
the debt, or vital stimulus funding to pump monkeys in North Carolina
full of cocaine (true, seriously, but don't ask me why).[56] Furthermore, if you
pay local tax but no federal income tax, you're more easily seduced by the
most malign of Big Government's distortions: its insistence that more and
more aspects of life have to be regulated by a centralized regime in Washington rather than by varieties of state, county, and municipal bodies. As a

general principle, if you pay nothing for government, why would you want less of it? More specifically, if you pay nothing for federal government, why would the relentless centralization of American statism bother you?

In 2009, Ken Rogulski of WJR Detroit reported on a federal aid "giveaway" at the city's Cobo Center:

> WJR: Why are you here?
> WOMAN #1: To get some money.
> WJR: What kind of money?
> WOMAN #1: Obama money.
> WJR: Where's it coming from?
> WOMAN #1: Obama.
> WJR: And where did Obama get it?
> WOMAN #1: I don't know. His stash. I don't know. [She laughs.] I don't know where he got it from, but he's giving it to us, to help us.
> WOMAN #2: And we love him.
> WOMAN #1: We love him. That's why we voted for him!
> WOMEN (chanting): Obama! Obama! Obama! [They laugh.]
> WJR:… and where did Obama get the funds?
> WOMAN #2: Ummm, I have no idea, to tell you the truth. He's the President.[57]

Well, he got it from me, and from you. Every dollar in Obama's "stash" comes from me, you, or the Chinese Politburo. And redistributing it on the grounds above only inflates these ladies' blithe assumptions. But so what? If the object is to increase government, and expand the power of those in government, then the "Obama's stash" route works just fine.

By contrast, if you fall into the taxation category and you're stuck with the tab for Obama's stash, you're not only paying for groups that get a better hearing in Washington, but ensuring that the socioeconomic conditions of the republic will trend, mercilessly, against you. The small business class—men and women in unglamorous lines of work that keep the

Flownover Country going—are disfavored by the Conformicrats. They are occasionally acknowledged by our rulers with rhetorical flourishes—"tax cuts for working families"—but, on closer inspection, these "tax cuts" invariably mean not reductions in the rate of income seizure but a "tax credit" reimbursed from the seizure in return for living your life the way the government wants you to, and expanding the size of the dependent class.

United States income tax is becoming the twenty-first-century equivalent of the "jizya"—the punitive tax levied by Muslim states on their non-Muslim citizens. In return for funding the Caliphate, the infidels were permitted to carry on practicing their faith. Under the American jizya, in return for funding Big Government, the non-believers are permitted to carry on practicing their faith in capitalism, small business, economic activity, and the other primitive belief systems to which they cling so touchingly.

In the Islamic world, the infidel tax base eventually wised up. You can see it literally in the landscape in rural parts of the Balkans: Christian tradesmen got fed up paying the jizya and moved out of the towns up into remote hills far from the shakedown crowd. In less mountainous terrain where it's harder to lie low, non-Muslims found it easier to convert. That's partly what drove Muslim expansion. Once Araby had been secured for Islam, it was necessary to move on to the Levant, and to Persia, and to Central Asia and North Africa and India and Europe—in search of new infidels to mug. I'm not so invested in my analogy that I'm suggesting America's Big Government shakedown racket will be forced to invade Canada and Scandinavia. For one thing, everywhere else got with the Big Government program well ahead of America and those on the receiving end long ago figured out all the angles: in the Stockholm suburb of Tensta, 20 percent of women in their late forties collect disability benefits.[58] In the United Kingdom, five million people—a tenth of the adult population—have not done a day's work since the New Labour government took office in 1997.[59]

America has a ways to go in catching up with those enlightened jurisdictions, but it's heading there. As Congressman Paul Ryan pointed out, by 2004, 20 percent of U.S. households were getting about 75 percent of their income from the federal government.[60] As a matter of practical politics, how receptive would they be to a pitch for lower taxes, which they don't pay, or for lower government spending, of which they are such fortunate beneficiaries? How receptive would another fifth of households, who receive about 40 percent of their income from the feds, be to such a pitch?

But for the productive class, the ongoing government shakedown leads to demoralization and disincentivization. In 2002, 61 percent of Americans believed their children would enjoy higher living standards. By 2009, that was down to 45 percent. This is a hole in America's soul, and it's growing bigger every day.[61]

In the Nineties, the "culture wars" were over "God, guns and gays." The overreach of the statists has added a fourth G: Government itself is now a front in the culture war, and a battle of the most primal kind. Is the United States a republic of limited government with a presumption in favor of individual liberty? Or is it just like any other western nation in which a permanent political class knows what's best for its subjects? In California, the people can pass a ballot proposition against gay marriage, but a single activist judge overrules them. In Arizona, the people's representatives vote to uphold the people's laws, but a pliant judge strikes them down at Washington's behest. It is surely only a matter of time before some federal judge finds the Constitution unconstitutional.

Some schlub in Fresno might wonder why a gay judge who seemed a more militant advocate for gay marriage than the plaintiffs were didn't recuse himself from the case. But that just shows how little they know: it's the voters of California who should have recused themselves. Their bigotry makes them unqualified to pronounce on the subject. They should be grateful Judge Walker didn't mandate re-education camp.

It is never a good idea to send the message, as the political class now does consistently, that there are no democratic means by which the people can restrain their rulers. As the (Democrat) pollster Pat Cadell pointed out, the logic of that is "pre-revolutionary."[62]

Once you've secured the other levers of power, elective politics becomes a kind of sham combat to distract from the real battlegrounds. There are degrees of dissembling: the presidential candidate running as a "fiscally responsible post-partisan healer" provides the cover for an agenda crafted by far more explicitly left-wing legislators, such as Pelosi and Frank. Behind the legislators are the judges, behind the judges the regulatory bureaucracy, and behind the bureaucracy the union muscle: left, lefter, leftest.

★ ★ ★ ★ ★

FIDDLING WHILE ROME BURNS MONEY

Of all the many marvelous Ronald Reagan lines, this is my favorite:

We are a nation that has a government—not the other way around.[63]

He said it in his inaugural address in 1981, and, despite a Democrat-controlled Congress, he lived it. It sums up his legacy abroad: across post-Communist Europe, from Slovenia to Bulgaria to Lithuania, governments that had nations were replaced by nations that have governments.

Today, in Reagan's own country, we are atrophying into a government that has a nation.

In the eighteen months after the collapse of Lehman Brothers in September 2008, over seven million Americans lost their jobs, yet the number of federal bureaucrats earning $100,000 or more went up from 14 percent to 19 percent.[64] An economic downturn for you, but not for them. They're upturn girls living in a downturn world. At the start of the "downturn," the Department of Transportation had just one employee earning more than $170,000 per year. Eighteen months later, it had 1,690.[65] In the year after the passage of Obama's "stimulus," the private sector lost 2.5 million jobs, but the federal bureaucracy gained 416,000.[66] Even if one accepts the government's ludicrous concept of "creating or saving" jobs, by its own figures four out of every five "created or saved" jobs were government jobs. "Stimulus" stimulates government, not the economy. It's part of the remorseless governmentalization of American life.

What sort of jobs were "created or saved"? Well, the United States Bureau of the Public Debt is headquartered in Parkersburg, West Virginia—and it's hiring! According to the Careers page of their website: "The Bureau of the Public Debt (BPD) is one of the best places to work in the federal government. When you work for BPD, you're a part of one of the federal government's most dynamic agencies."[67]

I'm sure. They're committed to a working environment of "Information, Informality, Integrity, Inclusion & Individual Respect." In the land of the blind, the five-I'd bureaucrat is king. Alas, no room on the motto for the sixth I (Insolvency). At some point in the near future, Big Government will have reached its state of theoretical perfection and all revenues will be going either to interest payments to China or to lavish pensions liabilities for retired officials of the Bureau of Public Debt.

When the subject of the leviathan comes up, the media and other statism groupies tend to say, "Oh, well, it's easy to talk about cutting government spending, until you start looking at individual programs, most of which tend to be very popular."

"Programs" is a sly word. Regardless of the merits of the "program," it requires human beings to run it. And government humans cost more than private humans. In 2009, the average civilian employee of the United States government earned $81,258 in salary plus $41,791 in benefits. Total: $123,049.[68]

The average American employed in the private sector earned $50,462 in salary plus $10,589 in benefits. Total: $61,051.[69]

So the federal worker earns more than twice as much as the private sector worker. Plus he has greater job security: he's harder to fire, or even to persuade to take a small pay cut.

Experts talk about the difficulty of restructuring entitlement programs, or of carving out a few billions in savings here and there. But here's a thought experiment: imagine if federal workers made the same as the private workers who pay their salaries. Imagine if they had to get by on 61K instead of 123 grand.

Ah, but such fancies dwell purely in the Land of Imagination. In theory, Americans govern themselves through elected representatives. In practice, the political class are no longer the citizen-legislators of a self-governing republic but instead the plump, pampered Emirs of Incumbistan. Hawaii's Daniel Inouye has been in Congress as long as the islands have been a state, which means he's been in office longer than the world's longest-running dictators-for-life. Lest comparisons with Colonel Gaddafi seem a little unkind, Inouye has been in Washington almost as long as the five monarchs of the Kamehameha dynasty ruled over a unified kingdom of Hawaii. If that's what Hawaiians are looking for in a political system, why bother overthrowing Queen Lili'uokalani? John Dingell Jr. has been a Michigan congressman since 1955. For the twenty-two years before that, his constituents were represented by John Dingell Sr. Between the first Duke of Dingell and the second, the Dingell family has held the seat for a third of the republic's history. If that's what Michiganders are looking for in a political system, why not stick with the House of Lords?

The late Robert C. Byrd sat in the Senate for half-a-century while the world transformed, and strung along: a former Klan leader ("Exalted Cyclops") and recruiter ("Kleagle") who opposed civil rights, he ended his days as a hero to Moveon.org for opposing the war on terror. He doesn't seem to have been a principled Klansman or a principled Moveon.orgiast. He simply moved on as required. You gotta know when to change the sheets. He did what was necessary to maintain himself in power. Everything in West Virginia apart from the Bureau of Public Debt and the Klan lodge is named after him. When he turned against the war in Afghanistan in 2002, I suggested that maybe if we agreed to rename the place Robert C. Byrdistan, he might see his way to staying onside for a couple more months. (I'm still in favor of that: his view of power was no less primitively tribal and venal than your average Pushtun village headman's.) Apart from naming more public buildings after himself than your average Latin American caudillo would, what else did Byrd accomplish in his "public service"? What do Michiganders have to show for the Dingell dynasty's four-fifths of a century in office? Opponents should simply put up graphs showing the debt when Inouye and the rest were elected, and what it is now.

Charlie Rangel has been there since 1970. Even his car has been there a long time. Apparently in Congress you're not meant to keep a vehicle in the House parking garage for more than six weeks without moving it. Rangel parked his Mercedes in one of the most "highly coveted" spaces in 2003, put a tarp on it, and left it there for six years.[70] If only we could have done that with him and the rest of the legislative class. The chairman of the powerful House Ways and Means committee, Rangel was the man who wrote the nation's tax laws yet did not consider himself bound by them. So, for example, he had a rental property in the Dominican Republic but did not declare the income he received from it. Good for him. Would you like to have a rental property in a foreign jurisdiction and keep all the dough to yourself? Too bad. If you were to do it, there wouldn't be enough money to maintain our rulers in the style to which they've become accustomed. Rangel isn't rich by congressional standards, but he is in the happy position of so many people one encounters in "public service" who rarely if ever have cause to write a personal check. After the congressman's grotesque self-pitying ululations on the House floor for the injustice of being "censured" for his conduct, Kerry Picket of the *Washington Times* invited him to imagine what punishment the "average American citizen" would have received had he done what Rangel did. "Please," the congressman told her. "I don't deal in average American citizens."[71]

If only. Pete Stark has been in the House of Representatives since 1973. For all those decades, he has sworn to uphold the Constitution of the United States. What's in there? Let Pete explain it. In 2010, running for his nineteenth term in Congress, Stark was asked about the constitutionality of ObamaCare. He replied: "I think there are very few constitutional limits that would prevent the federal government from rules that could affect your private life."[72]

His lady questioner wanted to be sure she'd understood: "Is your answer that they can do anything?"

Stark responded: "The federal government, yes, can do most anything in this country."

He's right. If the Commerce Clause can be stretched to require you to make arrangements for your health care that meet the approval of the national government, then the republic is dead.

What's the very least that we're entitled to expect of our legislators? That they know what they're legislating. John Conyers has been in the House of Representatives since 1965. Like most representatives, he didn't bother reading the 3,000-page health-care bill he voted for, because, as he said with disarming honesty, he wouldn't understand it even if he did: "I love these members, they get up and say, 'Read the bill,'" sighed Congressman Conyers. "What good is reading the bill if it's a thousand pages and you don't have two days and two lawyers to find out what it means after you read the bill?"[73]

Okay, so it would be unreasonable to expect a legislator to know what it is he's actually legislating into law. He's got wall-to-wall aides to do that for him. When you're rejiggering more than one-sixth of the economy and incurring massive future debt, that's the sort of minor task you can out-source to a flunkey. It would be churlish to direct readers to the video posted on the Internet of Representative Conyers finding time to peruse a copy of *Playboy* while on a commuter flight to Detroit.[74] Perhaps if the ObamaCare bill had had a centerfold of Kathleen Sebelius on page 1,872, or maybe a "Girls of the Health & Human Services Death Panel" pictorial...

Two-thousand-page bills, unread and indeed unwritten at the time of passage, are the death of representative government. They also provide a clue as to why, in a country this large, national government should be minimal and constrained. Even if you doubled or trebled the size of the legislature, the Conyers plea would still hold: no individual can read these bills and understand what he's voting on. That's why the bulk of these responsibilities should be left to states and subsidiary jurisdictions, which can legislate on such matters at readable length and in comprehensible language.

But there's a more basic objection: Conyers is correct. He doesn't need to read the bill because he is no longer a maker of law. Law rests on the principle of equality before it. When a bill is two thousand pages, there's no equality: instead, there's a hierarchy of privilege. One state is treated differently from another, out of raw political necessity. For ObamaCare, Nebraska got a "Cornhusker Kickback," but there was no "Granite State Graft" for New Hampshire, because there was no political need for one. Some citizens (i.e., members of powerful unions and approved identity groups) are treated differently from other citizens (i.e., you). It's not a law so much as a Forbes 500 List, a hit parade of who's most plugged in to who matters in Washington, with Nebraska senators and UAW honchos at the top, and a loser like you way down at the bottom. And even then, as happened almost as soon as ObamaCare had passed, the un-level playing field had to be re-landscaped with additional hillocks and valleys containing opt-outs for McDonald's, the United Federation of Teachers, and anyone else powerful enough to get past the Obama switchboard operator.[75] So Conyers has to worry only that his client groups have been taken care of: he doesn't deal in average American citizens, as Charlie Rangel would say. Joe Average and all the rest can be left to the agency of this, the board of that, the commission of the other, manned by millions of bureaucrats whose role is to determine, arbitrarily but authoritatively, which of the multiple categories of Unequal-Before-the-Law Second-Class (or Third-Class, or Fourth-Class) Citizenship you happen to fall into.

The lifetime professional legislative class boasts of its "experience." Experience of what? Of spending beyond not their means but ours. The Emirs of Incumbistan have presided over an explosion of government, an avalanche of debt, and the looting of America's future. Robert C. Byrd named buildings after himself; Eddie Bernice Johnson handed out a third of Congressional Black Caucus college scholarships to her own grandchildren and the family of her senior aide;[76] Charlie Rangel fiddled his expenses while Rome burned through our money. Focused on their petty privileges, they were happy to sub-contract law-making to others. The Emirs corrupted not just themselves but the very idea of responsible government. And far from the ballot box, alternative sources of power arose.

★ ★ ★ ★ ★

THE BUREAU OF COMPLIANCE

Behind our left-wing legislators are lefter judges. In a country where every other institution has lost legitimacy, only our robed rulers still command widespread deference. So these days the left advances its causes more effectively through the courts than through elections, for the fairly obvious reason that very few people are dumb enough to vote for this stuff. The judiciary legislates fundamental issues—abortion, gay marriage, illegal immigration, health care—and thereby supplies electoral cover for Democrats. As Nancy Pelosi explained, "It is a decision of the Supreme Court. So this is almost as if God has spoken."[77] So that's that. Love to help you, says Nancy, take your point, but there's nothing I can do.

That's not how Abraham Lincoln saw it: "If the policy of the government upon vital questions affecting the whole people is to be irrevocably fixed by decisions of the Supreme Court…the people will have ceased to be their own rulers."[78]

Which they have.

America is unique in this regard. In Europe, if the establishment wants to invent a new "right"—that is, yet another intrusion by government—it goes ahead and does so. If it happens to conflict with this year's constitution, they rewrite it. But the United States is the only western nation in which the rulers invoke the Constitution for the purpose of overriding it.

What Judge Bolton in the Arizona immigration case and Judge Walker in the California marriage case share with Mayor Bloomberg's observations on popular opposition to the Ground Zero mosque is a contempt for the people. Popular sovereignty may be fine in theory but not when the citizenry are so obviously in need of "re-education" by their betters. The alliance of political statists and judicial statists is moving us into a land beyond law—a land of apostasy trials. The Conformicrats have made a bet that the populace will willingly submit to subtle but pervasive forms of re-education camp. Over in England, London's transportation department has a bureaucrat whose very title sums up our rulers' general disposition toward us: Head of Behavior Change.

In 2008, when the Canadian Islamic Congress attempted to criminalize my writing north of the border by taking me to the "Human Rights" Commission, a number of outraged American readers wrote to me saying, "You need to start kicking up a fuss about this, Steyn, and then maybe Canadians will get mad and elect a conservative government that will end this nonsense."

Made perfect sense. Except that Canada already had a Conservative government under a Conservative prime minister, and the very head of the "human rights" commission investigating me was herself the Conservative appointee of a Conservative minister of justice. Makes no difference. Once the state swells to a certain size, the people available to fill the ever expanding number of government jobs will be statists—sometimes hard-core Marxist statists, sometimes social-engineering multiculti statists, sometimes fluffily "compassionate" statists, sometimes patrician *noblesse oblige* statists, but always statists. The short history of the post-war western democracies is that you don't need a president-for-life if you've got a bureaucracy-for-life: the people can elect "conservatives," as from time to time the Germans and British have done, and the left is mostly relaxed about it because, in all but exceptional cases (Thatcher), they fulfill the same function in the system as the first-year boys at wintry English boarding schools who for tuppence-ha'penny would agree to go and take the chill off the toilet seat in the unheated lavatories until the prefects were ready to stroll in and assume their rightful place. Republicans have gotten good at keeping the seat warm.

Thus, America in the twenty-first century—a supposedly "center-right" nation governed by a left-of-center political class, a lefter-of-center judiciary, a leftest-of-center bureaucracy, all of whom have been educated by a lefterooniest-of-all academy.

Liberalism, as the political scientist Theodore Lowi put it, "is hostile to law," and has a preference for "policy without law."[79] The law itself doesn't really matter so much as the process it sets in motion—or, as Nancy Pelosi famously told the American people regarding health care, "We have to pass the bill so you can find out what's in it."[80] When Lowi was writing in the Seventies, he noted that both the Occupational Safety and Health Administration (OSHA) and the Consumer Product Safety Commission (CPSC) were set up by a Congress that didn't identify a single policy goal for these agencies and "provided no standards whatsoever" for their conduct. So they made it up as they went along.

Where do you go to vote out the CPSC or OSHA?

Or any of the rest of the unaccountable acronyms drowning America in alphabet soup. For more and more Americans, law has been supplanted by "regulation"—a governing set of rules not legislated by representatives accountable to the people, but invented by an activist bureaucracy, much of which is well to the left of either political party. As the newspapers blandly reported in 2010, the bureaucrats weren't terribly bothered about whether Congress would pass a cap-and-trade mega-bill into law because, if faint-hearted Dems lose their nerve, the EPA will just "raise" "standards" all by itself.[81]

Where do you go to vote out the EPA?

Congress stripped provisions for end-of-life counseling (the so-called "death panels") out of the ObamaCare bill, but Kathleen Sebelius, the Secretary of Health and Human Services, put 'em back on her say so.[82] And why shouldn't she? As Philip Klein pointed out in the *American Spectator*, the new law contained 700 references to the Secretary "shall," another 200 to the Secretary "may," and 139 to the Secretary "determines." So the Secretary may and shall determine pretty much anything she wants. Plucked at random:

> The Secretary shall develop oral healthcare components that shall include tooth-level surveillance.[83]

"Tooth-level surveillance": from colonial subjects to dentured servants in a mere quarter-millennium.

Where do you go to vote out "the Secretary"?

And so "We the people" degenerates into "We the regulators, we the bureaucrats, we the permit-issuers, we the czars." Dancing with the czars is unrepublican. "Ignorantia juris non excusat" is one of the oldest concepts of civilized society: ignorance of the law is no excuse. But today we're all ignorant of the law, from John Conyers and the guys who make it down to li'l ol' you on the receiving end. How can you not be? Under the hyper-regulatory state, any one of us is in breach of dozens of laws at any one time without being aware of it. In a New York deli, a bagel with cream cheese is subject to food-preparation tax, but a plain bagel with no filling is not.[84] Except that, if the clerk slices the plain bagel for you, the food-preparation tax applies. Just for that one knife cut. As a progressive caring society, New York has advanced from tax cuts to taxed cuts. Oh, and, if he *doesn't* slice the plain bagel, but you opt to eat it in the deli, the food preparation tax also applies, even though no preparation was required for the food.

Got that? If you've got a deli, you better have, because New York is so broke they need their nine cents per sliced bagel and their bagel inspectors are cracking down. How does the song go? "If I can make it there/I'll make it anywhere!" If you can make it there, you're some kind of genius. To open a restaurant in NYC requires dealing with the conflicting demands of at least eleven municipal agencies, plus submitting to twenty-three city inspections, and applying for thirty different permits and certificates. Not including the state liquor license.[85] The city conceded that this could all get very complicated. So what did it do to help would-be restaurateurs? It set up a new bureaucratic body to help you negotiate your way through all the other bureaucratic bodies. Great! An Agency of Bureaucratic Expeditiousness! And, if that doesn't work, they'll set up an Agency of Bureaucratic Expeditiousness Regulation to keep it up to snuff.

In such a world, there is no "law"—in the sense of (a) you the citizen being found by (b) a jury of your peers to be in breach of (c) a statute passed by (d) your elected representatives. Instead, unknown, unnamed, unelected, unaccountable bureaucrats determine transgressions, prosecute infractions, and levy fines for behavioral rules they themselves craft and which, thanks to the ever more tangled spaghetti of preferences, subsidies, entitlements, and incentives, apply to different citizens unequally. But tyranny is always whimsical. You may be lucky: you may not catch their eye—for a while. But perhaps your neighbor does, or the guy down the street. No trial, no jury, just a dogsbody in some office who pronounces that you're guilty of an offense a colleague of his invented.

One morning, I strolled into my office in New Hampshire and noticed a letter on my assistant's desk from the State of New York's Bureau of Compliance informing us that we were in non-compliance with the Bureau of Compliance.

This was news to me. I don't live in New York, I don't own a business in New York, I don't make anything in New York, I don't sell anything in New York, I rarely visit New York except to fly in once in a while and catch a Broadway show (which I'll now be doing on its out-of-town tryout in New Haven). Nevertheless, the State of New York had notified me that I was in non-compliance with the Bureau of Compliance, and apparently the fine for that is $14,000.

"Fourteen grand?" I roared to my lawyer. "On principle, I'd rather go to jail and be gang-raped by whichever bunch of convicted Albany legislators I have the misfortune to be sharing a cell with."

"I take it then you don't want to settle?"

No, sir. I'm proud to be in non-compliance with the Bureau of Compliance. I've put it on my business card. Still, I was interested to read this a few days later in the *New York Times*:

> Albany—As Gov. David A. Paterson calls lawmakers back to work on the budget this week, he has announced that the fiscal situation is so serious that he must begin laying off state workers. But there is one wrinkle, as officials try to pare government

spending: No one knows for sure how big the state work force actually is.[86]

Oh, my. You'd think that that would also be in non-compliance with the Bureau of Compliance, wouldn't you? But no, it's just business as usual. They can audit you, but no one can audit them. You have to comply with them, but they don't have to comply with them. The *Times* attempted to get some ballpark figures from the hundreds of state agencies; a few provided employment numbers, but others "seemed unaccustomed to public inquiry," as the newspaper tactfully put it.

Why wouldn't they be? Government accounting is a joke. In one year (2009), Medicare handed out $98 billion in improper or erroneous payments.[87] A tenth of a trillion? Ha! Rounding error. Look for it in the line-items under "Miscellaneous." For an accounting fraud of $567 million, Enron's executives went to jail, and its head guy died there.[88] For an accounting fraud ten times that size, the two Democrat hacks who headed Fannie Mae and Freddie Mac, Franklin Raines and Jamie Gorelick, walked away with a combined taxpayer-funded payout of $116.4 million. Fannie and Freddie are two of the largest businesses in America, but they're exempt from SEC disclosure rules and Sarbanes-Oxley "corporate governance" burdens, and so in 2008, unlike Enron, WorldCom, or any of the other reviled private-sector bogeymen, they came close to taking down the entire global economy. What then is the point of the SEC?

By 2005, the costs of federal regulatory compliance alone (that is, not including state or local red tape) were up to $1.13 trillion—or approaching 10 percent of GDP.[89] In much of America, it takes far more paperwork to start a business than to go on welfare. In the words of a headline in the organic free-range hippie-dippy magazine *Acres*, "Everything I Want to Do Is Illegal."[90]

The most vital element in a dynamic society is the space the citizen has to live life to his fullest potential. Big Government encroaches on this space unceasingly. Under the acronyms uncountable, we have devolved from republican self-government to a micro-regulated nursery. The book *What's the Matter with Kansas?* gives the game away in its very title. What's the matter with Kansas is that it declines to vote as the statists would like. It surely cannot be that there is something the matter with the statists, so there must be something the matter with their subjects: they're too ill-educated, or manipulated by advertisers, or deceived by talk radio, or just plain lazy to understand their own best interests. Therefore, it is our duty, as enlightened progressives, to correct their misunderstanding of themselves and decide on their behalf. In a famous interaction at an early tea party, CNN's Susan Roesgen interviewed a guy in the crowd and asked why he was here: "Because," said the Tea Partier, "I hear a president say that he believed in what Lincoln stood for. Lincoln's primary thing was he believed that people had the right to liberty, and had the right …"[91]

But Miss Roesgen had heard enough: "What does this have to do with your taxes? Do you realize that you're eligible for a $400 credit?"

Had the Tea Party animal been as angry as Angry White Men are supposed to be, he'd have said, "Oh, push off, you condescending tick. Taxes are a liberty issue. I don't want a $400 'credit' for agreeing to live my life in government-approved ways." Had he been of a more literary bent, he might have adapted Sir Thomas More's line from *A Man for All Seasons*: "Why, Susan, it profits a man nothing to give his soul for the whole world… but for a $400 tax credit?"

But Miss Roesgen wasn't done with her "You may already have won!" commercial: "Did you know," she sneered, "that the state of Lincoln gets $50 billion out of this stimulus? That's $50 billion for this state, sir."

Golly! Who knew it was that easy? $50 billion! Where did it come from? Did one of those Somali pirate ships find it just off the coast in a half-submerged treasure chest, all in convertible pieces of eight or Zanzibari doubloons? Or is it perhaps the case that that $50 billion has to be raised from the same limited pool of 300 million Americans and their as yet unborn descendants? And, if so, is giving it to the (bankrupt) "state of Lincoln" likely to be of much benefit to the citizens? Government money is not about the money, it's about the government. It's about social engineering—a $400 tax credit for falling into line with Barack Obama, Susan Roesgen, and the "Head of Behavior Change." That's why these protests are called Tea Parties—because the heart of the matter is the same question posed two-and-a-third centuries ago: Are Americans subjects or citizens? If you're a citizen, then a benign sovereign should not be determining "your interests" and then announcing that he's giving you a "tax credit" as your pocket money.

In *Political Economy* (1816), Thomas Jefferson wrote that "to take from one because it is thought that his own industry and that of his father's has acquired too much, in order to spare to others, who, or whose fathers have not exercised equal industry and skill, is to violate arbitrarily the first principle of association—'the guarantee to every one of a free exercise of his industry and the fruits acquired by it.'" To do so on the scale modern western societies do leads to two obvious problems: First, you can't erect a system of socioeconomic redistribution as extravagant as Susan Roesgen favors without losing a lot of the money en route. How much money do you have to take from Smith to give a $400 tax credit to Jones? Government isn't an efficient delivery system; it's a leach-field pipe with Smith at one end and Jones at the other and holes every couple of inches with thousands of bureaucrats sluicing all the way along. That's why we've wound up with a situation worse than that foreseen by Jefferson. America is not a society comprising two groups—one that has "acquired too much" and one that has "not exercised equal industry and skill"—but a society dominated by a third group, a government bureaucracy that has "acquired too much" and, to add insult to financial injury, is not required to "exercise equal industry."

And, when the state is that large, it takes not only the fruits but the fruit pies of your labors.

★ ★ ★ ★ ★

AS UNAMERICAN AS APPLE PIE

On the first Friday of Lent 2009, a state inspector from the Pennsylvania Department of Agriculture raided the fish fry at St. Cecilia's Catholic

Church in Rochester. He had been there for his annual inspection of the church's kitchen, but, while going about his work, he espied an elderly parishioner unwrapping some pies.

He swooped. Would these by any chance be *homemade* pies? Sergeant Joe Pieday wasn't taking no for an answer. The perps fessed up:

Josie Reed had made her pumpkin pie.

Louise Humbert had made her raisin pie.

Mary Pratte had made her coconut cream pie.

And Marge Murtha had made her farm apple pie.

And, by selling their prohibited substances for a dollar a slice, these ladies and their accomplices were committing a criminal act. In the Commonwealth of Pennsylvania, it is illegal for 88-year-old Mary Pratte to bake a pie in her kitchen for sale at a church fundraiser. The inspector declared that the baked goods could not be sold.[92]

St. Cecilia's holds a fish fry every Friday during Lent, and regular church suppers during the rest of the year. That's a lot of pie to forego. What solutions might there be? The inspector informed the ladies they could continue baking pies at home if each paid a $35 fee for him to come 'round to her home and certify her kitchen as state-compliant. "Well, that's just ridiculous," Louise Humbert, seventy-three, told the *Wall Street Journal*.

Alternatively, they could bake their pies in the state-inspected kitchen at the church. As anyone who bakes pies, as opposed to regulating them, could tell the inspector, if you attempt to replicate your family recipe in a strange oven, it doesn't always turn out like it should.

A local bakery stepped in and donated some pies. But that's not really the same, is it? Perhaps a more inventive solution is required. In simpler times, Sweeney Todd, purveyor of fine foodstuffs to Mrs. Lovett's pie shop in Fleet Street, would have been proposing we drop the coconut cream and replace it with state-inspector pie, perhaps with a lattice crust, symbolizing the prison bars he ought to be behind. Problem solved. Easy as pie, as we used to say.

Instead, bye bye, Miss American Pie.

No matter how you slice it, this is tyranny. When I first came to my corner of New Hampshire, one of the small pleasures I took in my new state were the frequent bake sales—the Ladies' Aid, the nursery school, the church rummage sale. Most of the muffins and cookies were good; some were exceptional; a few went down to sit in the stomach like overloaded barges at the bottom of the Suez Canal. But even then you admired if not the cooking then certainly the civic engagement. In a small but tangible way, a person who submits to a state pie regime is a subject, not a citizen—because participation is the essence of citizenship, and thus barriers to participation crowd out citizenship. A couple of kids with a lemonade stand are learning the rudiments not just of economic self-reliance but of civic identity. So naturally an ever multiplying number of jurisdictions have determined to put an end to such a quintessentially American institution. Seven-year-old Julie Murphy was selling lemonade in Portland, Oregon, when two officers demanded to see her "temporary restaurant license." Which would have cost her $120. When she failed to produce it, they threatened her with a $500 fine, and also made her cry.[93] Perhaps like the officers of Saudi Arabia's *mutaween* (the "Commission for the Promotion of Virtue and Prevention of Vices") the cheerless scolds of Permitstan could be issued with whips and scourges to flay the sinners in the street. When life hands you lemons, make lemonade—and then watch the state enforcers turn it back into sour fruit.

It is part of a sustained and all but explicit assault on civic participation, intended to leave government with a monopoly not just of power but of social legitimacy. So, while thanking that local bakery in Pennsylvania for their generosity in stepping up to the plate, we should note that, just as gun control is not about guns but control, so pie control is likewise not about pies, but about ever more total control.

Indeed, we do an injustice to ye medieval tyrants of yore. As Tocqueville wrote: "There was a time in Europe in which the law, as well as the consent of the people, clothed kings with a power almost without limits. But almost never did it happen that they made use of it."

True. His Majesty was an absolute tyrant—in theory. But in practice he was in his palace hundreds of miles away. A pantalooned emissary might come prancing into your dooryard once every half-decade and give you a hard time, but for the most part you got on with your life relatively undisturbed. In Tocqueville's words: "Although the entire government of the empire was concentrated in the hands of the emperor alone, and although he remained, in time of need, the arbiter of all things, the details of social life and of individual existence ordinarily escaped his control."

Just so. You were the mean and worthless subject of a cruel and mercurial despot but, even if he wanted to, he lacked the means to micro-regulate your life in every aspect. Yet what would happen, Tocqueville wondered, if administrative capability were to evolve to make it possible "to subject all of his subjects to the details of a uniform set of regulations"?

That moment has now arrived. Thanks to computer technology, it's easier than ever to subject the state's subjects to "a uniform set of regulations."

Back in the 1990s, Bill Clinton famously said, "The era of Big Government is over."[94] What we have instead is the era of lots and lots of itsy-bitsy, teensy-weensy morsels of small government that cumulatively add up to something bigger than the Biggest Government of all—a web of micro-tyrannies which, in their overbearing pettiness, ensnare you at every turn.

Marge Murtha can make an apple pie. What can a regime that criminalizes such a pie make? That's easy: Big Government makes small citizens.

Like to mull that thought over a cup o' joe? Sorry, I'd love to offer you one, but it's illegal. With its uncanny ability to prioritize, California, land of Golden Statism for unionized bureaucrats, is cracking down on complimentary coffee. From the *Ventura County Star*:

> Ty Brann likes the neighborly feel of his local hardware store.
> The fourth-generation Ventura County resident and small
> business owner has been going to the B & B Do it Center on
> Mobile Avenue in Camarillo for many years.... So when he

learned the county had told B & B it could no longer put out its usual box of doughnuts and coffee pot for the morning customers, Brann was taken aback.[95]

Dunno why. He lives in California. He surely knows by now everything you enjoy is either illegal or regulated up the wazoo. The Collins family had been putting a coffee pot on the counter for fifteen years, as the previous owners of the store had done, too, and yea, back through all the generations. But in California that's an illegal act. The permit mullahs told Randy Collins that he needed to install stainless steel sinks with hot and cold water and a prep kitchen to handle the doughnuts. "What some establishments do is hire a mobile food preparation services or in some cases a coffee service," explained Elizabeth Huff, "Manager of Community Services" (very Orwellian) for the Ventura County Environmental Health Division. "Those establishments have permits and can operate in front of or even inside of the stores."

Even inside? Gee, that's big of you. "Those establishments have permits"? In California, what doesn't? Commissar Huff added that there are a range of permits of varying costs. No doubt a plain instant coffee permit would be relatively simple, but if you wished to offer a decaf caramel macchiato with complimentary biscotti additional licenses may be required.

"We're certainly working with the health department," said Mr. Collins. "We want to be in compliance with the law."

Why?

When the law says that it's illegal for a storekeeper to offer his customer a cup of coffee, you should be proud to be in non-compliance. Otherwise, what the hell did you guys bother holding a revolution for? Say what you like about George III, but he didn't prosecute the Boston Tea Party for unlicensed handling of beverage ingredients in a public place.

This is the reality of small business in America today. You don't make the rules, you don't get to vote for people who make the rules. But you have to work harder, pay more taxes, buy more permits, fill in more paperwork, contribute to the growth of an ever less favorable business environment, and prostrate yourself before the Commissar of Community Services—all for the privilege of taking home less and less money.

The prohibition of non-state-licensed coffee is a small but palpable loss to civic life—a genuine community service, as opposed to those "Community Services" of which Elizabeth Huff is the state-designated "Manager." Randy Collins and the other taxpayers of Ventura County pay Commissar Huff's salary. I would wager that, like most small business owners, the Collins family work hard. They take fewer vacations and receive fewer benefits than Commissar Huff. They will retire later and on a smaller pension. Yet they pay for her. Big Government requires enough of a doughnut to pay for the hole: you take as much dough as you can get away with and toss it into the big gaping nullity of microregulation. And it's never enough. And eventually you wake up and find your state is all hole and no doughnut.

★ ★ ★ ★ ★

BULLS IN A CHINA SHOP

What do we have to show for the political class' disruption of every field of endeavor? From education to energy, health care to homeowning, the Conformicrats bungled everything they touched. You can see the impact of the regulatory state in the structural transformation of the American economy. From 1947 to the start of the downturn in 2008, manufacturing declined from 25.6 percent of the economy to 11 percent, while finance, insurance, real estate, and "professional services" grew from 13.9 percent to 33.5 percent.[96] Much of that last category is about the paperwork necessary to keep whatever it is you do in compliance with the Bureau of Compliance. Of the remainder, the financial sector ballooned in support of the Age of Credit, and real estate was the one thing you could always rely on—"safe as houses," right?

So how are those growth "industries" doing today? A headline from the *New York Times*:

Real Estate's Gold Rush Seems Gone for Good [97]

Which is a problem. For all the novelty junkies twittering about the Internet age and virtual reality, the principal asset of most Americans remains the most basic of all: the bricks and mortar of their rude dwelling. For all the analysts proclaiming society's transition from manufacturing to the "knowledge economy," for the majority of Americans the surest way of building wealth at the dawn of the twenty-first century involved neither knowing nor making anything: you bought a house, and, simply by doing nothing but eating, sleeping, and watching TV in it, your net worth increased.

Not anymore. Dean Baker, of the Center for Economic and Policy Research, calculates that it will take two decades to recoup the $6 trillion of housing wealth lost between 2005 and 2010.[98] Which means that in real terms it might never be recouped. In the early Seventies, the United States had about 35 million homes with three or more bedrooms, and about 25 million two-parent families with children. By 2005, the number of two-parent households with children was exactly the same, but the number of three-or-more-bedroom homes had doubled to 72 million. As the Baby Boomers began to retire, America had perhaps as much as a 40 percent over-supply of family-sized houses.[99] As Mr. Baker puts it, "People shouldn't look at a home as a way to make money because it won't."[100]

Oh. So what does that leave?

The "financial sector"? In the *Atlantic Monthly*, Simon Johnson pointed out that, from 1973 to 1985, it was responsible for about 16 percent of U.S. corporate profits. By the first decade of the twenty-first century, it was up to 41 percent.[101] That's higher than healthy, but the "financial sector" would never have got anywhere near that size if government didn't annex so much of your wealth—through everything from income tax to small-business regulation—that it's become increasingly difficult to improve your lot in life through effort—by working hard, making stuff, selling it. Instead, in order to fund a more comfortable retirement and much else, large numbers of people became "investors"—

albeit not as the term was traditionally understood. Like homeowning, it was all very painless: you work for some company, and it puts some money on your behalf in some sort of account that somebody on the 12th floor pools together with all the others and gives to somebody else in New York to disperse among various parties hither and yon. You've no idea what you're "investing" in, but it keeps going up, so why do you care? That's not like a nineteenth-century chappie saying he's starting a rubber plantation in Malaya and, with the faster shipping routes out of Singapore, it may be worth your while owning 25 percent of it. Or a guy in 1929 barking "Buy this!" and "Sell that!" at his broker every morning. Instead, in both property prices and retirement plans, an exaggerated return on mediocre assets became accepted as a permanent feature of life.

It's not, and it never can be. In Sebastian Faulks' novel *A Week in December*, set during the great unraveling of 2008, the wife of a hedgefundy type muses:

> The essential change seemed to her quite simple: bankers had detached their activities from the real world. Instead of being a "service" industry—helping companies who had a function in the life of their society—banking became a closed system. Profit was no longer related to growth or increase, but became self-sustaining; and in this semivirtual world, the amount of money to be made by financiers also became unhitched from normal logic.

It's one thing to have a financial sector that provides a means for wealth creators to access equity to advance economic growth. But, by the time you're using the phrase "credit default swap" without giggling, by the time you're trading not only in derivatives of derivatives but in derivatives of derivatives of derivatives (seriously), you're several links unhitched from any tangible reality. Tom borrows money from Dick, who turns a nice profit by selling Dick's debt to Harry, who covers himself against the risk of Dick's failure to repay by insuring the debt with Nigel, who mentions it over lunch to Peregrine, who writes it up in his Moneywatch column as a sign that confidence is returning to the markets. Only when Peregrine brings it up with Ahmed, the affable imam who lives next door, does anybody rain on the parade. The Prophet Mohammed, among his many strictures, enjoins the believers to have no truck with the frenzied infidel trade in Xeroxed IOUs. Which may be why (in the financial sector's in-house version of the demographic Islamization of Europe) the Age of Credit also saw sharia-compliant finance plant itself in the citadels of the West.

We're in a worse state than Jonathan Swift's banker—we cannot reliably say who has our bonds and therefore our souls. Thanks to the packaging, repackaging, subcontracting, and outsourcing of even routine mortgages, millions of home "owners" have no idea who really holds their property or the terms by which they can be expelled from it. And nor do the banks. According to the Office of the Comptroller of the Currency, by 2010 the U.S. financial system "owned" more than 230 trillion dollars' worth of derivatives—or about four times the entire planet's GDP.[102]

It was Polonius who advised, "Neither a borrower nor a lender be," and America at the dawn of the Obama era was approaching that blessed state. A man who borrows $400,000 for a house he cannot afford isn't really a "borrower," is he? After all, by 2008 every politician agreed that the priority was to keep people in "their" homes, and the Congressional Progressive Caucus was soon calling for a "moratorium on foreclosures," which is a polysyllabic way of saying there's no need to make your monthly payments. In what sense then is such a man "borrowing"?

And the banker who loaned the 400 grand isn't a "lender" of anything terribly real, is he? Not in an era of banking as performance art. "We refused to touch credit default swaps," the author and investment adviser Nassim Taleb said. "It would be like buying insurance on the Titanic from someone on the Titanic."[103] But a lot of people did just that. The Canadian commentator Jay Currie, waxing lyrical, put it this way: "If two people make a bet on the fall of a raindrop and each puts up, say, their shoes, the bet is a real bet. If they put up cash it is very close to a real bet. IOUs are not much of a bet. Someone else's IOUs? Still less of a bet. A good deal of imaginary money is going to money heaven, which is sort of like saying that your stuffed animal is dead."[104]

Except that many people made real-world decisions with their dead imaginary money. You thought the house you bought for a hundred grand was now worth a quarter-mil and so you took out a home-equity loan to buy a camper or to send your kid to private school. Your stuffed animal has died, but you've still got a real vet's bill to pay.

And then, just to pile on, the government steps in to replace all that dead imaginary money with real (or realish) money. Having, in effect, colluded in the destruction of meaningful risk-evaluation, Washington decided it was obliged to act—not to prevent a Thirties-style "credit crunch" but to prop up an unsustainable form of mock credit that had led to the crisis in the first place. The state's response to the downturn was to insist that we needed to re-inflate the credit bubble. If someone punctures your balloon, you can huff and puff into it all you want, but you're never going to get it up in the air again. The Obama administration blew a trillion dollars of "stimulus" into the punctured credit balloon, and it flew out the gaping hole in the back, dropped into the Potomac, and floated out to sea.

"Borrowing," continues Polonius, "dulls the edge of husbandry"—and that goes double for government, whose husbandry is dulled in the best of times. The state spends too much. So the individual spends too much. The state hires too many people on whom it lavishes too many benefits. So those foolish enough to remain in the private sector have to pay for the benefits of the public sector, and fund both their basics (housing) and their baubles (plasma TVs) through debt. At the start of the Reagan administration, America was the world's largest creditor nation and its citizens had a 10 percent savings rate.[105] Not today: By 2007, the average U.S. household had debts equivalent to 130 percent of income.[106] Keynes' view of the economy derived from the premise that a government treasury was not a family purse, and so the state, unlike the household, could borrow to "invest." Now, the family purse has caught up: Governments and individuals alike borrow extravagantly—and to "consume" in the most transient sense rather than invest in anything meaningful.

★ ★ ★ ★ ★

SLOW BOAT TO CHINA

The intellectual cover for America's structural deformation was provided by "globalization." Some of us have always been in favor of the "global economy." If I want to buy a CD or a sofa, I don't think it's any business of the government whether it comes from Cleveland or Milan or Ougadougou. As Adam Smith and John Stuart Mill will tell you, free trade has been indispensable to economic vitality from the Netherlands to Bengal. But you no longer hear much about "free trade." That humdrum, prosaic supply-and-demand concept yielded to a glittering new coinage: "globalization," less a commercial mechanism than an ideology.

But what does this mysterious metaphysical force called "globalization" actually boil down to? At the end of 2008, a few weeks after Barack Obama's historic election, the media reported on America's Christmas shopping spree. "Retail Sales Plummet," read the headline in the *Wall Street Journal*. "Sales plunged across most categories on shrinking consumer spending."[107]

That's great news, isn't it? After all, everyone knows Americans consume too much. What was it that then Senator Obama had said on the subject only a few months before? "We can't just keep driving our SUVs, eating whatever we want, keeping our homes at 72 degrees at all times regardless of whether we live in the tundra or the desert and keep consuming 25 percent of the world's resources with just four percent of the world's population, and expect the rest of the world to say, 'You just go ahead, we'll be fine.'"[108]

And by jiminy, we took the great man's words to heart. SUV sales nosedived, and 72 is no longer your home's thermostat setting but its current value expressed as a percentage of what you paid for it. If I understand the president's logic, in a just world Americans would be 4 percent of the population and consume 4 percent of the world's resources. And in his first year in office we made an excellent start toward that blessed utopia: Americans were driving smaller cars, buying smaller homes, giving smaller Christmas presents.

And yet, strangely, the Obama administration wasn't terribly happy about the Obamafication of the U.S. economy. The Democrats immediately passed a bazillion dollar "stimulus" package to "stimulate" us back into our bad old ways, and, when that didn't work, Ben Bernanke at the Federal Reserve printed another gazillion dollars in "quantitative easing" to lure us back into the malls.

And how did the rest of the world, of whose tender sensibilities Senator Obama was so mindful, feel about the collapse of American consumer excess? They were aghast, and terrified—as you would be if you suddenly found yourself strapped into a nightmare ride on a one-way express elevator into the abyss.

They didn't put it that way, of course. Economics correspondents instead penned erudite thumbsuckers about how the global economy needed to restore aggregate demand. Which is a fancy term for you—yes, you, Joe Lardbutt, the bloated, disgusting embodiment of American excess, driving around in your Chevy Behemoth, getting two blocks to the gallon as you shear the roof off the drive-thru lane to pick up your $7.93 decaf gingersnap-mocha-pepperoni-zebra mussel frappuccino, which makes for a wonderful thirst-quencher after you've been working up a sweat watching the 78" TV in your rec room with the thermostat set to 87. The message from the European political class couldn't be more straightforward: if you crass, vulgar Americans don't ramp up the demand, we're kaput. Unless you get back to previous levels of planet-devastating consumption, the planet is screwed.

"Much of the load will fall on the U.S.," wrote Martin Wolf in the *Financial Times*, "largely because the Europeans, Japanese and even the Chinese are too inert, too complacent, or too weak."[109] The European Union has 500 million people, compared with America's 300 million.[110] Britain, France, Germany, Italy, and Spain are advanced economies whose combined population adds up to that of the United States. Many EU members have enjoyed for decades the enlightened progressive policies that Americans didn't find themselves on the receiving end of until the Obama-Pelosi-Reid era. Why then are these advanced societies so "inert" that their economic fortunes depend on the despised, moronic Yanks?

Well, that's globalization. All the stuff that used to be made in America is now made somewhere else. But the people who buy it are still Americans. That part hasn't changed.

So, if Americans don't make any of this stuff, where do they get the money to buy it?

By borrowing it. Once you're paying what citizens of free societies do in taxes, what's left barely covers room and board. So life's little luxuries—or cheap plastic Chinese-made luxuries—have to be paid for through debt. So Americans buy toys that so enrich the Chinese they can afford to lend huge amounts of money to America to help our government grow even bigger so that Americans will have to borrow even more money for the next generation of cheap Chinese toys.

Hey, it's globalization. What could go wrong?

Entire countries—not just the Third World assembly plants, but G7 members such as Canada—have economies overwhelmingly dependent on access to the U.S. market. "Globalization," translated out of globaloney, means the American shopping mall is all but singlehandedly propping up living standards from Ontario to Indonesia. In 2010 U.S. consumer debt (that means us: not the spendaholic rulers but the spendaholic subjects) was about $2.5 trillion, or the combined GDP of Canada and India.[111] That seems like a lot of money to borrow in order to buy electronic amusements for a lifestyle we can't afford.

But the Chinese are smart guys. They must know that, right?

Undoubtedly. But the dollar is the global currency and so, unlike Zimbabwe or even Iceland, America gets to borrow money in its own bills, which it has the exclusive right to print as much of as it wants. So, even if there's a decline in value, for foreigners there is perceived to be a limit to the risk: buying U.S. debt is not like buying Zimbabwe's debt.

Yes, but why is the dollar still the global currency if America's the biggest debtor nation?

That's about image, too: America is seen as the guarantor of global order.

But, as noted earlier, when money drains, so does power—and very quickly, as the British learned after World War II. Today, money is draining across the Pacific. China Minmetals is a Fortune 500 company owned and controlled by the People's Republic.[112] By the way, read that sentence again and imagine what an H. G. Wells time traveler from the early Sixties, from the time of Mao's Cultural Revolution, would make of it. Yet in the Fortune Top Ten there are three Chinese companies against two from the United States.[113] And China Minmetals is serious business: they own the Northern Peru Copper Company in Canada,[114] and the Golden Grove copper, lead, zinc, silver, and gold mines in Western Australia,[115] and the mining rights to a huge percentage of Jamaican bauxite.[116] China's Sinopec bought up Calgary's Addax petroleum[117] and 9 percent of the Alberta oil sands business Syncrude,[118] and have massively expanded oil production and development in Sudan and Ethiopia. China's Sinochem took over Britain's Emerald Energy.[119] You remember all the "No Blood for Oil" chants back in 2003? Relax, it's our blood, their oil. The biggest foreign investor in post-war Iraq is the developer of the Ahdab oil field, the China National Petroleum Corporation.[120]

Think of it as the first settlers did *vis á vis* the Indians: the ChiComs sell us trinkets in exchange for our resources. Lenin boasted that "the capitalists will sell us the rope with which we will hang them." His fellow Communists in Beijing inverted the strategy to lethal effect: they sell us the rope, and sit back to watch us hang ourselves.

And, where money flows, power follows. Having turned resource nations in Africa into de facto protectorates, China has moved on to the developed world, and bailed out Portugal for $100 billion in exchange for significant stakes in their national utility companies.[121] Beijing is also the biggest foreign investor in post-bailout General Motors: they bought 18 percent of the Obama administration's IPO in 2010.[122] If the Obama-approved Chevy Volt isn't environmentally friendly enough for you, wait for the new Chevy Rickshaw. Can you still, as Dinah Shore sang, see the USA in your Chevrolet? The Chinese can.

Like America, China has structural defects. It's a dictatorship whose authoritarian policies have crippled its human capital. It has too many oldsters and not enough youth, and among its youth it has millions of surplus boys and no girls for them to marry. If China were the inevitable successor to America as global hegemon, that would be one thing. But the fact that it is incapable of playing that role is likely to make things even messier, more unpredictable, and far more destabilizing.

They have our souls who have our bonds. In their decadence, much of the western elite now think the answer to our worsening problems is not merely Chinese money but Chinese-style dictatorial government. If you support Bush's "Patriot Act," you're endangering civil rights. But if you support eco-totalitarianism, it's totally groovy.

In 2008, David Suzuki, Canada's most famous environmentalist, suggested that "denialist" politicians should be thrown in jail.[123] Mayer Hillman, senior fellow at the Policy Studies Institute in London, thinks democratic dissent from conformocrat-enviro-hysteria needs to be suppressed: "When the chips are down I think democracy is a less important goal than is the protection of the planet from the death of life, the end of life on it. This has got to be imposed on people whether they like it or not."[124] If the people are too foolish to vote as their betters instruct, then it will have to be "imposed." The earth is your führer. James Hansen, head of NASA's Goddard Institute, agrees on the inadequacy of America's "democracy" (his scare quotes) and argues that (to quote the article he wrote for the *South China Morning Post*) "Chinese Leadership Needed to Save Humanity."[125]

The *New York Times'* Great Thinker Thomas Friedman regularly channels his inner Walter Duranty: "What if we could just be China for a day?" he fantasized. "Where we could actually, you know, authorize the right solutions...."[126] Ah, yes. "Authorize" the "right" solutions without all that messy multi-party democracy getting in the way: why, in Beijing, where they don't suffer the disadvantages of free elections, they banned the environmentally destructive plastic bag! In one day! Just like that! "One-party autocracy certainly has its drawbacks," wrote Friedman. "But when it is led by a reasonably enlightened group of people, as China is today, it can also have great advantages. That one party can just impose the politically difficult but critically important policies needed to move a society forward in the 21st century."[127]

Ooooo-kay. But, pardon my asking, forward to where?

When the *New York Times'* most prominent writer comes out in favor of dictatorship, and no one else in the smart set calls him on it, you get a glimpse at the very least of the scale of elite contempt for popular sovereignty and the republic's animating principles. In breaking faith with the American idea, the political class got everything wrong: they exported millions of low-skilled jobs but imported millions of low-skilled workers; they fund both sides of the war on terror out of a wanton hostility to domestic energy production that leaves us dependent on noxious oil dictatorships that use their profits to wage civilizational warfare. And, having gotten us into this mess, the way to get us out is "China for a day." This is the logical endpoint of a cocooned conformocracy: Big Government having "imposed" the problems in the first place, only Even Bigger Government can "impose" the solutions.

Never underestimate the totalitarian temptations of the smart set. We'll hear a lot more of that in the years ahead.

THE NEW ATHENS
The Drowning City

*MR DIMPLE: Believe me, Colonel, when you shall have seen
the brilliant exhibitions of Europe, you will learn to despise the
amusements of this country as much as I do.*

*COLONEL MANLY: I do not wish to see them, for I can never
esteem that knowledge valuable, which tends to give me a distaste
for my native country.*

—Royall Tyler, *The Contrast* (1787)

From the *Times* of London, May 6, 2010:

> The President of Greece warned last night that his country
> stood on the brink of the abyss after three people were killed
> when an anti-government mob set fire to the Athens bank
> where they worked.[1]

Almost right. They were not an "anti-government" mob, but a government mob, a mob comprised largely of civil servants. That they are highly uncivil and disinclined to serve should come as no surprise: they're paid more and they retire earlier, and that's how they want to keep it. So they're objecting to austerity measures that would end, for example, the tradition of fourteen monthly paychecks per annum.[2] You read that right: the Greek public sector cannot be bound by anything so humdrum as temporal reality. So, when it was mooted that the "workers" might henceforth receive a mere twelve monthly paychecks per annum, they rioted. Their hapless victims—a man and two women—were a trio of clerks trapped in a bank when the mob set it alight and then obstructed emergency crews attempting to rescue them.

Unlovely as they are, the Greek rioters are the logical end point of the advanced social democratic state: not an oppressed underclass, but a spoiled overclass, rioting in defense of its privileges and insisting on more subsidy, more benefits, more featherbedding, more government.

Who will pay for it? Not my problem, say the rioters. Maybe those dead bank clerks' clients will—assuming we didn't burn them to death, too.

America and Greece are at different stops on the same one-way street, all too familiar to us immigrants. There's nothing new about Obama: been there, done that. Nothing could be less hopeful, or less of a change. He's the land where we grew up, with its union bullies and marginal tax rates and government automobiles and general air of decay all re-emerging Brigadoon-like from the mists entirely unspoilt by progress. It's like docking at Ellis Island in 1883, coming down the gangplank, and finding everyone excited about this pilot program they've introduced called "serfdom."

Greece is at the point in the plot where the canoe is about to plunge over the falls. America is upstream and can still pull for shore, but has decided instead that what it needs to do is not just drift along with the general current but paddle as fast as it can to catch up with the Greeks. Chapter One (the introduction of unsustainable entitlements) leads eventually to Chapter Twenty (total societal meltdown); the Greeks are at Chapter Seventeen or Eighteen.

The problem facing advanced societies isn't very difficult to figure out: the twentieth-century welfare state has run out of people to stick it to. When you're spending four trillion dollars but only raising two trillion in revenue (the Democrat model), you've no intention of paying it off, and the rest of the world knows it. In Greece, the arithmetic is even starker, because they're at the next stage of social-democratic ruin. If America's problem is that it's spent tomorrow today, and can never earn enough tomorrow to pay for what we've already burned through, nations such as Greece have a more basic problem: they've spent tomorrow today, and there isn't going to be a tomorrow. To prop up unsustainable welfare states, most of the western world isn't "printing money" but instead printing credit cards and pre-approving our unborn grandchildren. That would be a dodgy proposition at the best of times. But in the Mediterranean those grandchildren are never going to be born. That's the difference: in America, the improvident, insatiable boobs in Washington, Sacramento, Albany, and elsewhere are screwing over our kids and grandkids. In Europe, there are no kids or grandkids to screw over. In the end the entitlement state disincentives everything from wealth creation to self-reliance to the survival instinct, as represented by the fertility rate. If the problem with socialism, as Mrs. Thatcher famously said, is that eventually you run out of other people's money,[3] the problem with Greece and much of Europe is that they've advanced to the next stage: they've run out of other people, period. All the downturn has done is brought forward by a couple decades the West's date with demographic destiny.

The United States has a fertility rate of around 2.1—or just over two kids per couple.[4] Greece, as I pointed out in *America Alone*, has one of the lowest fertility rates on the planet—1.3 children per couple, which places it in the "lowest-low" demographic category from which no society has recovered and, according to the UN, 178th out of 195 countries. In practical terms, it means 100 grandparents have 42 grandkids—in other words, the family tree is upside down.

Hooray, say the liberal progressives. No more overpopulation!

Here's the problem: Greek public sector employees are entitled not only to fourteen monthly paychecks per annum during their "working" lives, but also fourteen monthly retirement checks per annum till death. Who's going to be around to pay for that?

So you can't borrow against the future because, in the crudest sense, you don't have one. Greeks in the public sector retire at fifty-eight, which sounds great. But, when ten grandparents have four grandchildren, who pays for you to spend the last third of your adult life loafing around?

Welcome to My Big Fat Greek Funeral.

We hard-hearted, small-government guys are often damned as selfish types who care nothing for the general welfare. But, as the protests in Greece, France, Britain, and beyond make plain, nothing makes an individual more selfish than the generous collectivism of big government: give a chap government health care, government-paid vacation, government-funded early retirement, and all the other benefits, and the last thing he'll care about is what it means for society as a whole. People's sense of entitlement endures long after the entitlement has ceased to make sense. And, if it bankrupts the entire state a generation from now, so what? In his pithiest maxim, John Maynard Keynes, the most influential economist of the twentieth-century social-democratic state and the patron saint of "stimulus," offered a characteristically offhand dismissal of any obligation to the future: "In the long run we are all dead."[5] The Greeks are Keynesians to a man: the mob is rioting for the right to carry on suspending reality until they're all dead. After that, who cares?

You don't have to go to Greece to experience Greek-style retirement. The Athenian "public service" of California has been metaphorically face down in the ouzo for a generation. As Arnold Schwarzenegger, the terminally terminated Terminator, told the legislature in his fourth State of the State address, "California has the ideas of Athens and the power of Sparta."[6] That's half-right: California has the ideas of Athens. Unfortunately, it's late twentieth-century Athens. As for "the power of Sparta," unless he's referring to gay marriage, it's hard to see what he's on about.

Greek public servants have their nose to the grindstone 24/7. They work twenty-four hours a week for seven months of the year. It's not just that every year you receive fourteen monthly payments, but that you only do about thirty weeks' work for it. For many public-sector "workers," the work day ends at 2.30 p.m. Gosh, when you retire on your fourteen monthly pension payments, you scarcely notice the difference, except for a few freed-up mornings. Couldn't happen in America, right?

In Bell, California, an impoverished dump on the edge of Los Angeles whose citizens have a per capita annual income of $24,800, the city manager was paid $787,637. With benefits, Robert Rizzo's compensation came to $1.5 million per annum. I use the phrase "per annum" loosely, since among the other gratifying aspects of his "job" was twenty-eight weeks off for vacation and sick leave. So in practical terms it worked out to $1.5 million per five and a half months.[7]

What kind of "city management" did Bell get in return for remunerating their city manager so handsomely? By 2008, Mr. Rizzo's regime had piled up nearly $80 million of debt on its 38,000 residents.[8] You do the math: clearly it would be unreasonable to expect Manager Rizzo to—or the blue-chip insurers, bondholders, and guarantors (Citigroup, Wedbush Morgan) who continued to facilitate Rizzo's "city management" in defiance of its arithmetical implausibility.[9] U.S. municipal government is the subprime mortgage of big collective borrowing: Citigroup and the other bigshots wouldn't have dealt with *you* on this basis, but they took the then reasonable view that even deranged spendthrift government doesn't default, because there's always someone it can pass the buck to. To modify Lord Acton, for Bell's underwriters coziness with power corrupts very cozily.

Ask not for whom Bell tolls, it tolls for thee. As for murderous civil servants, you don't have to go to Athens for that. In the New York Christmas snowstorm of 2010, the casualties of the city government's incompetence went beyond the abandoned hot dog carts and buses and ambulances wedged into the snow banks of midtown Manhattan. A young woman gave birth in the lobby of a Brooklyn apartment house, but the baby died, because, in one of the most densely populated cities on earth, "first responders" were unable to get to her through the unploughed streets of Crown Heights until ten hours after her 911 call.[10] In Queens, Yvonne Freeman, seventy-five, woke up with breathing difficulties, but she too died because the ambulance took hours to reach her.[11] As the can't-do buffoon mayor floundered from one disastrous press conference to another, it emerged that the city might have been afflicted not merely by the weather but by something close to the municipal equivalent of treason. A councilman claimed that, when the storm began, Sanitation Department bosses instructed their plough drivers to delay snow clearance in New York's outer boroughs in order to protest some planned (and fairly desultory) budget cuts.[12] The streets of Crown Heights weren't unploughed because they were meteorologically stricken but as a conscious act of sabotage by public "servants." That would make Mrs. Freeman, the Brooklyn baby, and others, victims of unionized manslaughter. As their Athenian comrades did, the public servants of New York prevented emergency crews from reaching those in peril, with fatal consequences. On the other hand, they did manage to clear the snow from outside the Staten Island home of Sanitation Department head honcho John Doherty, while leaving all surrounding streets pristinely clogged.[13]

Public-sector shakedown states are always unsustainable, but, though easy to launch, they're hard to reel back. In 2010 the media reported the largest demonstration in a quarter-century had taken to the streets outside the Capitol in Springfield, Illinois, to demand, "Raise my taxes!"[14] If you caught it with half an ear on the radio news, the gist seemed to be that these people were responsible and communitarian.

"Yes, people are hurting. That's why we need a tax increase," insisted Henry Bayer.

Who's he? Well, he's executive director of Council 31 of the American Federation of State, County, and Municipal Employees. Ah, right. So it's not butchers, bakers, and candlestick makers chanting, "Raise my taxes!" It's government workers.

Who live off taxes.

Taxes pay their salaries, benefits, and pensions. Government levies taxes on you and gives it to them. So Mr. Bayer and his chums might as well be yelling, "Gimme your money!" It's no more communitarian than me standing in the street chanting, "Buy my book!"

Big unions fund Big Government. The union slices off 2 percent of the workers' pay and sluices it to the Democratic party, which uses it to grow government, which also grows unions, which thereby grows the number of 2 percent contributions, which thereby grows the Democratic party, which thereby grows government.... Repeat until bankruptcy. Or bailout.

The "Raise my taxes!" protest was a subtler version of the Athenian riots—or a Trojan horse full of unionized Greeks. If the new class war is between "public servants" and the rest of us, some countries no longer have enough of "the rest of us" even to put up a fight. When the "public service" becomes as dominant as Greece's, it *is* the market: you can't cut back public spending without moving toward economic crisis and social catastrophe. The bloated public service leached so much out of the Greek economy that the European Union decided that the least worst response was to allow them to do the same to the broader EU economy—just as the debauched public sector of California is pinning its hopes on federal largesse.

Greece is a great civilization, or it was. Now it's a basket case. They set up a caring, compassionate, progressive society, and it's bankrupted them. In Greece, a female working in a "hazardous" job can retire with a full government pension at fifty. Initially, "hazardous" meant jobs like bomb disposal and mining. Ever fancied a career in bomb disposal? No? Don't blame you, it's kinda hazardous.

But, as is the way of government entitlements, the "hazardous" category growed like Topsy. Five hundred and eighty professions now qualify as "hazardous," among them hairdressing.[15] "I use a hundred different chemicals every day—dyes, ammonia, you name it," 28-year-old Vasia Veremi told the *New York Times*. "You think there's no risk in that?" Not to mention all those scissors.

Like hairdressers, Greek TV and radio hosts can also retire at fifty—because of their high level of exposure to "microphone bacteria."[16] Were you inspired to buy this book by seeing me yakking into a mike about it up on the podium at a stop on the publicity tour? Well, that very microphone counts as a hazardous work environment in Greece. What a class action we authors will have! These publishing houses are like the tobacco companies: when they booked me and J. K. Rowling and the guy who does those Chicken Soup things and the rest of us on a coast-to-coast media blitz, they knew all about the risks of microphone bacteria, but they went ahead and ruined our life expectancy anyway.

It all sounds great. Who wouldn't want to be a Greek hairdresser? Alas, being a Greek, period, is now a hazardous profession. An Obamafied America, following California down the Athenian path, is Greecing its own skids.

The EU is now throwing an extra trillion dollars at countries which by any objective measure are insolvent, and are unlikely ever again to be anything but—at least this side of bloody revolution. How do you grow your economy in an ever shrinking market? Greece is a land of ever fewer customers and fewer workers but ever more retirees and more government. How do you increase GDP? By export? To where? You're entirely uncompetitive; you can't make anything at a price any foreigner would be prepared to pay for it.

When you binge-spend at the Greek level in a democratic state, there aren't many easy roads back. The government introduced an austerity package to rein in spending.[17] In response, Greek tax collectors walked off the job. Read that again slowly: to protest government cuts, striking tax collectors refuse to collect taxes. In a sane world, this would be an hilarious TV comedy sketch. But most of the western world is no longer sane. It's tough enough to persuade the town drunk to sober up, but when everyone's face down in the moonshine, maybe it's best just to head for the hills—if you can find anywhere to flee.

Let us take it as read that Greece is an outlier. As waggish officials in Brussels and Strasbourg will tell you, it only snuck into the EU due to some sort of clerical error. It's a cesspit of sloth and corruption even by Mediterranean standards. If you were going to cut one "advanced" social democracy loose and watch it plunge into the abyss *pour encourager les autres*, it would be hard to devise a better candidate than Greece. And yet and yet … riot-wracked Athens isn't *that* much of an outlier. Greece's 2010 budget deficit was 12.2 percent of GDP;[18] Ireland's was 14.7.[19] Greece's debt was 125 percent of GDP;[20] Italy's 117 percent. Greece's 65-plus population will increase from 18 percent in 2005 to 25 percent in 2030;[21] Spain's will increase from 17 percent to 25 percent.

Some of the oldest nations in the world are now in the situation of a homeowner who's fallen too far behind on the payments and has no prospect of catching up: you might as well just put the door keys in an envelope, shove 'em under the door of the bank, and move on—perhaps to an uninhabited atoll in the South Pacific as yet unspoilt by unsustainable levels of government. At some point, the least worst option becomes armed revolution, civil war, or at least an electro-magnetic pulse attack that conveniently obliterates every single bank account and wipes the slate clean. As lazy, feckless, squalid, corrupt, and vicious as Greece undoubtedly is, it's not that untypical. It's where the rest of Europe's headed—and Japan and North America shortly thereafter.

★ ★ ★ ★ ★

THE GREEK BONE CONNECTED TO THE KRAUT BONE

Greece is broke, and has run out of Greeks. So it's getting bailed out by Germany. But Germany also has deathbed demographics: as Angela Merkel, the Chancellor, pointed out in 2009, for Germany an Obama-sized stimulus was out of the question simply because its foreign creditors know there are not enough young Germans around ever to repay it.[22] Germany has the highest proportion of childless women in Europe: one in three *fräulein* have checked out of the motherhood business entirely.[23]

Absolved from having to pay for their own defense, Continentals beat their swords into welfare checks, and erected huge cradle-to-grave entitlements. Even under the U.S. security umbrella, they proved unsustainable. Why? Well, like Keynes said, in the long run we are all dead—so why not bilk the future? We won't be here, and our creditors won't have a forwarding address. No one has engaged in transgenerational theft on the scale that Europe has.

And these days Germany has to support a continent. It's the economic powerhouse that's supposed to be rescuing the euro and preventing the five soi-disant PIIGS (Portugal, Italy, Ireland, Greece, Spain) from having the Big Bad Wolf of reality blow their house of straw to smithereens. But what happens when your engine room is rusting? "Germany's working-age population is likely to decrease 30 percent over the next few decades," says Steffen Kröhnert of the Berlin Institute for Population Development. "Rural areas will see a massive population decline and some villages will simply disappear—Germany will become a weak economic power in the future."[24]

The EU committed (to borrow from Philip K. Dick) a kind of pre-crime: it mugged the next generation. For the moment, the victims are still walking around, mostly unaware of what they're in for. For many of them, life is good. Take Marina Casagrande of Bergamo.[25] In Italy, a court ordered her father to pay Marina an allowance of 350 euros—approximately $525—every month. Signor Casagrande was then sixty. His daughter was thirty-two. She was supposed to have graduated with a degree in philosophy eight years earlier but, though her classes ended way back at the beginning of the century, she was still working on her thesis. So Signor Casagrande is obliged to pay up, either in perpetuity or until the completion of Marina's thesis, whichever comes sooner. Her thesis is about the Holy Grail. Which Marina would have little use for, given that she's already found a source of miraculous life-transforming powers in Papa's checkbook.

Marina is what they call a "bambocciona," which translates, roughly, as "big baby"—the term for the ever-growing number of Italian adults still living at home, in the same bedroom they've slept in since they were in diapers. There was, as usual, a momentary spasm of ineffectual outrage over the judge's decision against Signor Casagrande, whose very name is mocked by this demographic trend: the *casa* would seem much more *grande* if only Junior would move out. But in Italy they rarely do: seven out of ten adults aged 18 to 39 live with their folks.[26] Sixtysomething Italians ordered to pay "child support" to thirtysomething kids might consider moving back in with their nonagenarian parents and suing for a monthly allowance back-dated to the early Seventies.

Italy's *bamboccioni* have their equivalents around the world. In Japan, they're called *parasaito shinguru*—or "parasite singles," after the horror film *Parasite Eve*, in which alien spawn grow in human bellies feeding off the host. In Germany, they're *Nesthockers* with no plans to move out of "Hotel Mama." In Britain, they're KIPPERS (Kids In Parents' Pockets Eroding Retirement Savings). In Canada, by 2006, 31 percent of men aged 25 to 29 were still sleeping in their childhood bedroom each night.[27]

The economics of demographics used to be relatively simple: in a traditional agricultural society, by the time you got too worn and stooped for clearing and plowing, you hoped to have sired able-bodied 13-year-olds to do it for you. Today, most developed nations have managed to defer adulthood and thus to disincentivize parenthood—quite dramatically so, if the judgment against Signor Casagrande holds. Why blame his daughter? No matter how long you stay in school in Italy, there's nothing waiting for you when you come out. Francesca Esposito was twenty-nine, spoke five languages, had two degrees, and could land no job other than an unpaid traineeship with a government agency facilitating millions of euros' worth of false disability claims.[28] "I have every possible certificate," she told the *New York Times*, which, in its poignant profile of Italy's young, never seemed to consider whether such expensively acquired "certification" is necessary for a government job—or most others. Young(ish) Francesca had a law degree from Italy, a master's from Germany, and had interned in Luxembourg at the European Court of Justice. A century ago, this leisurely, indulgent saunter through a tri-national varsity would have been the province of bored aristocratic scions with no interest in politics or soldiery, but somehow Europe got the idea to universalize it. Miss Esposito's father is a fireman, her mother a high school teacher. She is the first in her family to learn a foreign language and graduate from college.

And she may well be the last. There is absolutely no return on investment, either for her or the Italian taxpayers who funded it. How could there be? A world in which you're expensively educated till thirty to join a government agency justifying its own expansion by manufacturing welfare fraud is almost too perfect an emblem of the European Union. Francesca will live a worse life than her parents. She will do unpaid traineeships and low-paid short-term contract work because in Europe's catatonic labor market the young (if one calls twenty-nine "young") are already paying the price for the lavish salaries and benefits awarded to the unsackable middle-aged. Hence, *bamboccioni*, *Nesthockers*, and KIPPERS. There used to be an English expression, "kippers and curtains." In Europe today, it's KIPPERS—and curtains. "Hope 'n' change"? To be young in the EU is to live in a land beyond hope.

Debt operates on certain assumptions: if you need $500 and you don't have it, the bank will lend it to you because they think you're likely to have 500 bucks in the near future. The older you get, the less likely the bank will assume that. If you're seventeen and broke, it's because you haven't yet got your first foot on the ladder of success. But if you're sixty-three or seventy-eight and you're broke, it's because that's who you are and you're never not going to be broke. So why should the bank lend you 500 bucks? Where's it going to come from?

That's the question the developed world is facing: Where's it going to come from? A new tax? There's nothing left to tax. By 2009, Europe was reduced to considering a levy on bovine flatulence.[29] You heard that right—not a flat tax but a flatulence tax. Ireland was pondering a tax of 13 euros per cow, while in Denmark it was as high as 80 euros per cow. Is a Danish Holstein six times as flatulent as an Irish Hereford? Beats me. But somewhere in Brussels there's a Director of the European Flatulence Agency of Regulation and Taxation (EuroFart) who's got all the graphs. Apparently it's to offset looming penalties each nation faces from EU legislation to combat "global warming." The *Times* of London reported: "EU member states are obliged to cut the emissions from non-ETS sectors by 10 percent overall by 2020. While Romania and Bulgaria will be allowed to increase emissions, Ireland and Denmark are each faced with cuts of 20 percent in farming sector emissions."[30]

Even allowing for the regulatory yoke Europe's cowed citizenry labor under, the bureaucratic logic here is hard to follow. Why is some Bulgar's Holstein allowed to increase his flatulence while the poor Jutlander's Polled Hereford has to put a stopper in it? Is there a dearth of flatulence in the Balkans but a Code Red alert over the North Sea? Couldn't the EU introduce flatulence offsets and let the excessively flatulent Irish trade some of their flatulence to the Carpathians?

Go back to medieval times. The gnarled old peasant is in his hovel, and one day a fellow rides up in the full doublet and hose and says he's come from the palace to collect His Majesty's bovine flatulence tax. It's just three groats per cow, a footling sum of no consequence. Even the medieval simpleton rustic would say, "Aaargh, sire, I dunno. The King's flatulence tax? That don't sound right...." When you're taxing bovine flatulence emissions, there's nothing left to tax.

Greece, wrote Theodore Dalrymple, is "a cradle not only of democracy but of democratic corruption"[31]—of electorates who give their votes to leaders who bribe them with baubles purchased by borrowing against a future that can never pay it off. The advanced democracies with their mountains of sovereign debt are the equivalent of old people who've blown through their capital and are all out of ideas looking for young people flush enough to bail them out. And the idea that it might be time for the spend-thrift geezers to change their ways butts up against their indestructible moral vanity. In 2009, President Sarkozy prissily declared that the G20 summit provided "a once-in-a-lifetime opportunity to give capitalism a conscience."[32] European capitalism may have a conscience. It's not clear it has a pulse. And, actually, when you're burning Greek bank clerks to death in defense of your benefits, your "conscience" isn't much in evidence, either.

This is the first crisis of globalization, and it is a far more existential threat than the Depression. In living beyond its means, its times, and its borders, the developed world has run out of places to pass the buck.

★ ★ ★ ★ ★

THE KRAUT BONE CONNECTED TO THE YANK BONE

American admirers often talk about the European lifestyle. Alas, it's all style and no life. If the EU's deathbed demographics are becoming too obvious for even the dopier media outlets to ignore, you can bet the Chinese and other buyers of western debt are way ahead in their analyses. If you're an investor and you're not factoring in demography, more fool you. Tracking GDP versus median age in the world's major economies is the easiest way to figure out where this story's heading.

Take a "toxic asset." What would improve its current pitiful value? That's easy: more demand. Less supply. An asset is only an asset as long as there's a buyer willing to buy it. If you've got 50 houses and 100 would-be homeowners, that's good for property prices. If you've got 100 houses and 50 would-be homeowners, that's not so rosy.

Which is the situation much of the West is facing. A bank is a kind of demographic exchange, by which old people with capital lend to young people with ambition and ideas. Who are somewhat thin on the ground in modern consumer societies. Japan, Germany, and Russia are already in net population decline.[33] Fifty percent of Japanese women born in the Seventies are childless. Between 1990 and 2000, the percentage of Spanish women childless at the age of thirty almost doubled, from just over 30 percent to just shy of 60 percent.[34] In Sweden, Finland, Austria, Switzerland, the Netherlands, and the United Kingdom, 20 percent of 40-year-old women are childless.[35] In a recent poll, invited to state the "ideal" number of children, 16.6 percent of Germans answered "None."[36]

Well, that's a woman's right to choose. But, in the macroeconomic picture, who's going to be around to buy your assets? Mark Twain commended the purchase of land because "they're not making any more of it."[37] But, in the fast depopulating eastern half of Germany, they've made more than anyone's going to need for the foreseeable future. *Pace* the Führer, no country has ever been less in need of lebensraum. America has a milder case of the same syndrome—the Boomers didn't have enough kids to sustain the mid-twentieth-century entitlement regime—but EU governments are now frantically hurling natalist benefits at a shrinking base of fecund womanhood.

Now look at it from a business point of view. In the United States, depending on what line of work you're in, your sales territory may be your town or your state or the whole of America. But for Germany, Italy, and Japan, their only viable sales territory is the world. When your median age is forty-three and rising, any economic growth is down to exports. Wall Street experts talk about restoring "consumer confidence," but in much of Europe they won't restore "confidence" until they restore consumers—that is, figure out a way to generate sufficient numbers of them. Until then, the domestic market is too old and too small (or "inert," to reprise Martin Wolf's line) to support economic revival.

If you're a German bank, to whom do you lend money? With age distribution on your home turf heading north relentlessly, you don't have enough young people to grow your business. So you lend farther and farther afield. Not crazy farther, not Sudan or Rwanda. But far enough that you're operating in markets where your traditional forms of risk analysis don't apply, even if you were minded to apply them. To western bankers, Eastern Europe didn't seem that different or dangerous, if you steered clear of the more psychotic oligarchs. Unfortunately, the post-Soviet east is even further down the demographic death spiral than you are. America? By some estimates, Germany's Landesbanken could have to write off a trillion bucks' worth of subprime crud from the U.S.

So, from the individual homeowner with no one to sell his home to, and the business that's run out of domestic market, and the bank frantically loaning to jurisdictions it barely comprehends, nudge it up one last stage—to the state. In recessions, government is enjoined to spend—to go into deficit, ramp up the national debt in order to "stimulate" the economy. Adding to the national debt presupposes that there'll be someone to pay it off. But what if there isn't? And do the Chinese and the Saudis already know the answer to that question? The failures of British and German Treasury auctions (not to mention near misses in the U.S. prevented only by the Fed buying up Treasury securities) prefigure a world with too much debt and too few sugar daddies willing to cover it.

In 2003, the IMF conducted a study of Eurosclerosis and examined the impact on chronic unemployment and other woes if the Eurozone labor market were to be Americanized—increasing participation in the work force, reducing taxes, rolling back job-for-life security, and generally liberalizing the economy.[38] They concluded that the changes would be tough, but over the long-term beneficial.

It's interesting that it never occurred to the IMF that anyone would be loopy enough to try their study the other way around—to examine the impact on America of Europeanization. For that, we had to wait for the election of Barack Obama. You've probably heard liberal academics on NPR and the like drooling about "the European model," and carelessly assumed they were referring to Carla Bruni. If only. Under the European model, state spending accounts for roughly 50 percent of GDP.[39] Under the Swedish model, which isn't half as much fun as it sounds, state spending accounts for 54 percent of GDP. In the United States, it's already over 40 percent. Ten years ago, it was 34 percent. So we're trending very Swede-like. And why stop there? In Wales, government spending accounts for just under 72 percent of the economy.[40] Fortunately for what's left of America's private sector, "the Welsh model" doesn't have quite the same beguiling ring as "the Swedish model." But, even so, if Scandinavia really is the natural condition of an advanced democracy, then we're all doomed.

That was the general thesis of *America Alone*—that the jig is up for much if not most of the western world. "Alarmist," pronounced *The Economist*,[41] reflecting the general consensus of polite society in both Europe and North America. Polite society has spent the years since playing catch-up. So if you don't want your *fin de civilisation* analysis from a frothing right-wing loon you can now get it from the house-trained chaps at the *New York Times*: "Europeans have boasted about their social model, with its generous vacations and early retirements, its national health care systems and extensive welfare benefits, contrasting it with the comparative harshness of American capitalism…'The Europe that protects' is a slogan of the European Union."[42]

Protects from what? Right now, Europe mostly needs protection from itself and its worst inclinations: "With low growth, low birth rates and longer life expectancies, Europe can no longer afford its comfortable lifestyle."

Even in its heyday—the Sixties and Seventies—the good times in Europe were underwritten by the American security guarantee: the only reason why France could get away with being France, Belgium with being Belgium, Sweden with being Sweden is because America was America. For over sixty years America has paid for Europe's defense. And because the United States Army lives in Germany, that frees up Germany to spend its defense budget on government health care and all the rest. In essence, American taxpayers pay for German entitlements.

And it still isn't enough.

So the world has deemed Greece "too big to fail," even though in (what's the word?) reality it's too big not to fail. And the rest of us are too big not to follow in its path: "Another reform high on the list is removing the state from the marketplace in crucial sectors like health care, transportation and energy and allowing private investment," reported the *New York Times*. "Economists say that the liberalization of trucking routes—where a trucking license can cost up to $90,000—and the health care industry would help bring down prices in these areas, which are among the highest in Europe."[43]

Removing the state from health care brings down prices? Who knew? This *New York Times* is presumably unrelated to the *New York Times* that spent the previous year arguing for the U.S. government's annexation of health care as a means of controlling costs. And entirely unrelated to the *New York Times* whose Nobel Prize-winning economics guru, Paul Krugman, pronounced Europe "the Comeback Continent" in 2008.[44]

About half the global economy is living beyond not only its means but its diminished number of children's means. Instead of addressing that fact, countries with government debt of 125 percent of GDP are being "rescued" by countries with government debt of 80 percent of GDP. Good luck with that.

★ ★ ★ ★ ★

THE YANK BONE CONNECTED TO . . . ?

The day after the 2010 election, I found myself sharing a stage with Howard Dean, former Governor of Vermont and head of the Democratic National Committee.[45] Governor Dean mused that the European Union was one of the most interesting experiments in government ever attempted. As "interesting" as the experiment is, most Greeks, Frenchmen, and Germans were not aware that they were signing on as guinea pigs. In the postwar ruins of *la gloire de la république*, the French created the embryo EU to be a kind of Greater France—as a way of avoiding the truth about their own diminished status. It worked too well, and, when the EU took on many of the calcified qualities of its dominant founder, the elite thought it was time to pass the buck up yet again. The Eurocrats are now in favor of the European Unionization of the world. As Herman van Rompuy put it: "2009 is the first year of global governance."[46]

Herman van Hoozee? Well, he's this curious Belgian bloke who, shortly before uttering the above words, emerged as the first "President" of "Europe." Nobody elected him as President of Europe, whatever that means. One day he was an obscure Belgian. The next day he was an obscure Belgian with a business card saying "President of Europe." Just one of those things, could happen to anyone. It's not just that he's hardly a household name in the average European household. It's not clear he's a household name even in the van Rompuy household. I don't watch a lot of Belgian TV, so I'm not sure if they have a "Belgian Idol" or "Dancing with the Belgians" over there, but, if so, he'd be knocked out in round one. Like everything in a European

Union all but entirely insulated from democratic accountability, the so-called "presidency" was a backroom stitch-up: neither the French nor the Germans wanted a charismatic glamorpuss in the gig stealing their respective thunders. An obscure Belgian was just the ticket. Being a low-grade nondescript was the minimum entry qualification.

And yet the fact remains that he is "President" of "Europe," and in that capacity he announced that 2009 was the first year of global governance.

Incidentally, did you get that memo?

Me neither.

Still, I'm always appreciative when a fellow says what he really means. The upgrading of the G20; the plans for planetary-wide financial regulation; the Copenhagen climate-change summit and its (thankfully thwarted) proposals for a transnational bureaucracy to facilitate the multitrillion-dollar shakedown of the advanced democracies: all these are pillars of "global governance," of the European Unionization of the world—and Copenhagen alone would have been the biggest exercise in punitive liberalism the western democracies had ever been subjected to. Right now, if you don't like the local grade school, you move to the next town. If you're sick of Massachusetts taxes, you move to New Hampshire. Where do you move to if you don't like "global governance"? To what polling station do you go to vote it out?

Greece's unsustainable spending is propped up by Germany, and Germany's unsustainable spending is propped up by America. So who's left to prop up America's unsustainable spending? Yet Washington is pushing on to Europe's future when even the Europeans are figuring you can't make it add up.

As the fog of Obama's rhetoric lifted and the scale of his debt mountain became clear, the president's courtiers began to muse about the introduction of an EU-style "VAT."[47] Americans generally translate that as a "national sales tax," but it actually stands for "value-added tax," because you're taxing the value that is added to a product in the course of its path to market. Yet what Europe needs is to add "value" in a more basic sense.

There are two main objections to the wholesale Europeanization of America. The easy one is the economic argument. But the second argument is subtler: the self-extinction of Europe is not just a matter of economics. Advanced social democracies don't need a value-added tax; they need a value-added life. "The Europe that protects" may protect you from the vicissitudes of fate but it also disconnects you from the primary impulses of life. Government security does not in and of itself make for a satisfying, purposeful life. Studies from the University of Michigan and elsewhere suggest quite the opposite—that welfare makes one unhappier than a modest income honestly earned and used to provide for one's family.[48] "It drains too much of the life from life," said Charles Murray in a speech in 2009. "And that statement applies as much to the lives of janitors—even more to the lives of janitors—as it does to the lives of CEOs."[49] Capitalists sometimes carelessly give the impression that theirs is a materialistic argument. But anti-capitalists do not want for material comforts—you go to the poorest part of town and you see plenty of iPhones and plasma TVs. And Eutopia is distinguished mainly by a lethargic hedonism: shorter working hours, longer vacations, earlier retirements, bigger benefits. What do they do with all that free time? High-school soccer and 4-H at the county fair? No. As we've seen, kids not called Mohammed are thin on the ground. God? No. When you worship the state-as-church, you don't need to bother showing up to Mass anymore. Civic volunteerism? No. All but extinct on the Continent. Do they paint, write, compose? Not so's you'd notice. Never mind Bach or even Offenbach, these days the French can't produce a Sacha Distel or the Germans a Bert Kaempfert, the boffo Teuton bandleader who somewhat improbably managed to play a critical role in the careers of the three biggest Anglophone pop acts of the twentieth century—he wrote "Strangers in the Night" for Sinatra, "Wooden Heart" for Elvis, and produced the Beatles' first recording session. If that sounds like a "Trivial Pursuit" answer, it's not. Eutopia turned out to be the trivial pursuit; to produce a Bert Kaempfert figure right now would be a major cultural accomplishment Europe can't quite muster the energy for. Life is a matter of passing the time—or, indeed, of holding the moment: "Linger awhile, how fair thou art," in the words of Goethe's Faust, which would make a fine epitaph for the European Union.

"In the long run we are all dead": Keynes' flippancy disguises his radicalism. For most of human history, functioning societies honor the long run; it's why millions of people have children, build houses, plant gardens, start businesses, make wills, put up beautiful churches in ordinary villages, fight and if necessary die for king and country.... It's why extraordinary men create great works of art—or did in the Europe of old. A nation, a society, a community is a compact between past, present, and future, in which the citizens, in Tom Wolfe's words, "conceive of themselves, however unconsciously, as part of a great biological stream":

> Most people, historically, have not lived their lives as if thinking, "I have only one life to live." Instead they have lived as if they are living their ancestors' lives and their offspring's lives and perhaps their neighbors' lives as well.... The mere fact that you were only going to be here a short time and would be dead soon enough did not give you the license to try to climb out of the stream and change the natural order of things.[50]

Europe climbed out of the stream. You don't need to make material sacrifices: the state takes care of all that. You don't need to have children. And you certainly don't need to die for king and country. But a society that has nothing to die for has nothing to live for: it's no longer a stream, but a stagnant pool. How fair thou hast been—but only for the moment, and the moment is passing. Europe's economic crisis is a mere symptom of its existential crisis: What is life for? What gives it meaning? Post-Christian, post-nationalist, post-modern Europe has no answer to that question, and so it has 30-year-old students and 50-year-old retirees, and wonders why the small band of workers in between them can't make the math add up. Yet it's not about the arithmetic, but about instilling in people for whom life is a diversion a sense of purpose larger than themselves: What's it all about, Alfie? Cradle-to-grave nanny-state "protection"?

Europe is already dead—in the short run.

Linger awhile, how fair thou art. It's nice to linger at the brasserie, have a second café au lait, and watch the world go by. At the Munich Security Conference, President Sarkozy demanded of his fellow Continentals, "Does Europe want peace, or do we want to be left in peace?"[51] To pose the question is to answer it. But it only works for a generation or two, and then, as the gay bar owners are discovering in a fast Islamifying Amsterdam, reality reasserts itself.

We began this book with some thoughts from Bertie Wooster and Jonathan Swift regarding Belshazzar's feast and "the writing on the wall." But sometimes there's so much writing you can barely see the wall. On my last brief visit, Athens was a visibly decrepit dump: a town with a handful of splendid ancient ruins surrounded by a multitude of hideous graffiti-covered contemporary ruins. Sit at an elegant café in Florence, Barcelona, Lisbon, Brussels, almost any Continental city. If you're an American tourist, what do you notice? Beautiful buildings, designer stores, modern bus and streetcar shelters...and all covered in graffiti from top to toe. The grander the city, the more profuse the desecration. Go to Rome, the imperial capital, the heart of Christendom: the entire city is daubed like a giant New York subway car from the Seventies. Look at your souvenir snaps: here's me and the missus standing by the graffiti at the Trevi Fountain; there we are admiring the graffiti at the Coliseum.

A *New York Times* feature on Berlin graffiti reported it as an art event, a story about "an integral component of Berliner Strassenkultur."[52] But it's actually a tale of civic death, of public space claimed in perpetuity by the vandals (like graffiti, another word Italy gave the world, as it were). At the sidewalk cafés, Europeans no longer notice it. But it is in a small, aesthetically painful way a surrender to barbarism—and one made even more pathetic by the cultural commentators desperate to pass it off as "art." And it sends a signal to predators of less artistic bent: if you're unwilling to defend the civic space from these coarse provocations, what others will you give in to?

It's strange and unsettling to walk through cities with so much writing on the wall, and yet whose citizens see everything but. Bertie Wooster's Aunt Dahlia is right: once upon a time, you were certainly an ass if you didn't know where "the writing on the wall" came from. It was part of the accumulated cultural inheritance: in the old Europe, Handel and William Walton wrote oratorios about it. Rembrandt's painting of Belshazzar's Feast hangs in the National Gallery in a London all but oblivious to its significance. Instead of paintings and oratorios and other great art about the writing on the wall, Europeans have walls covered in writing, and pretend that it's art. Today, I doubt one in a thousand high-school students would have a clue whence the expression derives. And one sign that the writing's on the wall is when society no longer knows what "the writing on the wall" means.

CHAPTER FOUR

DECLINE
American Idyll

Looking more nearly into their features, I saw some further pecu-
liarities in their Dresden-china type of prettiness. Their hair,
which was uniformly curly, came to a sharp end at the neck and
cheek; there was not the faintest suggestion of it on the face, and
their ears were singularly minute. The mouths were small, with
bright red, rather thin lips, and the little chins ran to a point. The
eyes were large and mild; and—this may seem egotism on my
part—I fancied even that there was a certain lack of
the interest I might have expected in them.
—H. G. Wells, ***The Time Machine*** **(1895)**

We took a whirl on H. G. Wells' famous time machine a few pages back, riding from the 1890s to the 1950s to our own time. In the original novella, a fellow in late Victorian England saddles up the eponymous contraption, propels himself forward, and finds himself in a world where humanity has divided into two: the Eloi, a small, soft, passive, decadent, vegetarian elite among whom one can scarce tell the boys from the girls; and the Morlocks, a dark, feral, subterranean underclass. This is supposedly London in the year 802,701 AD.

That's the only thing Wells got wrong: the date. He was off by a mere 800,690 years. If he'd set his time machine to nip ahead just a hundred or so to the early twenty-first century, he'd have been bang on target. Today, an insular myopic Eloi while away the hours conversing with the flowers, while the American Morlocks are beyond the horizon and rarely glimpsed. These groups are not yet formally divided into vegetarian on the one hand and carnivorous on the other, but they are evolving into physiognomically distinct species—an attenuated, emaciated coastal elite nibbling arugula in Malibu and Martha's Vineyard, while the vast bulk of people with vast bulk are confined to the intervening and less fashionable zip codes waiting in the drive-thru lane for a 2,000-calorie KrappiPounder. In his Obama hagiography, the MSNBC analyst Richard Wolffe reported that, at lunch one day, a conspicuously overweight White House aide was ostentatiously presented with a light salad by the president himself. The staffer responded that he could take care of both his health and his menu selections himself, but Obama was having none of it. "I love you, man," said the Commander-in-Chief. "Eat the salad."[1]

As an Obama acolyte, Mr Wolffe characterized this vignette as an example of how "caring" the president is, but a whiff of aesthetic revulsion from a coercive Conformocracy hangs over the incident: I love you, man. But you don't want people to get the impression that perhaps you're...not one of us. In *Invasion of the Body Snatchers*, the conformity enforcers urged the hold-outs just to close their eyes and go to sleep. In *Invasion of the Body Shrinkers*, the last lardbutt in the Obama circle is enjoined to eat the salad.

Beyond the White House as within, these are the salad days of the West. Researchers at the University of British Columbia published an exhaustive analysis of all those stories you read in the paper that begin "A new study shows that...."[2] In effect, UBC did a study of studies. They found that between 2003 and 2007, 80 percent of the population sample in the studies of six top psychology journals were university undergraduates, a demographic evidently containing many persons who would rather take part in studies than study what they're supposed to be studying. But these same psychology journals had somewhat carelessly assumed that the behavior patterns of wealthy western co-eds speak for the wider world. In other words, studies show that people who take part in studies are not that typical. The UBC paper gave a cute name to this unrepresentative sample of humanity: WEIRDs—Western Educated Industrialized Rich Democratic. I'd have gone for Western Educated Idle Rich Deadbeats myself, but *chacun à son goût*. The researchers were concerned with a very specific point: How representative of humanity at large is a tranche of affluent western college students? But they may have stumbled on the key not just to "scientific" studies but to liberal foreign policy, domestic spending, and the advanced social democratic state in the twenty-first century. If you take the assumptions of almost any group of college students sitting around late at night having deep-thought-a-thons in 1975, 1986, 1998, and imagine what a society governed by that sensibility would be like, you'd be where we are now—in a western world in elderly arrested adolescence, passing off its self-absorption as high-mindedness.

How high-minded are we? After the publication of *America Alone*, an exasperated reader wrote to advise me to lighten up, on the grounds that "we're rich enough to be stupid." That, too, has about it the sun-dappled complacency of idle trust-funders whiling away the sixth year of Whatever Studies. But it's an accurate distillation of a dominant worldview. Since 9/11, there have been many citations, apropos radical Islam, of Churchill's observation that an appeaser is one who feeds the crocodile hoping he'll eat him last. But we have fed the crocodile at home, too: we threw money at the Big Government croc for the privilege of not having to think seriously about certain problems, and on the assumption that, whatever we paid to make him go away, there would still be enough for us—that we were rich enough to afford our stupidity. Since the collapse of Lehman Brothers in 2008, we have been less rich. But, if anything, even more stupid.

Nevertheless, a lot of people take my correspondent's view: if you have old money well-managed, you can afford to be stupid—or afford the government's stupidity on your behalf. If you're a carbon-conscious celebrity getting $20 million per movie, you can afford the government's stupidity. If you're a tenured professor or a unionized bureaucrat in a nominally

private industry whose labor contracts were chiseled in stone two generations ago, you can afford it. But a lot of Americans don't have the same
comfortably padded margin for error on the present scale. And, as our
riches vanish, the stupidity pours into the vacuum.

In any advanced society, there will be a certain number of dysfunctional
citizens either unable or unwilling to do what is necessary to support themselves and their dependents. What to do about such people? Ignore the
problem? Attempt to fix it? The former nags at the liberal guilt complex,
while the latter is way too much like hard work. The modern progressive
has no urge to emulate those Victorian social reformers who tramped the
streets of English provincial cities looking for fallen women to rescue. All
he wants to do is ensure that the fallen women don't fall anywhere near him.

So the easiest "solution" to the problem is to toss public money at it.
You know how it is when you're at the mall and someone rattles a collection
box under your nose and you're not sure where it's going but it's probably
for Darfur or Rwanda or Hoogivsastan. Whatever. You're dropping a buck
or two in the tin for the privilege of not having to think about it. The modern welfare state operates on the same principle: since the Second World
War, the middle classes have transferred historically unprecedented
amounts of money to the unproductive sector in order not to have to think
about it.

But so what? We were rich enough that we could afford to be stupid.
And so we threw money at the dependent class, and indulged a gang
of halfwit and/or malevolent ideologues as they hollowed out the
education system and other institutions. We were rich enough to afford
their stupidity.

That works for a while. In the economic expansion of the late twentieth
century, average citizens of western democracies paid more in taxes but
lived better than their parents and grandparents. They weren't exactly rich,
but they got richer. They also got more stupid. The welfare states they
endowed transformed society: to be "poor" in the twenty-first-century West
is not to be hungry and emaciated but to be obese, with your kids suffering

from childhood diabetes. When Michelle Obama turns up to serve food at a soup kitchen, its poverty-stricken clientele snap pictures of her with their cellphones.[3] In one-sixth of British households, not a single family member works.[4] They are not so much without employment as without need of it. At a certain level, your nine-to-five bourgeois understands that the bulk of his contribution to the state treasury is entirely wasted, if not actively destructive. It's one of the basic rules of life: if you reward bad behavior, you get more of it. But, in good and good-ish times, so what?

Very few people are fiercely political, which is reasonable enough. The point of politics is to enable life—the pleasures of family, the comforts of home, the rewards of work, good food, good company, music, golf, snow-boarding, horse-shoeing, whatever's your bag. So, among America's elite, there are many non-political members, comfortable, educated beneficiaries of the American Dream who just want to get on with their lives. For these people and many others, liberalism is the soft option, the one with all the nice words—"diversity," "tolerance," "peace," "social justice," "sustainabil-ity"—and the position that requires least defending if you happen to be at a dinner party and the conversation trends toward current events. If you have to have "opinions," these are the safe ones. They're not really "opinions," are they? Just the default settings of contemporary sensibility.

"I never met people more indolent or more easily fatigued," wrote H. G. Wells of the Eloi. "A queer thing I soon discovered about my little hosts, and that was their lack of interest. They would come to me with eager cries of astonishment, like children, but like children they would soon stop examining me and wander away after some other toy." They love every-thing—in small doses. After all, if you love everything, why pay attention to anything in particular? If you drive around with a "COEXIST" bumper sticker, you've relieved yourself of having to know anything about Islam. You went to an awareness-raising rock concert: it was something to do with Bono and debt forgiveness, whatever that means, but let's face it, going to the park for eight hours of celebrity caterwauling beats having to wrap your head around Afro-Marxist economics.

"Their sentences were usually simple and of two words," recalled the Time-Traveler, "and I failed to convey or understand any but the simplest propositions." Very true. But whereas Wells' Eloi could only speak in "concrete substantives" and had lost the use of abstract language, our Eloi drone nothing but:

What do you think of illegal immigration?

Celebrate diversity.

What do you think of gay marriage?

Celebrate diversity.

What do you think of Islam?

Celebrate diversity.

What do you think of burqas, honor killings, female genital mutilation, stoning for adultery, capital punishment for homosexuals?

Celebrate diversity.

What do you think of war?

War is never the answer.

What if the question is, "How did the United States of America achieve its independence?"

All we are saying is give peace a chance.

Is that all you're saying?

Did we mention "celebrate diversity"?

In *Fahrenheit 451*, Ray Bradbury wrote: "If you don't want a man unhappy politically, don't give him two sides to a question to worry him: give him one. Better yet, give him none. Let him forget there is such a thing as war. If the government is inefficient, top-heavy, and tax-mad, better it be all those than that people worry over it. Peace, Montag."

Climate change? It's not a question, and there aren't two sides: there's the side of "the environment," and then there's the "deniers." Illegal immigration? There's the side of "diversity," and then there's the racists. From kindergarten up, America's "educators" teach their young charges the no-side buzz-words: Peace, Montag. The seductive peace of comfort and complacency.

★ ★ ★ ★ ★

THE UTOPIA OF MYOPIA

"Diversity" is an attitude rather than a lived experience. Slap the "COEXIST" sticker on your Subaru and you're more or less done. No need to be nervous. For the most part, you'll still be COEXISTing with people exactly like you. It certainly doesn't mean COEXIST with that crackbrained guy who services your car and listens to Rush Limbaugh, which you found out when you picked it up from the shop and couldn't figure out what was going on until you realized he'd retuned the radio and you were frantically pounding the buttons trying to get back to NPR so you missed the off-ramp but by then you'd found your way back to "All Things Considered" so you did get to hear that interview with the singer who has a new album but mainly wanted to talk about how the concession stands on her tour will be required to serve only fair-trade coffee.

And so the state religion co-opts many of the best and brightest but politically passive. It anesthetizes them into forgetfulness. The historian Victor Davis Hanson thinks his fellow Californians are now trending in a very Wellsian direction: the new Eloi expect to be able to enjoy all the benefits of

an advanced prosperous society while erecting a regime of regulated sentimentalization that will make its continuation impossible. "The well-off like
nice cars, tasteful homes, good food, and appropriate vacations," writes
Hanson, "but not the oil, gas, coal, nuclear energy, transmission lines, timber,
cement, farmland, water pumps, etc, that bring that to them."[5] Indeed, they
actively wage war on the latter. Just like President Obama, we love our arugula, but we support the EPA ruling that shuts down the "human use" irriga-
tion canal that enables our farmers to grow it.

Wells' Time-Traveler had a similar reaction to the Eloi: they lived comfortable lives, yet disconnected from the world that sustained their comforts.
"I saw mankind housed in splendid shelters, gloriously clothed, and as yet
I had found them engaged in no toil," he wrote. "These people were clothed
in pleasant fabrics that must at times need renewal, and their sandals,
though undecorated, were fairly complex specimens of metalwork. Somehow such things must be made." And yet he saw "no workshops" or sign of
any industry at all. "They spent all their time in playing gently, in bathing
in the river, in making love in a half-playful fashion, in eating fruit and
sleeping. I could not see how things were kept going." So it is in our time:
things are "kept going" by forces largely out of sight, whether in the
Flownover Country of working America, or in the shadows of the Undocumented, or in the factories of China.

Conversely, as Professor Hanson sees it, the new Morlocks of the American underclass demand iPods and video games and other diversions they
regard as their birthright, but are all but incapable of making any useful
contribution to the kind of society required to produce them:

> I suppose the attitude of the directionless youth is something
> like the following, though never articulated: "Some nerd will
> dream up a new video game; the Chinese will build it for me
> cheaply; and I will play it at my leisure given my birthright both
> as an exalted American and the enormous debt 'they' (fill in the
> blanks) owe me."

At some point the world snaps back, "Nope, the Indian and Chinese young person knows more, works harder, produces more—and gets more than you, despite your American brand."

The new Morlocks are primitivizing, while the new Eloi are becoming more elite and refined. "But they share a disturbing commonality," says Hanson. "Both expect something that they are not willing to invest in."

In his book *Civilization and Its Enemies*, Lee Harris writes of a collective "forgetfulness" that over time settles in to peaceful societies. The so-called "Greatest Generation" made serious mistakes when they took control of the levers of the state, but always somewhere, however deeply buried, they remembered what it was like to live in a world at war and, before that, a world of mass privation. The Baby Boomers who followed knew nothing other than peace and prosperity. They weren't "forgetful," for they had nothing to forget.

"It was natural on that golden evening that I should jump at the idea of a social paradise," says Wells' Time-Traveler. As he subsequently reflects: "After the battle comes Quiet. Humanity had been strong, energetic, and intelligent, and had used all its abundant vitality to alter the conditions under which it lived. And now came the reaction of the altered conditions." In time, the Sixties rebels ascended to power and became the teachers, and then their children, until we were three generations removed from memories of World War and Depression.

During the 2010 World Cup, the eminent Egyptian imam Mus'id Anwar gave a sermon in Cairo attacking young men who follow soccer instead of memorizing the Koran:

> Ask one of those young men who are so crazy about soccer to name the names of twenty of the Prophet's companions. Only 20! The Prophet Muhammad's companions numbered over 100,000. All I'm asking for is the name of 20 companions.... But if you ask the same guy to give you the names of 20 soccer players,

he will…give you the names of the reserve team players, of those
who are still active, and those who have retired.[6]

Who's to blame for this? Well, the imam looked into it and quickly discovered who's seducing the Muslims away from their Korans:

As you know, the Jews have *The Protocols of the Elders of Zion.*
Over 100 years ago, they formulated a plan to rule the world,
and they are implementing this plan.

One of the protocols says: "Keep the [non-Jews] preoccupied
with songs, soccer, and movies." Is it or isn't it happening? It is.

Don't some of them die in the course of a soccer match? At
an important match in Egypt, a man was standing in the stadium, and when his team scored a goal, he screamed
"Gooooaaal!" got a heart attack, and died.… The Zionists manage to generate animosity among Muslims, and even between
Muslim countries, by means of soccer. Whose interests does this
serve? The Jews.

Oh, it's easy to be skeptical. After all, if soccer is part of the international
Jewish Conspiracy, how come Israel has only managed to qualify for the
World Cup on one occasion (1970) and got knocked out in Round One?[7]
Ah, but that just shows how cunning these Jews are. At the time the distinguished cleric was advancing his theory, I happened to be in Bordeaux and
found myself outside the Virgin Megastore, which brands itself in France
as "*La culture du plaisir*"—The Culture of Pleasure. As far as I know, the
chain doesn't operate in the Middle East. If you're a Muslim, you have to
wait till you self-detonate to hit the Virgin Megastore, big time and with
our entire inventory priced to clear. But it struck me that the western world's
self-evaluation isn't so very different from Imam Anwar's diagnosis: we
promote ourselves as "the Culture of Pleasure"—preoccupied, as the imam
says, with songs, sports, movies, and other sensual delights.

Or as H. G. Wells put it: "This has ever been the fate of energy in security; it takes to art and to eroticism, and then come languor and decay."

Because even the "culture" part of "la culture du plaisir" eventually becomes too much effort. Our age does not produce great symphonies or operas but merely electronic delivery systems, new toys for enjoying old strains. The "artistic impetus would at last die away," wrote Wells of the Eloi. "To adorn themselves with flowers, to dance, to sing in the sunlight: so much was left of the artistic spirit, and no more. Even that would fade in the end into a contented inactivity."

Odd how many philosophical singalongs of the Sixties that one sentence anticipates: "If you're going to San Francisco, be sure to wear some flowers in your hair"; "All we need is music…and dancin' in the streets"; "We'll sing in the sunshine, we'll laugh every day.…"

A culture of pleasure can be very convenient for the government class. In Huxley's *Brave New World*, the World State Controller, to whom the author gave the oddly prescient name of Mustapha Mond, understands that people prefer happiness to truth, "happiness" being defined as round-the-clock sensory gratification—food, drugs, sex, consumer toys. Given that he was writing in the late Twenties, Huxley's parody pop songs anticipate very well the sensual torpor of our own *culture du plaisir*:

> Hug me till you drug me, honey;
> Kiss me till I'm in a coma;
> Hug me, honey, snuggly bunny;
> Love's as good as soma.

"Soma," a word Huxley took from Sanskrit, is a drug that both intoxicates and tranquilizes. In his brave new world, we're seduced into passivity. And in such a society, as Charles Murray wrote of Europe, "ideas of greatness become an irritant."[8] Go to the heart of western civilization—Rome, the capital of Christendom; Madrid, Lisbon, and Paris, the seats of mighty empires that sent their men and ships to every corner of the world and implanted their language and culture. And yet these cities are all now back-waters—mostly pleasant and residually prosperous backwaters, but utterly irrelevant to the future of the world. And that suits their citizens just fine.

Is that the fate the United States is destined for? It's what a lot of Americans would like. In 2008 many people were just exhausted by the "war on terror." Not because it demanded anything of them—quite the opposite: it was entirely outsourced to a small professional soldiery the twenty-first-century Eloi rarely encounter. But so what? They still had to hear about the war, and they were bored by it. Having to be at Code Orange in perpetuity was just kind of a downer. So they voted for "change"—by which they meant a quiet life: I don't want to have to think about wacky foreigners trying to blow us up; I don't need that in my life right now.

As for the Eloi's mostly inactive "activism," professions of generalized concerns about "world poverty" or "saving the planet" do not testify to your idealism so much as what Adam Bellow calls "a certain blithe assurance about the permanence of freedom":[9] you worry about lofty and distant problems because you assume there are none closer to home. Our Eloi are smugly self-satisfied. I cite at random four stickers from the cars parked outside a children's "holiday" concert in small-town Vermont:

I THINK, THEREFORE I'M A DEMOCRAT

What kind of sentient being boasts on a bumper sticker about his giant brain? And cites as evidence thereof his unyielding loyalty to a political machine? Talk about putting Descartes before the whores. What that translates to is: "I'M A DEMOCRAT. THEREFORE, I HAVE NO NEED TO THINK."

QUESTION EVERYTHING

Including the need to question everything? Doubting everything gets kinda exhausting. In practice, questioning "everything" boils down to questioning nothing in particular—for, if everything is a social construct, a manufac-tured reality, why bother? Fortunately, "QUESTION EVERYTHING" ceased to be operative on January 20, 2009. After that date, dissent was no longer "the highest form of patriotism," but merely racism.

IMAGINE PEACE

That's a total failure of imagination—a failure, under the guise of universal-ist multiculturalism, to imagine that outside your fluffy cocoon there is a truly many-cultured world full of people so "diverse" they do not view things as you do. Underneath the "IMAGINE" sticker was another:

PEACE THROUGH MUSIC

That's true if you've got in mind someone like Scotland's Bill Millin, per-sonal bagpiper to Lord Lovat, commander of 1st Special Service Brigade, who piped the men ashore on D-Day as he strolled up and down the beach amid the gunfire playing "Hieland Laddie" and "The Road to the Isles" and other highland favorites.[10] Bill Millin was a musician and a truly heroic one. But I would doubt our myopic Vermonter has even heard of him. I wonder if he's aware that, under the Taliban, music is banned. For all the much vaunted "empathy" of the caring class and their insistence on "celebrating diversity," they seem blissfully ignorant of the great diversity out there in the world, and of how hostile much of it is to their preoccupations. "Peace through Music" is inertia masquerading as a mission: hey, I'll just sit on the porch, smoke a little dope, strum my guitar, and tell myself that it's a great contribution to humanity.

Because anything other than striking self-flattering, mock-dissident poses is too much like hard work.

Adam Bellow may be understating the problem: even as they take their own freedoms for granted, it's not clear the Eloi care much about freedom per se. And even the lofty and distant causes are merely a pretext for a pampering overweening conformism. So don't pick up *Poems Against the War* under the misapprehension that the poems might address the, you know, *war*. Kim Addonizio's "Cranes in August" is about her daughter making cranes out of paper while "outside/the gray doves/bring their one vowel to the air," ominously. Don't care for gray doves in August? No problem. The very next poem is about geese in October:

> Geese, October 2002.

The poet, Lucy Adkins, notes that even as "our country's leaders/are voting for war," outside her home in Nebraska "the geese fly over/the old wisdom in their feathers." Not into geese or doves? How about insects? Like Kim Addonizio, for Kelli Russell Agodon war poetry starts with your daughter's play activities, but in this case the young Miss Agodon is endeavoring to help fire ants and potato bugs in their "small seaside community outside of Seattle":

> She tries to help them
> before the patterns of tides
> reach their lives.

As Ms. Agodon writes:

> Here war is only newsprint.
> How easy it is not to think about it
> As we sleep beneath our quiet sky.

You don't say! But enough about war, let's talk about me, and my daughter, and whatever happens to be flying or crawling by the window. Would it kill you to include one lousy detail about Iraq—you know, the ostensible subject? Maybe you could have the geese and gray doves fly over and take a look at what Saddam did to the Iraqi marshlands. As Bruce Bawer wrote in his review, "Throughout these poems, the implicit argument is: Why can't the whole world be as peaceable as my little corner of it is?"[11] Yes, indeed. If only geopolitics were like a pledge drive on Vermont Public Radio: tedious and disruptive, but only for a few days, and if you give them $50 to leave you alone you get an organic tote bag.

Campaigning for the Democrats in 2004, Ben Affleck offered a pearl of wisdom to John Kerry and his consultants: "You have to enervate the base," the Hollywood heartthrob advised solemnly.[12] As it happens, if it's enervating the base you're after, Senator Kerry was doing a grand job. It would be easy to mock Mr. Affleck as a celebrity airhead, but these days even the airheads are expensively credentialed: Ben is an alumnus of one of the same colleges as President Obama (Occidental). And liberal progressivism has done a grand job of enervating its base. A self-absorbed passivity is now the default mode of the enlightened worldview. Behind those "IMAGINE PEACE" stickers lies a terrible failure to imagine.

★ ★ ★ ★ ★
CELEBRATE YOURSELF

Appearing at the University of Denver in 2010, the talk-show host Dennis Prager was asked to identify the single greatest threat to the future of America.[13] Several enthusiastic members of the audience bayed "Obama!" and Mr. Prager found himself obliged to correct them: "No, it's not Obama," he said. "It's not. If, God forbid, President Obama came down with an illness nothing would change. Nothing."

This is correct. Barack Obama is a symptom rather than the problem. He didn't declare himself president; America *chose* him. That's what should worry you, not whether he was born in Mombasa and had his minions fake a Hawaiian birth certificate. That just gets you off the hook: aw, gee, we were duped. No, you duped yourself, America. That's the problem. Mr. Prager explained that the single greatest threat facing the nation was that "we have not passed on what it means to be American to this generation…. A society does not survive if it does not have a reason to survive." For Prager, small government is a moral question:

> We give far more to charity per capita than Europeans do. Why? Are we born better? No. The bigger the government the worse the citizen. They are preoccupied in Europe with how much time off: Where will they vacation? When will they retire? These are selfish questions, these are not altruistic questions. So the goodness that America created is jeopardized by our not knowing what we stand for. That's our greatest threat. We are our problem.

Instead of teaching "what it means to be American," we teach anything but. We are obsessed with identity, but any identity other than "American"— female, gay, African-American, Muslim-American, Undocumented-American. At American universities, women take Women's Studies, Latinos take Latino Studies, queers take Queer Studies. For many Americans, the preferred academic discipline is navel-gazing, sometimes literally: people of girth take Fat Studies. The best way to celebrate diversity is by celebrating yourself, and the best way to celebrate yourself is without anyone else getting in the way. And why wait till college? In New York, gay, lesbian, and transgendered schoolchildren can attend Harvey Milk High.[14] Are there many transgendered 13-year-olds, even in Manhattan? Well, it's about every student's right to a "non-threatening learning environment," and, if he doesn't actually learn anything in the non-threatening learning environment, he's still better off than if he'd been in the non-learning threatening environment of most New York high schools.

In all its shallow obsession with sexual and racial politics, the ever more leisurely vacuity of education also puts a question mark over identity in a more fundamental sense. In January 2009, Canada's *Globe and Mail* (which is like the *New York Times* but without the jokes) chose to contrast the incoming U.S. president with, er, me. "He belongs to a demographic—it made his win possible—that doesn't even get the problem with a black, a woman or a gay president," wrote Rick Salutin. "They don't clutch old identifications with race or 'the west.' They glory in 'hybridity'.... For another demographic, this shift induces panic. They worry about 'shriveled birth rates' in the United States and its 'enervated allies' (Mark Steyn); they mourn the decline of 'the last serious western nation.'"[15]

Crumbs. I wasn't aware I was an entirely different "demographic" from Barack Obama. We're more or less the same generation, but plainly the president stands for hope and the future and I represent the past and fear. As for "not getting the problem," a lot of those black voters who turned out in huge numbers for Obama in California stayed in the polling booth to vote down gay marriage:[16] the rainbow coalition shimmers beguilingly but dissolves on close contact—and that's before you ask the shy Muslim girl in the corner of the classroom if she wouldn't be happier at Lesbo High. Still, in a broad sense Rick Salutin is correct: the demographic that is the change it's been waiting for doesn't want to be seen "clutching old identifications." What a yawneroo that'd be.

For decades, western elites have been bored by their own traditions and fetishized the exotic. Obama was both the beneficiary of this syndrome and its apotheosis. He was living his own COEXIST sticker: his parents were Kansan and Kenyan, as if paired by an alphabetically minded dating agency; he was Hawaiian, and Indonesian; for white liberals he offered absolution from racial guilt, but he wasn't one of those in-your-face types like the Reverend Al and the Reverend Jesse yelling grievance jingles all day long; he was a community organizer from the mean streets of Chicago, yet he was also by some happy if vague process an alumnus of half the schools in the Ivy League, and he had the great good fortune not to live in any of the "communities" he "organized" but instead in the more salubrious Hyde Park, a community organized by John D. Rockefeller's money; he embodied "change," but he peddled the same reassuringly shopworn bromides ("America, this is our moment") whose woozy evasions liberals chose to regard as the second coming of Cicero; he was kinda Christian (albeit of the paranoid, neo-segregationist, Afro-nationalist branch) but sorta Muslim (from a Jakarta madrassah, but don't worry, not one of the heavy-duty kind); he had a white grandmother but also an undocumented auntie served with an unenforced deportation order. If that's not the all-American resumé for the twenty-first century, what is?

After the inauguration, my old pal Boris Johnson, Mayor of London, tweeted ecstatically: "What a speech!! Speaking as citizen of the world that was exac what I wanted to hear from an Amer Pres't."[17]

What that seems to boil down to is an Amer Pres't who isn't hung up on being Pres't of Amer: that Obama can do. "People of the world,"[18] he droned to his audience for his famous Berlin speech, sounding as if his spacecraft had just landed from Planet Hopechangula and you earthlings had no choice but to submit to his awesome power. In postmodern terms, he's not as far gone as Michael Ignatieff, leader of Her Majesty's Loyal Opposition in Ottawa. Previously a professor at Harvard and a BBC late-night intellectual telly host, Mr. Ignatieff returned to Canada in order to become Prime Minister, and to that end got himself elected as leader of the Liberal Party. And, as is the fashion nowadays, he cranked out a quickie tome laying out his political "vision." Having spent his entire adult life abroad, he was aware that some of the natives were uncertain about his commitment to the land of his birth. So he was careful to issue a sort of pledge of a kind of allegiance, explaining that writing a book about Canada had "deepened my attachment to the place on earth that, if I needed one, I would call home."[19]

My, that's awfully big of you. As John Robson commented in *The Ottawa Citizen*, "I'm worried that a man so postmodern he doesn't need a home wants to lead my country. Why? Is it quaint? An interesting sociological experiment?"[20]

Indeed. But there's a lot of it about. Many Americans quickly began to pick up the strange vibe that for Barack Obama governing America was "an interesting sociological experiment," too. He would doubtless agree that the United States is "the place on earth that, if I needed one, I would call home."

But he doesn't, not really: it's hard to imagine Obama wandering along to watch a Memorial Day or Fourth of July parade until the job required him to. That's not to say he's un-American or anti-American, but merely that he's beyond all that. Way beyond. He is, as John Bolton says, post-American.[21] In his own book on the president, Dinesh D'Souza argues that Obama is defined by his father's anti-colonialism.[22] Speaking as an old-school imperialist, I find him exactly the opposite: in his attitude to America, Obama comes across as a snooty viceregal grandee passing through some tedious colonial outpost. He's the first president to give off the pronounced whiff that he's condescending to the job—that it's really too small for him and he's just killing time until something more commensurate with his stature comes along. When he lectures America on the Ground Zero mosque or immigration, he does not speak to his people as one of them. When he addresses the *monde*, he speaks as a *citoyen du* for whom the United States has no greater or lesser purchase on him than Papua or Peru. There is an absence of feeling for America—as in his offhand remark to Bob Woodward that the United States can "absorb" another 9/11.[23] During the long Northern Irish "Troubles," cynical British officials used to talk off-the-record about holding casualties down to "an acceptable level of violence," but it's eerie to hear the head of state take the same view—and about a far higher number of fatalities.[24] Ask the 3,000 families who had a huge gaping hole blown in their lives whether another 9/11 is something you want to "absorb" rather than prevent.

But why be surprised at the thin line between Obama's cool and his coldness? Jeremiah Wright (his race-baiting pastor), Van Jones (his Communist "green jobs" czar), William Ayers and Bernardine Dohrn (his hippie-terrorist patrons) are not exactly stirred by love of country, either. Nor, to be honest, are America's desiccated media—although they know enough to understand that you have to genuflect in that direction once in a while: Would it kill you to wear the stupid flag pin? The rubes'll lap it up. Hence, the commentariat's subsequent panic at Obama's indifference even to faking feeling.

With hindsight, this is what drove both the birthers and the countering cries of racism. Detractors and supporters alike were trying to explain something that was at first vaguely palpable and then became embarrassingly obvious: it's not so much that he's foreign to America, but that America is foreign to him. Outside the cloisters of Hyde Park and a few other enclaves, he doesn't seem to *get* America. Not because he was born in Kenya or wherever, but because he's the first president to be marinated his entire life in a post-modern, post-American cultural relativism. What's worrying about Obama is not that he's weird but that he's so typical of much of the Eloi; in that sense, his post-Americanness is all too American.

In both Chicago's Ward Four, where the Obamas lived, and Ward Five, where they worked, 95 percent of electors voted Democrat in 2004.[25] You would be hard put to find another constituency so committed to celebrating lack of diversity. Like most professional multiculturalists, Obama has passed his entire adulthood in a very narrow unicultural environment where your ideological worldview doesn't depend on anything so tedious as actually viewing the world. The aforementioned Michael Ignatieff, who actually *has* viewed the world, gets close to the psychology in his response to criticisms of him for spending so much time abroad. Deploring such "provincialism," he replied: "They say it makes me less of a Canadian. It makes me *more* of a Canadian."[26]

Well, yes, you can see what he's getting at. Today, to be an educated citizen of a mature western democracy—Canada or Germany, England or Sweden—is not to feel Canadian or German, English or Swedish, heaven forbid, but rather to regard oneself as a *citoyen du monde*, like Obama in Berlin. Obviously, if being "more Canadian" requires one actually to be a Harvard professor or a BBC TV host or an essayist for *The Guardian*, then very few actual Canadians would pass the test. They would be condemned to be eternally "less Canadian." What Ignatieff really means is that in a post-nationalist west, the definition of "Canadian" (and Dutch and Belgian and Irish) is how multicultural and globalized you feel. The UN, Greenpeace, Amnesty International, Bono: these are the colors a progressive worldly westerner nails to his mast. You don't need to go anywhere, or do anything: you just have to pick up the general groove, which you can do very easily at almost any college campus.

This Barack Obama did brilliantly. His rise and the dancing fountains of media adoration accompanying it are a monument to the fraudulence of so much elite "accomplishment." The smart set were bamboozled because he seemed like one of their own: Columbia, Harvard Law, sort of "editing" a journal yet the only editor in its history never to publish a signed article, giving a lecture or two on constitutional law, handing out leaflets on the South Side of Chicago, voting present, listening to Jeremiah Wright's conspiracy theories for twenty years, dining with terrorist educator William Ayers.... This is a life? These are achievements?

Well, yes. For the parochial one-worlders among the American elite, that's a resumé and Sarah Palin's isn't. The American Eloi elected one of their own, and, if a year into his reign it was possible to detect signs of embarrassment among some of those gullible enough to fall for such a transparent crock, well, thanks for nuthin'. "I thought he'd do a better job," whimpered telly genius Jon Stewart.[27]

"Based on what, his extensive experience?" responded Instapundit Glenn Reynolds. "Rube."[28] The election of Obama was a profoundly unserious act by an unserious nation, and, if you were Putin, the ChiComs, or the ayatollahs, you would have to be awfully virtuous not to take advantage of it.

Within months of his inauguration, I found a lot of Americans saying to me sotto voce that they had no idea the new president would feel so "weird." But, in fact, he's not weird. He's WEIRD in the sense of those students in the behavioral studies: Western Educated Idle Rich Deadbeat. He's not, even in Democrat terms, a political figure—as Bill Clinton and Joe Biden are. Instead, he's a creature of the broader culture: there are millions of people like Barack Obama, the eternal students of an unbounded lethargic transnational campus for whom global compassion and the multicultural pose are merely the modish gloss on a cult of radical grandiose narcissism.

Even as he denies American exceptionalism, he gets turned on by his own. Or as someone once said, "We are the ones we've been waiting for."

We were waiting for a man who would have been unthinkable as the leader of a serious nation until our civilization had reached such a level of bland bovine prosperity it truly believed that the platitudinous nursery chants it teaches our children as a substitute for education are now a blueprint for governance. Obama is not just a product of his time, but *the* product of his time.

★ ★ ★ ★ ★

THE STUDENT PRINCES

In 1940, a majority of the U.S. population had no more than a Grade Eight education.[29]

By 2008, 40 percent of 18- to 24-year-olds were enrolled in college.[30]

So we're on track to a world in which the typical American is almost twice as old by the time he completes his education as he was in 1940, and has spent over twice as long in the classroom—and, in theory, gotten twice as much attention from his schoolma'am: the pupil/teacher ratio is half of what it was a century ago.[31] Indeed, since 1970 overall public school employment has increased ten times faster than public school enrollment—with no discernible benefit to student performance.[32] Here's reporter Howard Blume in the *Los Angeles Times*: "Despite thousands of teacher layoffs and shrinking school budgets, Los Angeles Unified, the state's largest school system, posted gains on annual standardized tests. Schools statewide also posted overall gains in results released Monday."[33]

"Despite"?

Today's "educators" take no chances with their young charges, to the point of keeping as many as they can in "school" until well into what now passes for adulthood. What dragons have been slain by this semester-creep? In 1940, before this process got rolling, Americans had a literacy rate of over 97 percent.[34] Seventy years later, at a student demo to protest budget "cuts" at the University of Washington, the elderly demonstrators waved printed placards bearing the slogan:

WHO'S SCHOOLS? OUR SCHOOLS![35]

And you're welcome to them. Or, as their placards would no doubt put it, your welcome to 'em. Were they English majors?

Education is the biggest single structural defect in the United States. No country needs to send a majority (never mind "all," as is President Obama's ambition) of its children to college, and no country should: not every child has the aptitude to benefit from college, and not every child who has wants to go, or needs to. For most who wind up there, college is a waste of time, and money, and life. Hacks pretend to teach, slackers pretend to learn, and employers pretend it's a qualification. Full disclosure: I never went to college, which is why my critics usually preface their dissections with a reference to "the uneducated" or "the unlettered Mark Steyn." Guilty as charged: no letters on me. But I was doing ancient Greek in high school and Latin by middle school, not because I was "gifted" but because that's just the way it was back then. I long ago gave up marveling at how little American education asks of its inmates. By universalizing university, you let K-12 off the hook. College becomes the new high school—which is exactly the opposite of what a dynamic, efficient society would be doing: middle school should be the new high school. Early-year education is the most critical; if you screw up the first eight grades, keeping the kid in class till he's thirty isn't going to do much to fix things.

Beyond the academic arguments, no functioning state can afford to keep its kids at school till they're twenty-two. It leads to later workplace participation, later family formation, and societal infantilization. Take America in its most dynamic years—the period when it put great inventions within the reach of every citizen (the automobile, the telephone, the washer and dryer), and, for you *culture-du-plaisir* types, also developed the modern entertainment industry (radio, talking pictures, gramophone records, Tin Pan Alley, jazz, Broadway, Hollywood): it did all this with a population whose median education was 8.3 years. Eighth Grade America won a world war, and emerged afterwards as an economic superpower that dominated the post-war era until Eighteenth Grade America sleepwalked it off the precipice.

Oh, well. What does an American get for sticking with the system to Ninth Grade, Twelfth Grade, Sixteenth Grade, and beyond? Is he more "educated"? Not obviously so. But he is indisputably credentialed, and in the credential-fetishizing America of the early twenty-first century, that's what counts. So American families plunge themselves into debt and take huge amounts of money out of the productive economy in order to feed the ravenous diploma mill. It's not too demanding, and getting less so every year: by 2010, only 23 percent of courses offered at Harvard required a final exam.[36] For most of its "scholars," college is a leisurely half-decade immersion in the manners and mores of American conformism. Other than that, it doesn't matter what, if anything, you learn there, just so long as you emerge with the diploma. It used to be made of sheepskin. But these days the students are the sheep and the ones getting fleeced are their parents.

By the turn of the twenty-first century, America had per capita two-and-a-half times as many college students as Britain and Spain. Its college population was significantly larger than its high school population, mainly due to the fact that such fields of scholarship as "Jiggle in My Walk: The Iconic Power of the 'Big Butt' in American Pop Culture"[37] are so rigorous that to complete a bachelor's degree can take twice as long as it once would have. Say what you like about half a decade of "Peace Studies" but, while light on the studies, it's certainly peaceful. To acquire the ersatz sheepskin, Americans not only forego what might have been six years of profitable and career-advancing work, they also rack up a six-figure debt in order to access a job that is increasingly unlikely to justify that outlay. But then taking that first step on the debt ladder is as important an initiation into contemporary adulthood as the magic credential.

In fairness, there remain certain exceptions to these leisurely frauds. America retains world-class academic institutions in science and engineering.

But half the graduate students in these fields are foreigners, and more and more return home at the end of their studies.[38] Perhaps we could retrain a few Diversity Officers to replace retiring physicists. Beyond that, has universal credentialism created a golden age of American scholarship? Not so's you'd notice. Michelle Obama was born in 1964, so, unlike Condi Rice, she has no vivid childhood memories of racial segregation. She was among the first generation to benefit from "affirmative action," which was supposed to ameliorate the lingering grievances of racism but seems, in Mrs. Obama's case, merely to have transformed them into post-modern pseudo-grievance. "All my life I have confronted people who had a certain expectation of me," she told an audience in Madison. "Every step of the way, there was somebody there telling me what I couldn't do. Applied to Princeton. 'You can't go there, your test scores aren't high enough.' I went. I graduated with departmental honors. And then I wanted to go to Harvard. And that was probably a little too tough for me. I didn't even know why they said that."[39]

But hang on. Her test scores weren't "high enough" for Princeton? Yet, rather than telling her "You can't go there," they took her anyway. And all the thanks they get is that her test scores are now a recurring point of resentment: "The stuff that we're seeing in these polls," she told another audience, "has played out my whole life. You know, always being told by somebody that I'm not ready, that I can't do something, my scores weren't high enough."[40] If she had been Elizabeth Edwards and her scores weren't high enough, that'd be that (Teresa Heinz Kerry could probably leverage the whole Mozambican thing). Yet Mrs. Obama regards contemporary state-mandated compensation for institutional racism from before she was born as merely another burden to bear. In testament to an age of boundless self-infatuation, she arrived as a black woman at Princeton and wrote her undergraduate thesis on the difficulties of being a black woman at Princeton. "Princeton-Educated Blacks and the Black Community"[41] is a self-meditation by the then Miss Robinson on the question of whether an Ivy League black student drawn into the white world is betraying lower-class blacks. Or as she put it:

A separationist is more likely to have a realistic impression of
the plight of the Black lower class because of the likelihood that
a separationist is more closely associated with the Black lower
class than are integrationist [sic]. By actually working with the
Black lower class or within their communities as a result of their
ideologies, a separationist may better understand the desparation [sic] of their situation and feel more hopeless about a
resolution as opposed to an integrationist who is ignorant to
their plight.

Ah, the benefits of an elite education. Suppose Michelle Obama had not
suffered the crippling burden of being American but had instead been
born in France or Switzerland, India or China. In less enlightened lands,
when you're told "Your test scores aren't high enough," that's it, you can't
go. To get into other countries' elite institutions, you have to be objectively
excellent. To get into America's best schools and join its elite, you need
mediocre grades and approved social points. Harvard's defense of "affirmative action" rests on the benefits of "diversity": "A farm boy from Idaho
can bring something to Harvard College that a Bostonian cannot offer.
Similarly, a black student can usually bring something that a white person
cannot offer."

That's the argument, such as it is: "Affirmative action" discriminates
positively—in favor of certain groups that add an unspecified richness to
campus life. As we know, Michelle Obama fell into the latter category of
"black student." But what about the "farm boy from Idaho"? In 2010, the
Princeton sociologist Thomas Espenshade and his colleague Alexandria
Radford produced an analysis of applications for eight highly competitive
colleges and universities.[42] What was most revealing was the way "affirmative action" has progressed from mere race bias to ideological apartheid.
Espenshade and Radford found that participating in "red state" activities
such as 4-H, ROTC, or the Future Farmers of America substantially
reduced a student's chances of being accepted by these colleges. "Being an

officer or winning awards" with such groups had an even more severe impact, reducing your chances of admission by 60 to 65 percent.

So, if you're a white farm boy from Idaho, you're already at a disadvantage compared with the Michelle Obamas and Sonia Sotormayors of your generation. And, if you participate in 4-H or JROTC, you're only making things worse. And, if you hold a leadership position in 4-H, you're pretty much doomed. Over time "affirmative action" and "diversity" have so corrupted the integrity of American education that it now affirmatively acts in favor of ideological and cultural homogeneity. Or as the blogger Kate McMillan likes to say: What's the opposite of "diversity"? University.[43]

This is why the massive expansion of American education is evidence not of progress but of its exact opposite—its decay into ideological factory farms. It's a progressive 4-H: Hogwash, Hypersensitivity, Habituation, Homogeneity—for the price of which you wind up in Hock. "Our ruling class recruits and renews itself not through meritocracy but rather by taking into itself people whose most prominent feature is their commitment to fit in," wrote Angelo Codevilla of Boston University, noting the unprecedented uniformity of the new American elite. "Until our own time America's upper crust was a mixture of people who had gained prominence in a variety of ways, who drew their money and status from different sources and were not predictably of one mind on any given matter. The Boston Brahmins, the New York financiers, the land barons of California, Texas, and Florida, the industrialists of Pittsburgh, the Southern aristocracy, and the hardscrabble politicians who made it big in Chicago or Memphis had little contact with one another."[44] The social engineers changed all that, imposing a single orthodoxy on their pupils. For the most part, "diversity" is merely a sentimental cover for mediocrity. As Codevilla pointed out:

> Since the 1970s, it has been virtually impossible to flunk out of American colleges. And it is an open secret that "the best" colleges require the least work and give out the highest grade point averages.... The most successful neither write books and

papers that stand up to criticism nor release their academic records. Thus does our ruling class stunt itself through negative selection. But the more it has dumbed itself down, the more it has defined itself by the presumption of intellectual superiority.

It was interesting to listen to Candidate Obama lecture Americans on their failure to learn another language.[45] The son of a Ph.D. and a Harvard-educated economist, young Barack went to a fancy Hawaiian prep school, and then to Occidental, Columbia, and Harvard. And he's hectoring a guy who graduated high school in Nowheresville and shingles roofs all day about not speaking French or German? Well, what's Barack's excuse? The Obamas are the beneficiaries of the most expensive and luxuriant education on the planet. Where's their French?

Well, they were too busy cranking out sludge about the "desparation" [sic] of separationists, or whatever Michelle was droning on about at Princeton in unreadable maunderings all too typical of what passes for "education." Is the credentialing mill up to the job of producing an American leadership class capable of competing with those of China, India, and other emerging societies? Aw, we're rich enough that we can afford to be stupid. California's teachers are the highest paid in the United States, and its classrooms are among the worst.[46] But at least they're expensive—why, the Robert F. Kennedy Community School in Los Angeles is the first schoolhouse on the planet to cost over half-a-billion dollars ($578 million, to be exact).[47]

The Credentialed Age symbolizes an important transition in society. We've gone through those before, of course—from an agrarian society to an industrial society, and thence to the so-called "knowledge economy." But, when you think about it, is the "knowledge economy" really that knowledgeable? It would seem improbable that any society could undergo the massive expansion of college education that America has seen since the Second World War, and either effectively impart that much extra "knowledge" or create the jobs that require it. So, instead, we have witnessed an explosion in the ersatz-knowledge economy, where it is possible to pass one's entire life in an entirely bogus occupation—such as "community organizer" or "diversity consultant," to name only the First Couple's contributions to the scene. Addressing a group of financially strapped women in economically debilitated central Ohio, Michelle Obama told them: "We left corporate America, which is a lot of what we're asking young people to do. Don't go into corporate America."[48]

But isn't "corporate America" what pays for, among other things, the Gulf emir-sized retinue of courtiers the average U.S. senator now travels with? And in what sense did the Obamas "leave" corporate America? Before ascending to her throne, the First Lady worked for the University of Chicago Hospitals. She wasn't a nurse or doctor, or even a janitor. She was taken on by the hospitals in 2002 to run "programs for community relations, neighborhood outreach, volunteer recruitment, staff diversity, and minority contracting."[49] She was a diversicrat—a booming industry in Eloi America. In 2005, by happy coincidence, just as her husband was coming to national prominence, she received an impressive $200,000 pay raise and was appointed Vice President for Community and External Affairs and put in charge of managing the hospitals' "business diversity program." Mrs. Obama famously complained that America is "just downright mean,"[50] and you can see what she's getting at: she had to make do with a lousy $316,962 plus benefits for a job so necessary to the hospitals that when she quit to become First Lady they didn't bother replacing her.[51]

Leave "corporate America" and get a non-job as a diversity enforcement officer: that's where the big bucks are.

Abraham Lincoln, a predecessor of Barack Obama in both the White House and the Illinois state legislature, had eighteen months of formal education and became a soldier, surveyor, postmaster, rail-splitter, tavern keeper, and self-taught prairie lawyer. Obama went to Occidental College, Columbia University, and Harvard Law School, and became a "community organizer." I'm not sure that's progress—and it's certainly not "sustainable."

If he hadn't become president, his resumé wouldn't be anybody's idea of a return on investment. His life would read like one of those experimental novels that runs backwards. But who cares? At every stage along the way, he got the measure of his guilty white liberal patrons and played them for saps.

President Obama now wants the rest of America to follow in his and Michelle's footsteps. Under his student-loan "reforms," if you choose to go into "public service" any college-loan debts will be forgiven after ten years.[52] Because "public service" is more noble than the selfish, money-grubbing private sector. That's another one of those things that "everybody" knows. So we need to encourage more people to go into "public service."

Why?

In the six decades from 1950, the size of America's state and local work-force increased three times faster than the general population.[53] Yet the president says it's still not enough: we have to incentivize even further the diversion of our human capital into the government machine.

Like many career politicians, Barack Obama has never created, manu-factured, or marketed any product other than himself. So quite reasonably he sees government dependency as the natural order of things. And in his college-loan plan he's explicitly telling you: If you start a business, invent something, provide a service, you're a schmuck and a loser. In the America he's offering, you'll be working till you drop dead to fund an ever swollen bureaucracy that takes six weeks' vacation a year and retires at fifty-three on a pension you could never dream of.

Centralization, unionization, and credentialization have delivered American education into the grip of a ruthless and destructive conformity. America spends more per pupil on education than any other major indus-trial democracy, and the more it spends, the dumber it gets.[54] Ignorance has never been such bliss—at least for the teachers' union. As for the students, nearly 60 percent of U.S. high school graduates entering community college require remedial education.[55] In New York, it's 75 percent.[56] Obama's pro-posals are bold only insofar as few men would offer such a transparent guarantee of disaster. But, in his lavish, leisurely, over-lettered education, he embodies the failings of his class: credentialism isn't going to be enough in the post-abundance economy, and 90 percent of expensively acquired college "educations" won't see any return on investment.

★ ★ ★ ★ ★

THE FEELIES

Way back in 1993, in *The American Educator*, Lillian Katz, professor of early childhood education at the University of Illinois, got the lie of the land:

> A project by a First Grade class in an affluent Middle Western suburb that I recently observed showed how self-esteem and narcissism can be confused. Working from copied pages prepared by the teacher, each student produced a booklet called "All About Me." The first page asked for basic information about the child's home and family. The second page was titled "What I like to eat," the third was "What I like to watch on TV," the next was "What I want for a present."…
>
> Each page was directed toward the child's basest inner gratifications. Each topic put the child in the role of consumer—of food, entertainment, gifts, and recreation. Not once was the child asked to play the role of producer, investigator, initiator, explorer, experimenter, or problem-solver.[57]

Professor Katz recalled walking through a school vestibule and seeing a poster that neatly summed up this approach to education—a circle of clapping hands surrounding the slogan:

> We Applaud Ourselves.

And not for the Latin scores. Our students are certainly expert at applauding themselves, with levels of "self-esteem" growing ever more detached from more earthbound measures of achievement. A 2003 OECD study asked pupils of many lands whether they got "good marks in mathematics."[58] Seventy-two percent of U.S. students said yes. Only 56 percent of Finns did, and a mere 25 percent of Hong Kong pupils. Yet, according to another OECD study of the world's Ninth Graders, Hong Kong has the third best math scores in the world, Finland the second, and the top spot goes to Taiwan (which didn't participate in the earlier feelgood study, presumably because their self-esteem levels are so low they're undetectable).[59] Where do all those Americans so confident of their "good marks" in math actually rank in the global Hit Parade? Number 35, between Azerbaijan and Croatia. We barely scrape the Top 40 in actual math, but we're Number One in self-esteem about our math.

Lillian Katz made her observations in the early Nineties. Fifteen years later, a generation expertly trained in tinny self-congratulation went out and voted for a candidate who told them:

We are the ones we've been waiting for.

There's a lot of it about in the age of self-esteem. No satirist could invent a better parody of solipsistic sloth dignified as idealism than a bunch of people sitting around waiting for themselves. Hey, man, you're already there. What are you waiting for?

Many electors voted for Barack Obama in order to check "vote for a black president" off America's to-do list. Framed like that, it sounds worthy and admirable. But one could also formulate it less attractively: they voted for Obama in order to feel good about themselves. Which is what "celebrating diversity" boils down to.

As for feelings in general, Obama himself is the perfect emblem of the Age of Empathy. Unlike the hard-faced Bush regime, he "cared." After all, he told us so. Asked what he's looking for in a Supreme Court justice, he gave the correct answer: "The depth and breadth of one's empathy."[60]

In a TV infomercial a few days before his election, Obama declared that his "fundamental belief" was that "I am my brother's keeper."[61]

Hmm. Back in Kenya, his brother lives in a shack on 12 bucks a year.[62] If Barack is his brother's keeper, why can't he shove a sawbuck and a couple singles in an envelope and double the guy's income? Ah, well: When Barack Obama claims that "I am my brother's keeper," what he means is that the government should be his brother's keeper. Aside from that, his only religious belief seems to be in his own divinity:

"Do you believe in sin?" Cathleen Falsani, the religion correspondent for the *Chicago Sun-Times*, asked then Senator Obama.

"Yes," he replied.

"What is sin?"

"Being out of alignment with my values." [63]

That's one convenient religion: Obama worships at his own personal altar at the First Church of Himself. Unlike Clinton, he can't feel your pain, but his very presence is your gain—or as he put it in his video address to the German people on the twentieth anniversary of the fall of the Berlin Wall: "Few would have foreseen on that day that a united Germany would be led by a woman from Brandenburg or that their American ally would be led by a man of African descent."[64]

Tear down that wall … so they can get a better look at *me!!!* Is there no one in the White House grown-up enough to say, "Er, Mr. President, that's really the kind of line you get someone else to say about you"? And maybe somebody could have pointed out that November 9, 1989, isn't about him but about millions of nobodies whose names are unknown, who led dreary lives doing unglamorous jobs and going home to drab accommodations, but who at a critical moment in history decided they were no longer going to live in a prison state. They're no big deal; they're never going to land a photoshoot for *GQ*. But it's their day, not yours.

Is all of human history just a bit of colorful backstory in the Barack Obama biopic? "Few would have foreseen at the Elamite sack of Ur/Napoleon's retreat from Moscow/the assassination of the Archduke Franz Ferdinand/

the passage of the Dubrovnik Airport Parking Lot Expansion Bill that one day I would be standing before you talking about how few would have foreseen that one day I would be standing before you."

If he is not as esteemed in the world's chancelleries as an American president might have the right to expect, he is at least self-esteemed. He is the *ne plus ultra* of self-esteem, which may explain why, whenever Obama's not talking about himself, he sounds like he's wandered vaguely off-message. You could hardly devise a better jest on the Feeler generation, those Americans reared in the Cult of Empathy, who voted for Obama because he was supposed to embody both their empathy for him and his empathy for all the victims of the heartless Bush regime. Within months, liberal columnists complaining about his "detachment" found themselves confronting the obvious—that whatever they felt for him, he didn't feel for them. In this Obama was yet again the supreme embodiment of our times: in the Age of Empathy, "feeling good" is better than "doing good", and feeling good about yourself is best of all.

★ ★ ★ ★ ★

WE ARE THE WORLD . . .

In contemporary education's flight from facts to feelings, "empathy" has become a useful substitute for reality. In the schoolrooms of America, you'll be asked to empathize with a West African who's sold into slavery and shipped off to Virginia, or a loyal Japanese-American in a World War II internment camp, or a hapless Native American who catches dysentery, typhoid, gonorrhea, and an early strain of avian flu by foolishly buying beads from Christopher Columbus. This would be a useful exercise if we were genuinely interested in socio-historical empathizing. But instead the compliant pupil is expected merely to acknowledge the unlucky Indian as an early victim of European racism, and to assign the slave a contemporary African-American identity and thereby "empathize" with his sense of injustice. At this level, empathy is no more than the projection of contemporary and local obsessions over the rich canvas of the past and the other.

You didn't hear the word much a generation back. Now people who would once have sympathized with you insist on claiming to "empathize" with you. As Obama explained to his pro-abortion chums at Planned Parenthood: "We need somebody who's got the heart—the empathy—to recognize what it's like to be a young teenage mom. The empathy to understand what it's like to be poor or African-American or gay or disabled or old—and that's the criteria by which I'll be selecting my judges. Alright?"[65]

Alright. So let's take the fourth of those empathetic categories. If you're paralyzed in a riding accident, I can *sympathize* at the drop of a hat: my God, that's awful. Helluva thing to happen. But can I *empathize* (to quote a definition from David Berger's Clinical Empathy) "from within the frame of reference of that other person"?

Example: "Driving down there, I remember distinctly thinking that Chris would rather not live than be in this condition."[66]

That's Barbara Johnson recalling the immediate aftermath of her son Christopher Reeve's riding accident. Her instinct was to pull the plug; his was to live. Even the boundlessly empathetic Bill Clinton can't really "feel your pain." But the immodesty of the assertion is as pithy a distillation as any other of what's required in an age of pseudo-empathy.

The first definition in Webster's gets closer to the reality: "The imaginative projection of a subjective state into an object so that the object appears to be infused with it."

That's geopolitical empathy as practiced by the western world.

In the December 2007 edition of the *Atlantic Monthly*, Andrew Sullivan, not yet mired up Sarah Palin's birth canal without a paddle peddling bizarre conspiracy theories about the maternity of her youngest child, contemplated the ascendancy of Barack Obama and decided that his visage alone would be "the most effective potential rebranding of the United States since Reagan."[67] As he explained: "It's November 2008. A young Pakistani Muslim is watching television and sees this man—Barack Hussein Obama—is the new face of America. In one simple image, America's soft power has been ratcheted up not a notch, but a logarithm.... If you wanted the crudest but most effective weapon against the demonization of America that fuels Islamist ideology, Obama's face gets close."

I was *The Atlantic's* in-house obituarist for some years and I retain an affection for the magazine. But honestly, how could any self-respecting publication pass off such fatuous projection as geopolitical analysis? Let us grant that Mr. Sullivan is genuinely smitten by "Obama's face" and that his effusions are sufficiently widely shared that they help explain the appeal of a man of minimal accomplishments to a certain type of American liberal whose principal election issue is that he wants to feel good about himself. Nevertheless, the assumption that "a young Pakistani Muslim" in Karachi or Peshawar shares your peculiar preoccupations is the laziest kind of projection even by the standards of progressive navel-gazing.

For a start, the new pan-Islamism notwithstanding, there is an awful lot of racism in the Muslim world. If liberals stopped gazing longingly into "Obama's face" just for a moment, they might recall that little business of genocide in Darfur. What was that about again? Oh, yeah, Sudanese Muslim Arabs were slaughtering Sudanese Muslim Africans. Sure enough, a week after Obama's election, Ayman al-Zawahiri, Osama bin Laden's number two, issued a video denouncing the new president as "abeed al-beit," which translates literally as "house slave" but which the al-Qaeda subtitles more provocatively rendered as "house Negro."[68]

But, putting aside the racism, there is just a terrible banality underlying assumptions such as Sullivan's. Those who hate the Great Satan don't care whether he has a white face, a black face, a female face, or a gay face. In a multicultural age, we suffer from a unicultural parochialism: not simply the inability to imagine the other, but the inability even to imagine there is an other.

Donald Rumsfeld famously spoke of the "known knowns; there are things we know we know. We also know there are known unknowns; that is to say we know there are some things we do not know. But there are also unknown unknowns—the ones we don't know we don't know."[69] The old Cold Warrior's cool detachment is unfashionable in an age of ersatz empathy, but it has a rare humility. In an age of one-worldist fantasy, it helps to know that you don't know—and that, even in a therapeutic culture, you don't know how everybody *feels*.

For four decades America watched as politically correct fatuities swallowed the entire educational system, while conservatives deluded themselves that it was just a phase, something kids had to put up with as the price for getting a better job a couple years down the road. The idea that two generations could be soaked in this corrosive bilge and it would have no broader impact, that it could be contained within the precincts of academe, was always foolish. So what happens when the big colored Sharpie words on the vestibule posters—Diversity! Tolerance! Respect!—bust out of the grade school and stalk the land? On September 11, 2007, at the official anniversary observances in Massachusetts, Governor Deval Patrick said 9/11 "was a mean and nasty and bitter attack on the United States."[70]

"Mean and nasty"? He sounds like a kindergarten teacher. Or an oversensitive waiter complaining that John Kerry's sent back the aubergine coulis again. But that's what passes for tough talk in Massachusetts these days—the shot heard round the world and so forth. Anyway, Governor Patrick didn't want to leave the crowd with all that macho cowboy rhetoric ringing in their ears, so he moved on to the nub of his speech: 9/11, he went on, "was also a failure of human beings to understand each other, to learn to love each other."

We should beware anyone who seeks to explain 9/11 by using the words "each other." They posit not just a grubby equivalence between the perpetrator and the victim but also a dangerously delusional "empathy." The 9/11 killers were treated very well in the United States: they were ushered into the country on the high-speed visa express program the State Department felt was appropriate for young Saudi males. They were treated cordially everywhere they went. The lapdancers at the clubs they frequented in the weeks before the big day gave them a good time—or good enough, considering what lousy tippers they were. September 11 didn't happen because we were insufficient in our love to Mohammed Atta.

But the lessons of 9/11 were quickly buried under a mountain of relativist mush. Consider the now routine phenomenon by which any, um, unusual event is instantly ascribed to anyone other than the obvious suspects. When a huge car bomb came near to killing hundreds in Times Square, the first reaction of Michael Bloomberg, New York's mayor, was to announce that the most likely culprit was "someone with a political agenda who doesn't like the health care bill"[71] (that would be me, if his SWAT team's at a loose end this weekend). When, inevitably, a young man called Faisal Shahzad was arrested a couple days later, Mayor Bloomberg's next reaction was to hector his subjects that under no circumstances would the city tolerate "any bias or backlash against Pakistani or Muslim New Yorkers."[72]

How many times do the American people have to ace that test? They've been doing it for a decade now, and every time the usual suspects try to kill them the ruling class, with barely veiled contempt, insists that its own knuckledragging citizenry is the real problem. A couple months later Nanny Bloomberg went to the Statue of Liberty of all places to tell the plebs he has the misfortune to rule over to shut up. The man on whose watch Ground Zero degenerated from a target of war to a victim of bureaucracy was there to lecture dissenters that the site of the 9/11 attacks is a "very appropriate place"[73] for a mosque. The people of New York felt differently, but what do they know?

"To cave to popular sentiment," thundered Nanny, "would be to hand a victory to the terrorists—and we should not stand for that."[74] We used to hear this formulation a lot in the months after 9/11: If we do such-and-such, then the terrorists will have won. But this surely is the very acme of the template: If we don't build a mosque at Ground Zero, then the terrorists will have won! You're either with us or you're with the terrorists—and the American people are with the terrorists.

As is the way with the Conformity Enforcers, Nanny Bloomberg pulled out all the abstractions. "It was exactly that spirit of openness and acceptance that was attacked on 9/11."[75] Really? That's not what Osama bin Laden said. But, if we put away our abstract generalities and listen to what the enemy is actually telling us, then the terrorists will have won! For a fellow so open and accepting, Nanny Bloomberg seems awfully dogmatic and strident. This is the WEIRD syndrome—the determination to hammer the hard square peg of global reality into the hole of multicultural nullity, whatever it takes. Even after Faisal Shahzad's arrest for the attempted bombing of Times Square, the Associated Press, CNN, the *Washington Post*, and other grandees of the conformicrat media insisted on attaching huge significance to the problems the young jihadist had had keeping up his mortgage payments in Connecticut.[76] Subprime terrorism? Don't laugh. To the media, it's a far greater threat to America than anything to do with certain words beginning with I- and ending in -slam.

Incidentally, one way of falling behind with your house payments is to take half a year off to go to Pakistan and train in a terrorist camp. Perhaps Congress could pass some sort of jihadist housing credit?

Poor old Faisal Shahzad. Before heading off to Times Square, he made a pre-detonation video outlining the evils of the Great Satan.[77] Nothing about mortgage rates or foreclosure proceedings in there. He couldn't have been more straightforward, but still Nanny Bloomberg and the media cover their ears and go "La-la-la. Can't hear you."

Paul Berman, a lifelong liberal, says that the doctrine of relativism makes "everything the equal of everything else."[78] As a result, our ruling class— political, academic, cultural—have "lost the ability to make the most elementary distinctions." This is almost right. In fact, the cult of absolutist relativism is a kind of affirmative action against their own civilization: In any dispute between the boundlessly tolerant West and a highly intolerant Islam, it must be the fault of the former for being insufficiently tolerant of the latter's intolerance. A society led by men with such a self-destructive urge will get its wish, and very soon, and deservedly so.

Not so long ago I saw a two-panel cartoon: on the left hand panel, "This is your brain"; on the right hand panel, "This is your brain on political correctness"—a small and shriveled thing, but now standard issue.

Here's a random selection of headlines:[79]

Naval History Web Site Highlights Women's History Month
Senior Navy Leader Receives Black Engineer of the Year Award
Davede Alexander Receives Diversity Leadership Award
Navy Women in Aviation Show Diversity Is Rising
Top Pentagon Official Discovers Model of Diversity at Corona
Warfare Center, Says Navy's Doing Diversity Right
CNRH Seminar Teaches Lessons of Hope and Empowerment

The above were all plucked from the United States Navy newsletter. When the first newsletter showed up in my in-box, I thought it might contain under-reported tales of derring-do off the Horn of Africa battling Somali pirates. But instead it's one diversity-awareness story after another: "Senior Navy Leader Receives Most Diverse Engineer of the Year Award"; "Appointment of First Somali Pirate to Joint Chiefs Of Staff Shows Diversity Is Rising, Says Top Pentagon Official."

Fred Astaire in *Follow the Fleet*, 1935, words and music by Irving Berlin:

We joined the Navy to see the world
And what did we see?
We saw the sea...

Follow The Fleet, twenty-first century remake:

We joined the Navy to see the world
And what did we see?
We saw the Diversity Leadership Awards.

Well, you say, look, they're just doing what they need to do to keep the congressional oversight crowd off their back; it's just a bit of window dressing.

Hmm. In 2009, thirteen men and women plus an unborn baby were gunned down at Fort Hood by a major in the U.S. Army. Nidal Hasan was the perpetrator, but political correctness was his enabler, every step of the way. Major Hasan couldn't have been more straightforward about who and what he was. An Army psychiatrist, he put "SoA"—"Soldier of Allah"—on his business card.[80] At the Uniformed Services University of Health Sciences, he was reprimanded for trying to persuade patients to convert to Islam, and fellow pupils objected to his constant "anti-American propaganda."[81] But, as the Associated Press reported, "a fear of appearing discriminatory against a Muslim student kept officers from filing a formal written complaint."[82]

This is your brain on political correctness.

As the writer Barry Rubin pointed out, Major Hasan was the first mass murderer in U.S. history to give a PowerPoint presentation outlining the rationale for the crime he was about to commit.[83] And he gave it to a roomful of fellow Army psychiatrists and doctors—some of whom glanced queasily at their colleagues, but none of whom actually spoke up. And when the question arose of whether then Captain Hasan was, in fact, "psychotic," the policy committee at Walter Reed Army Medical Center worried, "How would it look if we kick out one of the few Muslim residents."[84]

This is your brain on political correctness.

So instead he got promoted to major and shipped to Fort Hood. And barely had he got to Texas when he started making idle chit-chat praising the jihadist murderer of two soldiers outside a recruitment center in Little Rock. "This is what Muslims should do, stand up to the aggressors," Major Hasan told his superior officer, Colonel Terry Lee. "People should strap bombs on themselves and go into Times Square."[85]

In less enlightened times, Colonel Lee would have concluded that, being in favor of the murder of his comrades, Major Hasan was objectively on the side of the enemy. But instead he merely cautioned the major against saying things that might give people the wrong impression. Which is to say, the right impression.

This is your brain on political correctness.

"You need to lock it up, major," advised the colonel.[86]

But, of course, he didn't. He could say what he wanted—infidels should have their throats cut, for example. Meanwhile, the only ones who felt any need to "lock it up" were his fellow psychiatrists, his patients, his teachers at the Uniformed Services University, officials at Walter Reed, and the brass at Fort Hood. So they locked it up for years, and fourteen people died.

And even when the slaughter had happened, much of the media found it easier to slander both the United States military and the general populace than to confront the evidence. Like Nanny Bloomberg, the Homeland Security Secretary Janet Incompetano professed to be most worried about an "anti-Muslim backlash" from the bozo citizenry she had the forlorn task of attempting to hold in check.[87]

As for the Army, well, obviously, they're a bunch of Bush-scarred psychos who could snap at any moment. *Newsweek* called the mass murder "A Symptom of a Military on the Brink."[88] "A psychiatrist who was set to deploy to Iraq at the end of the month, Hasan reportedly opened fire around the Fort Hood Readiness Center," wrote Andrew Bast. "It comes at a time when the stress of combat has affected so many soldiers individually that it makes it increasingly difficult for the military as a whole to deploy for wars abroad."

No mention of the words "Islam" or "Muslim," but Mr. Bast was concerned to "get at the root causes of soldier stresses." As in Post-Traumatic Stress Disorder. Operative word "post": you get it after you've been in combat. Major Hasan had never been in combat.

But, just as they effortlessly extended the subprime mortgage crisis to explain the Times Square bomber, the same conformicrat "experts" redefined "post-traumatic stress disorder" to apply to a psychiatrist who'd never been anywhere near a war zone. Until November 5, 2009, PTSD was something you got when you returned from battle overseas and manifested itself in sleeplessness, nightmares, or, in extreme circumstances, suicide. After November 5, PTSD was apparently spread by shaking hands and manifested itself in gunning down large numbers of people while yelling "Allahu akbar!" This is the first known case of Pre-Post-Traumatic Stress Disorder, but there could be thousands out there just waiting to blow.

This is your brain on political correctness.

Two joint terrorism task forces became aware almost a year before that Major Hasan was in regular e-mail contact with Anwar al-Awlaki, the American-born but now Yemeni-based cleric who served as spiritual advisor to three of the 9/11 hijackers and an imam so radical he's banned from Britain, a land with an otherwise all but boundless tolerance for radical imams. Al-Awlaki advocates all-out holy war against the United States. But the expert analysts in the Pentagon determined that there was no need to worry because this lively correspondence was consistent with Major Hasan's "research interests."[89] Which is one way of putting it.

Groups such as the Council on American-Islamic Relations (with its Potemkin membership but lots of Saudi funding) and the Organization of the Islamic Cooperation (the biggest voting bloc at the UN) want a world where Islam is beyond discussion—where "red flags" are ignored because to do anything about them would risk career-ruining accusations of "Islamophobia," or six months of "sensitivity training" to spay you into a docile eunuch of the PC state.[90] How's that project coming along? After Major Hasan's pre-Post-Traumatic Stress breakdown, General George W. Casey Jr., the Army's chief of staff, assured us that, despite the slaughter, it could have been a whole lot worse: "What happened at Fort Hood was a tragedy, but I believe it would be an even greater tragedy if our diversity becomes a casualty here."[91]

Celebrate diversity, yea unto death. The fact that a grown man not employed by a U.S educational institution or media outlet used the word "diversity" in a non-parodic sense should be deeply disturbing. "Diversity" is not a virtue; it's morally neutral. A group of five white upper-middle-class liberal NPR-listening women is non-diverse; a group of four white upper-middle-class liberal NPR-listening women plus Sudan's leading clitoridectomy practitioner is more diverse but not necessarily the better for it.

Nevertheless, asked "Who ya gonna believe—the Celebrate Diversity Handbook or your lyin' eyes?" more and more of us plump for the former, if only for a quiet life. Nine months after Major Hasan's killing spree, the Defense Secretary Robert Gates ordered "a series of procedural and policy changes that focus on identifying, responding to and preventing potential workplace violence."[92]

"Workplace violence"? Yes, it's the new official euphemism: "The changes include plans to educate military commanders on signs of potential workplace violence...."

Say what you like, but at least the Army's workplace violence is "diverse."

The brain-addled "diversity" of General Casey will get some of us killed, and keep all of us cowed. Old watchword: Better dead than red. Updated version: Better screwed than rude. In the days after the slaughter, the news coverage read like a satirical novel that the author's not quite deft enough to pull off, with bizarre new Catch-22s multiplying like the windmills of your mind: if you muse openly on pouring boiling oil down the throats of infidels, then the Pentagon will put that down as mere confirmation of your long-established "research interests." If you're psychotic, the Army will make you a psychiatrist for fear of provoking you. If you gun down a bunch of people, within an hour the FBI will state clearly that we can all relax, there's no terrorism angle, because, in a micro-regulated, credential-obsessed society, it doesn't count unless you're found to be carrying Permit #57982BQ3a from the relevant State Board of Jihadist Licensing.

And "Allahu akbar?" That's Arabic for "Nothing to see here."

Pace General Casey, what happened was not a "tragedy" but a national scandal.

Anwar al-Awlaki and his comrades have bet that such a society is too sick to survive. Watch the nothing-to-see-here media driveling on about "combat stress" and the Pentagon diversicrats issuing memos on "workplace violence" like gibbering lunatics in a padded cell, and then think whether you'd really want to take that bet. The craven submission to political correctness, the willingness to leave your marbles with the Diversity Café hat-check girl, the wish for a quiet life leads to death, and not that quietly. When the chief of staff of the United States Army has got the disease, you're in big (and probably terminal) trouble. And when the guy's on the table firing wildly and screaming "Allahu akbar!" the PC kindergarten teachers won't be there for you.

★ ★ ★ ★ ★
...WE ARE THE CHILDREN

Political correctness is the authoritarian end of a broader infantilization. Hardly a week goes by where you don't read a lifestyle feature such as this, from *New York* magazine:

> He owns eleven pairs of sneakers, hasn't worn anything but jeans in a year, and won't shut up about the latest Death Cab for Cutie CD. But he is no kid. He is among the ascendant breed of grown-up who has redefined adulthood as we once knew it and killed off the generation gap.[93]

Death Cab for Cutie, the band, took its name from "Death Cab for Cutie," the song. The Bonzo Dog Doo Dah Band sang it back in the Sixties, a parody of Top 40 death anthems ("Teen Angel," "Leader of the Pack") with Vivian Stanshall Elvising up the refrain as the taxi runs a red light and meets its rendezvous with destiny: "Someone's going to make you pay your fare."

One wouldn't want to place too great a metaphorical burden on an obscure novelty number, but to the jaundiced eye America's Eloi can easily seem like infantilized cuties unaware they're riding in a death cab. In the old days, there were, broadly, two phases of human existence: You were a child until thirteen. Then you were a working adult. Then you died. Now there are four phases: You're a child until twelve, eleven, nine—or whenever enlightened jurisdictions think you're entitled to go on the pill without parental notification. Then you're an "adolescent," an ever more elastic term of art now stretching lazily across the decades. Then you work, after a fashion. Then you quit at sixty-five, sixty, fifty-five in France, fifty in Greece, whatever you can get away with, and enjoy a three-decade retirement at public expense. The tedious business of being a grown-up is that ever-shrinking space between adolescence and retirement.

Let Barack Obama explain things: "I see some young people in the audience," began the president at one of his "town hall meetings" in Ohio.[94]

Not that young. For he assured them that, under ObamaCare, they'd be eligible to remain on their parents' health coverage until they were twenty-six.

The audience applauded.

Why?

Because, as the politicians say, "it's about the future of all our children." And in the future we'll all be children. For most of human history, across all societies, a 26-year-old has been considered an adult—and not starting out on adulthood but well into it. Not someone who remains a dependent of his parents, but someone who would be expected to have parental responsibilities himself. But not anymore. Sure, come your twenty-seventh birthday, it'll be time to move out of your parents' insurance agency—at least until Obama's next piece of child-friendly legislation. But till then, here's looking at you, kid.

This ought to be deeply insulting to any self-respecting 26-and-a-half-year-old. As for the rest of us, the kind of society in which 26-year-olds are considered children is a society in decline—in economic decline, cultural decline, spiritual decline, in demographic decline (as Europe already is), in terminal decline. The western world lives increasingly in a state of deferred adulthood. We enter adolescence earlier and earlier and we leave it later and later, if at all.

As everyone knows, our bodies "mature" earlier so it would be unreasonable to expect our grade-schoolers not to be rogering anything that moves, and the most we can hope to do is ensure there's a government-funded condom dispenser nearby. But even as our bodies reach "maturity" earlier and earlier, it would likewise be unreasonable to expect people who've been fully expert in "sexually transmitted infections" for a decade and a half to assume responsibility for their broader health-care arrangements.

And, come to think of it, isn't it unreasonable to expect 30-year-olds who've been sexually active since sixth grade to assume responsibility for their sexual activity? As the *Washington Post* reported:

> High school students and college-age adults have been complaining to District officials that the free condoms the city has been offering are not of good enough quality and are too small and that getting them from school nurses is "just like asking grandma or auntie."
>
> So DC officials have decided to stock up on Trojan condoms, including the company's super-size Magnum variety, and they have begun to authorize teachers or counselors, preferably male, to distribute condoms to students if the teachers complete a 30-minute online training course called "WrapMC"—for Master of Condoms.
>
> "If people get what they don't want, they are just going to trash them," said T. Squalls, 30, who attends the University of the District of Columbia. "So why not spend a few extra dollars and get what people want?"[95]

That last paragraph deserves to be chiseled on the tombstone of the Republic. As April Gavaza, the blogger Hyacinth Girl, responded: "Hey, T., why don't you spend a few extra dollars and buy your own, jackass?"[96]

Fair enough. Why should T. Squalls, thirty, bill D.C. taxpayers for his sex life? Thirty is so old you're not even eligible for Obama's child health-care coverage. Thirty is what less evolved societies used to call "early middle age." Why is *Washington Post* chairman Donald Graham (to pluck a D.C. householder at random) buying condoms for 30-year-old men he doesn't know?

Because that's Big Government for you: you start a free-condom program for sexually active fourth graders, and next thing you know elderly swingers in the twelfth year of Social Construct Studies want in. The D.C. condompalooza is a perfect example of progressive thinking's malign paradox: it both destroys childhood and infantilizes adulthood, leaving a big chunk of the populace as eternal teenagers.

What was it the hippies said? Never trust anybody over thirty? Advice to D.C. women: Never trust anybody over thirty who expects the government to buy his condoms.

As the recession hit, the *Los Angeles Times* ran a profile on a hip new social phenomenon: "funemployment."[97] They had good jobs, great pay, and then they lost them. But if you're not married and your parents have kept your old bedroom open, what's the diff? Two of the funemployed, Andy Deemer, thirty-six, and Amanda Rounsaville, thirty-four, connected through Facebook and took off in search of Asian mystics. They visited a fortuneteller in Burma, a tarot card reader in Thailand, some Saffron Revolution monks on the border, and, after spending ten days tracking her down, a reindeer-herding shaman in Mongolia.

Only the last advised them to "go back to work."

Whoa! Heavy, man! But maybe they went off to Bhutan to get a second opinion from a shaman-herding reindeer.

In the Sixties, privileged youth used to go off to find themselves in the year before college. Now they go off to find themselves when they're pushing forty. They seek the company of reindeer-herders at the age previous generations sought the company of Elks Lodgers.

"They are a generation or two of affluent, urban adults who are now happily sailing through their thirties and forties, and even fifties, clad in beat-up sneakers and cashmere hoodies," writes Adam Sternbergh in *New York*. "It's about a brave new world whose citizens are radically rethinking what it means to be a grown-up and whether being a grown-up still requires, you know, actually growing up."

I think we know the answer to that.

★ ★ ★ ★ ★

BOY MEETS GIRL

For H. G. Wells' late Victorian traveler, what was most striking about the Eloi was how they had evolved beyond sex:

> I perceived that all had the same form of costume, the same soft hairless visage, and the same girlish rotundity of limb.... In all the differences of texture and bearing that now mark off the sexes from each other, these people of the future were alike.... Seeing the ease and security in which these people were living, I felt that this close resemblance of the sexes was after all what one would expect; for the strength of a man and the softness of a woman, the institution of the family, and the differentiation of occupations are mere militant necessities of an age of physical force; where population is balanced and abundant, much childbearing becomes an evil rather than a blessing to the State; where violence comes but rarely and off-spring are secure, there is less necessity—indeed there is no necessity—for an efficient family, and the specialization of the sexes with reference to their children's needs disappears.

Victor Davis Hanson had a similar experience, some 800,000 years ahead of Wells' time-traveler. He noticed that "the generic American male accent" has all but died out, to be replaced by something affectedly "metrosexual" with "a particular nasal stress, a much higher tone than one heard 40 years ago...a precious voice often nearly indistinguishable from the female."[98] As for the old-school males, wrote Professor Hanson, "I watched the movie *Twelve O'Clock High* the other day, and Gregory Peck and Dean Jagger sounded like they were from another planet." (To be fair, the feminization of men is complemented by the masculinization of women. One recent Miss America winner, lantern-jawed, hipless, concrete implants, looks in the bikini shots like someone who should be suing the British NHS for a botched sex change.)

In 2006, Harvey Mansfield wrote a book called *Manliness* and was much mocked for it by the likes of Naomi Wolf, the feminist who picked out earth-toned polo shirts for Al Gore in his presidential campaign to make him seem more of an Alpha male—because nothing says "Alpha male" like hiring a feminist to tell you what clothes to wear.[99] "I define manliness," Professor Mansfield told one interviewer, "as confidence in the face of risk. And this quality has its basis in an animal characteristic that Plato called 'thumos.' Thumos means bristling at something that is strange or inimical to you. Think of a dog bristling and barking; that's a very thumotic response to a situation."[100]

Thumotic certainly. But not approved of terribly much nowadays: Bristling at the strange? Where've you been?

"I don't think manliness has gone away or become less manly," Professor Mansfield continued, "but it certainly has much less of a reputation. It's what I call 'unemployed,' meaning there's nothing responsible or respectable for it to do."

Quite so. Promoting her new film, about a fortysomething "choice mother" who decides to conceive a child by sperm donor, America's sweetheart *d'un certain age*, Jennifer Aniston, declared that women "don't have to settle with a man just to have that child.... Times have changed, and what is amazing is that we do have so many options these days."[101] Some women want a "new man" who'll be there at the birth. Others don't even want him there at conception. The progeny of such "choice mothers" have rather less choice in the matter, and research on the first generation (from the report "My Daddy's Name Is Donor") suggest a higher incidence of drug abuse, police run-ins, and the other now familiar side-effects of social rewiring. But hey, don't let that get in the way of your "many options."[102]

As for all those amazing options, don't try this one at home: marry young, have kids and a successful career. You'll be inviting a mountain of opprobrium. In the weeks before the 2008 election, I received an extraordinary number of emails from so-called "liberals" revolted by Sarah Palin's fecundity. One gentleman—well, okay, maybe not a "gentleman" but certainly an impeccably sensitive progressive new male—wrote to me from Shelton, Washington: "This abortion prohibitionist hag won't cut it among women with brains. And BTW she is a good example of reproduction run amok. 5 kids; 1 retard. I wonder if the bitch ever heard of getting spayed."

Golly, if Mister Sensitive is typical of the liberal male, you can understand why Jennifer Aniston would rather load up on turkey basters. By contrast, a few years back, it was reported that Mrs. Palin's contemporary, Alexis Stewart, daughter of Martha, was paying $28,000 a month in an effort to get pregnant.[103] She told *People* magazine that she'd "wanted a baby since she was 37," but that her ex-husband was "completely ambivalent about kids."[104] So these days she injects herself once a month with a drug that causes her to ovulate in thirty-six hours. "I go to the doctor's office and they put me under anesthesia and use an 18-inch needle to remove about ten eggs," she explained. "Then, I go home to my apartment in TriBeCa, change, and get ready for my Sirius Radio show, 'Whatever.'" The doctor then fertilizes the eggs by a method known as intra-cytoplasmic sperm injection. "I'm using an anonymous donor," Alexis confided to *People*, "but not from a genius bank. Those are creepy." Unlike giving celebrity interviews about your 28-grand-per-month intra-cytoplasmic sperm injection.

Each to her own. You can be a 45-year-old mother of five expecting her first grandchild and serving as Governor of Alaska. Or you can be a 45-year-old single "career woman" hosting a satellite radio show called "Whatever" and spending a third of a million dollars a year on intra-cytoplasmic sperm injection in hopes of becoming pregnant. What was it the feminists used to say? "You can have it all"? *Politico* reported that, to the enforcers at the National Organization for Women, Sarah Palin is "more a conservative man than she is a woman."[105] It seems "having it all" doesn't count if you do so within more or less traditional family structures. These days, NOW seems to have as narrow and proscriptive a view of what women are permitted to be as any old 1950s sitcom dad. Miss Stewart is untypical only in her budget in an age when, according to one survey, massive numbers of British women, their maternal instincts stymied by indifferent male "partners," are unfaithful in order to get pregnant.[106] One day Jennifer Aniston will make a glum romantic comedy about that exciting "option."

Alexis Stewart is probably wise to skip the genius bank. Her mom is genius enough—who else would have figured out there were millions of dollars in things like "coxcomb topiary"? Nevertheless, there is something almost too eerily symbolic about the fact that America's "domestic diva" is a divorcee with an only child unable to conceive. The happy homemaker has no one to make a home for. You look at the pictures accompanying *Martha Stewart's Thanksgiving* and think: Why bother just for her and Alexis? Why don't they just book a table at the Four Seasons?

A fortysomething single woman's $27,000-per-month fertility treatments are the flip side of the Muslim baby boom in Afghanistan, Somalia, Yemen, and elsewhere. Just as Europeans preserve old churches and farms as heritage sites, so our homemaking industry has amputated the family from family life, leaving its rituals and traditions as freestanding lifestyle accessories. Today many of the western world's women have in effect doubled the generational span, opting not for three children in their twenties but one designer yuppie baby in their late thirties.

Demographers talk about "late family formation" as if it has no real consequences for the child. But I wonder. The abortion lobby supposedly believes in a world where every child is "wanted." If you get pregnant at seventeen, nineteen, twenty-three, you most likely didn't really "want" a child: it just kinda happened, as it has throughout most of human history. But, if you conceive at forty-six after half-a-million bucks' worth of fertility treatment, you *really* want that kid. Is it possible to be over-wanted? I notice in my part of the country that there's a striking difference between those moms who have their first kids at traditional childbearing ages and those who leave it till Miss Stewart's. The latter are far more protective of their nippers, as well they might be: even if you haven't paid the clinic a bundle for the stork's little bundle, you're aware of how precious and fragile the gift of life can be.

Hence, the so-called "helicopter parents"—always hovering. When you contemplate society's changing attitudes to childhood—the "war against boys"[107] that Christina Hoff Summers has noted, and a more general tendency to keep children on an ever tighter chain—I wonder how much of that derives from the fact that "young moms" are increasingly middle-aged. Martha Stewart's daughter seems a sad emblem of a world that insists one should retain time-honored traditions when decorating the house for Thanksgiving but thinks nothing of dismantling the most basic building blocks of society.

As always, conservatives fight these battles by playing catch-up: "gay marriage" is seen as a threat to "traditional marriage." But, after the societal remaking of the last half-century, marriage is near kaput in most of the developed world, and hardly worth finishing off even in America. Rather, "gay marriage" offers a far more enticing target: today, a "family" is any living arrangement you happen to dig at that particular moment; a "marriage" is whatever tickles a California judge's fancy; and along with these innovations proceeds the de facto and de jure abolition of "the sexes." In his decision striking down California's Proposition 8, the most significant of Judge Walker's so-called "findings of fact" are about the elimination of sex, of male and female. After all, if a man can marry a man and raise a child, then the division of marital roles into "husband" and "wife" no longer applies, and the parental categories of "father" and "mother" are obsolete—"Parent One" and "Parent Two," as the new U.S. passport form now puts it, or, in the friskier designations of Spanish birth certificates, "Progenitor A" and "Progenitor B." And in that case in what sense do we still have "men" or "women"?

"The gender-neutral society is really a kind of experiment," says Mansfield, himself adopting the prissy liberal usage of mutable "gender" rather than immutable "sex." "It's something that hasn't been done before in human history."[108] If the aim is to create an androgynous people, then so far women are proving better at being men than men are at being women. For the first time in American history, there are more women than men in the workplace, and they dominate the professions.[109] The 2008 downturn accelerated the trend: the recession was for the most part a he-cession. There

are more women than men at college: for 2009 graduates, the college enrollment rate was 73.8 percent for girls, 66 percent for boys.[110] Almost 60
percent of Bachelor's Degrees go to women.[111] Speaking of bachelors, in
1980 the number of men who reached the age of forty without marrying
were 6 percent of the population.[112] A quarter-century later, they were 16.5
percent. How many by 2030? Currently some 55 percent of men aged 18 to
24 live with their parents.[113] Even before the recession, more than half of all
American college seniors moved back to the family home after gradua-
tion.[114] Thirteen percent of American males ("men" doesn't seem quite the
word) aged 25 to 34 live with their parents.[115]

From time to time, many ambitious regimes find themselves minded,
as Bertolt Brecht advised, to elect a new people. The immigration policies
of most western nations seem intended to accomplish that goal. But you
can also change the existing people, in elemental ways and over a surpris-
ingly short space of time. Give me a boy till seven, said the Jesuits, and I will
show you the man. Give me a boy till seventh grade, say today's educators,
and we can eliminate the man problem entirely.

Men are no longer hunter-gatherers, and have now ceased to be bread-
winners. It isn't such a bad deal. Though discriminated against in matters
such as child support, the average male—if he retains enough of the wily
survival instinct from the caveman days—can still have a pretty good time.
Most of these new-type gals still like a good old-fashioned shagging every
now and again, and there's no obligation to marry them anymore, or even
pretend you're dating seriously. You certainly don't have to meet their parents, and, if the stork decides to spring a little unwanted surprise on you,
there's always your friendly local abortionist. After all, being "pro-choice"
is a good way to show these babes what a sensitive new man you are.

So, even if constrained in all other rowdy boyish inclinations more or
less since nursery school, guys are still free to abandon women in greater
numbers than ever before. In 1970, 69 percent of 25-year-old white men
were married. By 2000, it was 33 percent.[116] The remainder don't have
wives, kids, homes—in the sense of mow-the-lawn wash-the-car paint-
the-spare-bedroom homes. So what do they do? Well, they drink, they

listen to music, they hook up, they lead teenage lives on an adult salary. Males 18 to 34 years old play more video games than kids: according to a 2006 Nielsen survey, 48.2 percent of men in that demographic amused themselves in that way for an average of two hours and forty-three minutes every day—that's thirteen minutes longer than the 12- to-17-year-olds.[117]

When these games were first produced, parents used to fret that they were taking boys away from baseball and tree-climbing and healthy outdoor activities. Now they're taking men away from ... what? their midlife crisis? "For whatever reason," concluded Kay Hymowitz in *City Journal*, "adolescence appears to be the young man's default state."[118] Anthropologists are generally agreed that wherever you go on the planet, what suppresses (to use an unfashionable concept) adolescence and turns boys into men is marriage and children. When you marry ever later and have children ever later, manhood also comes much later—if at all. "The conveyor belt that transported adolescents into adulthood has broken down," declared Dr. Frank Furstenberg after studying the "adultescence" phenomenon.[119] But the belt didn't really "break down." It was systematically slowed down, then cut up and recycled into extra-strength condoms. Among the general, swift, and transformative re-ordering of social structures, the percentage of homes with two parents and children has fallen by half since 1972, while the percentage of homes with unmarried, childless couples has doubled.[120]

As Gloria Steinem proclaimed, "A woman needs a man like a fish needs a bicycle." Today, in our feminized aquarium, we have all but eliminated the bicycle, save for a few rusting barnacle-encrusted spokes on the bottom. The full impact of our endlessly deferred adulthood is not yet known, although its contours can already be discerned. What kind of adults emerge from the two-decade cocoon of modern adolescence? Even as the western world atrophies, not merely its pop culture but its entire aesthetic seems mired in arrested development. In his book *Men to Boys: The Making of Modern Immaturity*, Gary Cross asks simply: "Where have all the men gone?"[121]

Like George Will, Victor Davis Hanson, and others who've posed that question, Professor Cross is no doubt aware that he sounds old and square. But in a land of middle-aged teenagers somebody has to.

★ ★ ★ ★ ★

NO MAN'S LAND

"It is easier," said Frederick Douglass, "to build strong children than to repair broken men." But what if, as a matter of policy, we're building our children to be broken men? And broken not just psychologically but biologically. Headline from the *Daily Mail*, 2004: "Concern as Sperm Count Falls by a Third in UK Men."[122]

Don't ask me why: I'd blame Tony Blair's cozying up to Bush were it not for "Sperm count drops 25 % in younger men"[123] (*The Independent*, 1996), so maybe it was John Major pulling out of the European Exchange Rate Mechanism.

Do we still need sperm? Oh, a soupçon here and there still has its uses. In 2009, a shortage of the stuff was reported in Sweden.[124] There had been an unexpected surge in demand, from lesbian couples anxious to conceive. So they headed off to the sperm clinic, whereupon the Sapphic demand ran into the problem of male inability to satisfy it. The problem seems to be higher than usual levels of non-functioning sperm. Even for a demographic doom-monger such as myself, you could hardly ask for a more poignant *fin de civilisation* image than a stampede of broody lesbians stymied only by defective semen, like some strange dystopian collaboration between Robert Heinlein and Russ Meyer.

H. G. Wells' Time-Traveler writes of the softened Eloi:

> It happened that, as I was watching some of the little people bathing in a shallow, one of them was seized with cramp and began drifting downstream. The main current ran rather swiftly, but not too strongly for even a moderate swimmer. It will give you an idea, therefore, of the strange deficiency in these creatures, when I tell you that none made the slightest attempt to rescue the weakly crying little thing which was drowning before their eyes.

Instead, it is Wells' Victorian gentleman who leaps in the river, rescues the poor girl, and brings her back to land. He did what any man would have done, didn't he?

Are you sure about that? As I say, the author's dystopian vision is off only insofar as the world he predicted showed up 800,000 years ahead of schedule. In Wells' Britain in the early twenty-first century, men routinely stand around watching girls drown.

In May 2010, a 37-year-old woman was drowning in the River Clyde while police officers called to the scene stood on the bank and watched.[125] "As a matter of procedure it's not the responsibility of the police to go in the water," explained a spokesperson, sniffily, "it's the Fire and Rescue Service." And, as they weren't there yet, tough. The woman would have died had not three Glasgow University students jumped in to save her. Needless to say, the students were in complete breach of "matters of procedure."

In February 2010, a 5-year-old girl was trapped in a car submerged in the icy River Avon for two hours while West Mercia Police stood around on the bank watching.[126] They were "prevented" from diving in to rescue her by "safety regulations." In 2007, two police officers watched as a 10-year-old boy, Jordon Lyon, drowned in a swimming pool in Wigan.[127] The same year, fireman Tam Brown dived into the River Tay to rescue a drowning girl and got her back to shore, only to find he was now subject to a disciplinary investigation by Tayside Fire Service.[128]

In 2008, Alison Hume fell sixty feet down an abandoned mine shaft. An 18-strong rescue crew arrived, but the senior officer said that a recent memo had banned the use of rope equipment for rescuing members of the public. It could only be used to rescue fellow firefighters. So Alison Hume died, in compliance with the memo.[129]

Could this sort of thing happen in America? Oh, it already does. In 2010, KING-TV in Seattle broadcast footage of three "security guards" at a downtown bus station standing around watching while a 15-year-old girl was brutally beaten for her purse, phone, and iPod.[130] But it's okay, the "guards" were "just following orders not to interfere." The victim later told police that she had deliberately stood next to the "guards" while waiting for her bus thinking it would be the safest place. As the video shows, she was punched and slammed against the wall while standing adjacent to so-called "security"—and still they did nothing. And King's County Sheriff's Department congratulated the "men" on their forbearance: "The guards were right to follow their training."

You have to be "trained" to stand around doing nothing?

Recall Harvey Mansfield's definition of manliness—"confidence in the face of risk"—and then look at the helmets grown men wear to take a Sunday bicycle ride 'round a suburban park. As for Plato's concept of "thumos"—an animal instinct to bristle at the sense of danger—the instinct seems all but lost.

To return to Gloria Steinem, when might a fish need a bicycle? The women of Montreal's École Polytechnique could have used one when Marc Lépine walked in with a gun and told all the men to leave the room. They meekly did as ordered. He then shot all the women.[131]

To those who succeeded in imposing the official narrative, Marc Lépine embodies the murderous misogynist rage that is inherent in all men, and which all must acknowledge.

For a smaller number of us, the story has quite the opposite meaning: Marc Lépine was born Gamil Gharbi, the son of an Algerian Muslim wife-beater. And no, I'm not suggesting he's typical of Muslim men or North African men: my point is that he's not typical of anything, least of all what we might call (if you'll forgive the expression) Canadian manhood. The defining image of contemporary maleness is not Monsieur Lépine/Gharbi but the professors and the men in that classroom, who, ordered to leave by the lone gunman, obeyed, and abandoned their female classmates to their fate—an act of abdication that would have been unthinkable in almost any other culture throughout human history. The "men" stood outside in the corridor and, even as they heard the first shots, they did nothing. And, when it was over and Gharbi walked out of the room and past them, they still did nothing. Whatever its other defects, Canadian manhood does not suffer from an excess of testosterone.

In 2009, the director Denis Villeneuve made a film of the story, *Polytechnique*. "I wanted to absolve the men," he said. "People were really tough on them. But they were 20 years old.... It was as if an alien had landed."[132]

But it's always as if an alien had landed. When another Canadian director, James Cameron, filmed *Titanic*, what most titillated him were the alleged betrayals of convention. It's supposed to be "women and children first," but he was obsessed with toffs cutting in line, cowardly men elbowing the womenfolk out of the way and scrambling for the lifeboats, etc. In fact, all the historical evidence is that the evacuation was very orderly. In real life, First Officer William Murdoch threw deckchairs to passengers drowning in the water to give them something to cling to, and then he went down with the ship—the dull, decent thing, all very British, with no fuss. In Cameron's movie, Murdoch takes a bribe and murders a third-class passenger. (The director subsequently apologized to the First Officer's home town in Scotland and offered £5,000 toward a memorial. Gee, thanks.)[133] Mr. Cameron notwithstanding, the male passengers gave their lives for the women, and would never have considered doing otherwise. "An alien landed" on the deck of a luxury liner—and men had barely an hour to kiss their wives goodbye, watch them clamber into the lifeboats, and sail off without them. The social norm of "women and children first" held up under pressure.

Today, in what Harvey Mansfield calls our "gender-neutral society," there are no social norms. Eight decades after the *Titanic*, a German-built ferry en route from Estonia to Sweden sank in the Baltic Sea. Of the 1,051 passengers, only 139 lived to tell the tale.[134] But the distribution of the survivors was very different from that of the *Titanic*. Women and children first? No female under fifteen or over sixty-five made it. Only 5 percent of all women passengers lived. The bulk of the survivors were young men. Forty-three percent of men aged 20 to 24 made it.

No two ship disasters are the same, but the testimony from the MV *Estonia* provides a snapshot of our new world: according to the Finnish Accident Investigation Board's official report, several survivors reported that "everyone was only looking out for himself." According to a Swedish passenger, Kent Harstedt, "A woman had broken her legs and begged others to give her a life jacket, but it was the law of the jungle."[135] "Some old people had already given up hope and were just sitting there crying," said Andrus Maidre, a 19-year-old Estonian. "I stepped over children who were wailing and holding onto the railing."

You "stepped over" children en route to making your own escape? There wasn't a lot of that on the *Titanic*. "There is no law that says women and children first," Roger Kohen of the International Maritime Organization told *Time* magazine. "That is something from the age of chivalry."

If, by "the age of chivalry," you mean the early twentieth century.

As I said, no two maritime disasters are the same. But it's not unfair to conclude that had the men of the *Titanic* been on the *Estonia*, the age and sex distribution of the survivors would have been very different. Nor was there a social norm at the École Polytechnique. So the men walked away, and the women died.

Whenever I've written about these issues, I get a lot of emails from guys scoffing, "Oh, right, Steyn. Like you'd be taking a bullet. You'd be pissing your little girlie panties," etc. Well, maybe I would. But as the Toronto blogger Kathy Shaidle put it: "When we say 'we don't know what we'd do under the same circumstances,' we make cowardice the default position."[136]

I prefer the word passivity—a terrible, corrosive passivity. Even if I'm wetting my panties, it's better to have the social norm of the *Titanic* and fail to live up to it than to have the social norm of the Polytechnique and sink with it.

These are Finnish men, Estonian men, Canadian men. Are you so confident after the blitzkrieg on manhood waged by the educational establishment that the same pathologies aren't taking hold in the U.S.? Consider the ease with which an extraordinary designation has been conferred upon the men who won America's last great military victory—long ago now, before

Afghanistan, before Mogadishu, before the helicopters in the Iranian desert, before Vietnam, before Korea. When Tom Brokaw venerates the young men who went off to fight in Europe and the Pacific seven decades ago as "the Greatest Generation," by implication he absolves the rest of us. For, if they are so great and so exceptional, it would be unreasonable to expect us to do likewise.

"Under the new conditions of perfect comfort and security, that restless energy, that with us is strength, would become weakness," wrote Wells. "Physical courage and the love of battle, for instance, are no great help—may even be hindrances—to a civilized man." As the Time-Traveler observed of the Eloi: "Very pleasant was their day, as pleasant as the day of the cattle in the field. Like the cattle, they knew of no enemies and provided against no needs. And their end was the same."

Wells describes the Eloi drifting into "feeble prettiness." Here is the writer Oscar van den Boogaard from an interview with the Belgian paper *De Standaard*. Mr. van den Boogaard is a Dutch gay "humanist," which is pretty much the trifecta of Eurocool. He was reflecting on the accelerating Islamization of the Continent and concluded that the jig was up for the Europe he loved. "I am not a warrior, but who is?" he shrugged. "I have never learned to fight for my freedom. I was only good at enjoying it."[137] In the famous Kübler-Ross stages of grief, Mr. van den Boogard is past denial, anger, bargaining, and depression, and has arrived at a kind of acceptance.

> I have never learned to fight for my freedom. I was only good at enjoying it.

Sorry, doesn't work—not for long. Cuties in a death cab eventually have to pay the fare.

THE NEW BRITANNIA
The Depraved City

The last sigh of liberty will be heaved by an Englishman.
—Charles-Louis de Secondat, Baron de la Brède et de Montesquieu, letter to William Domville (July 22, 1749)

Sometimes you do live to see it. In *America Alone*, I pointed out that, to a 5-year-old boy waving his flag as Queen Victoria's Diamond Jubilee procession marched down the Mall in 1897, it would have been inconceivable that by the time of his eightieth birthday the greatest empire the world had ever known would have shriveled to an economically emaciated, strike-bound socialist slough of despond, one in which (stop me if this sounds familiar) the government ran the hospitals, ran the automobile industry, controlled much of the housing stock, and, partly as a consequence thereof, had permanent high unemployment and confiscatory tax rates that drove its best talents to seek refuge abroad.

A number of readers, disputing the relevance of this comparison, sent me mocking letters pointing out Britain's balance of payments and other deteriorating economic indicators from the early twentieth century on. True. Great powers do not decline for identical reasons and one would not expect Britain's imperial overstretch to lead to the same consequences as America's imperial understretch. Nonetheless, my correspondents are perhaps too sophisticated and nuanced to grasp the somewhat more basic point I was making. Perched on his uncle's shoulders that day was a young lad who grew up to become the historian Arnold Toynbee. He recalled the mood of Her Majesty's jubilee as follows: "There is, of course, a thing called history, but history is something unpleasant that happens to other people. We are comfortably outside all of that I am sure."[1]

The end of history, 1897 version.

Permanence is always an illusion. Mighty nations can be entirely transformed mighty fast, especially when history comes a-calling. The "something unpleasant" doesn't have to be especially so: national decline is at least partly psychological—and therefore what matters is accepting the psychology of decline. Within two generations, for example, the German people became just as obnoxiously pacifist as they once were bloodily militarist, and as militantly "European" as they once were menacingly nationalist.

Well, who can blame 'em? You'd hardly be receptive to pitches for national greatness after half a century of Kaiser Bill, Weimar, the Third Reich, and the Holocaust.

Yet what are we to make of the British? They were on the right side of all the great conflicts of the last century; and they have been, in the scales of history, a force for good in the world—perhaps the single greatest force for good. In the second half of the twentieth century, even as their colonies advanced to independence, dozens of newborn nation-states retained the English language, English parliamentary structures, English legal system, English notions of liberty, not to mention cricket and all manner of other cultural ties. Insofar as the world functions at all, one can easily make the case that it's due largely to the Britannic inheritance. Today, from South Africa to India to Australia, the regional heavyweights across the map are of British descent, as are three-sevenths of the G7, and two-fifths of the permanent members of the UN Security Council—and in a just world it would be three-fifths. The usual rap against the Security Council is that it's the Second World War victory parade preserved in aspic, but, if that were so, Canada would have a greater claim to a permanent seat than either

France or China. The reason Ottawa didn't make the cut is because a third anglophone nation and a second realm of King George VI would have made too obvious a simple truth—that, when it mattered, the Anglosphere was the all but lone defender of civilization and of liberty.

And then there's the hyperpower. The transition from Pax Britannica to Pax Americana, from the old lion to its transatlantic progeny, was one of the smoothest transfers of power in history—and the practical, demonstrable reality of what Winston Churchill called the "English-speaking peoples," a Britannic family with America as the prodigal son, but a son nevertheless and the greatest of all. In his sequel to Churchill's *History of the English-Speaking Peoples*, Andrew Roberts writes:

> Just as we do not today differentiate between the Roman Republic and the imperial period of the Julio-Claudians when we think of the Roman Empire, so in the future no one will bother to make a distinction between the British Empire-led and the American Republic-led periods of English-speaking dominance between the late-eighteenth and the twenty-first centuries. It will be recognized that in the majestic sweep of history they had so much in common—and enough that separated them from everyone else—that they ought to be regarded as a single historical entity, which only scholars and pedants will try to describe separately.

As to what "separated them from everyone else," there has always been a distinction between the "English-speaking peoples" and the rest of "the West," and at hinge moments in human history that distinction has proved critical. Continental Europe has given us plenty of nice paintings and mellifluous symphonies, French wine and Italian actresses, but, for all our fetishization of multiculturalism, you can't help noticing that when it comes to the notion of a *political* West—with a sustained commitment to individual liberty and representative government—the historical record looks a lot more unicultural and indeed (given that most of these liberal democracies other than America share the same head of state) uniregal. Many Continental nations have constitutions dating all the way back to the disco era: the United States Constitution is not only older than the French, German, Italian, and Spanish constitutions, it's older than all of them put together. The entire political class of Portugal, Spain, and Greece spent their childhoods living under dictatorships. So did Jacques Chirac and Angela Merkel. We forget how rare in this world is sustained peaceful constitutional evolution, and rarer still outside the Anglosphere. "The English-speaking peoples did not invent the ideas that nonetheless made them great," writes Roberts. "The Romans invented the concept of Law, the Greeks one-freeman-one-vote democracy, the Dutch modern capital-ism...." But it is the English world that has managed to make these bless-ings seemingly permanent features of the landscape. Take England out of the picture and there are not just a lot of holes in the map—but the absence of most of the modern world.

As always, Britain's decline started with the money. When Europe fell into war in 1939, FDR was willing to help London fight it, but he was deter-mined to exact a price: not just a bit of quid pro quo (American base rights in British colonies) but a serious financial and geopolitical squeeze. The U.S. "Lend-Lease" program to the United Kingdom ended in September 1946. London paid off the final installment of its debt in December 2006, and the Economic Secretary, Ed Balls, sent with the check a faintly surreal accompa-nying note thanking Washington for its support during a war fast fading from living memory.[2] Look at how Britain shrank during those six decades. In 1942, Winston Churchill told the House of Commons, "I have not become the King's First Minister in order to preside over the liquidation of the Brit-ish Empire."[3] But in the end he had no choice. The money drained to Wash-ington, and power and influence followed.

In terms of global order, the Anglo-American transition was so adroitly managed that most of us aren't quite sure when it took place. Some scholars like to pinpoint it to the middle of 1943. One month, the

British had more men under arms than the Americans. The next, the Americans had more men under arms than the British. The baton of global leadership had been passed. And, if it didn't seem that way at the time, that's because it was as near a seamless transition as could be devised—although it was hardly "devised" at all, at least not by London. Yet we live with the benefits of that transition to this day: to take a minor but not inconsequential example, one of the critical links in the post-9/11 Afghan campaign was the British Indian Ocean Territory. As its name would suggest, that's a British dependency, but it has a U.S. military base—just one of many pinpricks on the map where the Royal Navy's Pax Britannica evolved into Washington's Pax Americana with nary a thought: from U.S. naval bases in Bermuda to the Anzus alliance Down Under to Canadian officers at Norad in Cheyenne Mountain, London's military ties with its empire were assumed by the United States, and life and global order went on.

One of my favorite lines from the Declaration of Independence never made it into the final text. They were Thomas Jefferson's parting words to his fellow British subjects across the ocean: "We might have been a free and great people together."[4] But ultimately, when it mattered, they were. Britain's eclipse by its transatlantic offspring, by a nation with the same language, same legal inheritance, and same commitment to liberty, is one of the least disruptive transfers of global dominance ever.

Think it's likely to go that way next time 'round? By 2027 (according to Goldman Sachs) or 2016 (according to the IMF), the world's leading economy will be a Communist dictatorship whose legal, political, and cultural traditions are as foreign to its predecessors as could be devised.[5] Even more civilizationally startling, unlike the Americans, British, Dutch, and Italians before them, the pre-eminent economic power will be a country that doesn't use the Roman alphabet.

They have our soul who have our bonds—and the world was more fortunate in who had London's bonds than America is seventy years later. Britain's eclipse by its wayward son was a changing of the guard, not a razing of the palace. By contrast, the fall of America would mark the end of a two-century anglophone dominance of geopolitics, of trade, of the global currency (sterling, and then the dollar), and of a world whose order and prosperity most people think of as part of a broad universal march of progress but which, in fact, derive from a very particular cultural inheritance and may well not survive it.

According to Lawrence Summers, America and China exist in a financial "balance of terror"—or, in Cold War terms, on a trigger of Mutually Assured Destruction.[6] You could have said the same for London and Washington in March of 1941, nine months before Pearl Harbor, back when Lend-Lease began. Without American money and materiel, Britain and the Commonwealth would have been defeated. On the other hand, if Britain and the Commonwealth had collapsed, German-Japanese world domination would not have proved terribly congenial to the United States, not least the Vichy regimes in Ottawa and the Caribbean. But, as the British learned, any balance shifts over time—and so does influence: by 1950, for Britannia's lion cubs in Canada and Australia, getting a friendly ear in Washington mattered more than one in London.

The Sino-American "balance of terror" is already shifting, and fast. By 2010, China was funding and building ports in Burma, Sri Lanka, Bangladesh, and Pakistan.[7] They, too, are Britannia's lion cubs, part of London's Indian Empire. Yet all four went from outposts of the British Raj to pit-stops on Chinese manufacturing's globalization superhighway within a mere sixty years. Ascendant powers take advantage of declining ones: FDR and his successors used Lend-Lease and the wartime alliance to appropriate much of the geopolitical infrastructure built by Britain. China, in turn, will do the same to the United States—initially for trade purposes, but eventually for much more. Here's just a few things London didn't have to worry about Washington doing: In recent years, Beijing has engaged in widespread intellectual-property theft and industrial espionage against the West;[8] attempted multiple cyber-attacks on America's military and commercial computer systems;[9] blinded U.S. satellites with lasers;[10] supplied arms to the Taliban;[11] helped North Korea deliver missiles to Iran and Pakistan;[12] assisted Teheran with its nuclear program;[13] and actively cooperated in a growing worldwide nuclear black market.[14]

In response, American "realists" keep telling themselves: Never mind, economic liberalization will force China to democratize. Lather, rinse, repeat.

If there is any single event that marked the end of Britain as an imperial power of global reach, it's the Suez Crisis of 1956. Egypt nationalized the Suez Canal and London intervened militarily, with the French and Israelis, to protect what it saw as a vital strategic interest, a critical supply line to and from the Asian and Pacific members of the Commonwealth. In the biggest single disagreement between Britain and America since the Second World War, Washington opposed the invasion. We can argue another day about what prompted Nasser to seize the canal and whether the American reading of the situation helped lead to the late twentieth-century fetid "stability" of the Middle East and, among other things, 9/11. But for now just concentrate on one single feature—what Eisenhower opted to do to the Brits once he'd decided to scuttle the Suez operation. He ordered his Treasury Secretary to prepare to sell part of the U.S. Government's Sterling Bond holdings (that is, the World War II debt).

In London, the Chancellor of the Exchequer, Harold Macmillan, reported to the Prime Minister, Anthony Eden, that Britain could not survive such an action by Washington. The sell-off would prompt a run on the pound, and economic collapse, very quickly. Britain, humiliated, withdrew from Suez, and from global power.

It starts with the money. But it won't end there. It never does.

And this was the friendliest shift of global hegemony—the one between family, from an elderly patriarch to its greatest scion, two great powers speaking the same language and with a compatible worldview. Its leaders were not just allies, but chums, wartime comrades, Sir Anthony as Churchill's deputy and Foreign Secretary, Ike as Supreme Allied Commander in London.

But Eisenhower had the money, so he called the shots. Eden's widow, the Countess of Avon, told me years ago that Ike came to regret his actions over Suez. Too late.

Britain accepted its diminished status with as much grace as it could muster. Like an old failing firm, its directors had identified the friendliest bidder and arranged, as best they could, for a succession in global leadership that was least disruptive to their interests and would ensure the continuity of their brand—the English language, English law, English trade, English liberties. It was such an artful transfer it's barely noticed and little discussed.

But we'll notice the next one.

"Next time 'round" is already under way. And one day Washington will be on the receiving end of Beijing's Suez moment.

★ ★ ★ ★ ★

AFTER THE BALL

To point out how English the globalized world is, is, of course, a frightfully unEnglish thing to do. One risks sounding like the old Flanders and Swann number:

> The English, the English, the English are best.
> I wouldn't give tuppence for all of the rest.

Which is the point of the song: English braggadocio is a contradiction in terms. You need some sinister rootless colonial oik like me to do it. No true Englishman would ever descend to anything so vulgar. But there's a difference between genial self-effacement and contempt for one's own inheritance. In 2009, Geert Wilders, the Dutch parliamentarian and soi-disant Islamophobe, flew into London and promptly got shipped back to the Netherlands as a threat to public order.[15] After the British Government had reconsidered its stupidity, he was permitted to return and give his speech at the House of Lords—and, as foreigners often do, he quoted

Winston Churchill, under the touchingly naive assumption that this would endear him to the natives.[16] Whereas, of course, to almost all members of Britain's current elite, quoting Churchill approvingly only confirms that you're an extremist lunatic. I had the honor a couple of years back of visiting President Bush in the White House and seeing the bust of Sir Winston on display in the Oval Office. When Barack Obama moved in, he ordered it removed and returned to the British.[17] Its present whereabouts are unclear. But given what Churchill had to say about Islam in his book on the Sudanese campaign, the bust was almost certainly arrested upon landing at Heathrow and deported as a threat to public order.

Somewhere along the way a quintessentially British sense of self-deprecation curdled into a psychologically unhealthy self-loathing. A typical foot-of-the-page news item from the *Daily Telegraph*:

> A leading college at Cambridge University has renamed its controversial colonial-themed Empire Ball after accusations that it was "distasteful." The £136-a-head Emmanuel College ball was advertised as a celebration of "the Victorian commonwealth and all of its decadences."
>
> Students were urged to "party like it's 1899" and organizers promised a trip through the Indian Raj, Australia, the West Indies, and 19th century Hong Kong.
>
> But anti-fascist groups said the theme was "distasteful and insensitive" because of the British Empire's historical association with slavery, repression and exploitation.
>
> The Empire Ball Committee, led by presidents Richard Hilton and Jenny Unwin, has announced the word "empire" will be removed from all promotional material.[18]

The way things are going in Britain, it would make more sense to remove the word "balls."

It's interesting to learn that "anti-fascism" now means attacking the British Empire, which stood alone against fascism in that critical year between the fall of France and Germany's invasion of Russia. And it's even sadder to have to point out the most obvious fatuity in those "anti-fascist groups'" litany of evil—"the British Empire's association with slavery." The British Empire's principal association with slavery is that it abolished it. Until William Wilberforce, the British Parliament, and the brave men of the Royal Navy took up the issue, slavery was an institution regarded by all cultures around the planet as a constant feature of life, as permanent as the earth and sky. Britain expunged it from most of the globe.

It is pathetic but unsurprising how ignorant all these brave "anti-fascists" are. Yet there is a lesson here not just for Britain but for America, too: when a society loses its memory, it descends inevitably into dementia. And, if *la crème de la crème* of the British education system so willingly prostrates itself before ahistorical balderdash, what then of its more typical charges? If you cut off two generations of students from their cultural inheritance, why be surprised that legions of British Muslims sign up for the Taliban? These are young men who went to school in Luton and West Bromwich and learned nothing of their country of nominal citizenship other than that it's responsible for racism, imperialism, colonialism, and all the other bad -isms of the world. If that's all you knew of Britain, why would you feel any allegiance to Queen and country? One of the July 7 Tube bombers left a famous video broadcast posthumously on Arab TV, spouting all the usual jihadist boilerplate but in a Yorkshire accent: Ee-oop Allahu akbar! Eaten away by Islam and welfare, much of Britain is on a fast track to Somalia with chip shops.[19]

And what if you don't have Islam to turn to? The transformation of the British people is in its pestilential way a remarkable achievement. Raised in schools that teach them nothing, they nevertheless pick up the gist of the matter, which is that their society is a racket founded on various historical injustices. The virtues Hayek admired? Ha! Strictly for suckers.

"We don't need no education," as Pink Floyd sang. When a broke British government attempted to increase the cost of university education, "students" rampaged through Parliament Square, set fire to the statue of Lord Palmerston and urinated on that of Winston Churchill.[20] The signature photograph of the riot showed a "student" swinging from the Union Flag on the Cenotaph, the memorial to Britain's 700,000 dead from the Great War. Who was this tribune of the masses? Step forward, Charlie Gilmour, stepson of Pink Floyd guitarist David Gilmour, a geriatric rocker worth $150 million or thereabouts.[21] When he went up to Cambridge University, Charlie's parents had two suits made for him by a Savile Row tailor so he could swank about the groves of academe in bespoke elegance. Yet young Mr. Gilmour still thinks the government should fund his education. "Hey, teacher, leave us kids a loan," as his dad's rock group almost sang.

What's he studying at Cambridge? History. Despite that, and despite the prominently displayed words "THE GLORIOUS DEAD," he had no idea that the monument he was desecrating was a memorial to Britain's fallen soldiers. As the columnist Julie Burchill observed, Charlie no doubt assumed "the Glorious Dead" was a rock band.[22]

In 2008, when the economy hit the skids, Gordon Brown and other ministers of the Labour Government fell back on stillborn invocations of "the knowledge economy" that will always make Britain an attractive place to do business because of the "added value" of its educated workforce.[23] (You hear the same confident bluster from American experts entirely ignorant of the academic standards of Asia.) Are you serious? Have you set foot in an English state school in the last fifteen years? The well of cultural inheritance in great nations is deep but not bottomless.

What happened to England, the mother of parliaments and a crucible of liberty? Britain, in Dean Acheson's famous post-war assessment, had lost an empire but not yet found a role. Actually, Britain didn't so much "lose" the Empire: it evolved peacefully into the modern Commonwealth, which is more agreeable than the way these things usually go. Nor is it clear that modern Britain wants a role, of any kind. Rather than losing an empire, it seems to have lost its point.

★ ★ ★ ★ ★

WORLD WITHOUT WANT

Having succeeded Britain as the dominant power, in what other ways might the mighty eagle emulate the tattered old lion? First comes reorientation, and the shrinking of the horizon. After empire, Britain turned inward: between 1951 and 1997 the proportion of government expenditure on defense fell from 24 percent to 7, while the proportion on health and welfare rose from 22 percent to 53. And that's before New Labour came along to widen the gap further.[24]

Those British numbers are a bald statement of reality: you can have Euro-sized entitlements or a global military, but not both. What's easier to do if you're a democratic government that's made promises it can't afford—cut back on nanny-state lollipops, or shrug off thankless military commitments for which the electorate has minimal appetite?

In the grim pre-Thatcher nadir of the 1970s, the then Prime Minister, Jim Callaghan, confided to a pal of mine that he thought Britain's decline was irreversible and that the government's job was to manage it as gracefully as possible. He wasn't alone in this: an entire generation of British politicians, on both sides of the aisle, felt much the same way. They rose onward and upward, "managing" problems rather than solving them. You can already see the same syndrome in Washington. While Obama seems actively to be willing U.S. decline as some sort of penance to the planet, many others have accepted American diminishment as a mere fact of life to be adjusted to as best one can. Yet, as noted, national decline is always at least partly psychological. Even in the long ebbing of imperial grandeur, there was no rational basis for modern Britain's conclusion that it had no future other than as an outlying province of a centralized Euro nanny state dominated by nations whose political, legal, and cultural traditions are entirely alien to its own. The embrace of such a fate is a psychological condition, not an economic one. Thus, Hayek's greatest insight in *The Road to Serfdom*, written with an immigrant's eye on the Britain of 1944:

There is one aspect of the change in moral values brought about by the advance of collectivism which at the present time provides special food for thought. It is that the virtues which are held less and less in esteem and which consequently become rarer are precisely those on which the British people justly prided themselves and in which they were generally agreed to excel. The virtues possessed by Anglo-Saxons in a higher degree than most other people, excepting only a few of the smaller nations, like the Swiss and the Dutch, were independence and self-reliance, individual initiative and local responsibility, the successful reliance on voluntary activity, noninterference with one's neighbor and tolerance of the different and queer, respect for custom and tradition, and a healthy suspicion of power and authority.

Within little more than half-a-century, almost every item on the list had been abandoned, from "independence and self-reliance" (40 percent of Britons receive state handouts[25]) to "a healthy suspicion of power and authority"—the reflex response now to almost any passing inconvenience is to demand the government "do something," the cost to individual liberty be damned. The United Kingdom today is a land that reviles "custom and tradition," requires criminal background checks for once routine "voluntary activity" (school field trips), and in which "noninterference" and "tolerance of the different" have been replaced by intolerance of and unending interference with those who decline to get with the beat: Dale McAlpine, a practicing (wait for it) Christian, was handing out leaflets in the town of Wokington and chit-chatting with shoppers when he was arrested on a "public order" charge by Police Officer Sam Adams (no relation), a gay, lesbian, bisexual, and transgender community outreach officer.[26] Mr. McAlpine had said homosexuality is a sin. "I'm gay," said Officer Adams. Well, it's still a sin, said Mr. McAlpine. So Officer Adams arrested him for causing distress to Officer Adams.

In Britain, everything is policed except crime. The government-funded National Children's Bureau has urged nursery teachers and daycare supervisors to record and report every racist utterance of toddlers as young as three.[27]

Like what?

Well, if children "react negatively to a culinary tradition other than their own by saying 'Yuk,'" that could be a clear sign that they'll grow up to make racist remarks that could cause distress to the anti-racism community outreach officer. Makes a lot of sense to get all their names in a big government database by pre-kindergarten.

While the gay, lesbian, bisexual, and transgender community outreach officer is busy arresting you for offending the gay, lesbian, bisexual, and transgender community outreach officer, in the broader scene London now has more violent crime than New York and Istanbul. From personal observation, an alarming number of the men on its streets seem to affect the appearance of the bad guys' crew in *Pirates of the Caribbean*, shaven headed with large earrings, and the sprightly swagger of a rum-fueled sea dog sighting one of the less pox-ridden strumpets in Tortuga. As for the English roses, at about 2:00 on a Wednesday afternoon, in order to enter a convenience store, I was obliged to step over a girl of about twelve dressed like a trollop and collapsed in her own vomit. But never fear, the government is taking action: in order to facilitate safer binge drinking, police announced that they would be handing out free flip-flops outside nightclubs in order to help paralytic dolly birds stagger home without stumbling in their high heels and falling into the gutter.[28]

In 2006, on a train in South London, a 96-year-old man was punched in the face and blinded in one eye.[29] His 44-year-old attacker had boarded the crowded tram, tried to push past Shah Chaudhury in the aisle and become enraged by the nonagenarian's insufficient haste in moving out of the way. "You bastard!" he snarled, and slugged him. Much of the commentary concerned the leniency of the sentence. Yet that wasn't what caught my eye about the story of poor Mr. Chaudhury. In a statement to the court, the victim "said he had been standing in the aisle of the tram because nobody would give up their seat for him." He was ninety-six years old and relied on two walking sticks. How can it be that not a single twenty/thirty/fortysomething in the car thought to offer his seat?

Some years ago the livelier members of the Royal Canadian Mounted Police were illegally burning down the barns of Quebec separatists. When this became public, Pierre Trudeau blithely responded that, if people were upset by the Mounties' illegal barn-burning, maybe he'd make it legal for the Mounties to burn barns. George Jonas, one of our great contemporary analysts, responded that Monsieur Trudeau had missed the point: barn-burning wasn't wrong because it was illegal; it was illegal because it was wrong.[30]

That's an important distinction. Once it's no longer accepted that something is wrong, all the laws in the world will avail you naught. The law functions as formal embodiment of a moral code, not as free-standing substitute for it. Beating up a 96-year-old isn't wrong because it's illegal; it's illegal because it's wrong. Not offering your seat to a 96-year-old isn't illegal at all, but it's also wrong. And, if a citizen of an advanced western social democracy no longer understands that instinctively, you can pass a thousand laws and issue a million ASBOs (the "Anti-Social Behavior Orders" introduced by Tony Blair) and they will never be enough. British society has come to depend on CCTVs—closed-circuit cameras in every public building, every shopping center, every street, even (in some remote rural locales) in the trees. In some cities, traffic wardens have miniature cameras in their caps to film ill-tempered motorists abusing them for writing a ticket.[31] Britain is said to be home to a third of all the world's CCTVs, and in the course of an average day, the average Briton is estimated to be filmed approximately 300 times.[32] So naturally the Croydon trolley had a camera, and it captured in vivid close-up the perpetrator attacking his victim. And a fat lot of good the video evidence did Mr. Chaudhury.

Churchill called his book *The History of the English-Speaking Peoples*—not the English-Speaking Nations. The extraordinary role played by those nations in the creation and maintenance of the modern world derived from their human capital. What happens when, as a matter of state policy, you debauch your human capital? The United Kingdom has the highest drug use in Europe,[33] the highest incidence of sexually transmitted disease,[34] the highest number of single mothers,[35] the highest abortion rate;[36] marriage is all but defunct, except for toffs, upscale gays, and Muslims. A couple of years ago, the papers reported that stabbings are so rampant in British schoolyards that a company that specializes in military body armor is now manufacturing school blazers lined with Kevlar.[37] For Americans, the quickest way to understand modern Britain is to look at what LBJ's Great Society did to the black family and imagine it applied to the general population.

American exceptionalism would have to be awfully exceptional to suffer a similar expansion of government and not witness, in enough of the populace, the same descent into dependency and depravity. As the United Kingdom demonstrates, a determined state can change the character of a people in the space of a generation or two. When William Beveridge laid out his blueprint for the modern British welfare state in 1942, his goal was the "abolition of want," to be accomplished by "cooperation between the State and the individual."[38] In attempting to insulate the citizenry from the vicissitudes of fate, Sir William succeeded beyond his wildest dreams: want has been all but abolished. Today, fewer and fewer Britons want to work, want to marry, want to raise children, want to lead a life of any purpose or dignity. "Cooperation" between the State and the individual has resulted in a huge expansion of the former and the ceaseless withering of the latter.

For its worshippers, Big Government becomes a kind of religion: the church as state. After the London Tube bombings, Gordon Brown began mulling over the creation of what he called a "British equivalent of the U.S. Fourth of July," a new national holiday to bolster British identity.[39] The Labour Party think-tank, the Fabian Society, proposed that the new "British Day" should be July 5, the day the National Health Service was created.[40] Because the essence of contemporary British identity is waiting two years for a hip operation. So fireworks every Glorious Fifth! They should call it Dependence Day.

One-fifth of British children are raised in homes in which no adult works.[41] Just under 900,000 people have been off sick for over a decade, claiming "sick benefits," week in, week out for ten years and counting.[42] "Indolence," as Machiavelli understood, is the greatest enemy of a society, but rarely has any state embraced indolence with such paradoxical gusto as Britain. There is almost nothing you can't get the government to pay for. Plucked at random from the *Daily Mail*:

> A man of 21 with learning disabilities has been granted tax-payers' money to fly to Amsterdam and have sex with a prostitute.[43]

Why not? His social worker says sex is a "human right" and that his client, being a virgin, is entitled to the support of the state in claiming said right. Fortunately, a £520 million program was set up by Her Majesty's Government to "empower those with disabilities." "He's planning to do more than just have his end away," explained the social worker. "Refusing to offer him this service would be a violation of his human rights."

Of course. And so a Dutch prostitute is able to boast that among her clients is the British Government. Talk about outsourcing: given the reputation of English womanhood, you'd have thought this would be the one job that wouldn't have to be shipped overseas. But, as Amsterdam hookers no doubt say, lie back and think of England—and the check they'll be mailing you.

To a visitor, one of the most telling features of contemporary London are the signs pleading with you not to beat up public employees. The United Kingdom seems to be evolving from a nanny state into a kind of giant remedial institution for elderly juvenile delinquents. At bus stops in London, there are posters warning, "DON'T TAKE IT OUT ON US." At the Underground stations, you see the slogan "IF YOU ABUSE OUR STAFF, LONDON SUFFERS" above a poster of Harold Beck's iconic Tube map rendered as a giant bruise—as if some Cockney yob has just punched London in the kisser and beaten it Northern Line black and Piccadilly Line blue, with other parts of the pulverized skin turning Circle Line yellow and even

Central Line livid red. I found this one of the bleakest comments on modern Britain: all the award-winning wit and style of the London advertising world deployed in service of a devastating acknowledgment of civic decay.

But why wouldn't you take it out on the state? In much of Britain, what else is there? In Wales, Northern Ireland, and parts of northern England, the state accounts for between 73 and 78 percent of the economy, which is about the best Big Government can hope to achieve without full-scale Sovietization.[44] In such a world, if something's bugging you enough to want to kick someone's head in, there's a three-in-four chance it's the state's fault. Beveridge's "abolition of want" starts with the abolition of stigma. Once you've done that, it's very hard to go back even if you want to—and there's no indication Britain's millions of non-working households do. The evil of such a system is not the waste of money but the waste of people. Tony Blair's ministry discovered it was politically helpful to reclassify a chunk of the unemployed as "disabled." A fit, able-bodied 40-year-old who has been on disability allowance for a decade understands somewhere at the back of his mind that he is living a lie, and that not just the government but his family and his friends are colluding in that lie. Big Government means small citizens: it corrodes the integrity of a people, catastrophically.

England is a sad case study because it managed to spare itself all the most obviously toxic infections of the age, beginning with Fascism and Communism. But, after Big Government, after global retreat, after the loss of liberty there is only pitiless civic disintegration. The statistics speak for themselves. The number of indictable offenses per thousand people was 2.4 in 1900, climbed gradually to 9.7 in 1954, and then rocketed to 109.4 by 1992.[45] And that official increase understates the reality: many crimes have been decriminalized, and most crime goes unreported, and most reported crime goes uninvestigated, and most investigated crime goes unsolved, and almost all solved crime merits derisory punishment.

Yet the law-breaking is merely a symptom of a larger rupture. In Anthony Burgess' famous novel *A Clockwork Orange*, the precocious psychopathic teen narrator at one point offers his dad some (stolen) money so his parents can enjoy a drink down the pub. "Thanks, son," says his father.

"But we don't go out much now. We daren't go out much now, the streets being what they are. Young hooligans and so on. Still, thanks."

Burgess published his book in 1962, when, on drab streets of cramped row houses, working-class men kept pigeons and tended vegetable allotments. The notion that the old and not so old would surrender some of the most peaceable thoroughfares in the world to young thugs was the stuff of lurid fantasy. Yet it happened in little more than a generation.

"We time-shift," a very prominent Englishman told me a few years ago. "Pardon me?" I said.

"We time-shift," he repeated. At certain hours, the lanes of the leafy and expensive village where he lives are almost as pleasant as they look in the realtors' brochures. But then the yobs come to from the previous night's revelries and swagger forth for another bout of "nightlife"—drinking, swearing, shagging, vomiting, stabbing. "So we time our walks for before they wake up," my friend told me. "It's so peaceful and beautiful at six in the morning." This is some of the most valuable real estate in the world, and yet wealthy families live under curfews imposed by England's violent, feral youth—just as Alex's parents do in Burgess' novel, a work as prophetic as Orwell's or Huxley's.

"The past is a foreign country: they do things differently there." But viewed from 2010, England the day before yesterday is an alternative universe—or a lost civilization. In 2009, the "Secretary of State for Children" (an office both Orwellian and Huxleyite) announced that 20,000 "problem families" would be put under 24-hour CCTV supervision in their homes. As the *Daily Express* reported, "They will be monitored to ensure that children attend school, go to bed on time and eat proper meals."[46] Orwell's government "telescreen" in every home is close to being a reality, although even he would have dismissed as too obviously absurd a nanny state that literally polices your bedtime.

Montesquieu's prediction that "the last sigh of liberty will be heaved by an Englishman" seemed self-evident after the totalitarian enthusiasms of the Continent in the mid-twentieth century. Today? The last sigh will be heaved by England's progeny, in the United States. Is its heaving inevitable?

Must there be a "last sigh of liberty"? A progressivist would scoff at the utter codswallop of such a fancy. Why, modern man would not tolerate for a moment the encroachments his forebears took for granted! And so we assume that social progress is like technological progress: one cannot uninvent the internal combustion engine, so how could one uninvent liberty?

★ ★ ★ ★ ★
THE LOTTERY OF LIFE

Unlike the French and the Russians, the British Revolution happened overseas, in their American colonies, when British subjects decided they wanted to take English ideas of liberty further than the metropolis wanted to go. You can measure the gap in the animating principles between the rebellious half of British North America and the half that stayed loyal to the Crown: the United States is committed to "life, liberty and the pursuit of happiness," Canada to "peace, order and good government." Britain has always been a more paternalistic society, with a different sense of the balance between "liberty" and "order." That's what comes with being an imperialist. The old British elite took it for granted that they had a planet-wide civilizing mission. As the empire waned, a new elite decided to embark on a new civilizing mission closer to home. It turned out to be a de-civilizing mission. There is less and less liberty and opportunity to pursue happiness in the new Britain, and little evidence of order and good government.

Does the fate of the other senior Anglophone power hold broader lessons for the United States? For many Americans, it will be a closer model of decline than Greece. It's not so hard to picture a paternalist technocrat of the Michael Bloomberg school covering New York in CCTV less for terrorism than to monitor your transfats. Britain is a land with more education bureaucrats than teachers, more health-care administrators than doctors, a land of declining literacy, a threadbare social fabric, and an ever more wretched underclass systemically denied the possibility of leading lives of purpose and dignity in order to provide an unending pool of living corpses for the government laboratory. A people mired in dependency turning into snarling Calibans as the national security state devotes ever more of its resources to monitoring its own citizenry.

You cannot wage a sustained ideological assault on your own civilization without grave consequence. We are approaching the end of the Anglo-American moment, and the eclipse of the powers that built the modern world. Even as America's spendaholic government outspends not only America's ability to pay for it but, by some measures, the world's, even as it follows Britain into the dank pit of transgenerational dependency, a failed education system and unsustainable entitlements, even as it makes less and less and mortgages its future to its rivals for cheap Chinese trinkets, most Americans assume that simply because they're American they're insulated from the consequences. There, too, are lessons from the old country. Cecil Rhodes distilled the assumptions of generations when he said that to be born a British subject was to win first prize in the lottery of life. On the eve of the Great War, in his play *Heartbreak House*, Bernard Shaw turned the thought around to taunt a ruling class too smug and self-absorbed to see what was coming. "Do you think," he wrote, "the laws of God will be suspended in favor of England because you were born in it?"

In our time, to be born a citizen of the United States is to win first prize in the lottery of life, and, as Britons did, too many Americans assume it will always be so. Do you think the laws of God will be suspended in favor of America because you were born in it? Great convulsions lie ahead, and at the end of it we may be in a post-Anglosphere world.

FALL
Beyond the Green Zone

*Gaius Gracchus proposed his grain law. It delighted the people for
it provided an abundance of food free of toil. The good men, by
contrast, fought against it because they reckoned that the masses
would be seduced from the ways of hard work and become sloth-
ful, and they saw that the treasury would be drained dry.*

**—Marcus Tullius Cicero, Speech on Behalf
of Publius Sestius (55 BC)**

A s disastrous as the squandering of America's money has been, the
squandering of its human capital has been worse. While our over-
refined Eloi pass the years until their mid-twenties in desultory
sham education in hopes of securing a place in professions that are ever
more removed from genuine wealth creation, too many of the rest, by the
time they emerge from their own schooling, have learned nothing that will
equip them for productive employment. Already, much of what's left of
agricultural labor is done by the undocumented; manufacturing has gone
to China and elsewhere; and so 40 percent of Americans now work in low-
paying service jobs.[1] What happens when more supermarkets move to
computerized checkouts with R2D2 cash registers? Which fast-food chain
will be the first to introduce automated service for drive-thru? Once upon

a time, millions of Americans worked on farms. Then, as agriculture declined, they moved into the factories. When manufacturing was outsourced, they settled into low-paying service jobs or better-paying cubicle jobs—so-called "professional services" often deriving from the ever swelling accounting and legal administration that now attends almost any activity in America. What comes next?

Or, more to the point, what if there is no "next"?

Jobs rarely "come back." When they go, they go for good. Something else takes their place. After the recession of the early Nineties, America lost some three million jobs in manufacturing but gained a little under the same number in construction.[2] Then the subprime hit the fan, and America now has more housing stock than it will need for a generation. So what replaces those three million lost construction jobs? What are all those carpenters, plasterers, excavators going to be doing? Not to mention the realtors, home-loan bankers, contract lawyers, rental-income accountants, and other "professional service" cube people whose business also relies to one degree or another on a soaraway property market.

What if we've run out of "next"? When the factories closed, Americans moved into cubicles and checkout registers. What happens when the checkouts automate and the cubicles go the way of the typing pool?

At America's founding, 90 percent of the labor force worked in agriculture.[3] Today, fewer than 3 percent do. Food is more plentiful than ever, and American farms export some $75 billion worth of their produce. But they don't need the manpower anymore.[4]

So the labor force moved to the mills and factories. And they don't need the manpower anymore. Manufacturing produces the same amount with about a third of the labor that it took in 1950.[5] By 2010, the U.S. economy had restored pre-recession levels of output but without restoring pre-recession levels of employment: it turned out there was no reason to hire back laid off workers, and a lot of reasons not to, once you factor in the taxes, insurance, and the other burdens the state imposes on you for putting even modest sums in the pocket of employees you don't really need.

In H. G. Wells' bifurcated future, the Eloi lounged around all day while the Morlocks did manual labor underground. In our dystopia, the Eloi face a subtly different bifurcation: there's nothing for the Morlocks to do. A society with tens of millions of people for whom there is no work, augmented by tens of millions of low-skilled peasantry from outside its borders, is unlikely to be placid.

The first year of the Obama era and its failed "stimulus" pushed the national unemployment numbers up to almost 10 percent—officially.[6] But if you were one of his core supporters—black or young or both—then the unemployment rate was at least half as much again, and higher than that in many other places. In the summer of 2010, as Barack was golfing and Michelle was having public beaches closed on the Costa del Sol to accommodate her sunbathing needs, the black unemployment rate in America climbed to just under 16 percent, as opposed to a general figure of 9.5 percent. That's two-thirds higher—again, officially. That year, the number of young people (16 to 24) in summer employment hit a record low. Big Government is a jobs killer.[7] Big Government augmented by a terrible education system and a tide of mass immigration is a life killer. So if—when—the United States' AAA credit rating is downgraded and the economy starts to contract, what happens? An increase in the unemployment rate to 30 percent, higher in the decaying cities. Core government services cut. Basic shortages and deteriorating infrastructure for delivery. Civil unrest. Most of those go without saying: if you lay off a bunch of sixtysomethings a couple of years before retirement, they sit at home and fester. If you fire—or never even hire—younger, fitter groups, they tend to express their dissatisfactions more directly.

As farm work and factory shifts and service jobs fade, what occupations are on the rise? An America comprised of therapeutic statists, regulatory enforcers, multigenerational dependents, identity-group rent-seekers, undocumented menials, stimulus grantwriting liaison coordinators, six-figure community organizers, millionaire diversity-outreach consultants, billionaire carbon-offset traders, an electronic-leisure "knowledge sector," John Edwards' anti-poverty consultancy, John Kerry's vintner, and Al Gore's holistic masseuse will offer many opportunities, but not for that outmoded American archetype, the self-reliant citizen seeking to nourish his family through the fruits of his labor. And nor for millions of others just struggling to stay afloat.

★ ★ ★ ★ ★

THERE GOES THE NEIGHBORHOOD

The ruling class divides its subjects into Representation and Taxation categories. Favored groups are those that will expand the dependent class and, therefore, the dependent-administration class. Single women vote 60-something percent for Big Government, in part because, for unwed mothers, government is an absentee father you can always rely on to mail the check.[8] About 20 percent of U.S. households are unmanned. Thirty percent of rural women living alone exist below the poverty line.[9] One-third of all female-headed households live in poverty.[10] Which suits government just fine, because then you're more willing to serve as a pliant, dependent subject of the benign Sovereign. These worsening statistics do not demonstrate a need for Big Government. They are a consequence of Big Government.

But how pliant will you be when the money runs out and the programs get cut? The "austerity" riots in Greece, France, and the United Kingdom suggest the answer to that.

As for the taxation class, when the statists confiscate more of your dwindling earnings to prop up the wages and pensions of the government workforce and the benefit checks of the dependent class, what do you get in return? The security of the Nanny State? You've still got a job, you've still got a home, and all that does is make your property and place of employment a target for those who don't.

Remember our gentleman from 1890 taking a whirl on the time-machine. First we shunted him forward to 1950: wow, was he astonished! Then we pushed him ahead another six decades: this time, not so much. The TV's flatter, the fridge has an ice-dispenser in the door, but there is no sense, as there was in mid-century, of a great transformative leap. American energy has ebbed palpably; he is seeing the republic in stasis. Suppose we nudge him on just a little further, not decades but a few years—to that same ordinary house lot on a residential street.

His old home still stands, but as he gets his bearings he notices everything seems a little shabbier; even the electronic toys are dinged and scratched, as if the owners have foregone the new models. He looks out back through the bay window: strung across the grass is a sagging clothes line, which he can't recall seeing back in 2011. But, compared to a washer, it's "environmentally friendly," right? So was the hedge, but that's gone, and the fence is topped with barbed wire. He turns 'round. The front window has bars on it. Outside the car is small and old, and has more color-coded government permits down the driver's side of the windshield than ever before. But the yard is a mess, as if passers-by are tossing trash in it. And the house across the road—the old Alden place, back in his day—is boarded up.

He steps outside. He's never seen the street like this. In 1890, it was a pleasant residential neighborhood, never wealthy but neat and maintained. Now half the homes look abandoned. There are "For Sale" and "Foreclosure" signs everywhere, but they're leaning and hanging and faded, as if not even the realtor's placards are maintained. One in four homes is shuttered and dead. Another one in four looks like a carcass picked clean by predators: window holes like eyeless sockets, roof shingles stripped, exterior fixtures gone. The rest appear to be lived in, but half have missing panes patched with board and other signs of decay. He moseys down the street, past a gaggle of sullen youths slumped against the wall and eyeing him appreciatively. He crosses over, past another kid, in a wheelchair. No, not a kid. Maybe late forties, but dressed like a child. Our visitor from 1890 has noticed a lot of that since he moved on from 1950. He has one of those T-shirts with an in-your-face attitudinal slogan. But his face doesn't have much attitude or energy in it, and his legs are missing below the knees. Along the sidewalk are some parched saplings with a few browning leaves, each tree bearing a sign saying, "This Community Improvement Project

brought to you by the Federal-Urban Bureau of Arborial Renewal—
FUBAR: Working Together on the Road Ahead."

Our time-traveler asks the present owner of his old home what happened. But nothing really "happened": it just turned out this way. It was
never luxurious, but it was a nice neighborhood, and you knew who your
neighbors were. The tough times were a few blocks away, with the repos-
sessed homes and the abandoned cars on bricks in the yard. But then the
couple three houses down got foreclosed on, and the bank put their property up for sale, and nobody bought. So now the boarded up homes aren't
a few streets away, but next door. And the night is full of sounds: the word
gets round that Number 23 and Number 29 are empty, and people break
in for copper wiring or anything else there's a market or a need for. And
sometimes they bust in just because they're up to something and require a
place where they know they won't be disturbed. So the drug dealers creep
a little closer, and then the shootings.

On Wall Street, recessions are "cyclical." Out in the hinterland, the
cycle settles in, and it's vicious: abandoned homes lead to more crime lead
to more abandoned homes lead to even more crime lead to even more
abandoned homes.... A lifetime's labor has gone to pay the mortgage on
a house that will never be worth in real terms what you paid for it and
that now stands in a neighborhood the old you—the young you, the one
with modest dreams of a better life earned through effort—would never
want to live in.

So our time-traveler listens to the present owner of his old home explain
that, yes, they could rent out the upstairs, but, even though the Bureau of
Compliance at the city Department of Furnished Accommodation approved
their fire retardant cushions, the state Agency of Access & Equality says they
need a wheelchair ramp, and an elevator. And, even if they could afford that,
the only place they could put it is where that ugly old poplar is, and taking
that down requires permission from the Board of Environmental Impact,
which has a three-year backlog of tree-removal cases. They could just cut
it down, and gamble that no one would check, but Ken and Ron down the

street did it and got fined, and, even though they're appealing to the Human Rights Commission on the grounds that the fine was homophobic, it wouldn't be the same for them because they're not in any minority category, not since the state Supreme Court ruled that diabetes no longer qualified because too many people have it....

The gentleman from 1890 suddenly realizes that for the last ten minutes he has had absolutely no idea what this lady is talking about, but he has an overwhelming desire to get back on his time-machine before the youths sitting on the wall opposite strip it for parts and he winds up stuck forever in...well, whatever country this is. "America" doesn't seem quite the word.

★ ★ ★ ★ ★

SEE THE U.S.A. IN YOUR CHEVROLET

You don't have to engage in H. G. Wells speculations about the near future. Put a time-traveler from 1950 in Detroit sixty years later. He, too, would doubt he'd landed in the same country. For decades, Americans watched the decline of a great city and told themselves it was an outlier. It didn't used to be: "When General Motors sneezes, America catches a cold." When Detroit gets the ebola virus, America is surely in line to catch something—unless you're entirely convinced that its contagion can be quarantined. Half-a-century ago, the city was the powerhouse of the world. Now it's a wasteland. It's a motor city with no motor, a byword for industrial decline and civic collapse that Big Government liberals seem determined to make their template. To residents of the mid-twentieth century it would have seemed incredible that one day the president of the United States would fire the CEO of General Motors and personally call the mayor of Detroit to assure him he had no plans to move the company's head office out of the city. By the time it actually happened, it provoked barely a murmur.[11]

In 2009, General Motors had a market valuation about a third of Bed, Bath & Beyond, and no one says your Swash 700 Elongated Biscuit Toilet

Seat Bidet is too big to fail.[12] For purposes of comparison, GM's market capitalization was then about $2.4 billion versus Toyota's $100 billion and change (the change being bigger than the whole of GM).[13] General Motors, like the other two geezers of the Old Three, is a sprawling retirement home with a small money-losing auto subsidiary. The United Auto Workers is the AARP in an Edsel: it has three times as many retirees and widows as "workers" (I use the term loosely).[14] GM has 96,000 employees but provides health benefits to a million people. How do you make that math add up? Not by selling cars: Honda and Nissan were making a pretax operating profit per vehicle of around $1,600; Ford, Chrysler, and GM a loss of $500 to $1,500.[15] That's to say, they lose money on every vehicle they sell. Like Henry Ford said, you can get it in any color as long as it's red.

President Obama, in that rhetorical tic that quickly became a bore, likes to position himself as a man who won't duck the tough decisions. So, faced with a U.S. automobile industry that so overcompensates its workers it can't make a car for a price anybody's willing to pay for it, the president handed over control to the very unions whose demands are principally responsible for that irreconcilable arithmetic. Presented with a similar situation thirty years earlier, Mrs. Thatcher took on the unions and, eventually, destroyed their power. That was a tough decision. Telling your political allies they can now go on overpaying themselves in perpetuity is a piece of cake.

When the going gets tough, the tough get bailed out. Your car business operates on a failed business model? Don't worry, the taxpayers will prop that failed business model up forever. You went bananas on your credit card and can't pay it back? Order another round and we'll pass a law to make it the bank's fault. Your once Golden State has decayed into such a corrupt racket of government cronyism that the remaining revenue generators are fleeing your borders faster than you can raise taxes on them? Relax, we're lining up a federal bailout for you, too. Your unreadable newspaper woke up from its 96-page Obama Full Color Inaugural Souvenir bender to discover that its advertising revenue had collapsed with the real-estate market and GM dealerships? Hey, lighten up, John Kerry's already been pleading your case in the Senate.[16] Is it really so hard to picture the President calling the Mayor to assure him he has no plans to move the *New York Times* out of New York?

America is now a land that rewards failure—at the personal, corporate, and state level. If you reward it, you get more of it. If you reward it as lavishly as the federal government does, you'll get the Radio City Christmas Spectacular of Failure, on ice and with full supporting orchestra. The problem is that, in abolishing failure, you also abolish the possibility of success, and guarantee only a huge sucking statist swamp. From Motown to no town, from the Golden State to Golden Statists. What happens when the policies that brought ruin to Detroit and decay to California are applied to the nation at large?

Nobody did this to Detroit. The city and its business and civic leaders did this to themselves. In once functioning parts of Africa, civil war, a resurgent Islam, and other forces have done a grand job of reversing all the progress of the twentieth century. But the deterioration of Sierra Leone or Somalia is as nothing compared to the heights from which Detroit has slid. Entire blocks are deserted, and the city is proposing to turn commercial land back into pasture—on the unlikely proposition that attracting Michiganders to graze Holsteins between crack houses will lead to urban renewal. For a coffee-table book of ineffable sadness, two French photojournalists, Yves Marchand and Romain Meffre, wandered through the rubble of lost grandeur: the ruined auditorium of the United Artists Theater, built in 1928 in the Spanish-Gothic style, abandoned in the Seventies.[17] The shattered ballroom, with upturned grand piano, of the Lee Plaza Hotel, an art deco landmark from 1929, derelict since the Nineties. The Woodward Avenue Presbyterian Church, pews splintered, dust-caked Bibles and hymnals scattered across the floors. Messieurs Marchand's and Meffre's predecessors would have seen such scenes in bombed-out European cities circa 1945. But this was America, and no bombs fell. And the physical decay is as nothing to the deterioration of human capital: 44 percent of adults in the city have a reading comprehension below Grade Six level.[18] Or to put it another way: nearly half the grown-ups in Detroit could not graduate from elementary school. And, believe me, what Sixth Grade requires of American 12-year-olds is no great shakes.

According to *Time* magazine: "The estimated functional illiteracy rate in the city limits hovers near 50 percent."

With that pool of potential employees, why would anybody start a business in Detroit? What could you hire people to do?

Detroit did this to itself.

Well, you say, maybe things'll brighten up with the next generation?

Don't hold your breath. In March 2010, the president of the School Board, Otis Mathis, sent out the following email:

> If you saw Sunday's Free Press that shown Robert Bobb the emergency financial manager for Detroit Public Schools, move Mark Twain to Boynton which have three times the number seats then students and was one of the reason's he gave for closing school to many empty seats.[19]

Here's another one from President Mathis:

> Do DPS control the Foundation or outside group? If an outside group control the foundation, then what is DPS Board row with selection of is director? Our we mixing DPS and None DPS row's, and who is the watch dog?

A while back, I heard the English writer Anthony Daniels read aloud some correspondence from Jack the Ripper's first victim, a 43-year-old domestic servant called Mary Anne Nichols. In 1888, the year of her murder, she wrote to her father:

> I just write to say you will be glad to know that I am settled in my new place, and going on all right up to now.… It is a grand

place inside, with trees and garden back and front. All has been newly done up. They are teetotalers, and religious, so I ought to get on....[20]

Mary Anne Nichols was born in 1845—a quarter-century before the Education Act brought universal elementary schooling to all children in England and Wales. The correspondence of an uneducated domestic servant in and out of workhouses and prostitution is nevertheless written with better expression, better spelling, better punctuation and, indeed, more human feeling than the president of the School Board in a major American city.

Otis Mathis is not only a Detroit high school graduate but a college graduate.[21] His degree from Wayne State was held up for over a decade because of his repeated failure to pass the English proficiency test. Eventually, he did things the all-American way: he sued the college. So Wayne State dropped the English proficiency, and Otis Mathis got his degree. By then, he'd already been elected to the School Board.

By the way, he's not the only beneficiary of America's joke academic standards. In the Eighties, Chowan College in Murfreesboro, North Carolina, also dropped its English proficiency requirements in hopes of attracting wealthy foreigners. It worked. As Michelle Malkin pointed out, a chap called Khalid Sheikh Mohammed enrolled, fell in with a group of hardcore Muslims, transferred to North Carolina Agricultural and Technical State University to study mechanical engineering, and used the knowledge he acquired to pull off the first World Trade Center attack, the African embassy bombings, the assault on the USS *Cole*, 9/11, and the beheading of Daniel Pearl.[22] A little larnin' is a dangerous thing—particularly for Americans on the receiving end.

Whether or not Khalid Sheikh Mohammed sees himself as a role model for American students, Otis Mathis certainly does. "Instead of telling them that they can't write and won't be anything, I show that that cannot stop you," Mr. Mathis told the *Detroit News*. "If Detroit Public Schools can allow kids to dream, with whatever weakness they have, that's something...."[23]

The only one dreaming here is the president of the School Board. Being illiterate "cannot stop you" in Detroit, but try it in Bombay or Bangalore or almost any city in China—and then ask yourself to whom the future belongs. On present projections, at some point around the year 2025 American teachers will be earning two million per annum, and American Twelfth Graders will be unable to count their toes.

Detroit did this to itself.

Its profligate past destroyed the present, and its present will ensure there is no future, because lavishly funded civic institutions are incapable of providing the educational standards of a one-room schoolhouse of 200 years ago. This is an American city at the dawn of the twenty-first century, and one in two of its citizens are illiterate. That's about the same rate as the Ivory Coast, and the Central African Republic, which for much of the Seventies and Eighties was ruled by a cannibal emperor. Whereas in the Seventies and Eighties Detroit was ruled by a Democrat mayor, a bureaucracy-for-life, and an ever more featherbedded union army, all of whom cannibalized the city. Say what you like about Emperor Bokassa but, dollar for dollar, his reign was a bargain compared to Mayor Coleman Young's. Hizzoner called himself the MFIC—the Muthafucker In Charge— and, by the time it was over, Detroit was certainly fucked, and the only mothers still around were on welfare.

Return to those auto statistics: GM has one worker for every ten retirees and dependents. That math is Detroit's math, too. The city's population has fallen by over 50 percent since 1950.[24] So who's left? Thirty percent of the population are government workers.[25] According to the *Detroit News*, another 29 percent are out of work, "using the broadest definition of unemployment."[26] According to Dave Bing, Mayor Young's successor as MFIC, the real unemployment number is "closer to 50 percent."[27]

An unemployable, dysfunctional citizenry, a rapacious government, crime-ridden streets, and an education system that dignifies moronization as a self-esteem program: in Detroit, everything other than government is dead.

Decay sets in imperceptibly, but it accelerates, and, by the time you notice it, it's hard to reverse. Somewhere like Detroit isn't Somalia, not yet. But like other parts of the country it is en route to Latin America—a society with a wealthy corrupt elite that controls the levers of power, and beneath it a great swamp of poverty, whose inhabitants divide into two species—predators and prey. The Motor City is the Murder City, with one of the highest homicide rates on the planet—and 70 percent of them go unsolved.[28]

It will not seem quite such an outlier in the future.

★ ★ ★ ★ ★

BIG LOVE

The end-game for statists is very obvious. If you expand the bureaucratic class and you expand the dependent class, you can put together a permanent electoral majority. In political terms, a welfare check is a twofer: you're assuring yourself of the votes both of the welfare recipient and of the mammoth bureaucracy required to process his welfare. But extend that principle further, to the point where government intrudes into everything: a huge population is receiving more from government (in the form of health care or college subventions) than it *thinks* it contributes, while another huge population is managing the ever expanding regulatory regime (a federal energy-efficiency code, a transfat monitoring bureaucracy, a Bureau of Compliance for this, a Bureau of Compliance for that) and another vast population remains, nominally, in the private sector but, de facto, dependent on government patronage of one form or another—the designated "community assistance" organization for helping poor families understand what minority retraining programs they qualify for, or the private manufacturer from whom the TSA buys disposable latex gloves for enhanced patdowns. Either way, what you get from government—whether in the form of a government paycheck, a government benefit, or a government contract—is a central fact of your life.

But, if you're not on welfare, or working in the welfare office, or working for a "green solutions" business that's landed the government contract for printing the recycled envelopes in which the welfare checks are mailed out, or the trial lawyers behind the class action suit after the green-friendly recycled latex gloves cause mass Chlamydia outbreaks at Newark, O'Hare, and LAX, it's not an attractive society to be in. It's not a place to run a small business—a feed store or a plumbing company or anything innovative, all of which will be taxed and regulated into supporting the state sector. After all, what does it matter to them if your business goes under? Either you'll join the government workforce, or you'll go on the dole. So you too will become part of the dependent class, or the class that's dependent upon the dependent class. Whichever it is, Big Government wins.

We're told that America's and the world's economy depends on "consumption." Hence, the efforts of the government and the Federal Reserve to stampede recalcitrant consumers back into the malls. But consumption is a manifestation of an economy, not the cause of it. In order for something to be consumed, it first has to be produced—which is why healthy societies make wealth before consuming it. Big Government prefers to "stimulate" the public into consuming because it's easier than stimulating them into producing. But the latter is what matters.

What happens when you consume without producing? You can see it on any American Main Street, whose very inhabitants would startle a time-traveler from 1890 long before he noticed any of the technological marvels. A time-traveler from 1950 might have a more specific reaction: back in those days, a signature image of sci-fi movies and comic books was the enlarged brain, the lightbulb cranium with which a more evolved humanity would soon be wandering around. Evolvo Lad had one in his tussles with Superboy. So did Superman's sidekick in a futuristic fantasy called "The Super-Brain of Jimmy Olsen." "With his super-intelligent brain, Jimmy has me at his mercy!" gasps Superman. But Clark Kent's gal pal felt differently about her colossal noggin when it showed up in "Lois Lane's Super-Brain." "The evolution ray that made me super-intelligent turned me into a freak!" she sobs, clutching her unsightly Edisonian incandescent of a head.

There's good news and bad news, Lois. As any visitor from the Fifties would soon discover, in a bleak comment on the limits of predictive fiction, our brains didn't get bigger. But our butts did. If DC Comics had gone with "The Super-Ass of Jimmy Olsen," they'd have been up there with Nostradamus. "Our culture's sedentary character—our strong preference for watching over doing, for virtual over real action—seems closely correlated to our changing physical shape," wrote the Harvard historian Niall Ferguson. "We now consume significantly more fats and carbohydrates than we actually need. According to the standard measure of obesity, the body-mass index, the percentage of Americans classified as obese nearly doubled, from 12 percent to 21 percent, between 1991 and 2001. Nearly two-thirds of all American men are officially considered overweight, and nearly three-quarters of those between 45 and 64. Only Western Samoans and Kuwaitis are fatter."[29] We are our own walking (or waddling) metaphor for consumption unmoored from production.

Dependistan is an unhealthy land. In America, obesity starts earlier and earlier: it's doubled since 1980.[30] According to some surveys, a third of all children over two are obese.[31] Libertarians instinctively recoil from a nanny state that presumes to lecture you on eating your vegetables, and red-state conservatives have a natural cultural antipathy to effete, emaciated coastal metrosexuals nibbling their organic endives—and that was before Michelle Obama decided to make an anti-obesity crusade the centerpiece of her time as First Lady. They're not wrong to be suspicious. Almost all public health behavioral campaigns end up as either bullying or brain-dead or both: half a century ago, nobody thought smokers would wind up huddled on the sidewalk outside windswept office buildings. Few foresaw that high-school "zero tolerance" policies for drugs would lead to students being punished for having Aspirin in their lockers. In 2008, a bill in the British House of Commons attempted to ban Tony the Tiger, longtime pitchman for Frosties, from children's TV because of his malign influence on young persons.[32] Why not just ban Frosties? Or permit it by prescription only? Or make kids stand outside on the sidewalk to eat it? Already, San Francisco's city council has voted against life, liberty, and the pursuit of Happy Meals by attempting to criminalize fast-food menu items that offer free children's toys.[33] It's not far-fetched to imagine government attempting to alter the contents of our stomachs: in fact, they already do. The Public Health Agency of Canada requires that white flour, enriched pasta, and cornmeal be augmented by folic acid to help women lessen the risk of neural-tube defects in their babies.[34] It's also not far-fetched to predict the usual unforeseen consequences: a Norwegian study published in *The American Journal of Medicine* found that folic-acid fortification could increase your risk of cancer.[35] Oh, well.

Our "changing physical shape" (in Ferguson's words) seems an almost literal rebuke to the notion of republican self-government. Never mind the constitution, where are *our* checks and balances?

What might restore the unprecedented size of contemporary Americans to something closer to mid-twentieth-century Americans? The family meal, with mom, dad, and the kids all 'round the kitchen table, like *The Partridge Family* or *The Brady Bunch*? More competitive sports at school? A paper round? "Social media" novelties that don't require you to sit on your butt and look at a screen all day? A summer of farm work before six years of Fat Studies at George Mason University?

None of these things is going to happen. So instead we're left with Mrs. Obama as Marie Antoinette for an age of PC Bourbons: "Don't let them eat cake." What will that do? Push the percentage of obese kids up to 60 percent? Seventy? Senator Richard Lugar, one of the GOP's Emirs of Incumbistan, demands more "federal child nutrition programs."[36] But the National School Lunch Act (whose very name nineteenth-century Americans would have regarded as a darkly satirical fancy from dystopian science fiction) dates back to 1946. The bigging up of American schoolchildren happened on Washington's watch. Yet we'll fight the "war on obesity" as we fight the "war on poverty"—with more dependency and more government programs. While we're "fighting" all these phony wars, it's not even clear we could fight the old-fashioned kind anymore: according to the U.S. Army's analysis of national data, 27 percent of Americans aged 17 to 24 are too overweight for military service.[37] Even running for our lives is beyond many of us.

There is already an almost surreal disconnect between the emaciated sirens of popular culture and those who gather in the dark to watch small stars on the big screen. The largest people on the planet outside the hearty trenchermen of Western Samoa pay ten bucks to watch all-American stories set in all-American towns featuring increasingly un-American boys and girls who bear less and less resemblance to them. It seems likely that trend will continue, and a vast mass of vast mass will sink to the bottom while an ever more cadaverous elite gets all the best jobs. It also seems inevitable that, in response, Big Nanny will decide that she's the one who needs to get bigger and bigger, and to micro-regulate her 350 to 400 million charges ever more coercively. It's not such a leap to imagine the GAUNT Act (Government Assistance for Universal Nutritional Transformation) passing Congress circa 2020 to lessen strains on health-care costs. It won't work. You can't reduce the citizen's waist through government waste—not absent anything this side of a nationwide famine. But it won't stop the statists trying.

The landscape will adjust to accommodate: there will be more class action suits, and your local multiplex and car manufacturers and discount airlines will change their seat configurations every ten, five, two years. This is a cultural phenomenon arising from socio-economic changes that would be difficult to reverse even if our elites accepted the legitimacy of attempting to reverse them.

★ ★ ★ ★ ★

DEPENDISTAN

From the English-language edition of *Pravda*:

Family Becomes Extinct, To Be Replaced with Feminism and Gender Equality[38]

Year on year, there are fewer Russian weddings and, for those that do take place, in regions from Kirov to Krasnoyarsk some three-quarters end in divorce. As the reporter put it, "It is not ruled out that the institute of marriage will vanish in the near future." That's the way to bet—and not just in post-Soviet dystopias. More and more children are raised by single mothers.

Well, huff the elites, what's wrong with that? Are you stigmatizing these women? Are you saying they shouldn't have the rewards of a fulfilling career?

Whether or not juggling (as many of my North Country neighbors do) three minimum wage jobs—a checkout clerk, some part-time waitressing, a bit of off-the-books house cleaning—is every woman's idea of a fulfilling career, it doesn't leave a lot of time for hands-on parenting. Yet instead of trying to correct the structural flaws we will increase dependency—because single women are the most reliable voters for Big Government, even as it turns them into junkies for the state pusher and ensures their kids will reach their adulthood pre-crippled.

When America was hit by economic depression in 1837, Ralph Waldo Emerson was fascinated by how the struggling republic's energy was visible even on the fringes of society: "The literature of the poor, the feelings of the child, the philosophy of the street, the meaning of the household life, are the topics of the time. It is a great stride. It is a sign—is it not?—of new vigor, when the extremities are made active, when currents of warm life run into the hands and feet...."[39]

In the disease-ridden Dependistans of the new America, there are fewer signs of currents in the extremities. Western societies already face an explosion in health costs. From a report on Canada in *The Economist*: "Health spending, which is administered by the provinces, has increased from nearly 35 percent of their budgets in 1999 to 46 percent today. In Ontario, the most populous province, it is set to reach 80 percent by 2030, leaving pennies for everything else the government does."[40]

Eighty percent, huh? Add Chinese debt interest payments and that would be the entirety of U.S. government revenues spoken for. Beleaguered health administrators drowning in deficits will be way beyond death panels by then, and into living-death panels: Diabetes? Take three aspirin and call us when your legs drop off.

For a peek at the future, wander 'round the public housing in any American city: look at the number of wheelchairs, and the predominantly black men and women with missing limbs. And then look in their faces, and see how young they are. In ten years' time, there will be more, and they will be younger, and they will be wheeling in from the projects and the derelict husks of post-industrial cities, and a familiar sight almost everywhere in the United States.

The unhealthiness of Dependistan underlines the real problem with the modern welfare state: it's not that it's a waste of money but that it's a waste of people. There is a phrase you hear a lot in Canada, Britain, and Europe to describe the collection of positive "rights" (to "free" health care, unemployment benefits, subsidized public transit) to which the citizens of western democracies have become addicted: the "social safety net." It always struck me as an odd term. Obviously, it derives from the circus. But life isn't really a high-wire act, is it? Or at least it didn't use to be. If you put the average chap—or even Barack Obama or Barney Frank—in spangled leotard and tights and on a unicycle and shove him out across the wire, he's likely to fall off. But put the average chap in spangled leotard and tights out into the world and tell him to get a job, find accommodation, raise a family, take responsibility, and he can do it. Or he used to be able to, until the government decided he was "vulnerable" and needed a "safety net."

When did human life become impossible without a "safety net"? My neighbor's family came to my corner of New Hampshire in the winter of 1767–68 when her great-great-great-whatever dragged his huge millstones up the frozen river from Connecticut to build the first gristmill on a swift-running brook in the middle of uncleared forest in a four-year-old township comprising a dozen families. And he did it without first applying for a federal business development grant. No big deal. Her family's nothing special, my town's nothing special: that's the point. It was routine—in a pre-"safety net" society.

In his book *Soft Despotism, Democracy's Drift*, Paul Rahe writes, "Human dignity is bound up with taking responsibility for conducting one's own affairs."[41] But today the state cocoons "one's own affairs" so thoroughly as to remove almost all responsibility from modern life, and much of human dignity with it. And, if personal consequences have been all but abolished, societal consequences are harder to dodge.

The welfare state is less a social safety net than a kind of cage—a large cage but a cage nonetheless. And its occupants are not a trapeze act but more like an expensive zoo animal. Think of a panda. He's the most expensive item in any zoo's budget: those American institutions lucky enough to host a big cuddly panda spend some three million per annum on the cute l'il feller. They feed him, they protect him, they give him everything he could possibly want—except a purpose. Eventually, like Europeans, he can't even be bothered to breed. You put the comeliest lady panda you can find in the cage with him, and he's not interested. He just lies around all day. To reprise Charles Murray's line, Big Government "drains too much of the life from life."

Look, by historical standards, we're loaded. We're the first society in which a symptom of poverty is obesity: every man his own William Howard Taft. Of course we're "vulnerable"—by definition, we always are. But to demand a government organized on the principle of preemptively "taking care" of potential "vulnerabilities" is to make all of us, in the long run, far more vulnerable. A society of children cannot survive, no matter how all-embracing the government nanny.

★ ★ ★ ★ ★

THE KINGDOM OF THE BONOBO

A few years ago, Kenneth Minogue of the London School of Economics wrote that ours is the age of "the new Epicureans" in which the "freedom to choose" trumps all.[42]

A childless couple can choose to conceive.

A female couple can choose to conceive.

A male couple can choose to conceive. Barrie and Tony from Chelmsford, England, had been trying for a child for ages but nothing seemed to work. Then it occurred to them this might be because they're both men. So they advertised for an egg donor on the Internet and then found a Californian woman with a nine-month opening in her womb. A court in the Golden State agreed to register both men as the fathers of their children not so much on the technical grounds that they had "co-mingled" their sperm before FedExing it to their Fallopian timeshare and her turkey baster, but out of a more basic sympathy that this is how Barrie and Tony "self-identify" and it would be cruel to deny them. The mother did not rate a credit on the birth certificate. Nor did the turkey baster. This would seem to be in defiance of reality, but what price biology when measured against self-esteem?[43]

A woman in Bend, Oregon, can choose to become a man, and then a "pregnant man."[44]

A man can choose to become a woman, get halfway there, and then decide it's more fun to "live in the grey area," like "award-winning Canadian writer" Ivan E. Coyote, who prefers to be addressed as he/she and self-identifies as a "very masculine reading estrogen-based organism," and resents the way the hicks at U.S. Customs and Border Protection don't have a check box for that.[45] In 2009 Mr./Ms. Coyote was detained by CBP along with an American friend, "a tall, feminine woman with a heavy moustache."

Biologically, Barrie or Tony, but not both, is the sole father of their child; the "pregnant man" is pregnant but not a man; the he/she living in "the grey area" is in reality black or white—at least according to what we used to call "the facts of life." But issuers of passports, drivers' licenses, and birth certificates increasingly defer to the principle of "self-identification."

In terms of sexual identity, we're freer than almost any society in human history, at least in terms of official validation of our choice to "redefine" ourselves in defiance of biological and physiological reality. But sexual liberty has provided the cover for a sustained assault on individual liberty in every other sphere—in speech rights, in property rights, we are less free than our parents, and getting more constrained every day. Big Government seems to understand that if you let your subjects shag anything that moves and a lot that doesn't they'll mistake their shackles for a complimentary session at the bondage dungeon. Give me liberty or give me sex! Live free or bi-! In an age of suffocating statism, sexual license is the only thing you don't need a license for.

As for the sex, for niche identities and boutique demographics like Mr./ Ms. Coyote and Oregon's pregnant man, things seem to be working out swimmingly. But, among the masses, it's harder to avoid the sheer mountain of human debris being piled up. The story of the last forty years is the mainstreaming of rock-star morality: instant gratification, do your own thing, whatever's your bag. Jodie Foster and her turkey baster are rich enough to weather any unintended consequences of their fling, but the evidence suggests that, for the general populace, defining celebrity down is more problematic. "Oops! I Did It Again" is easy for Britney to say. Less so for Kaylee at the hair salon.

The new school soldiers on, arguing that chastity, fidelity, monogamy, etc., are mere social constructs: we've been indoctrinated into them by repressed cultural hierarchies. Sexual promiscuity is part of our nature: you should be getting it on with that hot chick at Number 27. And her husband. And get your wife in to video it. Screwing whatever you want whenever you want in whatever combination you want is as natural as wearing a mammoth pelt and sitting round the cave rubbing two sticks together. Christopher Ryan and Cacilda Jethá wrote a rather laborious book on the subject, *Sex at Dawn: The Prehistoric Origins of Modern Sexuality*, that demonstrates by frequent recourse to biology, anthropology, ethnography, and primatology that the idea of lifelong heterosexual marriage is a crock imposed on the world by party poopers.[46] Your hunter-gatherer was the king of the swingers, the jungle VIP.

At this point in the argument, it's customary to bring up bonobos. No, not the bloke from U2. He loves Africa, too, but not in that way. The bonobo is some kind of chimp that lives south of the Congo River, and is apparently the closest extant relative to humans. And, like us, he's a bi-guy who can't get enough casual sex. So, if he's hip to it, why have we got so many hang-ups?

That's easy, say the anthropologists: agriculture. Man stopped hunting and gathering and started farming. Bummer, man: families, monogamy, way less action. How ya gonna keep 'em down on the farm after they've seen Paris Hilton? Agriculture was not merely an ecological "catastrophe" (as the author Jared Diamond sees it), but also a sexual one.[47] Sure, these pre-agricultural societies may have had a lot of rape, incest, and female genital mutilation, but at least they knew how to party.

Let us take this argument on its face—that moving from primitive hunter-gatherer societies to agriculture not only introduced to the world concepts of property, autonomy, civil society, and markets but also deeply repressed our libido. In other words, sexual propriety is a function of civilization. The question then arises: Is it possible to restore man's unbounded license without also de-civilizing us? And, if so, what else are we losing with our inhibitions? In a state of nature, without a legal code or even social norms, you're free to pursue all your desires. Then again, so's the guy in the next tree. And, if he's bigger and stronger and if what he happens to desire is you, you may not enjoy it so much when it's you on the receiving end. That's another consequence of the liberation from responsibility: some of us lie around the well-appointed Big Government cage like listless, lethargic pandas and polar bears; others are more like those tigers that, after years of somnolence, wake up one morning and devour their devoted keeper.

The wreckage is impressive. The Sexual Revolution was well-named: it was a revolt not just against sexual norms but against the institutions and values they supported; it was part of an assault against any alternatives to government, civic or moral. Utopianism, writes the philosopher Roger

Scruton, is "not in the business of perfecting the world" but only of demolishing it: "The ideal is constructed in order to destroy the actual."[48] Who needs families, or marriage, or morality? Who needs nations, especially nations with borders? We'll take a jackhammer to the foundations of functioning society and proclaim paradise in the ruins.

"Moderate" Republicans such as Arnold Schwarzenegger like to boast that they're fiscal conservatives and social liberals. But the social liberalism always ends up burying the fiscal conservatism. As Congressman Mike Pence put it, "To those who say we should simply focus on fiscal issues, I say you would not be able to print enough money in a thousand years to pay for the government you would need if the traditional family collapses."[49]

But the collapse of the traditional family is already well advanced—and as part of a conscious Big Government strategy. Big Daddy sings a siren song: a kiss on the hand may be quite continental, but statism is a girl's best friend. So it is in government's interest to diminish those men old-fashioned enough to marry women and thereby woo them away from the Big Stash of Big Daddy Statist. Big Government's bias against marriage and family isn't an unforeseen quirk of the tax code. It's in logical, strategic support of its mission—to expand government and diminish everything else. How's it going? Well, 40 percent of American children are now born out of wedlock.[50] A majority of Hispanic babies are born to unmarried mothers. So are 70 percent of black children. And so are 70 percent of the offspring of non-Hispanic white women with a high school education and an income under $20,000. Entire new categories of crime have arisen in the wake of familial collapse, like the legions of daughters abused by their mom's latest live-in boyfriend. Congressman Pence's doomsday scenario is already here: millions and millions of American children are raised in transient households and moral vacuums that make not just social mobility but even elemental character formation all but impossible. In an America of fewer jobs, more poverty, more crime, more drugs, more disease, and growing ethno-cultural resentments, the shattering of the indispensable social building block will have catastrophic consequences.

★ ★ ★ ★ ★

SPLITSVILLE

What prevents the "state popular" from declining into a "state despotic"? As Tocqueville saw it, what mattered was the strength of the intermediary institutions between the sovereign and the individual. In France, the revolution abolished everything, and subordinated all institutions to the rule of central authority. The New World was more fortunate: "The principle and lifeblood of American liberty" was, according to Tocqueville, municipal independence.

Does that distinction still hold? In the twentieth century the intermediary institutions were belatedly hacked away—not just self-government at town, county, and state level, but other independent pillars: church, civic associations, the family. After the diminution of every intervening institution, very little stands between the individual and the sovereign, which is why the latter now assumes the right to insert himself into every aspect of daily life and why Henrietta Hughes in Fort Myers, Florida, thinks it entirely normal to beseech the Wizard in the far-off Emerald City, where the streets are paved with borrowed green, to do something about her bathroom.

In its debased contemporary sense, liberalism is a universalist creed. It's why the left dislikes federalism. Federalism means borders, and borders mean there's always somewhere else to go: the next town, the next county, the next state. I'm pro-choice and I vote—with my feet. Universal liberalism would rather deny you that choice. America has dramatically expanded not just government generally, but nowhere-else-to-go government in particular. As Milton Friedman wrote in 1979:

> From the founding of the Republic to 1929, spending by governments at all levels, federal, state, and local, never exceeded 12 percent of the national income except in time of major war, and two-thirds of that was state and local spending. Federal spending typically amounted to 3 percent or less of the national income. Since 1933 government spending has never

been less than 20 percent of national income and is now over
40 percent, and two-thirds of that is spending by the federal
government.... By this measure the role of the federal government in the economy has multiplied roughly tenfold in the
past half-century.[51]

The object is to reduce and eventually eliminate alternatives—to subsume
everything within the Big Government monopoly. Statists prefer national
one-size-fits-all—and ultimately planet-wide one-size-fits-all. Borders create the nearest thing to a free market in government—as the elite well
understand when they seek to avoid the burdens they impose on you. John
Kerry, a Big Tax senator from a Big Tax state, preferred to register his yacht
in Rhode Island to avoid half-a-million bucks in cockamamie Massachusetts "boat sales and use" tax.[52] This is federalism at work: states compete,
and, when they get as rapacious as the Bay State, even their own pro-tax
princelings start looking for the workarounds.

Bazillionaire senators will always have workarounds—for their land,
for their yachts, for their health care. You won't. Meanwhile, they're relaxed
about cities and states going broke—because it's a great pretext for propel-
ling government ever upward. When California goes bankrupt, the Golden
State's woes will be nationalized and shared with the nation at large: the
feckless must have their irresponsibility rewarded and the prudent get stuck
with the tab. Passing Sacramento's buck to Washington accelerates the
centralizing pull in American politics and eventually eliminates any advantage to voting with your feet. It will be as if California and New York have
burst their bodices like two corpulent gin-soaked trollops and rolled over
the fruited plain to rub bellies at the Mississippi. If you're underneath, it's
not going to be fun.

What then are the alternatives? And, if you're a relatively sane, lightly
populated state such as Wyoming or a fiscally viable powerhouse like Texas,
are you prepared to beggar yourself for the privilege of keeping fifty stars
on Old Glory?

In 2010, just as a federal court was striking down the Arizona legislature's attempt to control the state's annexation by illegal aliens, far away in the Hague the International Court of Justice declared that the province of Kosovo's unilateral declaration of independence from Serbia two years earlier "did not violate any applicable rule of international law."[53] Certain European secessionist movements—in Spain, Belgium, and elsewhere—took great comfort in the ruling. Russia and China opposed it, because they have restive minorities—Muslims in the Caucacus, and the Uighurs in Xinjiang—and they intend to keep them within their borders.[54] The United States barely paid any attention: if the ICJ's opinion was of any broader relevance, it was relevant to foreigners, and that was that. But, taken together, the Hague and Arizona decisions raise an interesting question: What holds the United States together? And will it continue to hold?

In 2006, the last remaining non-Serb republic in Yugoslavia flew the coop and joined Croatia, Macedonia, Bosnia … hold on, isn't it Bosnia-Herzegovina? Or has Herzegovina split, too? Who cares? Slovenia's independent and so is Slovakia. Slavonia wasn't, or not the last time I checked. But Montenegro is, and East Timor, and Tajikistan, and Uzbekistan, and every other Nickelandimistan between here and Mongolia. Since the fall of the Berlin Wall, big countries (the Soviet Union, Yugoslavia, Indonesia) and not-so-big countries (Czechoslovakia) have been getting smaller. Why should the United States remain an exception to this phenomenon? Especially as it gets poorer—and more statist.

For the best part of a century, America's towns, counties, and states have been ceding power to the central metropolis—even though, insofar as it works at all, Big Government works best in small countries, with a sufficiently homogeneous population to have sufficiently common interests. In *The Size of Nations*, Alberto Alesina and Enrico Spolaore note that, of the ten richest countries in the world, only four have populations above one million: the United States (310 million people), Switzerland (a little under 8 million), Norway, and Singapore (both about 5 million).[55] Small nations, they argue, are more cohesive and have less need for buying off ethnic and regional factions. America has been the exception that proves the rule because it's a highly decentralized federation. But, as Messrs. Alesina and Spolaore argue, if America were as centrally governed as France, it would break up.

That theory is now being tested on a daily basis. To ram government health care down the throats of America, Congress bought off regional factions with deals like the Cornhusker Kickback and the Louisiana Purchase. It is certainly no stranger to buying off ethnic factions in pursuit of the black and Hispanic vote—with immigration un-enforcement and affirmative action. Yet to attempt to impose centralized government on a third of a billion people from Maine to Hawaii is to invite failure on a scale unknown to history.

In the years ahead America will have its Slovakias and Slovenias, formally and informally. But it cannot remain on its present path and hold its territorial integrity.

Let us grant that the United States is not such a patchwork quilt of different ethnicities as Yugoslavia; it's a "melting pot"—or it was. Let us further accept for the sake of argument that the United States' success was unconnected to the people who established it and created its institutions and culture. It is famously a "proposition nation," defined not by blood but by an idea:

> Here, both the humblest and most illustrious citizens alike know that nothing is owed to them and that everything has to be earned. That's what constitutes the moral value of America. America did not teach men the idea of freedom; she taught them how to practice it.[56]

Who said that? A Frenchman: Nicolas Sarkozy, addressing Congress in 2007. But what happens when America no longer teaches men how to practice freedom? What then is its *raison d'être*? Does it have any more reason to stick together than any other "proposition nation" that dumps the proposition? Such as, to take only the most obvious example, the Soviet Union. What is there to hold a post-prosperity, constrained-liberty, un-Dreamt America together? The nation's ruling class has, in practical terms, already seceded from the idea of America. In the ever more fractious, incoherent polity they're building as a substitute, why would they expect their discontented subjects not to seek the same solution as Slovenes and Uzbeks?

Once upon a time, the mill owner and his workers lived in the same town. Now American municipalities are ever more segregated: the rich live among the rich, the poor come from two or three towns away to clean their pools. Nor is the segregation purely economic. The aforementioned Bell, California, was the town whose citizens had a per capita income of $24,800 but a city management that awarded themselves million-dollar salary-and-benefits packages. It comes as no surprise to discover 90 percent of its inhabitants speak a language other than English at home. Bell is an impoverished Latin American city, and so, like thousands of others south of the border, it has corrupt, rapacious Latin American government. Celebrate diversity!

Ask not for whom Bell tolls. Joe Klein, the novelist and columnist, was one of the most adamant of media grandees that the Tea Party's millions of "teabaggers" were "racists and nativists." "Sarah Palin's fantasy America," he explained to his readers at *Time* magazine, "is a different place now, changing for the worse, overrun by furriners of all sorts: Latinos, South Asians, East Asians, homosexuals … to say nothing of liberated, uppity blacks."[57] Joe, naturally, is entirely cool with all that. "The things that scare the teabaggers—the renewed sense of public purpose and government activism, the burgeoning racial diversity, urbanity and cosmopolitanism—are among the things I find most precious and exhilarating about this country."

Joe Klein finds "the burgeoning racial diversity, urbanity and cosmopolitanism" of America so "exhilarating" that he lives in Pelham, New York, which is 87.33 percent white. By contrast, Sarah Palin's racist xenophobic hick town of Wasilla, Alaska, is 85.46 percent white. (Percentages courtesy

of the 2000 census.) As for those "furriners of all sorts" that Klein claims to
dig, Pelham's "uppity blacks" make up only 4.57 percent of the population,
and Asians, whether of the southern or eastern variety, just 3.96 percent.
Unlike Wasilla, which is a long way to go, Pelham is within reach of splen-
didly diverse, urbane, and cosmopolitan *quartiers*—the Bronx, for example—yet Joe Klein, Mister Diversity, chooses not to reside in any of them,
and prefers to live uppitystate of the uppity blacks. Statistically speaking,
he lives in a less diverse neighborhood overrun by fewer "furriners" than
that chillbilly bonehead's inbred redoubt on the edge of the Arctic Circle.
Yet she and her supporters are the "racists and nativists," while Joe preens
himself on his entirely theoretical commitment to "diversity."[58] He would
seem to be volunteering himself as a near parodic illustration of the late
Joseph Sobran's observation that "the purpose of a college education is to
give you the correct view of minorities, and the means to live as far away
from them as possible."[59]

I don't mean to single out Joe Klein, who I'm sure is the soul of kindness
to lame dogs, l'il ol' ladies, uppity blacks, and South Asian furriners, where'er
he encounters them. No doubt Pelham has the occasional African-American college professor, East Asian hedge-fund manager, and perhaps even a
Muslim software developer or two sprinkled among its 87.33 percent
upscale honky populace. But Joe Klein is like a lot of Americans of his class:
"diversity" is an attitude rather than a lived experience.

And it will be ever more so: the more starkly we Balkanize into Bells
and Pelhams, the more frenziedly the Kleins of the world will bang the
"diversity" drum. The more rarefied the all but all-white communities get,
the more "COEXIST!" stickers they'll plaster on their Priuses: hybridity is
for your cars, not your municipal demographic profile.

In an age of political correctness, older people sometimes express
bewilderment at the lack of "common sense." But you can't have common
sense in a society with less and less in common: What does a gay hedonist
in San Francisco have in common with a Michiganistan mullah? What
does a Mississippi Second Amendment gun nut have in common with a

Berkeley diversity enforcement officer? What social conventions can bind them all? Even as we degenerate into ever more micro-regulations ever more targeted for ever more bewildering permutations, assertive identities will figure out ways to wiggle free.

But forget gays and Muslims and consider two sixtysomething white-bread Wasps living side-by-side in Yonkers, New York: At Number 27 is a lady who retired from teaching in the local school at the age of fifty-nine and lives on an annual pension of $78,255, exempt from state and local tax, with gold-plated health benefits, and everything inflation-proofed. At Number 29 is a guy exactly the same age who owns a hardware store, can't afford to retire, has health issues and crummy provision for amelioration thereof, yet will be working till he dies, while his neighbor enjoys a lavish two-decade retirement that he paid for in his taxes. This is a recipe for civil war, and no gay hedonists or firebreathing mullahs need be involved.

The "happy" ending for a statist America is an ever more self-segregating patchwork of cultural ghettoes from the barrios of California to the mosques of Dearborn to the beaches of Fire Island, each with its own TV networks, fashions, churches, mores, history, even children's names (Connor, Mohammed, Tyrone), but presided over by a bloated centralized government that presents itself as the sole legitimate arbiter between these factions, as they compete for its favors while ever more onerously taxed. What kind of America would that be? E pluribus who-num?

★ ★ ★ ★ ★

BORDER COUNTRY

"Would it not be easier," wrote Bertolt Brecht after the East German uprising in 1953, "for the government to dissolve the people and elect another?"

The thought has occurred to several governments over the years, and I don't mean the dictatorships. The easiest way to elect a new people is to import them. So the Eloi not only turn a blind eye to mass "undocumented" immigration, but facilitate it, and use the beleaguered productive class to subsidize it. Grade schools are not allowed to ask parents if they're in the country legally, so there has been a massive expansion of "bilingual education" from the Rio Grande to municipalities within a few miles of the Canadian border: a school system that can't teach its charges in one language has smoothly diversified into not teaching them in two. Across America, school district taxpayers are funding the subversion of their own communities.

Almost every claim made for the benefits of mass immigration is false. "Sober-minded economists reckon that the potential gains from freer global migration are huge," writes Philippe Legrain in *Immigrants: Your Country Needs Them*. "The World Bank reckons that if rich countries allowed their workforce to swell by a mere three percent by letting in an extra 14 million workers from developing countries between 2001 and 2025, the world would be $356 billion a year better off, with the new migrants themselves gaining $162 billion a year, people who remain in poor countries $143 billion, and natives in rich countries $139 billion."[60]

$139 billion? From "a mere" 14 million extra immigrants? Wow!

As Christopher Caldwell points out in his book *Reflections on the Revolution in Europe*, the aggregate gross domestic product of the world's advanced economies for the year 2008 was estimated by the International Monetary Fund at close to $40 trillion. So an extra $139 billion works out to an extra, er, 0.0035. Caldwell compares the World Bank argument to Dr. Evil's triumphant announcement (in the film *Austin Powers*) that he's holding the world hostage for *one million dollars!!!* "Sacrificing 0.0035 of your economy would be a pittance to pay for starting to get your country back."[61] As for that extra $139 billion divided between the inhabitants of all the world's "rich countries," that works out to less than what the U.S. Government spent in 2010 on unemployment insurance ($160 billion).

So much for the economic argument in capitalist terms. In welfare terms, Europeans were told they needed immigrants to help prop up their otherwise unaffordable social entitlements: in reality, Germany's *Gastarbeiter* ("guest workers") are heavy on the *Gast-*, ever lighter on the—*arbeiter*. Turkish immigrants have three times the rate of welfare dependency as ethnic Germans, and their average retirement age is fifty.[62] Foreigners didn't so much game the system as discover, thanks to family "reunification" and other lollipops, that it demanded nothing of them. Entire industries were signed up for public subsidy. Two-thirds of French imams are on the dole.[63] Does the World Bank set their welfare checks on the debit side of that spectacular 0.0035 economic growth? Or does that count as valuable long-term investment in the critical economic growth sector of incendiary mullahs? A dependence on mass immigration is neither a goldmine nor an opportunity to flaunt your multicultural bona fides, but a structural weakness.

"Moderate" Republicans often say that the party base represents a declining demographic (too white) and that the GOP needs to do more to reach out to Hispanics and other fast-growing segments of the population. The argument would seem to assume that this dramatic demographic shift is an entirely natural development. Why, after all, are white guys in decline and Hispanics on the rise?

Because the governing class decided, with the 1965 immigration act and much that has followed, that that's the way it's going to be. In the not entirely likely event that the GOP could persuade Hispanics to vote in overwhelming numbers for small government, the Democrats would look elsewhere for new clients—Muslims, say, maybe from Somalia, a nation which, in barely more than a decade, has transformed the welfare profile even of such backwaters as Lewiston-Auburn, Maine.[64] "Moderate" Republicans would then argue that the party's white-Hispanic base was now stagnating, and that the GOP needs to do more to reach out to Lewistan-Auburnistan.

The problem with dissolving the people and electing another is that you'd have to be a genius to pull off such a transformation without any unintended consequences. On the scale and speed with which much of the West has attempted it, you quickly reach a tipping point, in which the cultural capital of a functional nation state has been exhausted and what follows is … something else. The particular nature of America's mass illegal immigration is almost consciously designed to fracture the republic, and lead to enormous tracts of the country becoming entirely dysfunctional.

For the corporate right, undocumented immigrants mean cheap labor. For the statist left, they mean dependents—and cheap votes. For sentimentalists in between, it's an act of ethnocultural penance: hence, the Cinco de Mayo observances in schoolhouses up and down the land. The left are right. Big Government centralists don't mind about the costs Undocumented America imposes, because in the main it imposes them on states, cities, and school districts—and thus makes previously self-sufficient branches of government ever more dependent on central authority. And just as Big Government doesn't care about the impact on local government, Big Business doesn't care about the impact of illegal labor on small business. This is a recipe for civil strife, if not, ultimately, civil war.

The corporate right wanted open borders for cheap workers in part because the statist left has made American workers too expensive: you can ship manufacturing jobs to cheaper labor overseas, but it's not so easy with hotel chambermaids and seasonal agricultural workers. Meanwhile, the statist left favored open borders as a way of importing voters: untold millions of poor, ill-educated people with little English would need government services, and untold hundreds of thousands of bureaucrats would need to be hired to service them. And so Big Government grows its base. Most illegal immigrants arrived in the Southwest, where states are not red like the Old South nor blue like the Northeast, but kinda purple—50/50 congressional districts and Senate seats where a few anchor babies here and English-as-a-Second-Language programs there and the Democratic Party can tip the demographics permanently in its favor. In such a world, what happens when the economy nosedives and you have competing groups of poor whites, poor blacks, and poor Hispanics chasing ever fewer jobs and crushing the welfare system through sheer numbers?

The left was smarter than the right: the business class told itself it was importing hardworking families who just want a shot at the American Dream. But welfare mocks the Ellis Island virtues, upending them as easily as the shattered Statue of Liberty Charlton Heston stumbled across in the sands of a ruined planet. In an America with ever bigger government and ever poorer people, the dependency rationale for illegal immigration will win out over the business rationale. Seventy percent of births at the San Joaquin General Hospital in Stockton, California, are the so-called "anchor babies" born to illegals.[65] In related news, by 2010 Stockton's school district had a deficit of $25 million.[66] Same thing at Dallas General: 70 per cent of newborns are "anchor babies."[67] Seven out of ten isn't any kind of "minority"; it's the dominant culture of America's tomorrow.

As for "racist" Arizona, the majority of its schoolchildren are already Hispanic.[68] So, even if you sealed the border today, the state's future is as a Hispanic society: that's a given. Maybe it'll all work out swell. The citizenry never voted for it, but they got it anyway. Because all the smart guys bemoaning the irrational bigots knew what was best for them.

To the coastal Eloi, "undocumented immigrants" are the unseen Morlocks who mow your lawn while you're at work and clean your office while you're at home. (That's the real apartheid: the acceptance of a permanent "undocumented" servant class by far too many "documented" Americans who assuage their guilt by pathetic self-serving sentimentalization of immigration.) But in border states illegal immigration is life and death. A few days after Arizona passed its new law, I gave a speech in Tucson for the Goldwater Institute, and a lady came up to me afterwards to talk about the camp of illegals that's pitched up on the edge of her land, a few miles from downtown, but where the Federal Government has posted highway "Danger" signs warning the public that travel beyond this point is "not recommended." My audience member had no choice in the matter: she's not passing through; this is her home—and, if the Government of the United States is now putting up signs explaining that its writ no longer runs, they didn't think to warn her ahead of time. So she lies awake at night, fearful for her children and alert to strange noises in the yard. President Obama, shooting from his lip, attacked the Arizona law as an offense against "fairness."[69] But where's the fairness for this woman's family? Because her home is in Arizona rather than Hyde Park, Chicago, she's just supposed to get used to living under siege? She has to live there, while the political class that created this situation climbs back into the limo and gets driven far away from the intimidation, and the cartel hits, and the remorseless ebbing of U.S. sovereignty. The fetishization of the Undocumented is a form of class warfare waged against poor whites by Eloi elites who don't have to live with the consequences of the socioeconomic experiments they impose on others.

As for "the jobs Americans won't do," most of them would be more accurately categorized as the jobs American employers won't hire Americans to do—because, in a business culture ever more onerously regulated, the immigration status of one's employees has become one of the easiest levers for controlling costs. Why would this change? After all, as the official unemployment climbed to 10 percent and the non-college-educated unemployment rate hit 15 percent and the unofficial rate among blacks and other groups rose even higher, the rote-like invocations of "the jobs Americans won't do" was affected not a whit. If Americans won't do them (or won't be hired to do them) even at a time of high unemployment, maybe *that's* the problem that needs to be addressed. Instead, to solve an artificially created labor shortage, the U.S. government deemed U.S. immigration law unenforceable and illegitimate. And so the armies of the Undocumented will swell exponentially as Mexico dissolves into a murderous narco-state feeding ever greater northern habits. What is happening on the southern border is the unmaking of America.

★ ★ ★ ★ ★

DESTINY'S MANIFEST

There was a story that zipped around the Internet a few years ago, about a Mexican Air Force pilot who'd supposedly photographed a UFO. North of the border the response to this amazing news, from professional comedians to website comment sections, was well nigh universal: *Mexico has an air force. Who knew?*[70]

Ha-ha. Mexico. Third World joke. Actually, two centuries back, it had a bigger military than the United States. Like America, it was a settler society, but older and larger: Mexico City was founded in 1524, and, when Madrid belatedly recognized the independence of "New Spain" in 1821, the city gave its name to a country—and, indeed, empire: Imperio Mexicano. Not as silly as it may sound. Before the Louisiana Purchase, if you'd been asked to predict which settler capital, Mexico City or Washington, would emerge as the seat of power in post-colonial North America, many an analyst would have plumped for the Spaniards. They had an imperialist's sweep: when they seceded from Madrid, they did so in a "Solemn Act of the Declaration of Independence of Northern America," which definition stretched all the way north to what's now the Oregon border and quite a ways south, to Panama. By comparison, the United States seemed a weak and vulnerable territory holed up east of the Appalachians. It was a land economically dependent on exports but with few strategic transportation routes and unable to protect its sea lanes.

And then Napoleon sold America the port of New Orleans. "I have given England a maritime rival who sooner or later will humble her pride," he said, making mischief.[71] But the Mexican border was less than 200 miles from the newly American port, and a mere hundred from the expanded republic's critical artery, the Mississippi River. The wannabe Imperio, for its part, had a problem of its own. The land west of New Orleans, in the Mexican department of Texas, was mostly desert or mountains, and consequently lightly inhabited. So it suited the southern power to let American immigrants settle in this unpromising terrain—"doing the jobs Mexicans won't do," one might say. When Sam Houston decided it was time for northern settlers to rebel, the distant imperial capital of Mexico City had a hell of a time just getting troops through to Texas in order even to be able to hold a war. The defeats that left the U.S.-Mexican border where it is now delegitimized New Spain's ruling class, destabilized the politics of Mexico City for the better part of a century, and led to the squalid and violent polity we know today.

There are, give or take, 200 countries in the world. If you had 20 million
"undocumented" immigrants more or less proportionately distributed
between those 200 countries—Irish, Uzbeks, Belgians, Botswanans—then
maybe they would be assimilable, although even then it would be an
unprecedented challenge. But borderland immigration is different. In British terms, consider not the rapidly Islamizing East London or Yorkshire,
where Muslims are aliens replacing a native population, but think instead
of Ulster: when Ireland came under the English Crown, Scots Protestants
settled the north. When the south seceded to become the Irish Free State in
1922, the United Kingdom got a land border for the first time in its history.
The loyalists could have had all nine counties of historic Ulster for their
Northern Ireland statelet, but insisted on a mere six because they knew they
did not have the numbers to hold the other three. And even in the six counties thousands were murdered in the decades ahead. A border settles things,
but only conditionally: for Irish nationalists in Fermanagh and Tyrone, the
line meant nothing. This was Ireland, not Britain, and they had been there
first. That's how many Mexicans feel about the southern frontier: Arizona
is Mexico, not the United States, and it was Mexico first. You don't have to
be a large minority to cause an awful lot of trouble—as the British found
out on a small patch of turf where Irish nationalists were outnumbered
two-to-one by Unionists. And you don't even have to believe so fervently
that you're willing to kill and bomb. You just have to believe enough to live
it, in your daily routine. In the Arizona of tomorrow, Hispanics will be not
a minority but a majority: they will not assimilate with the United States
because they don't need to. Instead, the United States will assimilate with
them, and is already doing so, day by day.

In July 2010, Maywood, California, became the first city in America
to lay off its entire workforce, including the police and fire departments,
and contract out all services.[72] It did this because the city was so misman-
aged that its insurers canceled the coverage and every alternative provider
declined to accept the city's business. I was interested to discover, via the
2000 census, that the city is 96.33 percent Hispanic. Celebrate lack of

diversity! What will it be by the time the 2010 census numbers are out? 98.7 percent? Maywood does not seem an obviously Spanish name, and in fact the city was named for Miss May Wood, a young lady who worked for the real estate developers responsible for the original subdivision that led to the incorporation of the city in 1924. If you lived there in the boom years of the Forties, Fifties, and Sixties, you'll remember a blue collar town with good jobs, a civic culture, and a population that reflected the ethnic mix of the time. Then the jobs disappeared, and the civic culture declined, and Maywood turned 96.33 percent Hispanic in little more than two decades. So much for the melting pot. Today, one third of the population is estimated to be "illegal."[73] I put it in quotations because possession is nine-tenths of the law and in this case there's no doubt who possesses Maywood. How many other towns will similarly transform, and how fast?

Culture is not immutable. But changing culture is tough and thankless and something America's ever weakening assimilationists no longer have the stomach for. So go with the numbers: the Southwest will be Mexican, and Washington's writ will no longer run. The Mexican-American War established the borders of the America we know today. It took a couple of centuries, but illegal immigration has reversed the results of that conflict. America won the war, Mexico won the peace.

For Eloi America, it's a short step from ethnocultural penance to ethnocultural masochism. Los Angeles, New York, and other "sanctuary cities" have formally erased the distinction between U.S. citizens and the armies of the undocumented. This is the active collusion by multiple jurisdictions in the subversion of United States sovereignty. In Newark, New Jersey, it means an illegal-immigrant child rapist is free to murder three high-school students execution-style for kicks on a Saturday night.[74] In Somerville, Massachusetts, it means two deaf girls are raped by MS-13 members.[75] And in the 7-Eleven parking lot in Falls Church, Virginia, where four young men obtained the picture ID with which they boarded their flight on September 11, 2001, it means Saudi Wahhabists figuring out that, if the "sanctuary nation" (in Michelle Malkin's phrase) offers such rich pickings to imported killers and imported gangs, why not to jihadists?[76]

So here is another proposition for the proposition nation: Is it more likely that these trends will reverse—or that they will accelerate? Consider life in a permanently poorer America with higher unemployment, less social mobility, and any prospect for self-improvement crushed by the burden of government. Will that mean more or less marijuana? More or less cocaine? More or fewer meth labs? Mexican cartels account for approximately 70 percent of the narcotics that enter the U.S. to feed American habits.[77] Arizona already has a kidnapping rate closer to Mexico's than to New England's. Are the numbers likely to rise or fall in an ever more Mexicanized United States? If you're lucky, San Diego will seem no worse than Cancun, eastern resort capital of the Caribbean Riviera and generally thought of as relatively far from the scene of Mexico's drug wars.[78] Yet even in Cancun, within the space of a year, the head of the city's anti-drugs squad was murdered; the chief of police was arrested on drugs-trafficking charges; and then the mayor was, too. We will start to read similar stories of wholesale corruption and subversion from the cities of the American Southwest. And similar tales of depravity, too: in 2010, the bodies of four men and two women were found in a cave on the outskirts of Cancun.[79] They had been tortured. Their abdomens were branded with a "Z." The mark of Zorro? No, the Zeta drug cartel. Three of them had had their chests ripped open and their hearts removed.

As I said, Cancun is regarded as one of the towns least afflicted by drug violence. More than 4,000 U.S. soldiers died in Iraq between 2003 and 2010. In 2010 alone, some 13,000 Mexicans were killed in the drug wars.[80] More than 3,000 died in just one town—Ciudad Juarez, across the border from El Paso.[81] America will be importing not just drugs from Mexico, but the dominant players, the municipal outreach, and the business practices.

It's foolish to assume "globalization" is a purely economic phenomenon. In 2006, a group of Muslim men raised in suburban Ontario were arrested and charged with a terrorist plot that included plans to behead the Prime

Minister.[82] Almost simultaneously, the actual heads of three decapitated police officers were found in the Tijuana River.[83] In 2010, four headless bodies were left dangling from a bridge in the picture-postcard tourist town of Cuernavaca.[84] The same year, authorities arrested a leading hit-man beheader for one of the Mexican drug cartels.[85] He was fourteen years old, and a U.S. citizen, too (the anchor baby of an undocumented Californian). The drug cartels weren't Muslim last time I checked, but decapitation isn't just for jihadists anymore: if you want to get ahead, get a head.

How about stoning? Isn't that something they do to women in Iran? Yes, but a good idea soon finds an export market. In 2010, the body of Gustavo Sanchez, mayor of Tancitaro, in the Mexican state of Michoacán, was found with that of an aide in an abandoned truck.[86] Both men had been stoned to death. Tancitaro isn't anywhere important: it's a town of 26,000 people. Nonetheless, in the year before the mayor's fatal stoning, the city council chief was kidnapped and tortured to death, and Sanchez' predecessor and seven other officials resigned after being threatened by drug gangs and left unprotected by local cops. The entire 60-man police department was subsequently fired. In Santiago, they found their mayor's corpse with his eyes gouged out.[87] Mexico is degenerating into a narco-terrorist enterprise with a sovereign state as a minor subsidiary. George W. Bush liked to say of Iraq that we're fighting them over there so that we don't have to fight them over here. In Mexico, America has no choice in the matter: the decapitations and stonings and eye-gougings will move north of the border.

Of course, the real narco-state is not Mexico but America: if we didn't take drugs, we wouldn't need someone to supply them, and running a cartel wouldn't be such a lucrative enterprise. America's hedonist stupor has real consequences for others, and we will be living with them north of the "border" all too soon. But it's not necessary to argue about the drug cartels, or the gang killers, the child rapists, the drunk-drivers. Even without these, the central fact of Hispanic immigration—the wholesale transformation of innumerable American municipalities at unprecedented speed—would place a huge question mark over the future. Don't take my word for it, take the *New York Times'*. In 2009, it ran a story of immigrants in Langley Park, Maryland, "Struggling to Rise in Suburbs" (as the headline put it).[88] Usual sludge, but in the middle of it, helpfully explaining Langley Park to his readers, the reporter, Jason DeParle, wrote as follows: "Now nearly two-thirds Latino and foreign-born, it has the aesthetics of suburban sprawl and the aura of Central America. Laundromats double as money-transfer stores. Jobless men drink and sleep in the sun. There is no city government, few community leaders, and little community."

At which point I stopped, and went back, and reread it. For it seemed to me at first glance that Mr. DeParle was airily citing laundromats doubling as money-transfer stores, jobless men drinking and sleeping in the sun, and dysfunctional metropolitan government all as evidence of "the aura of Central America." And that can't be right, can it? Only a couple of days earlier, some Internet wags had leaked a discussion thread from the Journo-List, the exclusive virtual country club where all the hepcat liberals hang out. In this instance, the media grandees were arguing vehemently that Martin Peretz of *The New Republic* was, in the elegant formulation one associates with today's J-school alumni, a "crazy-ass racist."[89] The proof that this lifelong liberal is a "fucking racist" came in his observations on our friendly neighbor to the south: "I am extremely pessimistic about Mexican-American relations," said Mr. Peretz. "A (now not quite so) wealthy country has as its abutter a Latin society with all of its characteristic deficiencies: congenital corruption, authoritarian government, anarchic politics, near-tropical work habits, stifling social mores, Catholic dogma with the usual unacknowledged compromises, an anarchic counter-culture and increasingly violent modes of conflict."[90]

Martin Peretz's assumptions about "the aura of Central America" are not so very different from Jason DeParle's, but Mr. Peretz brought down the wrath of his own side's politically correct enforcers. Even though his remarks are utterly unexceptional to anyone familiar with Latin America. But since when have the PC police cared about observable reality?

Langley Park is a good example of where tiptoeing around on multiculti eggshells leads: there is literally no language in which what's happening in suburban Maryland can be politely discussed, not if an ambitious politician of either party wishes to remain viable. America is a land where the NAACP complains about the use of the widely known scientific term "black hole" on a Hallmark greeting card, and Hallmark instantly withdraws the card;[91] a land so obsessed by race that, in order to reverse an entirely fictional manifestation of "racism," it invented the subprime mortgage and sat back as it came within a smidgeonette of destroying the housing market, banking system, and insurance industry. But, even if it had, at least we'd have demonstrated our anti-racist bona fides even unto self-destruction, so that's okay.

To exhibit any interest in immigration or its consequences is to risk being marked down as, if not a "racist," at least a "nativist." And "immigration" isn't really what it is, is it? After all, in traditional immigration patterns the immigrant assimilates with his new land, not the new land with the immigrant. Yet in this case the aura of Maryland dissolves like a mirage when faced with "the aura of Central America."

Two generations ago, America, Canada, Australia, and the rest of the developed world took it as read that a sovereign nation had the right to determine which, if any, foreigners it extended rights of residency to. Now only Japan does. Everywhere else, opposition to mass immigration is "nativist," and expressing a preference for one group of immigrants over another is "racist." Until the Sixties, governments routinely distinguished between Irish and Bulgar, Indian and Somali, but now all that matters is the glow of virtue you feel from refusing to distinguish, as if immigration is like a UN peacekeeping operation—one of those activities in which you have no "national interest."

Very few elderly, established residents of Langley Park knowingly voted for societal self-extinction, yet in barely a third of a century it's become a fait accompli. And in a politically correct world there is no acceptable form of public discourse in which to object to it.

And so it just kinda happened. Another proposition: When large tracts of the United States take on "the aura of Central America"—laundromats doubling as money-transfer stores, jobless men drinking and sleeping in the sun, civic collapse, to cite only *New York Times*-observed phenomena—will such a land still be the United States? Or will it increasingly be the northern branch office of Latin America? None of us can say for sure, but, underneath the smiley-face banalities about hard-working families wanting a shot at the American Dream, I think most of us know which way to bet.

Human capital is the most reliable indicator of what society you'll be. Even liberals, even Martin Peretz, even the *New York Times* acknowledge that, at least in unguarded moments. For almost half a century, the human capital of the United States has transformed faster than at any time since the founding of the republic.

"Poor Mexico," Porfirio Diaz, the country's longtime strongman, is supposed to have said. "So far from God, so close to the United States." Today Mexico is America's southern quagmire—farther from God than ever, and not close to the United States but in it.

After the Arizona court decision, Jon Richards published a cartoon in the *Albuquerque Journal*. It showed three Indians standing on the shore watching the Mayflower approach. "Are they legal?" wonders the chief. "What do we do if they have babies?" asks his squaw. "Is it too late to build a fence?" says the brave.[92]

What is the message of this cartoon? That America has always been a land of immigrants? Or that the tide of illegal settlement is going to work out as well for the United States as it did for the Algonquin nation? Is Richards' cartoon just the cheap triumphalism of a self-loathing Anglo's cultural relativism? Or is it actually a portent of the future? The latter isn't so hard to imagine: a largely impoverished Hispanic Southwest, with a few tony Anglo gated communities—or, if you prefer, "reservations."

★ ★ ★ ★ ★

SHADOWLANDS

The Conformicrats live off the fruits of the productive class and they need to keep them in a state of quiescence. They achieve this with their allies in the dependent class by a kind of pincer movement. From above, the ideological aristocracy can inflict any amount of pain through its administrative enforcers. From below, there is the seething dysfunctional jungle of the underclass. You can measure civilized societies by how easy it is to insulate yourself from the predators, and in America it is still easier than in Britain. But, lurking in the Conformicrats' coercion of the beleaguered productive class is the implicit threat of a good cop/bad cop routine—or good statist/dysfunctional statist: if you don't give us what we want—more money for more agencies and more bureaucrats—we may not be able to hold the underclass in check, and you're within easier reach of 'em than we are. It is a worthless guarantee: given the human wreckage piled up by half-a-century of diseducation, welfarism, sexual self-destruction, and much else, the Eloi aristocracy cannot hold a Morlock dependent class in check. "We have not yet seen what man can make of man," wrote the behaviorist B. F. Skinner.[93] Well, we're about to.

Under Big Government, the ruling class get power and perks, some of the ruled class have workarounds (gated communities, offshore accounts), but others among the ruled class just get unruly.

What will the statists do? We are already watching municipalities drown in the pensions liabilities of their bureaucracies. Do they fix the problem or do they cut core services? The latter's the way to bet: you don't fire the police officers, but you reassign them to desk jobs where they'll get out less and thus require fewer vehicles, less gas, less equipment, less ammunition. It's already happening in the poorer cities, but, like rot in the boarded-up houses, the signs of decay will creep further up. A lot of cities will take on the character of Third World swamps the colonial authorities are resigned to losing: the police hole up in well fortified headquarters venturing out in heavily armored vehicles ever more rarely. Think St. Louis, Missouri, or Gary, Indiana, with a Green Zone, and your house is twelve blocks outside the perimeter. When the neighborhood's up for grabs, all that expensive law enforcement of the Security State won't be there for you. Get yourself a gun, while you're still allowed to.

Picture an American airport on the Friday afternoon before a big public holiday—the long, slow trudge to gain admission to the secure area. The
"secure area" won't be just for airports anymore. More and more of America will seek to be "secured" in the interests of constraining the forces on
the other side of the fence. Think of those decapitated heads in Mexico and
hope the cartels don't decide to learn incompetent transit terror from the
jihad—because, inevitably, Big Government will respond with big, bloated,
manpower-intensive, ever more intrusive bureaucratic overreach. A citizenry that shrugged when government bureaucrats took to themselves the
power to poke around with no probable cause in the nooks and crannies
of its genitalia will discover that such extraordinary powers will not remain
penned up in Terminal Three, but will spread—to bus stations, and key
Interstate ramps, and eventually random Main Streets. As the Shoe Bomber
led to the shoeless shuffle and the Panty Bomber led to the federally man-
dated scrotal grope, so the first Suppository Bomber will lead to complimentary federal prostate exams from LAX to JFK.

Then factor in the end of the dollar as global currency. Oil heads up past
five, six, seven bucks a gallon, and everything else follows. That inflation-
proofed schoolmarm in Yonkers isn't going to want to stay at Number 27
when everybody else in the street is poor and hates her. Nobody travels very
much anymore—who can afford it?—but the lines are as long as ever: the
Security State barely bothers to pretend it's for anything other than domestic crowd control. As the armed forces shrink with the dollar, hundreds of
thousands of American troops are demobbed and come home to find that,
whether or not it's over over there, it's certainly over over here. A statist
America won't be a large Sweden—unimportant but prosperous—but
something closer to the Third World. As a dead-end economy drives its
surplus manpower deeper into poverty, addiction, and crime, parts of the
country will take on post-Soviet Russian characteristics, with a gangster
class manipulating social disintegration for its own ends. What's left will be
Latin America, corrupt and chaotic, broke and brutish—for all but a privileged few.

What to do? Where to go? In 1785, the British philosopher Jeremy Bentham began working on his famous "Pan-opticon"—a radial prison in which a central "inspector" could see all the prisoners, but they could never see him. In the computer age, we now have not merely panopticon buildings, but panopticon societies, like modern London, with its wall-to-wall CCTV cameras. Soon perhaps, excepting a few redoubts such as Waziristan and the livelier precincts of the Horn of Africa, we will have a panopticon planet.

Yet high-tech statism still needs an overarching narrative. The "security state" is a tough sell: if you tell people the government is compiling data on them for national security purposes, the left instinctively recoils. But, if you explain that you're doing it to save the planet by monitoring carbon footprints and emissions compliance and mandatory recycling, starry-eyed coeds across the land will twitter their approval, and the middle-class masochists of the developed world will whimper in orgasmic ecstasy as you tighten the screws, pausing only to demand that you do it to them harder and faster. Consider a recent British plan for each citizen to be given an official travel allowance.[94] If you take one flight a year, you'll pay just the standard amount of tax on the journey. But, if you travel more frequently, if you take a second or third flight, you'll be subject to additional levies—all in the interest of saving the planet for Al Gore's polar bear documentaries and his county-sized carbon footprint. The Soviets restricted freedom of movement through the bureaucratic apparatus of "exit visas." The British favor the bureaucratic apparatus of exit taxes: the movement's still free; it's just that there'll be a government processing fee of £412.95. And, in a revealing glimpse of the universal belief in enviro-statism, this proposal came not from the Labour Party but from the allegedly Conservative Party. At their Monday night poker game in hell, I'll bet Stalin, Hitler, and Mao are kicking themselves: "'It's about leaving a better planet to our children?' Why didn't I think of that?"

You remember how President Bush used to talk about illegal immigration—about how we needed to help all those undocumented people "living in the shadows"? Doesn't that sound kinda nice—and restful? Living in the shadows, no government agencies harassing you for taxes and numbers and paperwork. By comparison, those of us in the blazing klieg lights of the nanny state are shadowed everywhere we go: government numbers for this, government cards for that, a life of barcodes and retinal scans, the TSA Obergropinführers at the airport.... You'd almost think that, compared to the 15 or 30 or however many million fine upstanding members of the Undocumented-American community are out there, the 300 or so million in the overdocumented segment of the population get a lousy deal.

Incidentally, over half the illegal population supposedly came to America after September 11, 2001.[95] That's to say, they broke into a country on Code Orange alert. Odd that. Even under the panoptic surveillance of the "security state," certain identity groups seem to be indulged by Big Government. In California one notices that the same regulatory leviathan that thinks nothing of sending in the heavies if a hardware store is offering complimentary coffee to its customers seems somewhat shyer of enforcing its bazillions of building code/food prep/environmental/health and safety rules against ad hoc mobile kitchens serving piping hot Mexican dishes up and down the highway. Park your van, get out the plastic chairs, pull out a tarp for a bit of shade, and start selling. All those county kitchen inspectors and food-prep permit issuers? Not a problem. Victor Davis Hanson, a tireless bicycler round the Golden State's Central Valley, notices the ever proliferating slicks of fat and lard emptied out on the road by such mobile restaurants, as do the crows and squirrels who love lapping them up.[96] In the Panopticon State, the Shadowlands are thriving: a state that presumes to tax and license Joe Schmoe for using the table in the corner of his basement as a home office apparently doesn't spot the half-dozen additional dwellings that sprout in José Schmoe's yard out on the edge of town. Do-it-yourself wiring stretches from bungalow to lean-to trailer to RV to rusting pick-up on bricks, as five, six, eight, twelve different housing units pitch up on one lot. The more Undocumented America secedes from the hyper-regulatory state, the more frenziedly Big Nanny documents you and yours.

This multicultural squeamishness is most instructive. Illegal immigrants are providing a model for survival in an impoverished statist America, and on the whole the state is happy to let them do so. In Undocumented America, the buildings have no building codes, the sales have no sales tax, your identity card gives no clue as to your real identity. In the years ahead, for many poor Overdocumented-Americans, living in the Shadowlands will offer if not the prospect of escape then at least temporary relief. As America loses its technological edge and the present Chinese cyber-probing gets disseminated to the Wikileaks types, the blips on the computer screen representing your checking and savings accounts will become more vulnerable. After yet another brutal attack, your local branch never reconnects to head office; it brings up from the vault the old First National Bank of Deadsville shingle and starts issuing fewer cards and more checkbooks. And then fewer checkbooks and more cash. In small bills.

The planet is dividing into two extremes: an advanced world—Europe, North America, Australia—in which privacy is vanishing and the state will soon be able to monitor you every second of the day; and a reprimitivizing world—Somalia, the Pakistani tribal lands—where no one has a clue what's going on. Undocumented America is giving us a lesson in how Waziristan and CCTV London can inhabit the same real estate, like overlapping area codes. There will be many takers for that in the years ahead. As Documented America fails, poor whites, poor blacks, and many others will find it easier to assimilate with Undocumented America, and retreat into the shadows. It will not merely be states and sub-state jurisdictions that secede, but individuals, too.

★ ★ ★ ★ ★

COUGAR TOWN

In 2003, Bill Clinton and Mikhail Gorbachev got together for an all-star recording of Prokofiev's beloved children's classic, *Peter and the Wolf.*[97] In the original, Peter and his friend the duck are out frolicking in the meadow when the slavering wolf shows up and embarks on his reign of terror. He gulps down the duck as his hors d'oeuvre, and has the cat lined up to follow. But fortunately, Peter gets hold of a rope and uses it as a noose with which to muzzle the wolf and take him into captivity.

In the Clinton version, you won't be surprised to hear, Peter realizes the error of his lupophobia and releases the creature back into the wild. The wolf howls a friendly goodbye. Which is jolly sporting of him when you consider that it's all our fault in the first place. "Forgetting his triumph, Peter thought instead of fallen trees, parched meadows, choked streams, and of each and every wolf struggling for survival," narrates our Bill, addressing the root causes and feeling the wolf's pain. "The time has come to leave wolves in peace."

How about the duck? Is she left in peace? Or in pieces?

Do you recall the weeks before September 11, 2001? On the Eastern Seaboard, it was the summer of shark attacks. Jessie Arbogast, an eight-year-old lad from Pensacola, Florida, had his arm ripped off, but his quick-witted uncle wrestled the predator back to shore, killed him, and retrieved the chewed-up limb from his jaws. The *New York Times*, in an eerie aquatic pre-echo of the left's reaction to 9/11, came down on the side of the shark: "Many people now understand that an incident like the Arbogast attack is not the result of malevolence or a taste for human blood on the shark's part," explained the *Times* editorial. "What it should really do is remind us yet again how much we have to learn about them and their waters."[98]

Why do they hate us? (Underwater version.)

There is a fairly recent journalistic genre, specimens of which now turn up on the news pages with numbing regularity. A cougar kills a dog near the home of Frances Frost in Canmore, Alberta.[99] Miss Frost, an "environmentalist dancer" with impeccable pro-cougar credentials, objects strenuously to suggestions that the predator be tracked and put down. A month later, she's killed in broad daylight by a cougar who's been methodically stalking her.

"I can't believe it happened," wailed a fellow environmentalist. But why not? Cougars prey on species they're not afraid of. So, if they've no reason to be afraid of man, they might as well eat him. He's a lot easier to catch than a deer. Taylor Mitchell, a singer-songwriter, was killed by coyotes in Cape Breton National Park in Nova Scotia.[100] "It's hard to understand why this may be happening," said Derek Quann, a resource conservation manager, after a second attack. "We don't think there's been a significant increase in the population. There could be a larger problem in the ecosystem at play." That was his coy way of suggesting that coyotes are losing their traditional fear of man, and with it their tendency to stay out of his way.

Aside from the boom in Islamic terrorism, the Nineties and the Oughts were also the worst decades ever for shark, bear, alligator, and cougar attacks in North America. The obvious explanation is that there are more of these creatures than ever before—the bear and cougar populations have exploded across the continent. But the more sinister one is that animals have not just multiplied but evolved: they've lost their fear of man. They now see him for what he is: a tasty Jello pudding on legs.

In 2003, Disney brought us its latest animated feature, *Brother Bear*, the usual New Age mumbo-jumbo with a generic Native American gloss. It told the tale of Kenai, a young fellow in a bucolic Pacific Northwest at the end of the Ice Age. To avenge his brother's death, Kenai kills the brown bear responsible. But trouble's a-bruin: his late brother is wise enough to know that killing is not the answer and so gets the Great Spirit to teach Kenai a lesson by transforming him into a bear. He thereby learns that bears are not violent beasts but sensitive beings living in harmony with nature who understand the world they live in far more than man does. I would certainly agree that bears are wiser and more sensitive than man, if only because I've yet to meet a bear who's produced an animated feature as mawkishly deluded as this.

Among the technical advisers on the film, hired to ensure the accurate depiction of our furry friends, was Timothy Treadwell, the self-described eco-warrior from Malibu who became famous for his campaign "to promote getting close to bears to show they were not dangerous."[101] He did this by sidling up to them and singing "I love you" in a high-pitched voice. *Brother Bear* is certainly true to the Treadwell view of brown bears, and he would surely have appreciated the picture had he ever gotten to see it. But, just as Kenai found himself trapped inside a bear, so did Mr. Treadwell—although in his case he was just passing through. In September, a pilot arrived at the ursine expert's camp near Kaflia Bay in Alaska to fly him out and instead found the bits of him and his girlfriend that hadn't yet been eaten buried in a bear's food cache.

Treadwell had always said he wanted to end up in "bear scat," so his fellow activists were inclined to look on the bright side. "He would say it's the culmination of his life's work," said his colleague Jewel Palovak. "He died doing what he lived for."[102]

I wonder if he was revising his view in the final moments. And if his girlfriend was quite so happy to find she had a bit part in "the culmination of his life's work."

You'd have to have a heart of stone not to weep with laughter at the fate of the eco-warrior, but it does make *Brother Bear* somewhat harder to swallow than its technical adviser manifestly was. There are People for the Ethical Treatment of Animals, but sadly no Animals for the Ethical Treatment of People. And, just as bugs are becoming resistant to antibiotics, so the big beasts are changing, too. Wild animals are not merely the creatures of their appetites; they're also astute calculators of risk. Not so long ago, your average bear knew that if he happened upon a two-legged type, the chap would pull a rifle on him and he'd be spending eternity as a fireside rug. But these days it's just as likely that any human being he comes across is some pantywaist Bambi Boomer enviro-sentimentalist trying to get in touch with his inner self. And, if the guy wants to get in touch with his inner self so badly, why not just rip it out of his chest for him?

North American wildlife seems to have figured that out. Why be surprised if other predators do? A soft Eloi culture will bend and accommodate and prostrate—and still be consumed as easily as Timothy Treadwell.

At American airports, to avoid even the hint of a suggestion that people who want to blow up airplanes are more likely to have certain characteristics than others and to maintain the polite fiction that all seven billion inhabitants of the planet pose an equal security risk, the Government of the United States has decreed that federal officials are entitled to inspect your private parts and those of your children and your grandmother. All 300 million sets of American genitalia are up for grabs—without probable cause. God forbid you should be so insensitive as to use "enhanced pat-down" techniques on any Guantanamo detainees, but you can use them on three-year-old girls and octogenarian nuns. Cougars, lambs, sharks, baby seals: we must not profile.

Think of Frances Frost vigorously objecting to any suggestion the predator cougar be tracked down. Al-Qaeda understand that mentality—which is why they advise captured jihadists always to claim they've been tortured, and let the Frances Frosts of the grievance industry help them get lawyered up. So do the armies of the Undocumented. That sends a message about U.S. will, and not just to Latin-American peasants seeking economic betterment.

Picture Timothy Treadwell cooing love songs to his killers. You don't have to go to the Arctic to see that. In Philadelphia, there is an organization called the BDS Coalition. BDS? As in "Bush Derangement Syndrome"? No. It stands for "Boycott, Divestment, Sanctions," and it's an alliance of groups committed to working for "social justice" in "Palestine." So they staged a disruptive "flashdance" at a Philly supermarket to protest the store's "policy" of carrying brands of hummus made by companies perceived to have too close ties to Israel.[103] Watching these young white twentysomething American students "dance into action" around the hapless grocery clerks, you couldn't help noticing that (without wishing to stereotype from modes of dress and levels of hirsuteness) more than a few of the young ladies appeared to be stern feminists, if not, ah, persons of orientation. In America, so what? But try it in Hamas-run Gaza.

There is a group called Queers Against Israeli Apartheid. When they march in Gay Pride parades, they chant:

Butch, femme, bottom, top
Israeli apartheid has to stop.[104]

Queers Against Israeli Apartheid—now there's a cause. When he spoke to
Columbia University, President Ahmadinejad of Iran told his audience that
there are no homosexuals in Iran.[105] Not one. Where are they? On a weekend
visit to Gaza to see the new production of *Mame*? Alas, there was no time
for follow-up questions. In Mullah Omar's Afghanistan, homosexual men
were put to death by being crushed under a wall specifically built for that
purpose.[106] Under the Taliban, it was just about the only work you could
get in the otherwise depressed Afghan construction industry. Have you tried
being a lesbian in Yemen? Have you tried being a *woman* in Yemen?

A few years back, I thought even spaghetti-spined western liberals might
draw the line at "Female Genital Mutilation"—or "FGM," as it's already
known in far too many western hospitals from Virginia to Australia. After
all, it's a key pillar of institutional misogyny in Islam: its entire purpose is
to deny women sexual pleasure. True, a lot of us hapless western men find
we deny women sexual pleasure without even trying, but we don't demand
genital mutilation to guarantee it. On such slender distinctions does civilization rest. Yet already female genital "mutilation" has been replaced by the
less judgmental term of "female genital cutting." In 2010, the American
Academy of Pediatrics floated the suggestion that, because certain, ahem,
"immigrant communities" were shipping their daughters overseas to
undergo "cutting," in a spirit of multicultural compromise perhaps U.S.
pediatricians should amend their opposition to the practice, and provide
a "ritual nick" to young girls.[107]

Nonetheless, at the Gay Pride parade they know their priorities:

Butch, femme, bottom, top
Israeli apartheid has to stop.

Is there a Queers Against Sharia?

Butch, femme, top, bottom
Gay bars in Riyadh?
Hard to spot 'em.
Bottom, top, femme, butch
Pride parade's dull since the Taliban putsch.
Top, bottom, butch, femme
With complimentary FGM.
Top, bott, butch, femme, trans
Quit your chanting and read your Korans.

There is a moral frivolity to the Eloi's generalized concerns for "the planet." But it quickly advances to the next stage—a moral decadence that expresses itself by venerating those who will gladly kill them when they have served their purpose as useful idiots. Listen to Sheikh Muhammad al-Gamei'a, an Egyptian Muslim of such exemplary moderation that he was the head imam at the Islamic Cultural Center and Mosque in New York at the time of 9/11's, er, "controlled explosion." Shortly thereafter, he explained why he agrees with Philadelphia BDS Coalition and Queers Against Israeli Apartheid that it's all the fault of the Jews: "You see these people all the time, everywhere, disseminating corruption, heresy, homosexuality, alcoholism, and drugs. Because of the Jews there are strip clubs, homosexuals, and lesbians every-where. They do this to impose their hegemony and colonialism on the world...."[108]

So Jews are to blame for lesbians? Do the prancing sapphists in that Philly supermarket know they're just tools of the International Jewish Conspiracy?

Fortunately for them, they're taking their courageous stand for Palestin-ian "social justice" in Pennsylvania. Not everyone keeps such a discreet distance. In 2008, the Italian performance artist Pippa Bacca set off to hitch-hike from Milan to the Palestinian Territories to promote "world peace." She was dressed as a bride, and the purpose of her trip was to show that if only you put your trust in our common humanity then all will be well.

A month later, her naked body was found in the bushes near Gebze in Turkey. She had been gang-raped and then killed. Like Timothy Treadwell's, her illusions met reality.[109]

Most of us as individuals retain enough of a survival instinct that, if we find ourselves on a rough city block in a foreign land late at night, we mothball the PC pieties until we get back to the lobby of the Grand Hyatt. But what happens when Pippa Bacca's illusions become the dominant political discourse of a free society? And how many Timothy Treadwells crooning to their killers does a society have to have before it loses even the very idea of a survival instinct?

Eloi passivity offers a template not only to a resurgent Islam. In Europe, we can already see what happens when the ruling class is obliged to tell a citizenry mired in dependence that there's no more money. In France, the government announced the retirement age would be raised from 60 to 62 by 2018, and there were protests. In Britain, the government raised the cost of university education, and the elderly "students" rioted. En route to the Royal Variety Performance at the London Palladium, the heir to the throne, the Prince of Wales, and his consort the Duchess of Cornwall became separated from their police escort and had their Rolls besieged and battered by a mob chanting "Off with their heads!" That's a portent of America's future—except that for a failed and discredited elite there will be no pampered princes to serve as a focused target. After economic ruin, the Eloi will retreat from an unenforceable border and other areas of the country, not out of choice but from necessity. As the years go by, they will find it ever harder to insulate themselves from the pathologies they have fed. The collapse of the dollar as the global currency and the end of cheap imports will cause shortages in much of the land. But beyond that the abandonment of America's animating ideas will leave a large porous continent with insufficient social glue to make it governable. And then, as H. G. Wells' Eloi discovered, the Morlocks will take their opportunity, and in their "feeble prettiness" the elites will no longer even know how to rouse themselves.

An America that abandons the American idea will be a turbulent society. The present de facto segregation—in Maywood, California, and elsewhere—will decay into tribalism, both cultural and economic. The United States will quietly retreat from the southern borderlands and other redoubts of the Undocumented, in the way that the Government of France has retreated from those banlieues that Muslims regard as part of the Dar al-Islam. Other neighborhoods will opt for de facto secession, and still functioning states will opt for de jure secession, anxious to escape being buried by federal debt. Balkanization will cease to be a pejorative and become the least worst hope: united we're done for, but divided a few corners of the map might stand a chance. The Eloi elites who did this to America will hunker down within protected enclaves while outside life grows increasingly savage and violent. But eventually they will come for the elite communities, too—as the cougar came for Frances Frost, and the bear for Timothy Treadwell.

THE NEW JERUSALEM
The City Besieged

I have a premonition that will not leave me. As it goes with Israel
so will it go with all of us. Should Israel perish the holocaust will
be upon us.
—**Eric Hoffer,** *Los Angeles Times* **(May 26, 1968)**

In 2009 Benjamin Netanyahu, the Prime Minister of Israel, took to the podium of the UN General Assembly and observed that he was speaking just a few days after the president of Iran had claimed that the Holocaust was a lie. Mr. Netanyahu then explained that he'd recently visited a villa in Wannsee, a suburb of Berlin, and been shown the minutes of a meeting held there on January 20, 1942, at which senior German officials formulated precisely their plan for the extermination of the Jews. "Here is a copy of those minutes," the Prime Minister told the UN. "Is this a lie?"[1]

The day before, he'd been given another photocopy—this time of the original construction plans, signed by Heinrich Himmler, for the Auschwitz-Birkenau concentration camp, wherein one million Jews would be killed. "Here is a copy of the plans," Mr. Netanyahu said to the assembled ranks of world leaders. "Is this too a lie?"

And so at the dawn of the twenty-first century, one head of government holds up the documents for the "Final Solution" to "the Jewish problem" because another head of government insists, repeatedly, that no such event ever took place. This is the state to which the United Nations has fallen after six decades posing as Lord Tennyson's Parliament of Man: a sane man is obliged to prove to lunatics that the Holocaust actually happened.

One sympathizes with the Israeli Prime Minister, reduced, seventy years after Neville Chamberlain, to standing before the world waving pieces of paper from Herr Hitler. But he's missing the point. Ahmadinejad & Company aren't Holocaust deniers because of the dearth of historical documentation. They deny it because they can, and because it suits their own interests to do so, and because, in the regimes they represent, the state lies to its people as a matter of course and to such a degree that there is no longer an objective reality, only a self-constructed one.

And once you're in the business of constructing your own reality, even internal logic is not required. In Iran, many of the same people who deny the first Holocaust are planning the second one. Elsewhere in the Muslim world, I've run into folks who simultaneously believe (a) that there was no Muslim involvement in the attacks of September 11, and (b) it was a tremendous victory for the Muslim people. Incidentally, by "the Muslim world," I don't just mean the Middle East: according to one poll, only 17 percent of British Muslims believe there was any Arab involvement in 9/11, and a majority of British Muslims—56 percent—believe there was no Arab involvement.[2] And yet many British Muslims have marched in the streets under posters hailing the "Magnificent Nineteen" who carried out the attacks.

So we already live in a world in which there is insufficient agreed reality. After America, there will be even less. To be sure, whatever the president of Iran might believe, there are plenty of fellows, even at the UN General Assembly, who understand that, yes, Auschwitz was built and, yes, many Jews died there. EU prime ministers ostentatiously participating in the annual Holocaust Memorial Day observances are certainly aware. Yet even they felt it was not, in diplomatic-speak, helpful for Mr. Netanyahu to belabor the point with President Ahmadinejad. The New York Times offered an online analysis in its dull blog, the Lede: dredging up the Holocaust business was a bit of artful misdirection from the hardline Netanyahu.[3] As Robert Mackey explained, "his decision to engage so passionately with Iran's president ... helped to change the subject from a conversation that presents difficulties for Israel's leader—how to make peace with Palestinians without alienating his supporters."

Ah, so that's why he did it. The whole heads-of-state-who-deny-the-Holocaust thing was a cunning distraction by the Zionist Entity.

During Israel's famously "disproportionate" 2006 incursion into Lebanon, a reader reminded me of an old gag:

One day the UN Secretary General proposes that, in the interest of global peace and harmony, the world's soccer players should come together and form one United Nations global soccer team.

"Great idea," says his deputy. "Er, but who would we play?"

"Israel, of course."

Ha-ha. It always had a grain of truth, now it's the whole loaf.

Think of how the Prime Minister of Israel feels at the UN. And then picture what's left of the United States after global eclipse. Obama and the leftists notwithstanding, the effect of American retreat from superpower status will not be a quiet life but a future as the Zionist Entity writ large—no longer the Great Satan, but forever the Great Scapegoat. As Richard Ingrams wrote in Britain's *Observer* the weekend after 9/11:

Who will dare to damn Israel?[4]

Hey, take a number and get in line. Who won't dare to damn Israel? And for whatever bugs you. In late 2010, there was a series of shark attacks in the Red Sea off the Egyptian resort of Sharm el-Sheikh.[5] On an official Egyptian government news site, the governor of South Sinai, Mohamed Abdel Fadil Shousha, speculated that the fatal attacks in the hitherto peaceful waters were due to "the Mossad throwing in the deadly shark to hit tourism in Egypt." Other sources wondered if the Mossad had gone further and equipped the aquatic predators with GPS. Could be. Governor Shousha has undoubtedly seen the famous Hollywood film about a killer shark terrorizing a beach resort—*Jews*. Oh, c'mon, you're not gonna let a one-vowel typing error in the poster throw you off what it's really about, are you? Directed by the same infidel who made *Schindler's List*, if you get my drift.

The Governor of South Sinai is not the only political colossus to take the view that the world's troubles are due to a tiny strip of land that at its narrowest point is barely wider than my New Hampshire township. Only a few months before the shark attacks, Bill Clinton had been in Egypt and told an audience of local "businessmen" that solving the Israeli/Palestinian problem would "take away about half the impetus for terror in the whole world."[6]

Only 50 percent of global terrorism is all down to Israel? Are you sure you're not underestimating?

In rationalizing the irrational, you not only legitimize it but create a self-fulfilling prophecy. After the Bali nightclub bombings in 2002, Bruce Haigh, a retired Australia diplomat who'd served in Indonesia, Pakistan, and Saudi Arabia, went on TV and explained why hundreds of his compatriots had been blown up: "The root cause of this issue has been America's backing of Israel on Palestine."[7]

So we're conceding that if a fellow in Indonesia is "frustrated" by Israeli "intransigence," then blowing up Australian tourists, Scandinavian backpackers, and German stoners in Bali makes some kind of sense. For centuries, Jews were the handiest scapegoat in every two-bit duchy and principality across the map. In essence, the argument of Bill Clinton & Company simply affirms the ancient paranoia that the Jews are behind everything.

There is an element of humbug about all this. Just as Europe's rulers, while happy to pander to anti-American sentiment among the citizenry, are well aware that the United States has been the guarantor of the Continent's liberty since 1945, so Araby's rulers, happy to pander to their subjects' Judenhass in public, are privately rather appreciative of the Zionist Entity.

Diplomatic cables leaked in 2010 revealed that King Abdullah of Saudi Arabia was publicly urging the bombing of Iran's nuclear facilities, and had even indicated to the Israelis that come the big night he'd make sure his kingdom's radar facilities were switched off so nobody could tip off Teheran.[8] Were Israel to take up his offer, His Majesty would be the first in a long parade of Arab potentates and European foreign ministers lining up to denounce Zionist "disproportion." But it's heartening to know that, whatever lunacies they subscribe to in public, both Arabs and Europeans retain a few residual marbles in private.

Not all the scapegoaters are nuts, maybe not even the governor of South Sinai. Maybe he's just tossing a little red meat, a little shark bait to the Jew-hate crowd. But from Sharm al-Sheikh to the UN General Assembly, sane men find it politic to string along with the loons.

As the proverbial canary in the coal mine, Israel knows what America's in for. Like the United States, it is militarily superior to its enemies. If it were merely a matter of weaponry, they would have won decades ago. But, if that's all there is to it, where's the U.S. victory parade in Afghanistan? The Palestinians were among the first to realize that, in a media age, you can win on other battlefields. Stone-throwing youths have won more victories for Palestine—at least in the European press and on North American campuses—than the Egyptian, Syrian, and Jordanian armies ever did.

★ ★ ★ ★ ★

THE NEW NORMALIUT

One sympathizes with Americans weary of global responsibilities that they, unlike the European empires, never sought. You can understand why the entire left and much of the right would rather vote for a quiet life. The Jewish state felt the same way in the early Nineties. There's an Israeli coinage that was popular back then: "normaliut"—the desire to wake up each morning and live a normal political life, as John Podhoretz described it.[9] In the early Nineties, Israelis wanted normaliut, badly. They regarded themselves as a western democracy and wished to live like one. Instead of having to be on the military call-up list till you're European retirement age (fifty-five), they wanted to be like other westerners and worry about their vacation destinations and the quality of their stereo systems. The Oslo Accords were a vote for normaliut—a vote to be like Oslo, for the chance to live as a Middle Eastern Norway. In return, they got an Arafatist squat and then exterminationist Iranian proxies on their borders, and suicide bombers on their buses, and in the wider world isolation, demonization, and delegitimization, accompanied by a resurgent and ever more respectable anti-Semitism.

In 2008, the U.S. electorate voted to repudiate the previous eight years and seemed genuinely under the delusion that wars end when one side decides it's all a bit of a bore and they'd rather the government spend the next eight years doing to health care and the economy what they were previously doing to jihadist camps in Waziristan. In the old days, declining powers seeking to arrest either their own decline or another's rise would turn to war—see the Franco–Prussian, the Austro–Prussian, the Napoleonic, and many others. But those were the days when traditional great-power rivalry was resolved on the battlefield. Today we have post-modern post-great-power rivalry, in which America envies the way the beneficiaries of its post-war largesse have been able to opt out of the great game entirely. In reality-TV terms, the Great Satan would like to vote itself off the battlefield. It too yearns for normaliut.

So instead of unilateral Bush cowboyism, we elected President Outreach, a man happy to apologize for the entirety of American policy pre-January 2009.

How's that working out?

In 2010, Zogby International and the University of Maryland conducted an "Arab Public Opinion Poll" for the Brookings Institution.[10] They interviewed respondents in Egypt, Jordan, Lebanon, Morocco, Saudi Arabia, and the United Arab Emirates—the so-called "moderate" Arab Street. So how did President Obama do with the citizens of our allies after all the Islamoschmoozing and other outreach to the Muslim world?

In 2008, the last year of the Bush Texas-cowboy terror, 83 percent of Arabs had a very or somewhat negative view of the United States.[11] By 2010, the second year of the Obama apology tour, 85 percent had a very or somewhat negative view. So much for the outreach.

So if they don't like Obama, who do they like? The poll asked which world leader (other than their own) do you most admire? Here's the Top Twelve:

1) Prime Minister Erdogan of Turkey (20 percent);
2) Hugo Chavez, president of Venezuela (13 percent);
3) Mahmoud Ahmadinejad, president of Iran (12 percent);
4) Hassan Nasrallah, head honcho of Hizb'Allah (9 percent);
5) Bashar al-Assad, president of Syria (7 percent);
6) Nicolas Sarkozy, president of France (6 percent);
7) Osama bin Laden, Abbottabad's leading pornography aficionado (6 percent);
8) Jacques Chirac, the retired Gallic charmer (4 percent);
9) Sheikh Mohammed bin Zayed, Crown Prince of Abu Dhabi (4 percent);
10) Hosni Mubarak, president of Egypt (4 percent);
11) Sheikh Maktoum bin Rashid, Emir of Dubai (3 percent);
12) Saddam Hussein, Iraq War loser (2 percent).

What a hit parade! Twenty percent voted for the avowedly Islamist leader of a formerly secular pluralist Turkey; 57 percent voted for current dictators, dead dictators, thugs, terrorists, and a couple of wealthy minor princelings of the Muslim world; and the remainder celebrated diversity with Hugo Chavez and a pair of French roués. Maybe if Obama abased himself even more ostentatiously, maybe if next time he bows to the King of Saudi Arabia he licks the guy's feet, maybe then he can boost his numbers up to Jacques Chirac level.

But, just as fascinating was the so-called "realist" reaction of the pollsters' clients, the Brookings Institution. They took all the above as a sign

that America needs to work harder to distance itself from negative percep-
tions that it's too closely allied with Israel.

I don't think so. America could join Iran in a nuclear strike on the Zionist Entity, and those numbers wouldn't shift significantly. Because sometimes who you are is more important than anything you do. America will
discover, as Israel did, that a one-way urge for normaliut will lead to a more
dangerous world. In the vacuum of U.S. retreat, anti-Americanism will
nevertheless metastasize and crowd in from our borders. In 2010 *Die Welt*
reported that, on his recent visit to Teheran, Hugo Chavez had signed an
agreement to place Iranian missiles at a jointly operated military base in
Venezuela.[12] In the years ahead, distant enemies will seed new proxies in
Latin America (as Iran did to Israel with Hamas and Hizb'Allah), and suicide bombers will board our city buses, too.

American isolation is already under way. China is the world's biggest
manufacturer, the world's biggest exporter, the post-colonial patron of
resource-rich Africa, the post-downturn patron of cash-strapped Mediterranean Europe, and the biggest trading partner of India, Brazil, and
other emerging powers. Why be surprised that in such a world, getting
on with America matters less and less? Sometimes that's good news:
Washington and its geriatric EU allies wanted the bonkers Copenhagen
"climate change" deal; Brazil and India joined with China to block it.
Sometimes it's not so good: the leaders of Brazil (again) and Turkey, two
supposed American allies assiduously courted and flattered by Obama
during his first year, flew in to high-five Mahmoud Ahmadinejad and
subsequently took China's position on Iranian nukes.[13] But, either way,
second-tier powers around the globe are making their dispositions, and
telling us very plainly about what awaits. In 2010, the Royal Australian
Navy participated in its first ever naval exercises with Beijing;[14] a few weeks
later, Britain and Germany declined to support the U.S. in its efforts to
get China to increase the value of the yuan.[15] Even for America's closest
allies, the dominance of both the Pentagon and the almighty dollar is
conditional.

The world after America is beginning to take shape, a planet where the loons and the hard men make the running and the rest go along to get along. Picture the UN a few years down the road: for three of the Security Council's permanent members (Britain, France, Russia), an accommodation with Islam will be a domestic political imperative, and getting along with China will be the overriding foreign priority. In the practical sense, this will shrink "the West" and destroy the post-war balance of power in which three permanent members from the free world balanced two authoritarian powers. Nudge things a little further down the road—a fractious planet of hostile forces—Russia, China, a semi-Islamized Europe, the aspiring caliphate, whatever the new Chavismo bequeaths Latin America—all mutually antipathetic yet for whom the flailing America remains the biggest and most inviting target. There will be no "new world order," only a world with no order, in which pipsqueak failed states go nuclear while the planet's wealthiest nations are unable to defend their borders and are forced to adjust to the post-American era as they can. Yet, in such a geopolitical scene, whatever survives of the United States will still be the most inviting target—first because it's big; and second because, as Britain knows, the durbar moves on but imperial resentments linger long after imperial grandeur.

Listen to the way Washington's European "allies" and Sunni Arab "allies" and UN "human rights" bigwigs talk about the Jewish state today. That's how they'll be talking about the U.S. tomorrow. In a post-American world, the kind of world Barack Obama is committed to building, America will be surrounded on all sides by hostile forces and more globally demonized than ever. Another half-a-decade on, and there'll be an informal Islamoveto over European policy. Russia and China have already determined that, whatever their own little local difficulties with Muslims, their long-term strategic interest lies in keeping the jihad as an American problem. The internal logic of the demographic shifts will be to make much of the world figure it makes sense to be on the side America's not.

They got the post-American world they always dreamed of, and, as they adjust to a poorer and more violent planet, they will blame Washington for the horrors of the new age more furiously than ever. Think of Netanyahu alone at the podium trying to demonstrate objective facts to a roomful of madmen, liars, and appeasers. He's the warm-up act, and that's the reception Washington will get in a world after American power.

Western civilization is a synthesis—a multicultural synthesis, if you like: Athenian democracy, Roman law, the Hebrew Bible, dispersed by London to every corner of the globe. If Rome, Athens, and Jerusalem are the three temple mounts of the modern world and all its blessings, none has had a rougher ride than the last: attacked, besieged, captured, and recaptured dozens of times across the centuries—and twice destroyed. Today, Jerusalem is home to the Knesset and all Israeli government ministries, and the universally unrecognized capital of a universally delegitimized nation. Because the civilized world could not summon up the will to prevent Iran going nuclear, Israel will live on a thin line between the advanced civilized state they have built and oblivion, a permanent state of high alert in which the difference between first-world prosperity and extinction will come down to the hair-trigger reactions of bureaucratic monitoring of an implacable foe.

But in leaving Israel to its fate we have told our enemies something elemental and devastating about the will of a decaying West, and of the supposed global superpower. Around the world our foes will draw their own conclusions. Just as there are neglected and rubble-strewn Jewish cemeteries from Tangiers to Czernowitz to Baghdad, one day there will be abandoned American cemeteries, too. Across the globe there will be towns and countries where once were Americans and now are none—from Kuwait and Saudi Arabia to Germany and Japan. What's left of the republic will hunker down and finally understand what's it's like to be Israel. Washington will be the new Jerusalem—a beleaguered citadel in a world that wants to kill it.

AFTER

A Letter from
the Post-American World

Again upon the sea.
This time for Persia, bearing our wounded and the ashes of the
dead.... The skull of the last
Mehrikan I shall present to the museum at Teheran.
—J. A. Mitchell, *The Last American* (1889)

W*hat follows purports to be a missive from the future. Author*
unknown. It was found tucked into the glovebox in the remnants
of what appeared to be a Victorian-era contraption:

This is a letter from the day after tomorrow, from the world after
America. I would have entrusted it to the genial gentleman on a "time
machine" who turned up last week with excited tales of the marvels of an
American golden age circa 1950. Less than a hundred years ago! But the
young 'uns told him he sounded like those Islamophile "scholars" boring
on about the glories of Córdoba and el-Andalus in the tenth century. His
machine looked promising, but it attracted the attention of rival gangs
and they wound up with half of it apiece, neither of which functioned.

Much like what happened to America. But they left behind what I believe is the key time-traveling mechanism, and, while it is no longer sufficient to transport a person, I'm hopeful this letter will make it back to you in 1950—assuming, that is, that, like so much else of interest, the time-transporting device isn't stymied by the Sino-Russo-Islamic cybershield that has reduced the Internet to little more than an archive of cautionary tales of all but forgotten minor American celebrities. (The Internet was a turn-of-the-century phenomenon, like your hula hoop, if that's been invented by the time you get this.)

Before he got mugged, the time traveler wanted to know how we were getting by without the United States. Well, for want of any choice in the matter, we adjusted. As it beggared itself, cannibalized itself, and finally consumed itself, the hyperpower's networks of globalization remained largely in place. We know their names still—Starbucks, Wal-Mart, Google.... Many of the famous multinationals survived the collapse of the United States. In economic terms, they were bigger than most nation-states, and so they had no trouble finding small countries to serve as company towns of convenience. Some aspects changed. McDonald's and KFC and the rest are now halal. It's just easier that way. Otherwise, you wind up like the Russians, with two of everything—the Muslim-compliant Burger King, and the branch across the street that still serves vodka: "Have it your way—*da*?" And all that does is make it easier for Chechen gangs to blow up sad gaggles of Red Army alcoholics while minimalizing collateral damage of photogenic moppets and devout burqa-clad women. I no longer imbibe myself. Like the late American entertainer Dean Martin, I drank to forget. But we forgot almost everything very quickly, so the excuse is less persuasive.

Much of the world would still seem familiar to you. Have you ever been in the executive lounge of an upmarket American chain hotel in the Middle East? The Grand Hyatt in Amman perhaps? Very congenial in the old days. At breakfast you could get pancakes and hash browns, and the TV would be tuned to CNN International, while Saudi sheikhs and Russian "businessmen" and the representatives of Chinese state corporations conducted their affairs. For a while, that's what it felt like: an American-built international network but with fewer and fewer Americans. The Europeans had always enjoyed sneering at those polls about the ever dwindling percentage of Yanks who held valid passports. Who could blame you? You were the "ugly Americans," the only foreigners who upon landing in Paris, Rome, Berlin, and many other capitals could reliably expect to have their country openly insulted by the cab driver en route to the hotel. Once the dollar ceased to be the global currency, and America became both yesterday's man and the scapegoat for all the new woes afflicting the post-American world, fewer and fewer of your citizens ventured abroad. At power tables in the exclusive restaurants one sees Chinamen, Arabs, Venezuelans, even the occasional Jeremy or Derek from Eton or Upper Canada College hired as the retro-chic Wasp frontman for an international agglomeration of emirs and oligarchs. But not a lot of Americans.

Even travel within North America became prohibitively expensive, and dangerous. Virtuous Americans forswore nuclear power and coal mining, and, when the crisis of the early Seventies exposed your vulnerability to Middle Eastern oil dictatorships, you spent the next thirty years letting your dependence on foreign petroleum double from one-third to two-thirds of your energy needs while you busied yourselves piously declining to drill in the Arctic lest it sully the pristine breeding grounds of the world's largest mosquito herd. So today the Arabs still have the oil; Russia and Iran between them control half the world's natural gas; and China and India need more and more of both. It never seemed to occur to America's ruling class that an economy requires fuel to run it, and that one day the sellers might be in a position to pick and choose their customers. The decision by the Gulf emirates to lease bases to Beijing to enable the Chinese to secure the Asian oil routes was entirely predictable. Not a lot of Middle Eastern oil heads west these days.

The world after America is a sicker world. In 1999, the British Government set up NICE—the National Institute for Clinical Excellence, the country's nicely named "death panel." If one works for NICE these days, one no longer has to waste all that time inventing reasons as to why this or that innovative but costly American drug or procedure does not fit the overarching strategic goals of the National Health Service, because American medical innovation quickly dwindled away and nobody picked up the slack. The Chinese are said to have amazing new inventions to keep their leaders hale and hearty, but would prefer their aging peasantry keeled over sooner rather than later. A few other countries have carved out boutique markets: Japan for state-of-the-art post-human augmentation, the Swiss for luxury euthanasia. As I say, niche businesses. For the non-elites, for the multitudes of humanity crammed into the vast, diseased megalopolises of Africa or the *favelas* of Latin America, almost anything unexpected that happens anywhere kills huge numbers of people. Today the typical novelty virus develops in rural China, its existence is denied for weeks on end by the government, during which window of opportunity a carrier spreads it to the lobby of an international hotel in Hong Kong, and thence by jet it takes off for the world beyond—much as SARS did in 2003. But this time, instead of getting on a flight to Toronto, the returning tourist flies to Johannesburg, and the disease runs riot among a population whose immune systems are already weakened by HIV.

Tragic, but only for a moment, and then next month's surprise disaster comes along like clockwork. Even without the cooperation of mendacious despots, life is nasty, brutish, and shortened in dramatic ways. Tsunamis and earthquakes kill on impressive scales. There is no superpower with the carrier groups or the C-130s or, indeed, the inclination to have "boots on the ground" (quaint expression, now unknown) within hours to start rescuing people, feeding them, housing them. So today we are all impeccably multilateral and work through the UN bureaucracy, which holds state-of-the art press conferences to announce it will soon be flying in (or nearby, or overhead, or in the general hemisphere) a top-level situation-assessment team to the approximate vicinity to conduct a situation assessment of the situation just as soon as an elite team of corporate mercenaries has flown in and restored room service to the five-star hotel. Shouldn't be more than a few weeks.

If the tsunami doesn't get you, the relief operation usually does the trick. In 2010, an earthquake hit Haiti, and the UN dispatched peacekeepers, including cholera-infected Bangladeshi troops. So Haiti had a cholera epidemic introduced to the island by the transnational body supposedly rescuing it from the previous catastrophe. That was the test run for a world of hemisphere-hopping disasters. The Russians are pressuring the Chinese to develop a form of airborne quarantine: unmanned drones would spray the infected megalopolis from the skies, the way early morning aerial maintenance crews used to zap your DisneyWorld with bug spray from the heavens each dawn.

The world after America is a poorer place. The second half of the twentieth century saw the emergence of "a new world middle class," as Professor Xavier Sala-i-Martin called them in his study *The World Distribution of Income*. This class was made up of some 2.5 billion citizens of the developing world whose standards of living were rapidly approaching those of the West.[1] By the beginning of the twenty-first century, as Virginia Postrel reported in the *New York Times*, "the largest number of people earned about $8,000—a standard of living equivalent to Portugal's."[2] Not everybody was part of this success story: In your time—the 1950s—Egypt and South Korea had had more or less identical per capita incomes. By the first decade of the new century, Egypt's was less than a sixth of South Korea's.[3]

Which of these models would prevail in the years ahead? Access to western markets had given South Korea a western lifestyle, complete with western-sized families: soon, like many of the so-called "Asian tigers," they had one of the lowest fertility rates in the world. They were tigers without cubs. Whereas Egypt, like most of the Muslim world, was in a demographic boom and its poverty helped export its surplus population, either in the express lane (a gentleman called Mohammed Atta flying through the office window on a Tuesday morning) or through less dramatic but relentless mass immigration. (I believe they have a new "community center" named after Mr. Atta in Tower Hamlets, East London.)

The collapsed birth rates of Europe and the Asian tigers left an insufficient domestic market for economic growth. They were ever more dependent on access to the U.S. market, even as the American consumer became too broke to go to the mall. As for the rest of the planet, sub-Saharan Africa doubled its population between 2010 and 2030. Unlike enviro-feminists in London fretting about "overpopulation," the Africans were in no hurry to tie their tubes, and the West's ecochondriacs declined to hector them. Why, sub-Saharan babies "consumed" fewer resources. Which was true. They still do, man for man. Excepting South Africa, the Dark Continent's per capita income averaged $355 in 2004, but had fallen below $275 by 2030.[4] Good for the planet? Well, it depends how you think about it. A few years earlier, a Unicef report had found that more than one billion children in the developing world were suffering from the most basic "deprivations"—lack of food, lack of education, lack of rights.[5] Yet by 2020 each of them—or at any rate the half who were girls—had had an average of three children each. Who in turn lacked food and education and much else, and had a much higher incidence of genetic disorders. It would have been asking an awful lot for them to remain in the teeming, pathogenic shanty megalopolises into which the Third World's population was consolidating—rather than simply to sail over to Spain or Italy or the Côte d'Azur.

But never mind African-Asian or Cairo-Seoul comparisons, and consider the available models within Korea itself: in the south, a prosperous, educated, advanced nation; to the north, a dark, starving, one-man psychostate tyranny that exported nothing but knock-off Viagra and No Dong. The former is an erectile dysfunction treatment, the latter sounds like one but is in fact a long-range missile the Norks made available to interested parties such as Iran. Seoul was always vulnerable: it could be flattened by Pyongyang within minutes. Why ever would the Norks do that? Well, why in 2010 did they loose a couple hundred artillery shells at South Korea's Yeonpyeong Island, killing four civilians and injuring many more?[6]

Who knows? No analyst was able to articulate a rationale. Because a rationalist needs a rationale, but a psycho-state doesn't.

This peripheral peninsula was a snapshot of the world to come: South Korea had one of the highest GDPs per capita on the planet, yet was all but defenseless without American military protection.[7] North Korea had a GDP per capita that was all but unmeasurable, down in Sub-Basement Level Five with Burundi and the Congo—and yet it was, after a fashion, a nuclear power. In the years ahead, these contradictions would resolve themselves in entirely predictable ways.

★ ★ ★ ★ ★

IDENTITY AND AUTHENTICITY

The future belongs to those who show up for it. Yet in the multicultural West the question of human capital was entirely absent from most futurological speculation. "A growing number of people," wrote James Martin in *The Meaning of the 21st Century: A Vital Blueprint for Ensuring Our Future* (2006), "will think of themselves as citizens of the planet rather than citizens of the West, or Islam, or Chinese civilization."[8]

Mr. Martin provided no evidence for his assertion, and it should have been obvious even then that it was (to use a British archaism I rather miss) bollocks on stilts: the notion that an identity rooted in nothing more than the planet as a universal zip code would ever be sufficient should have been laughable. Yet nobody laughed, and certainly none of the experts so much as giggled even as the opposite proved true. The more myopic westerners promoted the vacuous banality of post-nationalist identity—what Mr Martin called "multicultural tolerance and respect"—the more people looked elsewhere and sought alternatives. Islam and "Chinese civilization" (to return to the author's specific examples) both did a roaring trade, while "citizens of the planet" degenerated to a useful designation for the millions of unfortunates in collapsed cities and regions who fell between the cracks of the hardening ideological blocs. "Stateless persons," we would once have said.

It is only human to wish to belong to something larger than oneself, and thereby give one's life meaning. For most of history, this need was satisfied by tribe and then nation, and religion. But by the late twentieth century the Church was in steep decline in Europe, and the nation-state was abhorred as the font of racism, imperialism, and all the other ills. So some (not all) third-generation Britons of Pakistani descent went in search of identity and found the new globalized Islam. And some (not all) 30th-generation Britons of old Anglo-Saxon stock also looked elsewhere, and found "global warming." What was it they used to say back then? "Think globally, act locally"? It worked better for jihad than for environmentalism. Adherents of both causes claimed to be saving the planet from the same enemy—decadent capitalist infidels living empty consumerist lives. Both faiths insisted their tenets were beyond discussion. As disciples of the now obscure prophet Gore liked to sneer, only another climate scientist could question the climate-science "consensus": busboys and waitresses and accountants and software designers and astronomers and physicists and mere meteorologists who weren't officially designated climatologists were unqualified to enter the debate. Correspondingly, on Islam, for an unbeliever to express a view was "Islamophobic."

As to which of these competing global identities was more risible, the 44th President of the United States promised to lower the oceans, while Hizb ut-Tahrir promised a global caliphate; *The Guardian*'s ecopalyptic correspondent Fred Pearce declared that within a few years Australia would be uninhabitable,[9] while Islam4UK declared that within a few years Britain would be under sharia.[10] I was never a betting man, even when it remained legal in Europe, but, if I had been forced to choose one of these scenarios, and had found an obliging bookie, I could have made a tidy sum …

So here we are with the oceans more or less exactly where they were, and Australia still habitable, and everything else utterly transformed. How pathetic it seems to have to state the obvious—that pseudo-identities cannot stand up to genuine identities. The "international community" proved to be fake, and hardheaded Russian and Chinese nationalism all too real.

The collective "European" consciousness promoted by the European Union shimmered and dissolved like a desert mirage, unlike the collective Islamic consciousness of the Organization of the Islamic Cooperation. When push came to shove, when bailout came to bankruptcy, there was no "Europe" beyond the official fictions of the Eurocrat elite. But, notwithstanding Sunni loathing for Shia, and Turk for Arab, and Arab for Persian, and Persian for Pakistani, Pakistani for black, Wahhabi for "moderate," and fervent jihadist for non-observant semi-apostate, most Muslims were nevertheless happy to identify themselves as part of what the author Christopher Caldwell called "Team Islam."

By 2010, the Organization of the Islamic Cooperation was already the largest single voting bloc at the UN, and controlled among other bodies the Human Rights Council. Which is why it quickly became an anti-human rights council, fiercely opposed to free speech, freedom of religion, women's rights, and much more. The international institutions built by an un-imperial America after the Second World War were effortlessly co-opted by nations and alliances that barely existed then. The OIC's conception of human rights came from their Cairo Declaration. Article 24: "All the rights and freedoms stipulated in this Declaration are subject to the Islamic Shari'a."[11]

Quite so. The OIC took the view that Islam, in both its theological and political components, should be beyond question, and its members supported the UN's rapid progress toward the planet-wide imposition of a law against "defaming" religion—which meant in effect a global apostasy law that removed Islam from public discourse. Imagine if someone had proposed an "Organization of the Christian Conference" that would hold summits attended by prime ministers and presidents, and vote as a bloc in transnational bodies. But, of course, by the twenty-first century there was a "Muslim world" (as presidential speechwriters and *New York Times* headline editors casually acknowledged) but no "Christian world" (heaven forfend!): Europe was militantly post-Christian, Russia had applied for observer membership of the OIC, and, as the 44th president—Obama—

bizarrely asserted to a European interviewer, America was "one of the larg-est Muslim countries in the world."[12]

And, if there was a "Muslim world," what were its boundaries? The OIC was formed in 1969 with mainly Middle Eastern members plus Indonesia and a couple more. By the Nineties, former Soviet Central Asia had signed on, plus Albania, Mozambique, Guyana, and various others. By the time the EU applied for observer status in the second decade of the twenty-first century, it seemed a mere formality.

And America? In 2007, the 43rd president had announced the appoint-ment of the first U.S. Ambassador to the OIC.[13] There was little fuss when Michigan applied for membership.

And so it went. You didn't need to go to "the Muslim world" to see "Team Islam" in action, only to what we used to call Christendom. When the subject of a fast Islamizing Europe first arose in the Oughts, sophisticates protested that one shouldn't "generalize" about Muslims. And it was true that, if you took a stamp collector's approach to immigration issues, there were many fascinating differences: the French blamed difficulties with their Muslim population on the bitter legacy of colonialism; whereas Germans blamed theirs on a lack of colonial experience at dealing with these exotic chappies. And, if you were a small densely populated nation like the Neth-erlands, the difficulties of Islam were just the usual urban/rural frictions that occur when people from the countryside—in this case, the Moroccan countryside—move to the cities. It was the consequence of your urban planning, or your colonialism, or your wealth, or just plain you. But, if you were in some decrepit housing project on the edge of almost any Continen-tal city from Malmö to Marseilles, it made little difference in practice. "If you understand how immigration, Islam, and native European culture interact in any western European country," wrote Christopher Caldwell, "you can predict roughly how they will interact in any other—no matter what its national character, no matter whether it conquered an empire, no matter what its role in World War II, and no matter what the provenance of its Muslim immigrants."[14] European Islam turned out to be less divided

than Greeks from Germans, Swedes from Portuguese. Many ethnic Continentals only discovered the post-nationalist identity they'd been long
promised after they converted to Islam: when the mirage of the "European
Union" faded, the Eurabian Union was the desert beyond.

Nor could the over-Europeanized cult of transnationalism survive in
the wider world. As the EU, the UN, and the G7 seized up, the tranzis turned
elsewhere, ever on the lookout for the Newest Established Permanent Float-
ing Crap Game on the geopolitical circuit. For a while, in the wake of the
2008 downturn, they pinned their hopes on the G20: same great poseur
multilateralism, brand new secretariat. You could see what was in it for EU
prime ministers: the transnational talking-shops were the equivalent of
those all-star charity fundraisers that spent so much money chauffeuring
the stars to the stadium there was no cash left for the charity. Diplomacy
used to be, as Canada's Lester Pearson liked to say, the art of letting the other
fellow have your way.[15] By the twenty-first century, "soft power" had become
more of a discreet cover for letting the other fellow have his way with you.
The Europeans "negotiated" with Iran over its nuclear program for years,
and in the end Iran got the nukes and Europe got to feel good about itself
for having sat across the table talking to no purpose for the best part of a
decade.

In Moscow, Vladimir Putin, self-promoted from president to de facto
czar, decided it was well past time to reconstitute the old empire and start
re-hanging the Iron Curtain—not formally, not initially, but certainly as a
sphere of influence from which the Yanks would keep their distance. Russia,
like China, was demographically weak but geopolitically assertive. The
Europe the new czar foresaw was one not only energy-dependent on Moscow but security-dependent, too. Hence, his mischievous support for a
nuclear Iran—because mullahs with nukes served Russia's ambitions to
restore its hegemony over Eastern Europe. Only Washington was surprised
at how far west "Eastern" Europe extended by the time Moscow was done.
In an unstable world, the Russians offered themselves as the protection
racket you could rely on, and there were plenty of takers for that once every

European city was within range of Teheran and the other crazies. Look at it from their point of view: as America's "good cop" retreated to the precinct house, there was something to be said for a "bad cop" who still had some credibility when it came to head-cracking.

In the nineteenth century the Anglophone powers killed or captured pirates. Two centuries later, with primitive vessels seizing tankers the length of carriers off the Horn of Africa, it was all more complicated. The Royal Navy, which over the centuries had done more than anyone to rid the civilized world of the menace of piracy, declined even to risk capturing their Somali successors. They had been advised by Her Majesty's Government that, under the European Human Rights Act, any pirate taken into custody would be entitled to claim refugee status in the United Kingdom and live on welfare for the rest of his life.[16] There was a film series popular at the time: *Pirates of the Caribbean*. I doubt it would have cleaned up at the box office if the big finale had shown Mr. Geoffrey Rush and his crew of scurvy sea dogs settling down in council flats in Manchester and going to the pub for a couple of jiggers of rum washed down to cries of "Aaaaargh, shiver me benefits check, lad." For his part, the U.S. Attorney-General, the chief law-enforcement official of the world's superpower, was circumspect about the legal status of pirates, as well he might be. Obviously, if the United States Navy had seized some eyepatched peglegged blackguard off the coast of Somalia and hanged him from the yardarm or made him walk the plank, pious senators would have risen as one to denounce an America that no longer lived up to its highest ideals ... and the network talking-heads would have argued that Plankgate was recruiting more and more young men to the pirates' cause ... and judges by the dozen would have ruled that pirates were entitled to the protections of the U.S. constitution and that under ObamaCare their peglegs had to be replaced by high-tech prosthetic limbs at taxpayer expense.

Conversely, a 2010 headline from the Associated Press: "Pirates 'Have All Died,' Russia Says, After Decrying 'Imperfections' In International Law."[17] Perhaps it seemed just as funny at the time.

The Somalis had made the mistake of seizing a Russian tanker. When Moscow's commandos took it back, they found themselves with ten pirates on their hands and the prospect of submitting them to an "imperfect" international legal regime. So, as a Defense Ministry spokesman explained, they "released" them. The Russians supposedly put them in a boat and pointed it in the general direction of Somalia. "They could not reach the coast and apparently have all died," said the official, poker-faced.

Oh.

Bad cop or metrosexual Euro-cop? On the high seas of reality, it was not a tough call.

★ ★ ★ ★ ★

FIVE BILLION GUYS NAMED MO

To state the obvious, the world after America is a lot more Muslim. Between 2010 and 2030, the *ummah*—the worldwide Muslim community—was predicted to increase from somewhere between a fifth and a quarter of the global population to one third of humanity.[18] By the time we got there, they wound up with a little more than that, the demographers having failed to take into account such icing on the *ummah*'s cake as the accelerating Muslim conversion rates on the Continent. But one third of humanity turned out to be a good ballpark figure, give or take. Non-Muslims did most of the giving, and Islam did the taking, especially of Europe. According to the UN, global population is supposed to peak at about nine billion in 2050, then level off and start to decline.[19] If you were one of those now mostly extinct eco-fetishists who thought of humanity as a species, then that nine billion was the number to watch, up from six billion at the turn of the century. But, if you didn't think of the world as one unified global parking lot, you were less interested in the big number and more in its constituent parts: on the road to that nine billion, almost all the increase in global population came from Islam and sub-Saharan Africa. Muslims would represent a third of the world's population, yet, aside from a handful of rapacious emirs and a few thousand layabout Saudi princes gambling and whoring in Mayfair and Macau, enjoy almost none of its wealth.

That would come as no surprise if you recall that statistic about Egypt's economic decline relative to South Korea. And Mubarak's thug state was considerably less decayed than Sudan and other Islamic hinterlands where by the dawn of the third millennium they had done a cracking job of killing almost all human progress of the modern age. Nevertheless, they are one in three of the global citizenry. In the first decade of the twenty-first century, Niger, which is over 90 percent Muslim, increased its population by almost half—from just over 10 million to just over 15 million.[20] In 2000, half a million of its children were estimated to be starving, but that was no reason not to add a few million more.[21] Its population is predicted to hit just under 100 million by the end of this century—in a country that can't feed a people one-tenth that size. Was it ever likely that an extra 90 million people would choose to stay within Niger? Samuel Huntington, in *The Clash of Civilizations* (now banned in Europe, following a "human rights" complaint), wrote vividly about "Islam's bloody borders"—"the boundary looping across Eurasia and Africa that separates Muslims from non-Muslims" and provided so many of the horror stories on the nightly news.[22] But by 2020 you could no longer delineate with any clarity that looping boundary: the border was a blur. By 2010, there were more Muslims in Germany than in Lebanon.[23] Within a few years, Germany would be semi-Muslim in its political character. That doesn't mean a majority of the population is Muslim, but the prevailing culture is. Recently, I saw an old film called *Cabaret*, with a memorable scene in a beer garden, in which an Aryan youth sings "Tomorrow Belongs to Me" and everybody joins in. It is a long time since I have been to a German beer garden. Tomorrow would belong to chaps less into draining their steins.

Though less bibulous, the new Europe is an unhealthier continent. I am not speaking metaphorically. By the beginning of the twenty-first century, in the city of Bradford, 75 percent of Pakistani Britons were married to their first cousins.[24] Even the Neanderthal racists warning against the horrors of mass immigration in the late 1960s never thought to predict that in the Yorkshire grade-school classes of the early twenty-first century a majority of the pupils would be the children of first cousins. Yet it happened.

The western elites stuck till the end to their view of man as homo economicus, no matter how obvious it was that cultural identity is a primal indicator that mere economic liberty cannot easily trump. If a man is a Muslim mill worker, which is more central to his identity—that he is a Muslim or that he works in a mill? So the mill closed down, and the Muslim remained, and arranged for his British-born sons to marry cousins imported from the old country, and so a short-term need for manual labor in the mid-twentieth century led to Yorkshire adopting Mirpuri marriage customs. Beyond Bradford, in the nation as a whole, 57 percent of British Pakistanis were married to their first cousins by the turn of the twenty-first century.[25] If, like most of the experts, you were insouciant about that number and assumed that the seductive charms of assimilation would soon work their magic, well, in 1970 the percentage was half that. But back then there were a lot fewer cousins to marry.

Many non-Pakistani Britons were a little queasy about the marital preferences of their neighbors but no longer knew quite on what basis to object to it. "The ethos of relativism," wrote the novelist Martin Amis, "finds the demographic question so saturated in revulsions that it is rendered undiscussable."[26] That was why, even though the marital customs of the Pakistani community of New York were little different, you heard not a peep on the subject from brave American urban liberals still cheerfully making sneering cracks about inbred fundamentalist redneck southern hillbillies.

British Pakistanis were then officially less than 2 percent of the population, yet accounted for a third of all children born with rare recessive genetic diseases—such as Mucolipidosis Type IV, which affects brain function and prevents the body expelling waste.[27] Native Scots families aborted healthy babies at such a rate they're now all but extinct; Pakistani first-cousin families had two, three, four children born deaf, or blind, or requiring spoon-feeding and dressing their entire lives. Learning disabilities among this community cost the education system over $100,000 per child. They cost the government health system millions of pounds a year. And this was the only way a culturally relativist West could even broach the topic: nothing against cousin marriage, old boy, but it places a bit of a strain on the jolly old health-care budget. Likewise, don't get me wrong, I've nothing against the polygamy, it's just the four welfare checks you're collecting for it. An attempt to confine spousal benefits to no more than two wives was struck down as discriminatory by the European Court of Human Rights.

But this was being penny-wise and pound-blasé. When 57 percent of Pakistani Britons were married to first cousins, and another 15 percent were married to relatives, and a fair number of those cousin couples were themselves the children of cousins, it surely signaled that at the very minimum this community was strongly resistant to traditional immigrant assimilation patterns. Of course, in any society, certain groups are self-segregating: the Amish, the Mennonites, and so on. But when that group is not merely a curiosity on the fringe of the map but the principal source of population growth in all your major cities, the challenge posed by that self-segregation is of a different order.

A combination of entitlements and demography would cripple much of the developed world both fiscally and physically. The new Europe is sickly, and its already unsustainable health systems have buckled under the strain. Unless you are in the government nomenklatura, or a member of an approved identity group with an effective lobbying organization, or a celebrity, "universal access to quality health care" means universal access to an ever lengthier, ever more bureaucratically chaotic waiting list.

As for the aging native populations, they were the ones who found it increasingly difficult to self-segregate. There was an entertaining Swedish public health professor called Hans Rosling who liked to use his "Trendalyzer" software to present zippy four-minute demographic computerizations of how the world had progressed over the last two centuries.[28] He used to pop up on YouTube back before the "gatekeeping" or whatever euphemism the Chinese owners now use for their "family-friendly filtering." Professor Rosling produced fun stuff, showing how Botswana by 2010 had advanced, on major socioeconomic indicators, to where Portugal once was, and how Singapore had overtaken Scandinavia. But it would have been interesting to see him apply his Trendalyzer to parts of his own country. Founded as a dock for the Archbishop of Lund, Malmö was one of the first Christian cities in Denmark. In our time it would become the first Muslim city in Sweden. In the old days, around 2011, 2012, I sat and had a coffee in a nice little place in a beautiful medieval square in the heart of town. Aside from a few modernist excrescences, it would not have looked so different in the early days of the Lutheran church. I got lucky, and fell into conversation with a couple of young Swedes. Fine-looking ladies. They're not entirely extinct, not quite, but already I miss Nordic blondes. At dusk, and against their advice, I took a 20-minute walk to Rosengard. As one strolled the sidewalk, the gaps between blondes grew longer, and the gaps between fierce, bearded Muslim men grew shorter. And then eventually you were in the housing projects, and all the young boys kicking a soccer ball around were Muslim, and every single woman was covered—including many who came from "moderate" Muslim countries and did not adopt the headscarf or hijab until they emigrated to Sweden, where it was de rigeur, initially in Rosengard but increasingly throughout. Even then, ambulances and fire trucks did not respond to emergency calls without police escort. What was the rationalization Israel used at the Oslo Accords? "Land for peace"? In Sweden, about as far as you can get from Gaza and the West Bank, they would also trade land for peace, and wound up with neither. The Jews were the first to flee Malmö: soon it was just another town with a weed-strewn, decaying "old Jewish cemetery." Nevertheless, it was not merely the Jewish graveyard that was destined to be abandoned, but the Lutheran ones, too.

★ ★ ★ ★ ★

DARKNESS FALLS

In 2006, Ezra Levant was the only publisher in Canada to allow his readers to see the so-called "Mohammed cartoons," originally printed in

the Danish newspaper *Jyllands-Posten*. As a result he was investigated by the
Government of Alberta and subjected to three long years of judicial harass-
ment. Halfway through his ordeal, Mr. Levant observed that one day the
Danish cartoons crisis would be seen as a more critical event than the
attacks of September 11, 2001.[29] Not, obviously, in terms of the comparative
death tolls, but in what each revealed about the state of western civilization
in the twenty-first century.

After the slaughter of 9/11, the civilized world fought back, hit hard, went
on the attack, rolled up the Afghan terrorist camps, toppled the Taliban. In
the battle cry of a soon forgotten man called Todd Beamer, "Let's roll!"

After the Danish cartoons, we weaseled and equivocated and appeased
and apologized, and signaled that we were willing to trade core western
values for a quiet life. *Let's roll over!* It's a lot less effort.

For the shrewder strategists of the new Caliphate, it wasn't hard to
figure out which was the more telling event about the resolve of the West.
Terrorism was useful as a distraction. Terror attacks so obsessed the
national security state that it poured billions—trillions—into living per-
petually at Code Orange alert, creating gargantuan bureaucracies that
never caught a single terrorist yet managed to persuade the citizenry to
accept the right of government officials to insert their latex-gloved fingers
into your underwear and fondle your scrotum in the interests of "security." Even today, when America is no longer worth blowing up, when the
United States has to all intents blown itself up, it still takes longer than
anywhere on the planet to board a plane, thanks to ancient security kabuki
ever more removed from reality. The more alert the security state was to
shoe-bombers, panty-bombers, implant-bombers, and suppository-
bombers, the more indulgent it grew of any Islamic initiative that stopped
short of self-detonation. Which suited the savvier imams just fine. They
had no desire to be holed up in a smelly cave in the Hindu Kush sharing
a latrine with a dozen halfwitted goatherds while plotting how to blow
up the Empire State Building. Why fly jets into luxury skyscrapers? The
real estate would be theirs soon enough. Eschewing the means, Islam's

shrewder strategists nevertheless shared the same end as the cave dwell-
ers—the wish to expand the boundaries of "the Muslim world." Why
impose Islamic law by the sword and get the infidels all riled up? Mothball
your Semtex belt, and western liberals will volunteer for dhimmitude in
order to demonstrate their multicultural bona fides.

In the Middle East, Islam had always been beyond criticism. It was only
natural that, as their numbers grew in Europe, North America, and Australia, observant Muslims would seek the same protections in their new lands.
But they could not have foreseen how eager western leaders would be to
serve as their enablers. There was the Swedish minister of integration, Jens
Orback, who said we must be nice to Muslims now so that when they're in
the majority they'll be nice to us,[30] and the Dutch justice minister, Piet Hien
Donner, who said he would have no problem with Sharia if a majority of
people voted for it,[31] and of course all those American eminences from
President Obama down eager to proclaim that a mosque at Ground Zero
would be the living embodiment of the First Amendment. As the more
cynical Islamic imperialists occasionally reflected, how quickly the supposed
defenders of liberal, pluralist, western values came to sound as if they were
competing to be Islam's lead prison bitch.

The Netherlands—"the most tolerant country in Europe," to revive
the long obsolete cliché—proved an especially instructive example. In a
peculiarly enthusiastic form of prostration, the Dutch state adopted
"shoot the messenger" as a universal cure-all for "Islamophobia." To some,
Holland had once meant tulips, clogs, windmills, fingers in the dike. To
others, it meant marijuana cafés, long-haired soldiers, legalized hookers,
fingers in the dyke. But by the second decade of the twenty-first century
it was an increasingly incoherent polity where gays were bashed, uncovered
women got jeered in the streets, and you couldn't do *The Diary of Anne
Frank* as your school play lest the Gestapo walk-ons be greeted by audience
cries of "She's in the attic!" There was, of course, some pushback from
extreme right-wing racist extremists, if by "extreme right-wing racists" you
mean the gay hedonist Pim Fortuyn, the anti-monarchist coke-snorting

nihilist Theo van Gogh, and the secular liberal black feminist Ayaan Hirsi Ali. If they objected to the "extreme" labeling, it wasn't for long: in the Low Countries Islam's critics tended to wind up either banned (Belgium's Vlaams Blok), forced into exile (Miss Ali), or dead (Fortuyn and van Gogh).

It was not "ironic" that the most liberal country in western Europe should be so eager to descend into a revoltingly illiberal servitude. It was entirely foreseeable. Justifying extraordinary levels of mass immigration first as narrowly defined economic self-interest and then as moral vanity, Europe made its principal source of new Europeans a population whose primal identity derived from a belief system that claimed total jurisdiction over every aspect of their lives. They were then amazed to discover that that same population of new "Europeans" assumed that all European social, cultural, and political life should realign itself with that belief system. Perhaps they should have considered that possibility earlier. Geert Wilders, a Member of Parliament, was prosecuted, ostensibly for "Islamophobia" but essentially because he was an apostate, a dissenter from the state religion of multiculturalism.[32] It was a heresy trial, the first of many. And, in that sense at least, the European establishment unwittingly eased the transition from "multicultural tolerance" to the more explicitly unicultural and intolerant regimes that followed.

To state the obvious again, the world after America is less Jewish. "Sixty percent of Amsterdam's orthodox community intends to emigrate from Holland,"[33] said Benzion Evers, the son of the city's chief rabbi, five of whose children had already left by 2010. When he walked the streets of his hometown, the young Mr. Evers hid his skullcap under a baseball cap. Seemed like old times. "Jews with a conscience should leave Holland, where they and their children have no future, leave for the U.S. or Israel," advised Frits Bolkestein, former EU Commissioner and head of the Dutch Liberal Party. "Anti-Semitism will continue to exist, because the Moroccan and Turkish youngsters don't care about efforts for reconciliation." Minheer Bolkestein was not (yet) asking what else those "youngsters" didn't care for, but like many other secular Dutchmen with no interest in Jews one way or the other, he soon found out.

The droller Saudi princes and other bankrollers of the new Caliphate occasionally marveled at posterity's jest: as paradoxical as it might sound, the Holocaust had enabled the Islamization of Europe. Without post-war guilt, and the revulsion against nationalism, and the embrace of multiculturalism and mass immigration, the Continent would never have entertained for a moment the construction of mosques from Dublin to Dusseldorf and the accommodation of Muslim sensitivities on everything from the design of British nursing uniforms to Brussels police doughnut consumption during Ramadan. The principal beneficiaries of European Holocaust guilt turned out to be not the Jews but the Muslims.

It took the West some time to accept another obvious truth—that a society that becomes more Muslim will have fewer homosexuals. In 2009, the Rainbow Palace, formerly Amsterdam's most popular *homo-hotel* (in the Dutch vernacular), had announced it was renaming itself the Sharm and reorienting itself to Islamic tourism. Or as the felicitously named website allah.eu put it: "Gay Hotel Turns Muslim."[34]

If you were a nice young couple from San Francisco planning a honeymoon in "the most tolerant city in Europe," it was helpful to make sure your travel brochure was up to date. Within a decade, many of the Continent's once gay-friendly cities were on the brink of majority-Muslim status. But, long before that statistical milestone was reached, the gay moment in Amsterdam, Oslo, and elsewhere was over.

As for the Jews and gays, so for the feminists. In the Muslim housing projects of France, according to the official statistics, the number of rapes rose by an annual 15 to 20 percent throughout the first decade of the twenty-first century.[35] One victim of routine rape in *les banlieues*, the late Samira Bellil, had published an autobiography called *Dans l'enfer des tournantes*—"In the hell of the take-your-turns," the *tournante* being the slang term used by Muslim youths for gang-rape.[36] "There are only two kinds of girls," wrote Mlle. Bellil, who was gang-raped all night at the age of fourteen.

"Good girls stay home, clean the house, take care of their brothers and sisters, and only go out to go to school." Whereas those who "wear make-up, to go out, to smoke, quickly earn the reputation as 'easy' or as 'little whores.'" Lest Muslim girls find themselves in a moment of weakness tempted toward the Paris Hilton side of the tracks, the British National Health Service began offering "hymen reconstruction" surgery in order not to diminish their value to prospective husbands.[37]

When Miss Bellil published her book, her parents threw her out and her community disowned her. But her story discomforted those far beyond the Muslim ghettoes. These facts were too cold and plain to be expressed in a multicultural society which had told itself that, thanks to the joys of diversity, a nice gay couple and a polygamous Muslim with three wives in identical niqabs can live side by side at 27 and 29 Elm Street. In the *New York Times*, the eminent philosopher Martha Nussbaum explained why she objected to moves to ban the burqa in European cities: "My judgment about Turkey in the past," Nussbaum wrote, "was that the ban on veiling was justified, in those days, by a compelling state interest—derived from the belief that women were at risk of physical violence if they went unveiled, unless the government intervened to make the veil illegal for all. Today in Europe the situation is utterly different, and no physical violence will greet the woman who wears even scanty clothing."[38]

How absurd those lazy assumptions read today. But why did they not seem so to Ms. Nussbaum and her editors back in 2010? Even then, no young girl could safely walk in "scanty clothing" through Clichy-sous-Bois or Rosengard. In La Courneuve in France, 77 percent of covered women said they wore the veil to "avoid the wrath of Islamic morality patrols," as the writer Claire Berlinski put it. She added: "We are talking about France, not Iran."[39]

As a young man, long ago, I would often find myself at dinner sitting next to a Middle Eastern lady of a certain age. And the conversation went as it often does when you're with Muslim women who were at college in the Sixties, Seventies, or Eighties. In one case, my dining companion had just been at a conference on "women's issues," of which there were many in the Muslim world, and she was struck by the phrase used by the "moderate Muslim" chair of the meeting: "authentic women"—by which the chair meant women wearing hijabs. And my friend pointed out that when she and her unveiled girlfriends had been in their twenties *they* were the "authentic women": "covering" was for old village biddies, the Islamic equivalent of gnarled Russian babushkas. It would never have occurred to her that the assumptions of her generation would prove to be off by 180 degrees—that in middle age she would see young Muslim women wearing a garb largely alien to their tradition not just in the Middle East but in Brussels and London and Montreal.

I have before me two photographs—first, the Cairo University class of 1978, with every woman bare-headed; second, the Cairo University class of 2004, with every woman hijabed to the hilt.[40]

Even as late as 2020, you would still hear some or other complacenik shrug, "Oh, but they haven't had time to westernize. Just you wait and see. Give it another twenty years, and the siren song of westernization will work its magic." The argument wasn't merely speculative, it had already been proved wrong by what had happened over the previous twenty years. I have a third photograph: the Cairo University class of 1959, with every woman in a blouse and skirt or summer frock, and hair styled no differently from suburban housewives in Westchester County.[41] Cairo University in 1959 looked like London. Now London University looks like Cairo. But western liberals stuck with inevitablist theories of social evolution till the end, convinced that women's rights and gay rights were like the wheel or the internal combustion engine—that once you'd invented them they can't be un-invented. Instead, tides rise, and then ebb.

In the second decade of the twenty-first century, major cities in the heart of the "free world" became less free, and then unfree. An American tourist— a 28-year-old blonde child-woman from Professor Nussbaum's class at the University of Chicago—would not be able to walk through the streets of Amsterdam and Brussels without either being accompanied by men fit enough to ward off any predators or, alternatively, being "covered," initially in the minimalist headscarf style once favored by Hillary Clinton making an official visit to a moderate Arab emirate but soon in something far more smothering. To do otherwise was to risk ending up like Samira Bellil. Western feminist groups, victors in the war against the stern patriarchy of 1950s sitcom dads, for the most part retreated silently—or persuaded themselves, like the Australian feminist Germaine Greer in her effusions about female genital mutilation, to applaud the new oppressor.[42]

And so the world after America celebrates less diversity. It had been fascinating to watch the strange men and women who led the western world in twilight pass off their groveling cowardice as debonair courage. As President Obama was making his now forgotten prostrations in Cairo, his Secretary of State was hectoring the Zionist Entity, regarding the West Bank, that there has to be "a stop to settlements—not some settlements, not outposts, not natural-growth exceptions."[43] No "natural growth"? You mean, if you and the missus have a kid, you've got to talk gran'ma into moving out? To Tel Aviv, or Brooklyn, or wherever? Consciously or not, Mrs. Clinton had endorsed "the Muslim world's position on infidels who happen to find themselves within what it regards as lands belonging to Islam: the Jewish and Christian communities are free to stand still or shrink, but not to grow. Would Obama have been comfortable mandating "no natural growth" to Israel's million-and-a-half Muslims? No. Yet the administration had no difficulty embracing the "the Muslim world's confident belief in one-way multiculturalism, under which Islam expands in the West but Christianity and Judaism shrivel inexorably in the Middle East, Pakistan, and elsewhere. When General Maude's British Indian Army took Baghdad from the Turks in 1917, they found a city whose population was 40 percent Jewish.[44] By the end of the twentieth century, Iraq was just another spot on the map where the only Jews are in the cemetery. And why stop there? In 2003 President Bush's "coalition of the willing" took Baghdad from Saddam Hussein. There were at that time an estimated million or so Christians in Iraq. By 2010, their numbers had fallen by half.[45] In October that year,

Muslim terrorists entered Our Lady of Salvation church in Baghdad and murdered two priests and over fifty congregants.[46] That December only one Christian church in the city formally observed Christmas, but Christian families were still singled out for violence and death in their homes.[47] This happened on America's watch—while Iraq was a protectorate of the global hyperpower. Soon Baghdad's Christians would join Baghdad's Jews as an historical footnote, a community to be found only in weed-choked, garbage-strewn graveyards.

Even as Christians were explicitly targeted from Nigeria to Egypt to Pakistan, Katie Couric, the stupefying purveyor of conventional wisdom on CBS News, proclaimed "Islamophobia" to be one of the year's most unreported stories.[48] Like the earlier coinage of "homophobia," Islamophobia was a mental illness whose only symptom was the accusation of having it. Islam reviled homosexuality but not so much that it wasn't above appropriating the tropes of identity-group victimhood for its own purposes. It worked. President Obama made fawning speeches boasting that "I reject the view of some in the West that a woman who chooses to cover her hair is somehow less equal."[49] How brave of him! But what about the Muslim women who choose not to cover themselves and wind up beaten, brutalized, and the victims of "honor killing"? No, not just in Waziristan and Yemen, but in Germany and Scandinavia and Ontario—and in Buffalo and Peoria, too. Ah, but that would have required real courage, not audience flattery and rhetorical narcissism masquerading as such. When Matthew Shepard was hung out to die on a fence in Wyoming, he became instantly the poster child for an epidemic of "anti-gay" hate sweeping America: books, plays, films were produced about him. Frank Rich, the distinguished columnist of the *New York Times*, had to be restrained from writing about him every week. If there had been a Matthew Shepard murder every few months, Mr. Rich et al would have been going bananas about the "climate of hate." Yet you could run over your daughter in Peoria (Noor Almaleki),[50] decapitate your wife in Buffalo (Aasiya Hassan),[51] drown your three teenage daughters and your first wife in Kingston, Ontario (the Shafia family),[52] and progressive opinion and the press were entirely indifferent. Why were Miss Almaleki and Mrs. Hassan not as famous as Matthew Shepard? They weren't living in up-country villages in the Pakistani tribal lands. They were Americans—and they died because they wanted to live as American women.

But, in an "Islamophobic" West, the new ground rules were quickly established: Islam trumped feminism, trumped homosexuality, trumped everything. In speeches around the globe, the 44th President of the United States affected a cool equidistance between his national interests and those of others. He was less "the leader of the Free World" than the Bystander-in-Chief, and thus the perfect emblem of a western world content to be spectators in their own fate.

The world after America is more violent. In 2011, *Der Spiegel* reported:

> Young Muslim women are often forced to lead double lives in Europe. They have sex in public restrooms and stuff mobile phones in their bras to hide their secret existences from strict families. They are often forbidden from visiting gynecologists or receiving sex ed. In the worst cases, they undergo hymen reconstruction surgery, have late-term abortions or even commit suicide.[53]

This is "living"? *Der Spiegel*'s vignette suggests less a "double life" than a double non-life—westernized slut by day, body-bagged chattel by night. "Forgetfulness occurs," Lee Harris wrote, "when those who have been long inured to civilized order can no longer remember a time in which they had to wonder whether their crops would grow to maturity without being stolen or their children sold into slavery by a victorious foe."[54] They would soon be reacquainted. *Der Spiegel* was fretting over the internal contradictions of sexual hedonism in a multicultural age: Can you have thousands of young men in northern England in loveless marriages to women they never previously knew from their families' home villages back in Mirpur living alongside underdressed Brit slatterns staggering around in mini-skirts and fishnets?

Not without consequences, not for a while. As a culture of unbounded sexual license for women surrendered to one of greater constraints, the sex ed and restroom copulation and hymen reconstruction faded from the scene in Berlin and Amsterdam and Yorkshire. But a world full of male frustrations will always find a market for sex slavery. As the western cities where once they'd procured their blonde "escorts" became Islamized and as erotically enticing as Riyadh, Saudi princes proved a rich market for "European companions," voluntary or conscripted.[55] In China, there would be millions of young men for whom (as a consequence of the government's "one-child" policy) there were no women, and to whom even the sad, dead-eyed trollops of northern England looked good. We were returning to an age where crops are stolen and children enslaved.

As a headline in the impeccably non-far-right *Spiegel* wondered: "How Much Allah Can the Old Continent Bear?"[56]

In the interests of managing this transformation, Europe and Australia and Canada had enthusiastically constrained ancient liberties. At first, it seemed bizarre to find the progressive left making common cause with radical Islam. One half of the alliance professed to be pro-gay, pro-feminist, pro-whatever's-your-bag secularists; the other half were homophobic, misogynist, anti-any-groove-you-dig theocrats. Even as the tatty bus'n'truck roadshow version of the Hitler-Stalin Pact, it made no sense. But in fact what they had in common overrode their superficially more obvious incompatibilities: both the secular Big Government progressives and political Islam recoiled from the concept of the citizen, of the free individual entrusted to operate within his own space, assume his responsibilities, and exploit his potential. But there was a central difference: Islam meant it, and its sense of purpose would be of an entirely different order from the PC statists. And so, as some segments of American and western life sputtered and failed, others would strengthen, growing ever more fiercely self-segregating, demanding at least acquiescence from those they regard as inferior—and using PC institutions to advance their goals.

As Islam well understood, for an enfeebled West, incremental pre-emptive concession was the easiest option. To do anything else would have been asking too much. Appearing before Congress in 2010, the Attorney General of the United States denied repeatedly that the Times Square Bomber, the Fort Hood shooter, and other wannabe jihadists were moti-vated by "radical Islam."[57] Listening to America's chief law enforcement officer, one was tempted to modify Trotsky: You may not be interested in Islam, but Islam is interested in you. The Saudis, having already bought up everything they needed to buy in Christendom, had created a climate that would strangle free speech, even in America. And that was only the begin-ning. Just as the left had embarked on its long march through the institu-tions, so too had Islam. Its Gramscian subversion of transnational bodies, international finance, human rights institutions, and the academy would soon advance to such pillars of the American idea as the First Amendment. Liberty and pluralism do not fall in an instant, in America any more than in Nigeria. Nor does sharia triumph overnight. But Islam's good cop was cannier than its bad: Millenarian Iran wanted to nuke us. Wahhabist Saudi Arabia wanted to own us. Stealth jihad and creeping sharia were to prove more effective.

★ ★ ★ ★ ★

AFTER MAN

What was left of the "developed" world thought it could live as a Greater Switzerland, albeit without the federalism and the gun ownership: like the Swiss, the West was prosperous but neutral, even about itself. Like Geneva, it was attracted to transnational institutions. As the Swiss had lived off banking and chocolates, so the West thought it could live off high finance and delicacies. Switzerland was a place where once one went to prolong life—in expensive sanatoria—but by the twenty-first century had diversified into a one-stop shop for state-of-the-art assisted suicide, both for the terminally ill and for any next of kin in robust physical health who nevertheless were sufficiently depressed to wish to join their loved ones in the express check out.

As Africa and the Muslim world got younger, the West got older. Once America fell apart and it became clear that there was no longer a U.S. cavalry to ride to the rescue, many around the world slumped into fatalism. In the new Europe, death was a living, and euthanasia clinics (the "dignified departure" lounges) boomed. For those less despondent, the trickle of Muslim "reversions" became a flood, as the middle class did what was necessary to get by. One day the office in which you work installs a Muslim prayer room, and a few of your colleagues head off at the designated times, while the rest of you get on with what passes for work in the EU. A couple of years go by, and it's now a few more folks scooting off to the prayer room. Then it's a majority. And the ones who don't are beginning to feel a bit awkward about being left behind. What do you do? The future showed up a lot sooner than you thought. If you were a fundamentalist Christian like those wackjob Yanks, signing on to Islam might cause you some discomfort. But, if you're the average post-Christian Eurosecularist, what does it matter? Who wants to be the last guy sitting in the office sharpening his pencil during morning prayers?

The rowdier remnants of the old working class clutched at new political straws, variously neo-nationalist, quasi-fascist, and downright thuggish. The death-cult left plowed on, insisting that the world was overpopulating and the best thing you could do to save "the planet" was tie your tubes and abort your babies—or kill yourself. Nobody believes the planet-saving bit anymore, but they still abort their babies, out of a more general malaise. Even if you're not suicidal, hospitals are prone to sudden power failures, tragic but economically beneficial: if you thought seniors were expensive at the turn of the century, wait until they're demanding replacement organs grown by nanotechnology.

Untroubled by immigrants, unburdened by grandchildren, dying alone and unloved, the aging Japanese were the first to take a flyer on the post-human future. By the dawn of the new century, they were living longer than ever. The only glitch was that, as the Japanese got older, their young got fewer: the land of the setting sun was already in net population decline, and octogenarians aren't the demographic you turn to to maintain your roads, police the subways, work the supermarket checkout—or look after you in the old folks' home.[58]

A few years earlier, Japan Logic Machine had developed the Yurina—not the most appealing name, especially for a robot that spreads your legs and changes your diaper.[59] But it was a huge success with the elderly and bedridden. It could turn down your bed, run your tub, and then lift you up and carry you over to it for an assisted bath. It wasn't like the old robots of early sci-fi, with cold metallic claws pinching your aged, withered flesh. The Yurina's hands were soft, softer than the calloused digits of the harassed human nurse one saw less and less of.

Saitama University developed an advanced model—a robot that could anticipate your wishes by reading your face.[60] It could tell you were looking at it, and knew enough about you to understand whether a particular facial expression meant you'd like a cup of tea or a tuna sashimi. Professor Yoshinori Kobayashi said this new "humanoid" (his term) was not just for senior centers, but for Tokyo restaurants, too. After all, an aging society has plenty of seniors who like to eat out on wedding anniversaries, but a smaller and smaller pool of potential waitresses. Professor Kobayashi's prototype dressed like a French maid with white pinafore, cap and gloves, and black dress. A full wig of hair framed her wide-eyed Manga features. There are worse ways to end your days than as the surviving human element in an anime/live-action feature.

The Japanese called these humanoids "welfare robots." And I suppose, if you look at it like that, it was a more cost-effective welfare operation than the ugly bruisers of America's public sector unions with their unaffordable benefits and pensions. But it was a melancholy comment on the *fin de civilisation* West that even this most futuristic innovation was driven by the fact that there were too many members of the dependent class and not enough people for them to depend on.

And so the Japanese helped us end our days with our very own French maid and English butler, the real thing being all but extinct by then. Even the early models felt human when you touched them—or, anyway, as human as your average pair of silicone implants feel, and, in Beverly Hills and beyond, the rich soon got used to those.

Even as millions upon millions of poor brutalized Africans attempted to reach the West, a new conventional wisdom developed that the advanced world was running short of emigrants to be our immigrants. Given their citizens' withered birthrates and disinclination to work and their worsening of the already calamitous demographic distortion by using "GRIN" (genetics, robotics, information systems, and nanotechnology) to extend their lives into the nineties and beyond, the state likewise found such technology too seductive to resist. The lazier elected officials soon fell back on the platitude that we need roboclones to do "the jobs that humans won't do"—or can't do. Just as abortion, contraception, and low birthrates were advanced by the demand for women to enter the workforce in massive numbers, so genetic evolution would be advanced by the demand not just for men, women, immigrants, but *anything* to enter the workforce and save the progressive social-democratic state from total collapse. For Japanese and European governments, it was asking too much to expect them to wean their mollycoddled populations off the good life and re-teach them the lost biological impulse. Easier to give some local entrepreneur the license to create a new subordinate worker class.

For years the futurologists had anticipated the age of post-humanity—or super-humanity: the marriage of man to his smartest machines in what Ray Kurzweil had called "the Singularity," a kind of computerized Rapture, in which believers would be digitized and live not forever but as long as they wished, as algorithms in a new form.[61] If you combined the increasing anti-humanism of western environmentalism with western welfarism's urge to hold the moment, to live in an eternal present, as Europe and parts of America seemed to want, the Singularity would seem to be the perfect answer. Instead of dying out because we had no children, we would live our children's and grandchildren's and great-great-great-great-great-grandchildren's lives for them. Kurzweil himself planned on living 700 years: his would be both the last generation of humanity, and the first of super-humanity.

You're probably wondering what these first supermen do? Nothing super, I regret to say. A consistent theme of western twilight, from the grade-school poster of clapping hands circled around the words "We applaud ourselves!" to the woman in Starbucks Blackberrying and Facebooking and Twittering to herself, was of humanity turned inward, "revolving on themselves without repose," in Tocqueville's phrase. The prototype Singulars, pioneering a form of immortality that extends the moment forever, are similarly self-preoccupied, Tweeting into Tweeternity—while physical labor falls to the Welfare Robots, doing the jobs Post-Humans are too busy self-uploading to do.

And so the last generation of ever more elderly westerners goes on—and on and on, like the joke about the gnarled old rustic and the axe he's had for seventy years: he's replaced the blade seven times and the handle four times, but it's still the same old trusty axe. They have achieved man's victory over death, not in the sense our ancestors meant it—the assurance of eternal life in the unseen world—but in the here and now. Which is what it's all about, isn't it? An eternal present tense.

You would be surprised by how fast demographic destiny, economic reality, and technological escape-hatches intersect. Compare the turn-of-the-century's suspicion and denigration of genetically modified foods with what was either enthusiasm for or indifference to genetically modified people. Mess with our vegetables and we would burn down your factory. Mess with us, and we passed you our credit card. And by the time we wondered whether it was all such a smart idea it was the robots that had the Platinum Visa cards.

★ ★ ★ ★ ★

THE SOMALIFICATION OF THE WORLD

The world after America is more dangerous, more violent, more genocidal. The fulfillment of Iran's nuclear ambitions was more than simply the biggest abdication of responsibility by the great powers since the 1930s. It confirmed the Islamo-Sino-Russo-Everybody Else diagnosis of Washington as a hollow superpower that no longer had the will or sense of purpose to enforce the global order.

What changed? At first, it seemed that nothing had. When a year or two went by without Israel getting nuked, people concluded that there had been no reason to worry in the first place. Washington's "realists" said it demonstrated that "containment" (the fallback policy) worked. If the destruction of the Zionist Entity and, indeed, the West as a whole were Iran's goals, they were theoretical—or, at any rate, not urgent. Pre-nuclear Iran had authorized successful mob hits on Salman Rushdie's publishers and translators, and blown up Jewish community centers in Buenos Aires, and acted extraterritorially to the full extent of its abilities for a third of a century, suggesting at the very minimum that it might be prudent to assume that when its abilities go nuclear Iran would be acting to an even fuller extent. But to acknowledge that simple truth would have asked too much of the "great powers," preoccupied as they were with health care reform, and gays in the military, and universal nuclear disarmament.

Everything changed, instantly. But we pretended not to notice. At a stroke, Iran had transformed much of the map—and not just in the Middle East, where the Sunni dictatorships faced a choice between an unsought nuclear arms race or a future as Iranian client states. The "realists" argued that Iran was a "rational" actor and so, because blowing Tel Aviv off the map was totally "irrational," it obviously couldn't be part of the game plan. Whether or not Iran was being "contained" from killing the Jews, there was no strategy for "containing" Iran's use of its nuclear status to advance its interests more discreetly, and no strategy for "containing" the mullahs' generosity to states and groups more inclined to use the technology. It should have been obvious that, even before obliterating Israel, Teheran intended to derive *some* benefit from its nuclear status. Entirely rational leverage would include: controlling the supply of Gulf oil, setting the price, and determining the customers; getting vulnerable emirates such as Kuwait and Qatar to close

U.S. military bases; and turning American allies in Europe into de facto members of the non-aligned movement. Whatever deterrent effect it might have had on first use or proliferation, there was no reason to believe any U.S. "containment" strategy would prevent Iran accomplishing its broader strategic goals. And sure enough all came to pass, very quickly. Why wouldn't they? Soviet containment had been introduced a couple years after Washington had nuked Japan. Iranian "containment" followed years of inaction, in which America and its allies had passively acquiesced in the ayatollahs' ambitions. Unlike the 1940s, there was a fundamental credibility issue.

Saudi Arabia began its own nuclear acquisition program, and continued with it even after it became clear that, on balance, Shia Persian nuclearization worked, like so much else, to Wahhabi Arab advantage. It clarified the good cop/bad cop relationship. The Saudi annexation of the West was now backed by Iranian nuclear muscle.

For the most part, China stands aloof from these disputes. It has no pretensions to succeed America as the global order maker, and, while preferring likeminded authoritarian regimes, is happy to do business with whomsoever finds themselves in power in Africa, South America, or anywhere else. For their part, China's trading partners have no desire to provoke Beijing, not with all those surplus young men it's so eager to dispatch abroad. In a world in which American battleships no longer ply the Pacific, Australia understands that it lives on a Chinese lake. How silly was the assumption that "globalization" meant "westernization" or even "Americanization"—for little reason other than that, when a Danish businessman conversed with his Indonesian supplier, he did so in English. There have always been lingua francas—Latin, French—and their moments came and went. In 1958, just under 10 percent of the world's people spoke English and 15.6 percent spoke Mandarin.[62] By 1992, Mandarin was 15.2 percent, and English was down to 7.6. Today, business computers from Canada to New Zealand have keyboards in Roman and Chinese characters.

Even as it de-anglicizes, so the world after America is reprimitivizing, fast. In the early years of the century, in many columns filed from the VIP lounges of the world's airports, Thomas L. Friedman, the in-house "thinker" at the *New York Times*, had an analogy to which he was especially partial. From December 2008:

> Landing at Kennedy Airport from Hong Kong was, as I've argued before, like going from the Jetsons to the Flintstones.[63]

And it wasn't just space-age Hong Kong! From May 2008:

> In JFK's waiting lounge we could barely find a place to sit. Eighteen hours later, we landed at Singapore's ultramodern airport, with free Internet portals and children's play zones throughout. We felt, as we have before, like we had just flown from the Flintstones to the Jetsons.[64]

And it wasn't just stone-age JFK! From 2007:

> Fly from Zurich's ultramodern airport to La Guardia's dump. It is like flying from the Jetsons to the Flintstones.[65]

I gather that "The Flintstones" and "The Jetsons" were two popular TV cartoon series of the mid-twentieth century. If you still have difficulty grasping Mr. Friedman's point, here he is in 2010, bemoaning the "faded, cramped domestic terminal" in Los Angeles, yet another example of America's, er, terminal decline:

> Businesses prefer to invest with the Jetsons more than the Flintstones.[66]

More fool them. Scholars of twentieth century popular culture say you'd have made a ton more money if you'd invested in "The Flintstones," which was a classic, instead of "The Jetsons," which was a stale knock-off with the veneer of modernity. But, if you were as invested in this theory of terminal decline as Friedman was, it would have helped to think it through a little. Here's one more from the *New York Times*' cartoon thinker, from January 2002, when Americans were, for once, the Jetsons:

> For all the talk about the vaunted Afghan fighters, this was a war between the Jetsons and the Flintstones—and the Jetsons won and the Flintstones know it.[67]

But they didn't, did they? To reprise the old Taliban saying: "Americans have all the watches, but we've got all the time." The American Jetsons had all the high-tech gizmos, but the Afghan Flintstones had the string and fertilizer. The United States had accounted for almost half the world's military expenditures. But somehow it didn't feel like that. In Afghanistan, a few illiterate goatherds with IEDs had tied down the hyperpower for over twice as long as it took America to win victory in the Second World War. To be sure, counterinsurgency campaigns are difficult. But D-Day difficult? Liberating-a-continent difficult? Liberating a continent from a serious enemy with well-trained troops and state-of-the-art technology?

If the jihadists' problem was an inability to forget the Crusades, perhaps the West suffered from an inability to remember. After Muslim provocations against Christians, Pope Urban II spoke to the Council of Clermont in 1095 and called for what we now know as the First Crusade. Within four years, an army had been raised, got to the Middle East (on foot for most of the journey), liberated the Holy Land, and established a Christian Kingdom of Jerusalem that lasted for two centuries. Four years, eight years, twelve years after George W. Bush spoke in the rubble of Ground Zero, Ground Zero was still rubble, and all the smart thinkers insisted that it was a waste of time to discuss whatever it was America was doing in Afghanistan in terms of outmoded concepts such as "victory." Nobody had any desire to be in Kabul for another two centuries, or even another two years.

Well, the First Crusade was too long ago, and so was D-Day, and the wars were different now: America had more ships and more planes than anybody else on the planet. So, entirely reasonably, nobody wanted to get into a dogfight or a naval battle with them. Instead, the geopolitical Gulliver was up against legions of Liliputians—fiercely motivated youths generated by an ideology with all but unlimited manpower. It had been that way since Somalia in the early Nineties. The Americans made a film on the subject (*Black Hawk Down*) and then never gave it another thought. And so, two decades on, the world's most luxuriously funded military showed no sign of having adapted to the world it was living in. Its enemies had: an IED was an "improvised" explosive device. Why couldn't America improvise? In the early stages of its wars, IEDs were detonated by cell phones and even garage-door openers. So the Pentagon jammed them. The enemy downgraded to more primitive detonators: you can't jam string. In 2010 it was reported that the Taliban had developed metal-free IEDs, which made them all but undetectable: instead of two hacksaw blades and artillery shells, they began using graphite blades and ammonium nitrate.[68] If you had tanks and battle-ships and jet fighters, you were too weak to take on the hyperpower. But, if you had string and hacksaws and fertilizer, you could tie him down for a decade. America had fallen for the Friedman thesis: in Afghanistan, the Taliban had invested in "The Flintstones," while the West had invested in "The Jetsons," and we were the ones desperate to negotiate our way out.

So, in the fall of 2001, the Jetsons toppled the Flintstones. And the Flintstones bided their time, and quickly figured out that the Jetsons didn't have the stomach to do what it takes, and their space-age occupation of Bedrock would rapidly dwindle down into a thankless semi-colonial polic-ing operation for which the citizenry back on the home front in Orbit City would have no appetite. Jetson-wise, the West was all jets and no sons. The sociologist Gunnar Heinsohn pointed out that 1,000 German men had 480 sons, while 1,000 Afghan men had 4,000 sons.[69] To lose your only son in a distant war is devastating. For your third, fourth, and fifth sons, what else is there for them to do?

The Pentagon was post-human before post-human was cool. Having pioneered unmanned drones to zap the natives from the skies, it developed more sophisticated models—drones that flew in the exosphere, and were even more invisible to the goatherds far below. When you're dependent on technology in an age of globalized computerization, it's hard to make everything "secure," and certainly not as secure as a group of inbred jihadists sitting around a camp fire. The unceasing Chinese cyber-probing grew more and more probing, and daring. Drones would suddenly drop from the skies for no apparent reason. Nobody minded: if it was a casualty of war, it was not one to be memorialized or exploited for political gain. Eventually the cost of replacing them became prohibitive. The land of the unmanned drone gradually abandoned the drone, while remaining unmanned.

Recall H. G. Wells' Time-Traveler. When he makes his first foray into the Morlocks' subterranean lair, he is impressed to find that, unlike the effete Eloi, they are not vegetarian. On the other hand, he is not clear exactly what large animal it is that they're roasting on the spit.

And then the penny drops.

"Even now man is far less discriminating and exclusive in his food than he was—far less than any monkey," he reflects. "His prejudice against human flesh is no deep-seated instinct. And so these inhuman sons of men—!"

He calms himself and tries to look at it in a scientific spirit. "After all, they were less human and more remote than our cannibal ancestors of three or four thousand years ago."

I gather that, for TV comics and newspaper cartoonists of your time—the mid-twentieth century—there were few more reliable laughs than putting a white man wearing a pith helmet in a big pot surrounded by dancing natives. Yet, oddly enough, there was virtually no empirical basis for such a persistent stereotype. "The rest of the world had always believed that there was cannibalism in Africa," wrote Charles Onyango-Obbo in *The East African* in 2003, "but there wasn't much hard evidence for it."[70]

Yet by the early days of the twenty-first century, when the PC enforcers would clobber you for even the mildest evocation of the old cooking-pot gag, cannibalism was flourishing. Mr Onyango-Obbo had been reporting that the Congolese Liberation Movement was slaughtering huge numbers of people and feeding the body parts to their relatives. In North Kivu, a group called les Effaceurs (the Erasers) had wanted to open up the province's mineral resources to commercial exploitation and to that end had engaged in ethnic cleansing by cannibalism. The Congo Civil War raged for most of the first decade of this century uncovered by CNN and the *New York Times* for want of any way to blame it on George W. Bush. Among the estimated six million dead, many were eaten. The two parties to the conflict agreed on very little except that pygmies make an excellent entrée. Both sides hunted them down as if they were the drive-thru fast-food of big game. While regarding them as sub-human, they believed that if you roasted their flesh and ate it you would gain magical powers. In return, the pygmies asked the UN Security Council to recognize cannibalism as a crime against humanity, for all the good that did.[71]

After all, a society that will resume cannibalism is unlikely to observe any UN resolutions. As Mr. Onyango-Obbo saw it, the resurgence of the two-legged menu option was a function of Africa's reprimitivization. "Cannibalism," he wrote, "happens commonly where there is little science, and people don't see themselves as creatures of a much higher order than other animals around them. When you have gone to the moon, you consider yourself and other humans to be very different from the chimp at the zoo."

But in the twilight of the West, Americans no longer went to the moon, and environmental activists loudly proclaimed that man was no different from the chimps (who by the way shouldn't be in the zoo).

The state of nature made huge advances in the early years of the century. Why did we never wonder what might happen when such forces went nuclear? Ah, well. The transnational jet set had other filet o' fish to fry. They had convinced themselves that economic and technological factors shape the world all but exclusively, and that the sexy buzz words—"globalization," "networking"—could cure all ills. The famous Golden Arches Thesis of Thomas Friedman posited that countries with McDonald's franchises don't go to war with each other. Shortly thereafter, Bill Clinton bombed Belgrade, a city richly endowed with western fast-food outlets. A few years earlier, when the Iron Curtain had fallen, Yugoslavia had been, economically, the best-positioned of the recovering Communist states. But, given the choice between expanding the already booming vacation resorts of the Dalmatian coast for their eager Anglo-German tourist clientele or reducing Croatia and Bosnia and Kosovo to rubble over ethno-linguistic differences no outsider can even discern ("Serbo-Croat"?), Yugoslavia opted for the latter. They didn't eat their enemies' private parts, but they certainly sliced off plenty of breasts and genitals.

Another thinker, Thomas P. M. Barnett, the widely admired author of *The Pentagon's New Map: War and Peace in the Twenty-First Century* and *Blueprint for Action: A Future Worth Creating*, liked to divide the world into a functioning "Core" and a "Non-Integrating Gap."[72] He favored using a "SysAdmin" force—a "pistol-packin' Peace Corps"—to transform the "Gap" countries and bring them within the "Core." Like many chaps who swan about dispensing high-end advice to international A-listers, he viewed the world's problems as something to be sorted out by more effective elites— better armed forces, international agencies, that sort of thing. The common herd was noticeable by its absence from his pages. If he had given them any thought, he might have realized that his vision of a "SysAdmin" force— European allies that would go into countries after American hard power has liberated them—was simply deluded. Whatever the defects of the Continent's elites, the real problem was not the lack of leaders but the lack of followers.

It soon became clear that Professor Barnett was holding his thesis upside down. Rather than Europe's leadership class helping move countries from the Non-Integrating Gap to the Core, it would have its work cut out preventing large parts of the Core doing a Bosnia and moving to the Non-Integrating Gap. For all the economic growth since World War II, much of the world had gone backwards—almost the whole of West Africa, and Central Africa, and Sudan, Somalia, Pakistan, Bosnia. Yet none of the elite asked themselves a simple question: What's to stop that spreading? In a world after America, the reprimitivization of the map would accelerate: the new Jew-hating Sweden…the French banlieues where the state's writ ceased to run…Clapton, East London, where Shayna Bharuchi cut out her four-year-old daughter's heart while listening to an MP3 of the Koran…

A famous American First Lady wrote a bestseller called *It Takes a Village* (to raise a child)—an African proverb, supposedly. Why our leaders should have been commending tribal life as a model for advanced societies is a mystery. But even Africans didn't want to raise their children in an African village. They abandoned them for shanties in what (if you flew over West Africa by night) looked like one giant coastal megalopolis. And, with respect to child-rearing, they left behind most of their traditions, too. We are a planet without a past—or, at any rate, memory. Like the European trans-nationalists wedded to their Ponzi welfare state, like the American spenda-holics burning through trillions as if it was still 1950 and they were the only economic power on earth, like the Singularity post-humans revolving on themselves without repose, reprimitivized man lives in an eternal present tense, in the dystopia of the moment. In *The Atlantic Monthly* a few years back, casting around for a phrase to describe the "citizens" of such "states," Robert D. Kaplan called them "re-primitivized man."[73] Demographic growth, environmental devastation, accelerated urbanization, and civic decay have reduced them to a far more primitive state than their parents and grandparents. As Andrew McCarthy wrote: "Civilization is not an evolution of mankind but the imposition of human good on human evil. It is not a historical inevitability. It is a battle that has to be fought every day, because evil doesn't recede willingly before the wheels of progress."[74]

By the dawn of the twenty-first century, Liberia, the Congo, Somalia, Sudan, Iran, Pakistan, and North Korea were all less "civilized" than they had been a couple of generations ago. And yet in one sense many of them had made undeniable progress: they had globalized their pathologies.

Somali pirates seized container ships flying the ensigns of the great powers. Iranian proxies ran Gaza and much of Lebanon. North Korea's impoverished prison state had provided nuclear technology to Damascus and Teheran, and Teheran had agreed to station missiles in Venezuela. Even the nude warlords of west Africa had managed to destabilize on a scale no second-tier western power could contemplate. Celebrating diversity unto the end, wealthy nations that could no longer project meaningful force to their own borders watched the two-bit basket-cases nuclearize, and assumed this geopolitical diversity would have no consequences. By 2005, Iran was offering to share its nuclear technology with Sudan.[75]

Sudan? Oh, surely you remember: the other day I found a program for a "Save Darfur" interpretative-dance fundraiser in the attic. Massachusetts, I think. Perhaps you attended. Someone read out a press release from the activist actor George Clooney, and everyone had a simply marvelous time. Meanwhile, back in Sudan, the killing went on: hundreds of thousands of people were murdered. With machetes. That's pretty labor-intensive.

But a nuclear Sudan would supposedly be a model of self-restraint?

The mound of corpses piled up around the world at the turn of the century was not from high-tech nuclear states but from low-tech psycho states. Yet the Pansy Left (in George Orwell's phrase) continued to insist that the problem was technological, a question of nuclear "proliferation." Even from a post-American world, it seems sad to have to point out that the problem was not that America had nukes and that poor old Sudan had to make do with machetes. It's that the machete crowd were willing to kill on an industrial scale and the high-tech guys could not muster the will to stop them. To horrified western liberals, nuclear technology was bad in and of itself. But nukes are means. What you do with them depends on your ends. And if, as in the Congo and Sudan, killing is your end, then you will find the means. Perhaps it was only sensitivity to cultural diversity that prevented President Obama taking up a machete non-proliferation initiative.

There is a fine line between civilization and the abyss. North Korea had friends on the Security Council. Powerful states protected one-man psycho

states. And one-man psycho states provided delivery systems to apocalyptic ideological states. And apocalyptic ideological states funded non-state
actors around the world. And in Somalia and elsewhere non-state actors
were constrained only by their ever increasing capabilities.

As America should have learned the hard way in Iraq and Afghanistan,
stupid, ill-trained illiterates with primitive explosives who don't care who
they kill can inflict a lot of damage on the technologically advanced highly
trained warriors of civilized states. As one of Nick Berg's kidnappers
explained both to his victim and to the world in the souvenir Islamic snuff
video, "You know, when we behead someone, we enjoy it."[76] Thus, "asym-
metric warfare" on a planet divided into civilized states with unusable
nuclear arsenals and barbarous regimes happy to kill with whatever's to
hand. We had moved into a world beyond American order, but in which,
as large swathes of the map reprimitivized, the shrinking superpower would
remain the most inviting target.

Many westerners were familiar with Nietzsche's accurate foretelling of
the twentieth century as an age of "wars such as have never happened on
earth."[77] This was a remarkable prediction to make from the Europe of the
1880s, a time of peace and prosperity. But too many forget the context in
which the philosopher reached his conclusion—that "God is dead."
Nietzsche was an atheist but he was not simply proclaiming his own contempt for faith, as Richard Dawkins, Sam Harris, and other bestselling
atheists would do in our own century. "God is dead" was not a statement
of personal belief, but a news headline—in the author's words, a "tremendous event." If, as he saw it, educated people had ceased to believe in the
divine, that entailed certain consequences. For God—or at any rate the
Judeo-Christian God whose demise he was reporting—had had a civilizing
effect during his (evolutionarily speaking) brief reign. Without God,
Nietzsche wondered, without "any cardinal distinction between man and
animal," what constraints are there? In the "arena of the future," the world
would be divided into "brotherhoods with the aim of the robbery and
exploitation of the non-brothers." That was the purpose of his obituary

announcement: "The story I have to tell," he wrote in 1882, "is the story of the next two centuries."

We know he called the twentieth century right. So what did he have to say about the twenty-first? He foresaw a time even worse than the "wars such as have never happened," wars that were after all still fought according to the remnants, the "mere pittance" of the late God's moral codes. But after that, what? The next century—our century—would see "the total eclipse of all values." Man would attempt a "re-evaluation," as the West surely did through multiculturalism, sexual liberation, eco-fetishization, and various other fancies. But you cannot have an effective moral code, Nietzsche pointed out, without a God who says "Thou shalt not."

Thou shalt not what? Eat pygmies? Rip out children's hearts? Wire up your own infant as a bomb? Express mild disapproval of the cultures that engage in such activities? Multiculturalism was the West's last belief system. Its final set of values accorded all values equal value. Which is to say that it had no values—for, if all values have equal value, what's the point? There was still enough of the "mere pittance" of the old values for skanky tweens in hooker chic or burqa-ed women escorting their daughters to the FGM clinic to cause feminists some momentary disquiet. But they could no longer summon up a moral language to object to it. They valued all values, and so relentlessly all values slipped into eclipse—and then a valueless age dawned.

It's never a good idea to put reality up for grabs. I remember my last visit to Monte Carlo, to see an old friend who had retired there for tax reasons. Enjoying a café au lait under an awning on a pedestrianized street, we watched the world go by and discussed the demographic death spiral that "alarmist" early-century tracts had played up. And, after chewing over the numbers for Italy, Spain, and so on, my friend had said jokingly, "Well, what about Monaco? Could Monte Carlo spearhead the rebirth of Europe?"

Alas, no. Monaco had the lowest birth rate on the planet: seven births per thousand people.[78] That was because it was a chichi little enclave of wealthy tax exiles, and who wants snot-nosed kids getting underfoot and spoiling things? The town was impressive—clean, prosperous, civilized, and no children. What could be more amiable?

That's what more and more of Europe felt like, at least outside the surging Muslim enclaves. Much of the western world had made a bet that it could survive as a giant Monte Carlo—rich, plump, happy, and insulated from all the unpleasantness of life. As I said to my friend that day: What's holding Monte Carlo in place?

It's a short sail from impoverished North Africa. What was there to prevent, say, a bunch of Algerians just walking in and taking it?

The first victims of American retreat were the many parts of the world that had benefited from an unusually benign hegemon. But eventually the consequences of retreat came home, too.

How quickly the world turns:

Western Europe is semi-Islamic.

A resurgent Russia is also Islamizing fast but under a stern petro-czar confident he can control them. He has reestablished Eastern Europe and Central Asia as the bear's sphere of influence.

Iran is the dominant power in the Middle East, actively supported by a post-Kemalist Turkey and with the reluctant acquiescence of the Sunni dictatorships. Its missiles can reach western Europe, and its technology is being dispersed to friendly nations and non-state actors alike.

Pakistan has fallen to the local branch of the Taliban, and India is preoccupied by a nuclear stand-off. North Korea is clinging on as a nuclear Wal-Mart for anyone who wants a No Dong missile at unbeatable prices.

China is growing old, and is in a hurry. Resource-short as always, it has bought up much of Africa. The least worst parts of the Dark Continent are a de facto Beijing protectorate, while those territories that are too much trouble for China to annex are exporting their people and their problems north.

Latin America is for sale to whoever's buying—the Chinese, the Russians, the new Caliphate. Islam has made modest inroads into the continent—not huge but just enough to add a whole new wrinkle to America's unenforced southern border. A failing superpower doesn't have the guards to keep track of the line, even if it wanted to. One time there was talk of getting state-of-the-art sensors like the Chinese have, to keep their Uighurs in place. But no one in the crumbling union of however many states remain in Old Glory has the budget any more. The Border Patrol do their best, but it's getting harder to tell José from Mohammed what with the opportunist "reversions" going on among the drug cartels.

Going over the computer footage one morning, the guards see a truck managed to get across during the night. Not a big deal, probably just a couple dozen peasants heading north to join their families.

Funny thing, though. The truck didn't stop in the Arizona desert and let out its human cargo. The border guys found out a couple days later it had headed north, picked up Interstate 40 eastbound, all the way through New Mexico, Oklahoma, Arkansas, Tennessee until it hit Greensboro and swung north on I-85.

Towards Washington.

They figured it out when they saw it on the news.

THE HOPE OF AUDACITY

I do not believe that the solution to our problem is simply to elect the right people. The important thing is to establish a political climate of opinion which will make it politically profitable for the wrong people to do the right thing. Unless it is politically profitable for the wrong people to do the right thing, the right people will not do the right thing either, or if they try, they will shortly be out of office.
—Milton Friedman, *Milton Friedman in Australia* (1975)

In February 2009, a few weeks after his inauguration, President Obama went to Congress to deliver America's first State of the European Union address. It included the following:

I think about Ty'Sheoma Bethea, the young girl from that school I visited in Dillon, South Carolina—a place where the ceilings leak, the paint peels off the walls, and they have to stop teaching six times a day because the train barrels by their classroom. She had been told that her school is hopeless, but the other day after class she went to the public library and typed up a letter to the people sitting in this chamber. She even asked her principal for

the money to buy a stamp. The letter asks us for help, and says,
"We are just students trying to become lawyers, doctors, con-
gressmen like yourself and one day president, so we can make a
change to not just the state of South Carolina but also the world.
We are not quitters." That's what she said. "We are not quitters."[1]

There was much applause, and this passage was cited approvingly even by
some conservatives as an example of how President Obama was yoking his
"ambitious vision" (also known as record-breaking spending) to traditional
appeals to American virtues. In fact, the Commander-in-Chief was deftly
yoking the language of American exceptionalism to the cause of European
statism. Apparently, nothing testifies to the American virtues of self-reliance
and entrepreneurial energy like joining the monstrous army of robotic
extras droning in unison, "The government needs to do more for me...."
The animating principles of the American idea were entirely absent from
Obama's vision—unless by American exceptionalism you mean an exceptional effort to harness an exceptionally big government in the cause of
exceptionally massive spending.

Consider first the least contentious part:

> We are just students trying to become lawyers, doctors,
> congressmen...

The doctors are now on track to becoming yet another group of government employees; the lawyers sue the doctors for medical malpractice and,
when they've made enough dough, like ambulance-chaser par excellence
John Edwards, they get elected to Congress. The American Dream, twenty-
first-century version? Is there no one in Miss Bethea's school who'd like to
be an entrepreneur, an inventor, a salesman, a generator of wealth? *Someone*'s got to make the dough the government's already spent. Maybe Dillon
High School's most famous alumnus, Federal Reserve chairman Ben Bernanke, could explain it to them.

As for the train "barreling by their classroom," the closest the railroad track comes to the school is about 240 yards, or over an eighth of a mile.[2] The president was wrong: trains are not barreling by any classroom six times a day. And, even if they were, that's fewer barrelings per diem than when the school was built in 1912, or the new wing added in 1957. Incidentally, multiple press reports referred to the "113-year old building." Actually, that's the building *behind* the main school—the original structure from 1896, where the School District bureaucracy now has its offices. But if, like so many people, you assume an edifice dating from 1896 or 1912 must ipso facto be uninhabitable, bear in mind that the central portion of the main building was entirely rebuilt in 1983.

That's to say, this rotting, dilapidated, mildewed Dotheboys Hall of a Gothic mausoleum dates all the way back to the Cyndi Lauper era.

Needless to say, the Obama stenographers up in the press gallery were happy to take the Hopeychanger-in-Chief at his word on the facts of the case. But even more striking is how indifferent they were to the bigger question: "She had been told her high school is hopeless," said the president.

But surely a school lavishly funded by world and historical standards that needs outside help from the national government for a paint job is, by definition, "hopeless"?

What of the students' alleged ambition to "make a change to not just the state of South Carolina but also the world"? Well, why not start closer to home? Instead of "changing the world," why not try to change your crummy school and your rundown town? Or does that lack the Obama-esque glamour of healing the planet? Come to that, why would the rest of humanity want to have the world changed by someone who can't organize a paint job?

In practice, one-worldism conveniently absolves one of doing anything about more localized and less exotic concerns—such as peeling paint and leaking ceilings. And, if a schoolhouse is so afflicted, what's the best way to fix it? Applying for federal funds and processing the building maintenance through a huge continental bureaucracy? Or doing what my neighbors in

New Hampshire did when the (older than Dillon) grade-school bell-tower was collapsing? The carpenters and painters donated their time, and the materials were paid for through the proceeds of such non-world-changing activities as community square dances and bean suppers.

If that sounds sick-makingly Norman Rockwell, well, take it from me, small town life is hell and having to interact with folksy-type folks in a "tightly knit community" certainly takes its toll, and the commemorative photo montage in the restored tower of gnarled old Yankees in plaid looking colorful while a-hammerin' and a-shinglin' doesn't fully capture many of the project's arcane yet fractious disputes. Still, forget the cloying small-town sentimentality: it's the quickest and cheapest way to get the job done. It always is.

Dillon, South Carolina, is a city of about 6,000 people. Is there really no way they can organize acceptable accommodation for a two-grade Junior High School without petitioning the Sovereign in Barackingham Palace?

Like many municipalities with a significant black population, Dillon has an absence of men: in a quarter of its households, the only adult is a female; in the town as a whole, there are 80 men for every 100 women. Then again, painting walls does not require a burly old brute, and, with a county employment rate of 15 percent, there are surely residents of Dillon with time available.[3] Wouldn't it have made an inspiring tale if, instead of beseeching King Barack the Two-Coats, the people of Dillon had just got on with it and done it themselves? It's the sort of thing they'd once have made a heartwarming TV movie about: *The Little Junior High That Could.*

Ah, but instead of the can-do spirit we now have the can-do-with-some-government-funding spirit. And it's hard to get an inspirational heart-warmer out of that.

From *The New England Primer* to federally disbursed primer: Tocqueville would weep. "It is in the township that the strength of free peoples resides," he wrote. "Municipal institutions are for liberty what primary schools are for science; they place it within reach of the people.... Without municipal institutions, a nation is able to give itself a free government, but it lacks the spirit of liberty."

Even if the federal behemoth were capable of timely classroom repainting from D.C. to Hawaii, consider the scale of government and the size of bureaucracy that would be required. Once such an apparatus is in place, it won't content itself with paint jobs. The issue is not the decrepitude of the building but the decrepitude of liberty. Maybe Big Government can spend enough of our children's money to halt the degradation of infrastructure. But the degradation of citizenship—of the "spirit of liberty"—is harder to reverse.

As dispiriting as Miss Bethea's letter was, Obama's citation of it was even more so. How could any citizen-president of a self-governing republic quote approvingly a plea for remote, centrally regulated, continent-wide dependency?

Because that's what he likes about it: the willingness of freeborn citizens to be strapped in to the baby seats of Big Nanny. Ty'Sheoma Bethea's application for federal dependency justifies the ruling class' belief in its own indispensability. That's why it got read out in Congress. Almost two years later, in a strikingly whiney response even by his own standards, Obama pleaded to a liberal interviewer that he was merely the president, not the king.[4] Well, how did large numbers of people such as young Miss Bethea get so confused on that point? For both the ruling class and a huge number of its subjects, it is not just routine but (as Obama suggested) somehow admirable to look to central government to supply your needs—shelter, sustenance, clothing, medication, painless sedatives both pharmaceutical and figurative. To Ty'Sheoma Bethea and her school chums, it sounds liberating: if the benevolent state takes care of all your needs, you're free to concentrate on "changing the world." In reality, you've already changed it—from a state of raw, messy liberty to one on the path to despotic insolvency. What would be the price of a gallon of paint once it's been routed through a massive centralized education bureaucracy?

For the moment that remains a purely hypothetical thought. On the other hand, the first major item of congressional business after the Democrats' midterm shellacking in 2010 was to pass a "Food Safety" Act, among whose items was federal regulation of schoolhouse bake sales.[5] If the students of Dillon ever rouse themselves to do something about their peeling paint and train-rattled windows by selling blueberry pies and cranberry muffins, they can at least do so knowing their baked goods are now under the supervision of the Imperial Court in Washington.

★ ★ ★ ★ ★

IT'S NOT HOW YOU QUIT, IT'S WHERE YOU START

"I think of Ty'Sheoma Bethea," said Barack Obama. I think I think of her rather more than he does these days, and I wonder how two generations of American students came to think like this at all.

I doubt I'll be invited to give the commencement address in Dillon any time soon. Even at the best of times, "upbeat and inspirational" isn't really my bag. I went to one of those old-school English boys' institutions where instead of prioritizing "self-esteem" the object was to lower it to imperceptible levels by the end of the first week. Still, I've spoken at enough American schools to know that you're supposed to jolly 'em along with something uplifting like "You can be anything you want to be." Here's the problem, and here's what I would tell the student body of Dillon in the unlikely event they book me for a motivational speech:

> You can't always be anything you want to be. I wanted to be a great tap-dancer. Instead I'm a mediocre tap-dancer. But that's my problem. Your problem is that my generation and your teachers' generation have put a huge obstacle in the way of you being anything you want to be: We've spent your future. Generationally speaking, yours truly, the principal, the guidance

counselor, the school board, the old, the late middle-aged and the early middle-aged have cleaned you out before you've got going.

"It's about the future of all our children." And the future of all our children is that you'll be paying off the past of all your grandparents. In the assisted-suicide phase of western democracy, voters are seduced by politicians who bribe them with government lollipops, but they're not willing to pay the cost of those lollipops. Solution: Kick it down the road, and stick it to the next generation. That's you.

So government has spent your future. This is the biggest generational transfer of wealth in the history of the world. Look at the way your parents and grandparents live: it's not going to be like that for you. You're going to have a smaller house, and a smaller car—if not a basement apartment and a bus ticket. But thanks a bundle, it worked out great for us. We of the Greatest Generation, the Boomers, and Generation X salute you, the plucky members of the Brokest Generation, the Gloomers, and Generation Y, as in "Why the hell did you old coots do this to us?", which is what you're going to be asking in a few years' time. You're being lined up for a twenty-first-century America of more government, more regulation, less opportunity, and less prosperity—and you should be mad about it: when you come to take your seat at the American table (to use another phrase politicians are fond of), you'll find the geezers, the boomers, and the Gen X-ers have all gone to the bathroom, and you're the only one sitting there when the waiter presents the check. That's you: Generation Checks.

"You can be anything you want to be!" "Dream your dreams!" You won't be able to dream your dreams, because you'll be the gray morning after of us oldtimers' almighty bender. The American Dream will be as elusive and mythical as the Greek Dream. Andrew Biggs of the American Enterprise Institute calculated that if the federal government were to increase every single tax by 30 percent it would be enough to balance the books—in 25 years.[6] Except that it wouldn't. Because if you raised taxes by 30 percent, government would spend even more than it already does, on the grounds that the citizenry needed more social programs and entitlements to compensate for their sudden reduction in disposable income.

In the Sixties, the hippies used to say, "Never trust anyone over 30." Now all the Sixties hippies are in their sixties, and they've gone quiet about that, but it's good advice for you: never trust anyone over 30 with the societal checkbook. You thought you were the idealistic youth of the Obama era, but in fact you're the designated fall-guys. You weren't voting for "the future," but to deny yourself the very possibility of one—like turkeys volunteering to waddle around with an *Audacity of Thanksgiving* bumper sticker on your tush. Instead of swaying glassy-eyed behind President Obama at his campaign rallies singing "We are the hopeychange," you should be demanding that the government spend less money on smaller agencies with fewer employees on lower salaries. Because if you don't, there won't be a future. "You can be anything you want be"—but only if you first tell today's big spenders that, whatever they want to be, they should try doing it on their own dime.

That's the most basic truth the young could impose on the old—the immorality of spending now and charging it to Junior. Next time Obama tells Joe the Plumber he wants to "spread the wealth around," it should be pointed out that you can't spread it until you've earned it. "Redistribution" from the future to the present is a crock, and if you happen (like the student body at Dillon High School) to have been assigned to the "future" half of that equation, you should be merciless in your contempt for the present-tensers who've done that to you.

Next to the gaseous abstractions of "hope" and "change" these are cruel, hard truths. But truths is what they are. Big Government makes everything else small, and rolling it back will be difficult. But a few core principles are useful guides:

★ ★ ★ ★ ★

DE-CENTRALIZE

To return to Obama's plea that he is not the king, but only the president: the American colonists overthrew the Crown because they believed the people are sovereign. If that means anything at all, it means that power is leased up from the citizen to town, to county, to state, to the nation, and ever more sparingly at each step along the way. In Canada, by contrast, the Crown is sovereign, and power is leased down through nation, province, and municipality to the subjects. The unceasing centralization of power nullifies the American Revolution. Even surviving local institutions aren't as local as they used to be. The nearly 120,000 school boards of America in 1940 have been consolidated into a mere 15,000 today, leaving them ever more to the mercies of the professional "educator" class.[7] Which is not unconnected to the peeling-paint problem in Dillon, South Carolina.

If this trend is going to be reversed, it will be by states and municipalities both ignoring Washington and, when necessary, defying it. "It is important to recognize the distinction," said President Reagan in 1987, "between problems of national scope (which may justify Federal action) and problems that are merely common to the States."[8] The former ought to be a very limited category: the best way to save "the United States" is to give it less to do, and the best way to do that is with a Tenth Amendment movement. "Let a hundred flowers bloom!" said Mao, who didn't mean it. So let fifty bloom—and then even more.

As we discussed earlier, in a liberal world much of our language decays into metaphor, disconnected from physical reality. A few years ago, a Fleet Street colleague accidentally booked himself into a conference on "building bridges" assuming it would be some multiculti community outreach yak-fest. It turned out to be a panel of engineers discussing bridge construction. If only more "bridge building" was non-metaphorical: the ability to build real bridges is certainly an attribute of community, and one Americans used to be able to do for themselves.

A friend of mine is a New Hampshire "selectman," one of those munic-ipal offices Tocqueville found so admirable. In 2003, a state highway inspec-tor rode through town and condemned one of the bridges, on a dirt road that serves maybe a dozen houses.

That's the bad news. The good news was the 80/20 state/town funding plan, under which, if you applied to Concord for a new bridge, the state would pay 80 percent of the cost, the town 20. So they did. The state esti-mated the cost at $320,000, so the town's share would be $64,000. Great. So the town threw up a temporary bridge just down river from the condemned one, and waited for the state to get going. Six years later, the temporary bridge had worn out, and the latest revised estimate was $655,000, so the town's share would be $131,000.

That's the bad news. The good news was that, under the "stimulus" bill, they could put in for the 60/40 federal/state bridge funding plan, under which the feds pay 60 percent, and the state pays 40, and thus the town would be on the hook for 20 percent of the 40 percent, if you follow. If they applied for the program now, the bridge might be built by, oh, 2018, 2020, and it'll only be $1.2 million, or $4 million, or $12 million, or whatever the estimate'll be by then.

But who knows? By 2018, there might be some 70/30 UN/federal bridge plan, under which the UN pays 70 percent, and the feds pay 30, and thus the town would only be liable for 20 percent of the state's 40 percent of the feds' 30 percent. And the estimate for the bridge will be a mere $2.7 billion.

While the Select Board was pondering this, another bridge was condemned. The state's estimate was $415,000, and, given that the previous bridge had been on the to-do list for six years, they weren't ready to pencil this second one in on the schedule just yet. So instead the town put in a new bridge from a local contractor. Cost: $30,000. Don't worry; it's all up to code—and a lot safer than the worn-out temporary bridge still waiting for the 80/20/60/40/70/30 deal to kick in. As my friend said at the meeting:

Screw the state. Let's do it ourselves.

"Screw the state" is not a Tocquevillian formulation, but he would have certainly agreed with the latter sentiment. When something goes wrong, a European demands to know what the government's going to do about it. An American does it himself. Or he used to—in the Jacksonian America a farsighted Frenchman understood so well. Big Government is better understood as remote government. If we can't "do it ourselves" when it comes to painting schoolrooms or building bridges, we should certainly confine it to the least remote level of government.

★ ★ ★ ★ ★
DE-GOVERNMENTALIZE

Much of America is now in need of an equivalent to Mrs. Thatcher's privatization program in 1980s Britain, or post-Soviet Eastern Europe's economic liberalization in the early Nineties. It's hard to close down government bodies, but it should be possible to sell them off. And a side benefit to outsourcing the Bureau of Government Agencies and the Agency of Government Bureaus is that you'd also be privatizing public-sector unions, which are the biggest and most direct assault on freedom, civic integrity, and fiscal solvency.

★ ★ ★ ★ ★

DE-REGULATE

A couple of years back, I was talking to a stonemason and a roofer who were asked to do a job for a certain large institution in New Hampshire. They were obliged to attend "ladder school," even though both men have been working at the top of high ladders for over forty years. The gentleman from OSHA (the Occupational Safety and Health Administration) cautioned them against mocking his transparent waste of their time: under the new administration, he explained, his bureaucracy would be adopting a more enforcement-oriented approach to private business. So they rolled their eyes merely metaphorically and accepted the notion that they should give up a working day because the federal government has taken to itself the right to credentialize ladder-climbing from the Great North Woods to Honolulu.

At a certain point, why bother? As fast as you climb the ladder, you'll be taxed and regulated down the chute back to the bottom rung. You'll be frantically peddling the treadmill seven days a week so that the statist succubus squatting on your belly as you sleep can sluice the fruits of your labors to untold millions of bureaucrats from the Bureau of Compliance micro-regulating you till your pips squeak while they enjoy a lifestyle you never will. "The business of America is business," said Calvin Coolidge. Now the business of America is regulation. It is necessary for once free people to take back responsibility for their own affairs. Ultimately, judge-made law and bureaucrat-made regulations and dancing with the czars strike at the compact between citizen and state. By sidestepping the consent of the governed, as regulators do, or expressing open contempt for it, as judges do, the governing class delegitimizes itself. When government is demanding the right to determine every aspect of your life, those on the receiving end should at least demand back that our betters have the guts to do so by passing laws in legislatures of the people's representatives. Micro-regulation is micro-tyranny, a slithering, serpentine network of insinuating Ceaucescu and Kim Jong-Il mini-me's. It's time for mass rejection of their diktats. A political order that subjects you to the caprices of faceless bureaucrats or crusading "judges" merits no respect. To counter the Bureau of Compliance, we need an Alliance of Non-Compliance to help once free people roll back the regulatory state.

★ ★ ★ ★ ★

DE-MONOPOLIZE

We also need a new trust-busting movement to bust the dominant trust of our time—the Big Government monopoly that monopolizes more and more of life. It is depressing that the government monopoly is now so taken for granted that much of our public discourse simply assumes the virtues of collectivism. For example, it's often argued that, as a proportion of GDP, America spends more on health care than countries with government medical systems.[9] As a point of fact, pre-ObamaCare "America" doesn't spend anything on health care: hundreds of millions of people make hundreds of millions of individual decisions about what they're going to spend on health care. Whereas up north a handful of bureaucrats determine what Canada will spend on health care—and that's that: health care is a government budget item. If Joe Hoser in Moose Jaw wants to increase Canada's health-care spending by $500 drawn from his savings account, he can't. The law prevents it. Unless, as many Canadians do, he drives south and spends it in a U.S. hospital for treatment he can't get in a timely manner in his own country.

While we're on the subject, why is our higher per capita health spending by definition a bad thing? We spend more per capita on public education than any advanced nation except Luxembourg, and at least the Luxembourgers have something to show for it.[10] But no one says we need to bring our education spending down closer to the OECD average. *Au contraire*, the same people who say we spend too much on health care are in favor of spending even more on education. You can make the "controlling costs" argument about anything. After all, it's no surprise that millions of free people freely choosing how they spend their own money will spend it in different ways than government bureaucrats would be willing to license on their behalf. America spends more per capita on food than Zimbabwe. America spends more on vacations than North Korea. America spends more on lap-dancing than Saudi Arabia (well, officially). America spends more per capita on health than Canada, but Canada spends more per capita on doughnuts than America. Yet the Canadian Parliament doesn't say, well, that shows that we need to control costs so we've drawn up a 2,000-page doughnut-reform bill, which would allow children to charge their dough-nuts to their parents until they're twenty-six years old. Ottawa would introduce a National Doughnut Licensing Agency. You'd still see your general dispenser for simple procedures like a lightly sugared cruller, but he'd refer you to a specialist if you needed, say, a maple-frosted custard—and it would only be a six-month wait, at the end of which you'd receive a stale cinnamon roll.

During the 2004 election, John Kerry and John Edwards went around telling people there are no jobs out there, even though at the time America had much lower unemployment than Canada, France, Germany, or almost any other developed country. But, catching Senator Edwards on the stump in an old mill town in New Hampshire, I saw what he was getting at. There are no jobs like the jobs your pa had, where you could go to the mill and do the same thing day in, day out for forty-five years, and it made it so much easier for swanky senators come election time because there were large numbers of you losers all in the same place when they flew in for the campaign stop, and the crowd was impressive, whereas now they have to prowl around town ferreting out small two- or three-man start-ups, which takes a lot longer and to be honest never looks so good on the evening news. Watching Senator Edwards pining for the mills, I wondered if he wasn't having a strange premonition of his own obsolescence. The rise of big business was also the rise of Big Government. This isn't 1934. In an age of small start-ups and home businesses and desktop publishing, we don't need a one-size-fits-all statist monopoly.

★ ★ ★ ★ ★

DE-COMPLICATE

We have unnecessarily complicated too many areas of human existence. Complexity justifies even more government intervention, leading to even more impenetrable complexity. After all, if health-care costs are the issue, it isn't very difficult. As every economist knows, third-party transactions are always more expensive, whether the third party is an insurer or the government. If I go to a movie, I've got a general idea of what it ought to cost me. If I'm expecting to pay ten bucks and the clerk says "That'll be $273.95," I would notice. But most of the people in a hospital waiting room have no idea whether the procedure costs $200 or $2,000 or $20,000—and they don't care: their only concern is whether the third party will grant access to it. I know what a movie ticket costs, I've no idea what a broken leg costs. Nor does anybody else—because there are so many third parties interceding themselves between your bone and the doctor that there is no longer a real market price for a broken leg. So if, as Massachusetts has done, you mandate universal third-partyism, your costs by definition will increase. There's no mystery about it. As a businessman, Mitt Romney should have known that.

Third-party transactions are always inflationary. So let's return as much of daily life as possible to a two-party system—buyer and seller. You'll be amazed how affordable it is. Compare cellphone and laptop and portable music system prices with what they were in the Eighties, and then ask yourself how it would have turned out with a government-regulated system of electronic insurance plans.

★ ★ ★ ★ ★

DE-CREDENTIALIZE

The most important place to start correcting America's structural defects is in the schoolhouse. The Democrats justified ObamaCare on the grounds of "controlling costs." What about applying the same argument to education? The object should be not to universalize college and therefore defer adulthood even further, but to telescope schooling. Even if one overlooks the malign social engineering, much of what goes on in the American schoolhouse is merely passing the time. In 2011, a study by Richard Arum and Josipa Roksa found that fewer than half of America's undergraduates had taken a single course in the previous semester that required twenty pages of written work. A third had not taken a single course demanding forty pages of reading. Forty-five percent of students showed no improvement in critical thinking, reasoning, or writing by the end of their sophomore years.[11] Writing, reading, thinking: who needs it? Certainly not the teachers of tomorrow: students majoring in education showed the least gains in learning.

Six-figure universal college education will only reinforce a culture of hermetically sealed complacency. Instead, it should be possible to teach what a worthless high school diploma requires by the age of fourteen. You could then do an extra two years on top of that and give people a *real* certificate of value, unlike today's piece of paper, to prospective employers. College should be for those who wish to pursue genuine disciplines, not the desultory salad bar of Women's "Studies," Queer "Studies," or 99 percent of the other "studies." As a culture, we do too much "studying" (mostly of our navels, if not lower parts) and not enough doing. Vocational education, even for what we now dignify as "professions," would be much better. So would privatizing education entirely.

★ ★ ★ ★ ★

DIS-ENTITLE

It's not so extraordinary that on the brink of fiscal catastrophe the Obama Democrats should propose the Ultimate Entitlement—health care. After all, the Entitlement Utopia is where they reside. What's more remarkable is that a couple of years earlier the Bush Republicans should have introduced a brand new entitlement all of their own—prescription drugs.

Entitlements are the death of responsible government: they offend against every republican precept. Regardless of government revenues or broader economic conditions, they "mandate" spending: they are thus an offense against one of the most basic democratic principles—that a parliament cannot bind its successors. In a sense, they negate the American revolution. They are taxation without representation—for, as we well know, no matter how the facts on the ground evolve over the decades, entitlements are insulated from both parliamentary oversight and election results. That is why the battle has to be won in the broader culture. Entitlements have to be delegitimized. "Human dignity," writes Paul Rahe, "is bound up with taking responsibility for conducting one's own affairs."[12] When the state annexes that responsibility, the citizenry are indeed mere sheep to the government shepherd.

★ ★ ★ ★ ★

DE-NORMALIZE

You can win this. Statists overreach. They did on "climate change" scaremongering, and the result is that it's over. Hollywood buffoons will continue to lecture us from their mega-mansions that we should toss out our washers and beat our clothes dry on the rocks singing native chants down by the river, but only suckers are listening to them.

They overreached fiscally, too. On January 20, 2009, Year Zero of the Democrat utopia, it seemed like a smart move to make "trillion" a routine part of the Washington lexicon. After all, what's easier to spend than a trillion we don't have? If most of us cannot conceive of what a "trillion" is in any meaningful sense anyway, how can we conceive of ever having to "repay" a trillion? There was method in the madness of the Democrats' baseline inflation. Yet they never quite closed the deal, and now all its many citations do is remind even the most innumerate that the Democrat project is a crock, and the word itself is merely shorthand for "money we don't have and will never have." The spendaholics tried to normalize "trillion." They failed. Let's keep it de-normalized and, while we're at it, de-normalize "billion," too—or, at any rate, "tens of." Units that are beyond the size of your pocket calculator should not be part of the public discourse.

Nevertheless, both these victories were close-run things. Had it not been for the leaked emails of the East Anglia Climate Research Unit warm-mongers (showing the collusion and corruption of scientific "peer review") and had it not been for a small band of grossly abused "climate denialists" to leak them to and get the word out, the Copenhagen deal might well have passed. Liberty cannot survive if only a few are eternally vigilant. We need more. We took our eyes off the colleges, and the high schools, and the grade schools, and these and many other institutions were coopted by forces deeply hostile to the American idea. So push back, beginning in kindergarten. Changing the culture (the schools, the churches, the movies, the TV shows) is more important than changing the politics.

An election is one Tuesday every other November. The culture is every day, every month, every year. Politicians are, for the most part, a craven, finger-in-the-windy bunch. Like Milton Friedman says, don't wait for the right people to get elected; create the conditions whereby the wrong people are forced to do the right thing.

DO

During Scott Brown's insurgent election campaign in deep blue Massachusetts, he was joined at one rally by a rare non-Democrat celebrity, John Ratzenberger, who played Cliff Claven on the sitcom *Cheers*. Back in 1969, it turned out, Mr. Ratzenberger had been at Woodstock. No, he wasn't the bass player with Country Joe and the Fish, assuming they have a bass player. Rather, he was a working carpenter. And four decades later, stumping for Brown, he offered the all-time greatest comment on those three days of "peace and love":

This isn't the Democratic party of our fathers and grandfathers. This is the party of Woodstock hippies. I was at Woodstock—I built the stage. And when everything fell apart, and people were fighting for peanut butter sandwiches, it was the National Guard who came in and saved the same people who were protesting them. So when Hillary Clinton a few years ago wanted to build a Woodstock memorial, I said it should be a statue of a National Guardsman feeding a crying hippie.[13]

Oh, my. Was Mr. Ratzenberger an officially licensed carpenter? Maybe whoever leaked Joe the Plumber's files could look into it.

I mentioned earlier that I always advise aspiring writers to not only write but *do* something. I have a particular respect for fellows who are brilliant at one thing but nevertheless like to potter at something else entirely. Frank Loesser was one of the greatest figures in American popular music, a man whose songs include "Heart And Soul," "Baby, It's Cold Outside," and the score for *Guys and Dolls*. That would be enough for most of us. But I remember being very impressed to discover that he was also a prodigious carpenter and cabinetmaker whose home was filled with amazing pieces of his own design and construction. He once got one of those pompous letters from some Hollywood vice-president or other headed "From the Desk of...." So he went into his shop and spent the weekend crafting a beautiful life-size desk corner complete with inlay and moldings, and put it in the mail with a sheet of paper headed "From the Desk of Frank Loesser."

On a broader socio-cultural point, people who don't know where stuff comes from or how it works are more receptive to bigger government. That's one reason why Canada and much of western Europe, both of which are more urbanized and in which more people live in small apartments, vote leftier than America. In my part of New Hampshire, we have to drill our own wells and supply our own water. Obviously, that's not feasible on Fifth Avenue, or not without greatly spoiling Central Park. So water becomes just another thing that government takes care of for you.

The aforementioned John Ratzenberger isn't merely an actor. He's also the founder of the Nuts, Bolts & Thingamajigs Foundation, dedicated to reviving the lost art of tinkering.[14] Familiar with the word? Messing about with stuff—taking it apart, figuring out how it worked, putting it together again with some modification of your own. What boys (and a few girls) used to do in the garage or the basement before the Internet was invented. "If we give up tinkering," says John Derbyshire of *National Review*, "we *might* survive, but only as a bureaucratic empire of paper-pushers and lotus-eaters."[15] Tinkerers built America. Benjamin Franklin, Thomas Edison, Henry Ford, all were tinkerers in their childhood. Everything from the airplane to the computer started in somebody's garage. Go back even further: the Industrial Revolution was a revolution of tinkerers. The great scientific thinkers of eighteenth-century England couldn't have been less interested in cotton spinning and weaving. Why would you be? It was left to a bloke on the shop floor who happened to glance at a one-thread wheel that had toppled over and noticed that both the wheel and the spindle were still turning. So James Hargreaves invented the spinning jenny, and there followed other artful gins and mules and frames and looms, and Britain and the world were transformed. By tinkerers rather than thinkerers. "Technological change came from tinkerers," wrote Professor J. R. McNeill of Georgetown, "people with little to no scientific education but with plenty of hands-on experience."[16] John Ratzenberger likes to paraphrase a Stanford University study: "Engineers who are great in physics and calculus but can't think in new ways about old objects are doomed to think in old ways about new objects."[17] That's the lesson of the spinning jenny: an old object fell over and someone looked at it in a new way.

In 2008, America elected a man with no "hands-on experience" of anything who promptly cocooned himself within a circle of advisors with less experience of business, of the private sector, of *doing* than any previous administration in American history. You want "change," so you vote for a bunch of guys who've never done nuthin' but sit around talking?

That letter from the post-American world a few pages back was addressed to those Americans of 1950. By the beginning of the new century, "1950s" had become a pejorative. Conservative pundits are routinely accused of wanting to turn the clock back to the Fifties. Not me. There is, after all, no need to turn the clock back because, fiscally and geopolitically, America's clock is stuck in the Truman administration. At the U.S. Treasury, the State Department, the Pentagon, it's forever chiming 1950. At the dawn of the American era, Washington was the last man standing, the victor of the Second World War and with its cities and factories intact, unlike Europe. It had a unique dominance of the "free world," and it could afford to be generous, so it was. America had more money than it knew what to do with, so it funded the UN and a dozen subsidiary bodies, and it absolved post-war Europe of paying for its own defense. And, as Germany and Japan and the rest of the West recovered, we continued to pay, garrisoning not remote colonies but some of the richest nations in history. Having forsworn imperialism, we sat back as the UN fell into the hands of our enemies and their appeasers, and still we picked up the check. Western economic ideas were taken up by Asia and Eastern Europe and Brazil and Turkey, and enriched many lands, but we saw ourselves as the unipolar hyperpower, so at Nato and the G7 and everywhere else, each time the bill came and the rest of the gang skipped to the bathroom, we were happy to stick it on our tab. We threw money at our friends (to defend them against hostile powers that had collapsed a generation earlier) and at our enemies (to enable them to use their oil revenues to fund anti-Americanism worldwide) and at dozens of countries in between who were of no geopolitical significance but wouldn't say no to a massive subsidy for an AIDS prevention program or whatever.

And we never even noticed we were no longer paying cash but with foreign credit cards.

1950 never ended. Even after the 2008 crash, even after the multi-trillion dollar deficits, it's still 1950. At the 2009 Copenhagen summit, America (broke, bankrupt, drowning in debt) offered to pay for China (the country in whose debt we're drowning) to *lower its carbon footprint*.[18] As Jonah

Goldberg said to me on FOX News that week, that's like paying your loan shark to winterize his home.

The further we get from 1950, the more Washington spends like 1950 is forever.

This is the real "war on children" (to use another Democrat catchphrase)—and every time you bulk up the budget you make it less and less likely they'll win it. Conservatives often talk about "small government," which, in a sense, is framing the issue in leftist terms: they're for Big Government—and, when you're arguing for the small alternative, it's easy to sound pinched and mean and grudging. But small government gives you big freedoms—and Big Government leaves you with very little freedom. The opposite of Big Government is not small government, but Big Liberty. The bailout and the stimulus and the budget and the trillion-dollar deficits are not merely massive transfers from the most dynamic and productive sector to the least dynamic and productive. When governments annex a huge chunk of the economy, they also annex a huge chunk of individual liberty. You fundamentally change the relationship between the citizen and the state into something closer to that of junkie and pusher—and you make it very difficult ever to change back. In the end, it's not about money, but about something more fundamental. Yes, you can tax people to the hilt and give them "free" health care and "free" homes and "free" food. But in doing so you turn them into, if not (yet) slaves, then pets. And that's the nub of it: Big Government leads to small liberty, and to small men. If a 26-year-old is a child, as President Obama says; if a 50-year-old hairdresser can retire and live at the state's expense for over half her adult life, as the Government of Greece says, then you are no longer free. "You can be anything you want to be"? Not at all. Not when you're owned by the government.

Freedom is messy. In free societies, people will fall through the cracks—drink too much, eat too much, buy unaffordable homes, fail to make prudent provision for health care, and much else. But the price of being relieved of all those tiresome choices by a benign paternal government is far too high. Big Government is the small option: it's the guarantee of smaller freedom, smaller homes, smaller cars, smaller opportunities, smaller lives.

★ ★ ★ ★ ★
LIVE FREE OR DIE

I'm an immigrant to this great land. For fellows like me, this is where the bus terminates. There's nowhere else to go. Everywhere else tried this, and it's killed them. There's nothing new about Obama-era "hope" and "change." For some of us, it's the land where we grew up: government hospitals, government automobiles, been there, done that. This isn't a bright new future, it's a straight-to-video disco-zombie sequel: the creature rises from the grave to stagger around in rotting bell-bottoms and cheesecloth shirt terrorizing a new generation. Burn, baby, burn, it's a Seventies-statist disco-era inferno!

When I first moved to New Hampshire, where "Live free or die" appears on our license plates, I carelessly assumed General Stark had said it before some battle or other—a bit of red meat to rally the boys for the charge; a touch of the old Henry V-at-Agincourt routine. But I soon discovered that the Granite State's great Revolutionary War hero had made his *cri de coeur* decades after the cessation of hostilities, in a letter regretting that he would be unable to attend a dinner. And in a way I found that even more impressive. In extreme circumstances, many people can rouse themselves to rediscover the primal impulses: the brave men on Flight 93 did. They took off on what they thought was a routine business trip, and, when they realized it wasn't, they went into General Stark mode and cried, "Let's roll!"

But it's harder to maintain the "Live free or die!" spirit when you're facing not an immediate crisis but just a slow, unceasing ratchet effect. Which is, in stable societies unthreatened by revolution or war within their borders, how liberty falls, traded away to the state incrementally, painlessly, all but imperceptibly. "Live free or die!" sounds like a battle cry: we'll win this thing or die trying, die an honorable death. But in fact it's something far less dramatic. It's a bald statement of the reality of our lives in the prosperous West. You can live as free men, but, if you choose not to, your society will surely die.

So, if you don't want to die, you need to force the statists either out of office or into dramatic course correction. For a start, if a candidate is not publicly committed to fewer government programs from fewer government agencies enforcing fewer government regulations with fewer government bureaucrats on less lavish taxpayer-funded pay, he's not serious. He's not only killing your grandchildren's and children's future, he's killing yours— and you will live to see it. It will be hard enough to apply pressure on America's bureaucracy-for-life once he's elected, but if he's not prepared to argue for smaller government en route to office he's certainly not going to do so afterwards. This applies to all levels of government: not just federal but state, county, town, and school district. Follow Friedman's rule: make the wrong people do the right thing. Forcing candidates to make no-tax pledges has had some success, not least in my own state. Let's try some spending pledges, and regulation pledges.

Americans face a choice: you can rediscover the animating principles of the American idea—of limited government, a self-reliant citizenry, and the opportunities to exploit your talents to the fullest—or you can join most of the rest of the western world in terminal decline. To rekindle the spark of liberty once it dies is very difficult. The inertia, the ennui, the fatalism is even more pathetic than the demographic decline and fiscal profligacy of the social democratic state, and, because it's subtler and less tangible, even harder to rally against.

And a final word to "the children": do you want to get suckered like your big brothers and sisters? Those saps who spent 2008 standing behind the Obamessiah swaying and chanting, "We are the dawning of the Hopeychange" like brainwashed cult extras? Sooner or later you guys have to crawl out from under the social engineering and rediscover the contrarian spirit for which youth was once known. If you're a First Grader reading this by flashlight under the pillow, don't wait till Middle School to start pushing back on this junk. This will be the great battle of the next genera-tion—to reclaim your birthright from those who spent it. If you don't, the entire global order will teeter and fall. But, if you do, you will have won a great victory. Every time a politician proposes new spending, tell him he's already spent your money, get his hand out of your pocket. Every time a politician says you can stay a child until your twenty-seventh birthday, tell him, "No, you're the big baby, not me—you've spent irresponsibly, and me and my pals are the ones who are gonna have to be the adults and clean up your mess. Don't treat me like a kid when your immaturity got us into this hole." This is a battle for the American idea, and it's an epic one, but—to reprise the lamest of lame-o lines—you can do anything you want to do. So do it.

ACKNOWLEDGMENTS

I would like to thank Marji Ross, Harry Crocker, Kathleen Sweetapple, and their colleagues at Regnery for their encouragement and advice. As always, I'm indebted to readers in America, Britain, Canada, Australia, Europe, Asia, and beyond for filling my in-box with sharp insights and pertinent anecdotes every morning. And I would be entirely adrift were it not for my trusty sidekicks Tiffany Cole, Chantal Benoît, and Katherine Ernst and their dogged research and expertly compressed statistical summaries. They could be taking it easy in a cushy government union job, so I'm grateful to them for laboring down the Steyn salt mines instead.

NOTES

Prologue

1. Town hall meeting in Greeley, Colorado, August 21, 2010; available online at http://www.greeleygazette.com/press/?p=5029.
2. Terrence P. Jeffrey, "111th Congress Added More Debt Than First 100 Congresses Combined: $10,429 Per Person in U.S.," CNSNews.com, December 27, 2010; available online at http://www.cnsnews.com/news/article/111th-congress-added-more-debt-first-100.
3. Herbert Stein, "Herb Stein's Unfamiliar Quotations," Slate.com, May 16, 1997; available online at http://www.slate.com/id/2561/.
4. Herbert Stein, "Herb Stein's Unfamiliar Quotations," Slate.com, May 16, 1997; available online at http://www.slate.com/id/2561/.
5. Remarks to reporters at a Christian Science Monitor breakfast, April 8, 2010; available online at http://www.politico.com/news/stories/0410/35546.html.
6. Brian Riedl, "President Obama Set to Exceed President Bush's Deficits," The Heritage Foundation, February 11, 2009; available online at http://blog.heritage.org/2009/02/11/president-obama-set-to-exceed-president-bush%E2%80%99s-deficits/.
7. Remarks at Thompson Creek Manufacturing in Landover, Maryland, January 7, 2011; available online at http://m.whitehouse.gov/the-press-office/2011/01/07/remarks-president-december-jobs-report-and-economic-personnel-announceme.

8. White House, "Table 15.3— Total Government Expenditures as Percentages of GDP: 1948-2010"; available online at http://www.whitehouse.gov/omb/budget/Historicals.

9. CBO report, "The Budget and Economic Outlook: Fiscal Years 2011 to 2021," January 2011; available online at http://www.cbo.gov/ftpdocs/120xx/doc12039/01-26_FY2011Outlook.pdf.

10. CBO report, "The Long-Term Budget Outlook: Federal Debt Held by the Public Under Two Budget Scenarios," June 2010; available online at http://www.cbo.gov/ftpdocs/115xx/doc11579/06-30-LTBO.pdf.

11. Niall Ferguson, "Sun could set suddenly on superpower as debt bites," *The Australian*, July 29, 2010; available online at http://www.theaustralian.com.au/news/opinion/sun-could-set-suddenly-on-superpower-as-debt-bites/story-e6frg6zo-1225898187243.

12. CBO report, "The Long-Term Budget Outlook: Federal Debt Held by the Public Under Two Budget Scenarios," June 2010; available online at http://www.cbo.gov/ftpdocs/115xx/doc11579/06-30-LTBO.pdf.

13. The Stockholm International Peace Research Institute, 2011; available online at http://www.rickety.us/2011/01/2009-defense-spending-by-country/.

14. Niall Ferguson, "Sun could set suddenly on superpower as debt bites," *The Australian*.

15. US Treasury, "Major Foreign Holders of Treasury Securities," March 15, 2001; available online at http://www.treasury.gov/resource-center/data-chart-center/tic/Documents/mfh.txt.

16. The Stockholm International Peace Research Institute, 2011; available online at http://www.rickety.us/2011/01/2009-defense-spending-by-country/.

17. US Department of Defense, "Annual Report to Congress: Military and Security Developments Involving the People's Republic of China," 2010; available online at http://www.defense.gov/pubs/pdfs/2010_CMPR_Final.pdf.

18. Sam Lister, ""NHS is world's biggest employer after Indian rail and Chinese Army," March 20, 2004; available online at http://www.timesonline.co.uk/tol/news/uk/health/article1050197.ece.

19. Lawrence B. Lindsey, "The Fiscal Trap," *The Weekly Standard*, December 6, 2010; available online at http://www.weeklystandard.com/articles/fiscal-trap_519582.html.

20. Testimony before the House Budget Committee, January 27, 2010; available online at http://www.c-spanvideo.org/program/2010BudgetandEconomicOutlook2.

21. The National Commission on Fiscal Responsibility and Reform, "The Moment of Truth," December 2010; available online at http://www.fiscalcommission.gov/sites/fiscalcommission.gov/files/documents/TheMomentofTruth12_1_2010.pdf.

22.   Tax Policy Center, "Historical Federal Receipt and Outlay Summary," March 25, 2011; available online at http://www.taxpolicycenter.org/taxfacts/displayafact. cfm?Docid=200; and the Congressional Budget Office, "Budget and Economic Outlook: Historical Budget Data," January 2011; available online at http://www. cbo.gov/ftpdocs/120xx/doc12039/HistoricalTables%5B1%5D.pdf.

23.   Brian Riedl, "Federal Spending by the Numbers 2010," June 1, 2010, Heritage Foundation; available online at http://www.heritage.org/Research/ Reports/2010/06/Federal-Spending-by-the-Numbers-2010.

24.   Terrence P. Jeffrey, "Conservatives Now Outnumber Liberals in All 50 States, Says Gallup Poll," CNSNews.com, August 17, 2009; available online at http://www. cnsnews.com/node/52602.

25.   Stephen Moore and Stephen Slivinski, "The Return of the Living Dead: Federal Programs That Survived the Republican Revolution," July 24, 2000, Cato Institute Policy Analysis; available online at http://www.cato.org/pubs/pas/pa375.pdf.

26.   Andrew Nagorski, "The Troubles," *Newsweek*, March 16, 2010; available online at http://www.newsweek.com/2010/03/15/the-troubles.html.

27.   Gregory White, "Bill Gross: Fed To Buy $100 Billion In Government Debt A Month Until It Hits $1.2 Trillion," *Business Insider*, October 8, 2010; available online at http://www.businessinsider.com/bill-gross-fed-to-buy-100-billion-in-government-securities-a-month-2010-10.

28.   John Kitchen and Menzie Chinn, "Financing U.S. Debt: Is There Enough Money in the World – and At What Cost?" University of Wisconsin, August 2010; available online at http://www.ssc.wisc.edu/~mchinn/Kitchen_Chinn_apr11.pdf.

29.   Christopher S. Johnson, "How Much Ruin is in a Nation?: The Spain of Philip IV," *First Things*, March 24, 2011; available online at http://www.firstthings.com/ onthesquare/2011/03/how-much-ruin-is-in-a-nation.

30.   Samuel P. Huntington, *Who Are We?: The Challenges to America's National Identity* (New York: Simon & Schuster, 2005).

31.   Lawrence Kudlow, "France's Problem is a Statist-Run Socialist Economy," RealClearPolitics.com, March 27, 2006; available online at http://www. realclearpolitics.com/articles/2006/03/paddle_the_french_fanny.html.

32.   Organisation for Economic Co-operation and Development, "Education at a Glance 2009: OECD Indicators," (Indicator B1 How much is spent per student?), 2009; available online at http://www.oecd.org/document/24/0,3343 ,en_2649_39263238_43586328_1_1_1_37455,00.html.

33.   Edward Luce, "The crisis of middle-class America," *Financial Times*, July 30, 2010; available online at http://www.ft.com/cms/s/2/1a8a5cb2-9ab2-11df-87e6-00144feab49a.html.

34.   Bureau of the Public Debt, "Commissioner's Welcome," 2011; available online
       at http://www.publicdebt.treas.gov/whoweare/welcome.htm.
35.   Niall Ferguson, "An Empire at Risk," *Newsweek*, November 28, 2009; available
       online at http://www.newsweek.com/2009/11/27/an-empire-at-risk.html.
36.   Samuel P. Huntington, *The Clash of Civilizations and the Remaking of World Order*
       (New York: Simon & Schuster, 1998).

Chapter One

1.   University of Toronto Library, "Hughes (Elizabeth) Papers"; available online at
       http://www.library.utoronto.ca/fisher/collections/findaids/hughes_elizabeth.
       pdf.
2.   "Mary Carmichael and Sharon Begley, "Desperately Seeking Cures," *Newsweek*,
       May 15, 2010; available online at http://www.newsweek.com/2010/05/15/
       desperately-seeking-cures.html.
3.   Henkles & McCoy, "1969"; available online at http://www.henkels.com/Timeline/
       Pages/TL1969.aspx.
4.   Remarks during Special Joint Session of Congress in Washington, D.C., May 25,
       1961; facts available online http://spaceflight1.nasa.gov/history/.
5.   William Safire, "In Event of Moon Disaster," memo to President Richard Nixon,
       July 18, 1969; available online at http://www.thesmokinggun.com/file/white-
       house-lost-space-scenarios.
6.   Bruce Charlton, "Human capability peaked before 1975 and has since declined,"
       Bruce Charlton's Miscellany blog, June 22, 2011; available online at http://
       charltonteaching.blogspot.com/2010/06/human-capability-peaked-about-
       1975-and.html.
7.   Remarks on Al Jazeera's Talk to Al Jazeera, June 30, 2010; available online at http://
       english.aljazeera.net/programmes/talktojazeera/2010/07/201071122234471970.
       html.
8.   *The Guardian*, "Astronauts Were 'Trinity of Evil', Says Banned Cleric," February
       3, 2003; available online at http://www.guardian.co.uk/science/2003/feb/03/
       spaceexploration.columbia13.
9.   Jeanne Sahadi, "Obama sketches out recovery plan," CNNMoney.com, January
       3, 2009; available online at http://money.cnn.com/2009/01/03/news/economy/
       obama_stimulus/index.htm?postversion=2009010306.
10.   Katrina vanden Heuvel, "A Trillion Dollar Recovery," *The Nation*, December 30,
       2008; available online at http://www.thenation.com/blog/trillion-dollar-
       recovery?page=0,0,0,3.

11. Mark I. Pinksy, "Write Now," *The New Republic*, December 8, 2008; available online at http://www.tnr.com/article/politics/write-now.

12. Franklin D. Roosevelt, "Address at the Dedication of the Boulder (Hoover) Dam," September 30, 1935; available online http://books.google.com/books?id=SYeE mU2aW9EC&pg=PA311&lpg=PA311&dq=This+morning+I+came,+I+saw,+ and+I+was+conquered,+as+everyone+would+be+who+sees+for+the+first+ time+this+great+feat+of+mankind&source=bl&ots=_ei3wFH- 9M&sig=zAhdn5KDbUAmQWQM9oNv6-UAN-8&hl=en&ei=3wLUTZOaIej 30gGQ1JTYCw&sa=X&oi=book_result&ct=result&resnum=1&ved=0CBYQ6 AEwAA#v=onepage&q=This%20morning%20I%20came%2C%20I%20 saw%2C%20and%20I%20was%20conquered%2C%20as%20everyone%20 would%20be%20who%20sees%20for%20the%20first%20time%20this%20 great%20feat%20of%20mankind&f=false.

13. Remarks made during an Urban Land Institute symposium in Las Vegas, Nevada, December 8-9, 2009; facts available online at http://www.politico.com/news/ stories/1110/45376_Page2.html, http://atlincolnhouse.typepad.com/ weblog/2009/12/talking-water.html, and http://www.uli.org/sitecore/content/ ULI2Home/ResearchAndPublications/CenterfortheWest/WaterSummit.aspx.

14. Mushtaq Yufzai, "Taliban Commanders See Victory in the Sacking of U.S. General," *The Daily Beast*, June 25, 2010; available online at http://www.thedailybeast. com/blogs-and-stories/2010-06-25/taliban-mcchrystal-sacking-a-victory/.

15. Remarks during State of the Union Address in Washington, DC, January 20, 2004; available online at http://www.washingtonpost.com/wp-srv/politics/ transcripts/bushtext_012004.html. The actual quote is: "I believe that God has planted in every human heart the desire to live in freedom. And even when that desire is crushed by tyranny for decades, it will rise again."

16. Anthony Tommasini, "Music; The Devil Made Him Do It," *New York Times*, September 30, 2001; available online at http://www.nytimes.com/2001/09/30/ arts/music-the-devil-made-him-do-it.html.

17. *The Telegraph*, "Obituary: Karlheinz Stockhausen," December 8, 2007; available online at http://www.telegraph.co.uk/news/obituaries/1571861/Karlheinz- Stockhausen.html.

18. Remarks on WOR radio in New York, New York, February 19, 2010; available online at http://articles.nydailynews.com/2010-02-19/local/27056722_1_port- authority-larry-silverstein-world-trade-center.

19. CNN, "38 Years Ago, World Trade Center Opened," April 4, 2011; available online at http://news.blogs.cnn.com/2011/04/04/38-years-ago-world-trade-center- opened/.

20. Jim Yardley, "Chinese Dam Projects Criticized for Their Human Costs," *New York Times*, November 19, 2007; available online at http://www.nytimes.com/2007/11/19/world/asia/19dam.html.

21. Facts available online at Burj Khalifa's website; http://www.burjkhalifa.ae/.

22. Henry Mance, "Brazil's huge river diversion project divides opinion," BBC News, April 12, 2010; available online at http://news.bbc.co.uk/2/hi/8575010.stm.

23. James Lileks, "NRO Symposium: Did It Change Us?" *National Review* Online, September 11, 2006; available online at http://www.nationalreview.com/articles/218680/did-it-change-us-nro-symposium.

24. Leslie H. Gelb, "Necessity, Choice, and Common Sense," *Foreign Affairs*, May/June 2009; available online at http://www.foreignaffairs.com/articles/64966/leslie-h-gelb/necessity-choice-and-common-sense.

25. The British Museum, "Christopher Wren, Design for the Dome of St Paul's Catherdral, a drawing in brown ink over pencil"; available online at http://www.britishmuseum.org/explore/highlights/highlight_objects/pd/c/christopher_wren,_design_for_t.aspx.

Chapter Two

1. Interview with David Wigg in London, England, October 8, 1969; available online at: http://www.beatlesinterviews.org/db1969.1008.beatles.html.

2. Reuters, "Key Facts About Fannie Mae and Freddie Mac," *USA Today*, July 13, 2008; available online at http://www.usatoday.com/money/economy/housing/2008-07-12-facts-fannie-freddie_N.htm.

3. Matthew Daneman, "Kodak Still a Vital Cog," *Rochester Democrat & Chronicle*, February 4, 2008; available online at http://www.rochesterbusinessalliance.com/core/contentmanager/uploads/PDFs/News%20articles/0204%20Kodak%20DANDC.pdf.

4. Michael P. Fleischer, "Why I'm Not Hiring," *Wall Street Journal*, August 9, 2010; available online at http://online.wsj.com/article/SB10001424052748704017904575409733776372738.html.

5. Maria Glod, "Va. Yogis Seek Rapture, Not Regulation," *Washington Post*, August 24, 2009; available online at http://www.washingtonpost.com/wp-dyn/content/article/2009/08/23/AR2009082302152.html.

6. Morris M. Kleiner, *Licensing Occupations: Ensuring Quality or Restricting Competition?*, Upjohn Institute Press, 2006; facts available online at http://www.bizpacreview.com/index.cfm?fuseaction=news.details&ArticleId=19421.

7. Patricia Reaney, "Washington, D.C. favorite area for wealthy young," Reuters, September 16, 2009; available online at http://www.reuters.com/article/2009/09/16/us-wealth-young-idUSTRE58F3GF20090916.

8. Ibid.

9. "The Richest Counties in America," *Newsweek*, November 10, 2010; available online at http://www.newsweek.com/2010/11/10/the-richest-counties-in-america.all.html.

10. Laurence J. Kotlikoff and David Rapson, "Does It Pay, at the Margin, to Work and Save? Measuring Effective Marginal Taxes on Americans' Labor Supply and Saving," National Bureau of Economic Research, May, 2007; available online at http://www.nber.org/chapters/c0048.pdf?new_window=1.

11. Town hall meeting in Fort Myers, Florida, February 10, 2009; available online at http://www.whitehouse.gov/the_press_office/Remarks-by-the-President-at-Fort-Myers-Town-Hall/.

12. Peter Nicholas, "Obama's 'New Foundation' gives way – maybe to a catchier catchphrase," *Los Angeles Times*, February 9, 2011; available online at http://articles.latimes.com/2011/feb/09/nation/la-na-new-foundation-20110209.

13. *Marion Daily Star*, 1899; also see William Safire, *Safire's Political Dictionary* (Oxford University Press, 2008); available online at http://books.google.com/books?id=c4UoX6-Sv1AC&pg=PA78&lpg=PA78&dq=Our+various+and+sundry+supplies+of+gray+matter+may+as+well+be+controlled+by+a+central+syndicate.Our+various+and+sundry+supplies+of+gray+matter+may+as+well+be+controlled+by+a+central+syndicate.&source=bl&ots=V1wh3zqsLl&sig=F6A3N2pGsMoneiBYkL1fxzenR20&hl=en&ei=AjmzTb6rBaKD0QGYvdiqCQ&sa=X&oi=book_result&ct=result&resnum=2&ved=0CBsQ6AEwAQ#v=onepage&q&f=false.

14. Remarks at a fundraiser in San Francisco, California, April 6, 2008; available online at http://www.politico.com/blogs/bensmith/0408/Obama_on_small-town_PA_Clinging_religion_guns_xenophobia.html.

15. Remarks at a campaign stop in Muncie, Indiana, April 12, 2008; facts available online at http://www.reuters.com/article/2008/04/12/us-usa-politics-idUSN1116676020080412.

16. Remarks at a campaign stop in Roseburg, Oregon, May 16, 2008; facts available online at http://afp.google.com/article/ALeqM5h-wpxs1Re-8vx2Zk5xnYygW1W67w.

17. Neil Irwin, "Economic growth slows to 2.4 percent in 2Q," *Washington Post*, July 30, 2010; available online at http://voices.washingtonpost.com/political-economy/2010/07/economic_growth_slows_to_24_pe.html.

18.   Interview with Don Imus; facts available online at http://washingtonexaminer.
      com/op-eds/2009/07/douglas-mackinnon-don-t-bother-these-guys-facts.

19.   David Brooks, "The Insider's Crusade," *New York Times*, November 21, 2008;
      available online at http://www.nytimes.com/2008/11/21/opinion/21brooks.html.

20.   Jonathan Alter, *The Promise: President Obama, Year One* (New York: Simon &
      Schuster, 2010); facts available online at http://www.claremont.org/publications/
      crb/id.1764/article_detail.asp.

21.   Remarks to the Greater Boson Chamber of Commerce in Boston, Massachusetts,
      October 28, 2010; facts available online at http://www.boston.com/news/local/
      massachusetts/articles/2010/10/28/kerry_says_democrats_have_been_fixing_
      gop_problems/.

22.   Speech in Boston, Massachusetts, April 22, 2006; available online at http://www.
      scoop.co.nz/stories/WO0604/S00399.htm; Monticello.org, "Spurious Quotes,"
      available online at http://www.monticello.org/site/research-and-collections/
      spurious-quotes.

23.   Jamie Stiehm, "Oval Office Rug Gets History Wrong," *Washington Post*, Septem-
      ber 4, 2010; available online at http://www.washingtonpost.com/wp-dyn/con
      tent/article/2010/09/03/AR2010090305100.html.

24.   Remarks at the Democrat National Gala, September 29, 2002; facts available online
      at http://www.snopes.com/quotes/caesar.asp and http://www.barbrastreisand.com/
      us/truth-alert/julius-caesar-quote-used-democratic-national-gala-speech.

25.   Michael C. Moynihan, "The Extreme Rhetoric about Extreme Rhetoric (With
      Bonus Fake Sinclair Lewis Fascism Quote!)," *Reason*, January 11, 2011; available
      online at http://reason.com/blog/2011/01/11/the-extreme-rhetoric-about-ext.

26.   Michael Young, "Down With Meritocracy," *The Guardian*, June 29, 2001; available
      online at http://www.guardian.co.uk/politics/2001/jun/29/comment.

27.   Associated Press, "Kerry, Bush GPAs At Yale Similar," CBSNews.com, February
      11, 2009; facts available online at http://www.cbsnews.com/stories/2005/06/07/
      politics/main700170.shtml.

28.   Winston Churchill, *The Hinge of Fate* (Rosetta Stone, LLC edition, 2002); avail-
      able online at http://books.google.com/books?id=CEK6h9lzK3wC&pg=PA75&
      lpg=PA75&dq=mere+advisors+at+large+with+nothing+to+do+but+think+a
      nd+talk+churchill&source=bl&ots=4xccE4bJdG&sig=-_O62AUhVhoskUVLR
      CE38HrBjuA&hl=en&ei=eXezTeyUFILu0gHD4sjMDw&sa=X&oi=book_resu
      lt&ct=result&resnum=2&ved=0CBwQ6AEwAQ#v=onepage&q&f=false.

29.   Tim Shipman, "Barack Obama sends bust of Winston Churchill on its way back
      to Britain," *UK Telegraph*, February 14, 2009; available online at http://www.
      telegraph.co.uk/news/worldnews/barackobama/4623148/Barack-Obama-sends-
      bust-of-Winston-Churchill-on-its-way-back-to-Britain.html.

30. Nick Schulz, "Help Wanted, No Private Sector Experience Required," The Enterprise Blog of the American Enterprise Institute, November 25, 2009; available online at http://blog.american.com/?p=7572.

31. Remarks in St. Paul, Minnesota, June 3, 2008; available online at http://www.breitbart.com/article.php?id=D912VD200.

32. Remarks at St. James's Palace in London, England, July 8, 2009; facts available online at http://www.independent.co.uk/environment/green-living/just-96-months-to-save-world-says-prince-charles-1738049.html.

33. Michael Grunwald, "The New Action Heroes," Time, June 14, 2007; available online at http://www.time.com/time/nation/article/0,8599,1632736,00.html.

34. CBS News New York, "Bloomberg Admits NYC Flubbed Blizzard Response," December 29, 2010; available online at http://newyork.cbslocal.com/2010/12/29/bloomberg-admits-nyc-flubbed-blizzard-response/.

35. Charlie LeDuff, "Los Angeles County Weighs Cost of Illegal Immigration," New York Times, May 21, 2003; available online at http://www.nytimes.com/2003/05/21/us/los-angeles-county-weighs-cost-of-illegal-immigration.html.

36. Remarks at a campaign event for Martha Coakley, Northeastern University in Boston, Massachusetts, January 17, 2010; available online at http://www.whitehouse.gov/the-press-office/remarks-president-event-with-massachusetts-attorney-general-martha-coakley.

37. Inside Edition, "White House Veggie-Gate," January 15, 2010; available online at http://www.insideedition.com/news.aspx?storyId=3855.

38. Stephen F. Hayes, "Scott Brown's Road to Victory," The Weekly Standard, January 20, 2010; available online at http://www.weeklystandard.com/blogs/scott-browns-road-victory.

39. MSNBC, "Countdown with Keith Olbermann," January 19, 2010; facts available online at http://hotair.com/archives/2010/01/20/olby-massachusetts-suddenly-turned-racist/.

40. Chris Woodyard, "Scott Brown drives his GMC pickup to U.S. Senate victory," USA Today, January 20, 2010; facts available online at http://content.usatoday.com/communities/driveon/post/2010/01/scott-brown-drives-his-gmc-pickup-truck-to-us-senate-victory/1.

41. Roderick Random, "Kanjorski ponders 'nuts,' bolts from blue," Scranton Times Tribune, October 23, 2010; available online at http://thetimes-tribune.com/opinion/editorials-columns/roderick-random/kanjorski-ponders-nuts-bolts-from-blue-1.1052739#axzz1A4hLabIP.

42. Michael Young, "Down With Meritocracy," The Guardian, June 29, 2001; available online at http://www.guardian.co.uk/politics/2001/jun/29/comment.

43. Peter Berkowitz, *"The New Dogma of Fairness," from New Threats to Freedom*, ed. Adam Bellow (Templeton Press, May, 2010); available online at http://www.peterberkowitz.com/thenewdogmaoffairness.pdf.

44. Neil Munro, "The Diversity Economy," *National Journal*, July 24, 2010; available online at http://nationaljournal.com/magazine/the-diversity-economy-20100724?print=true.

45. Frank Rich, "The Rage is Not About Health Care," *New York Times*, March 27, 2010; available online at http://www.nytimes.com/2010/03/28/opinion/28rich.html.

46. Karen Brown, "Mass. Health Care Reform Reveals Doctor Shortage," NPR, November 30, 2008; available online at http://www.npr.org/templates/story/story.php?storyId=97620520.

47. FOX News, "New Rules Coming for Payments Out of Health Savings Accounts," October 15, 2010; available online at http://www.foxnews.com/politics/2010/10/15/new-health-care-rules-require-doctors-note-pay-otc-drugs-fsas/.

48. NPR, "What's The Role Of Race In Health Care Fracas?" August 14, 2009; available online at http://m.npr.org/news/front/111899507?page=2.

49. Remarks to the Atlanta Press Club in Atlanta, Georgia, October 21, 2010; facts available online at http://www.npr.org/blogs/thetwo-way/2010/10/21/130728202/npr-ceo-williams-views-of-muslims-should-stay-between-himself-and-his-psychiatrist.

50. Comments posted on "JournoList", November 7, 2008; facts available online at http://dailycaller.com/2010/07/21/obama-wins-and-journolisters-rejoice/2/ and http://www.theatlantic.com/entertainment/archive/2010/07/on-eric-altermans-fucking-nascar-retards/60556/.

51. Greg Bluestein, "Firefighters stuck in Ga. awaiting orders," *Associated Press*, September 7, 2005; available online at http://www.usatoday.com/news/nation/2005-09-07-firefighters-ga-katrina_x.htm.

52. David Warren, "Two Solitudes," *Ottawa Citizen*, October 5, 2008; available online http://davidwarrenonline.com/index.php?id=927.

53. John Tierney, "Nader Searches for His Roots," *New York Times*, February 15, 2004; facts available online at http://www.nytimes.com/2004/02/15/politics/campaign/15POIN.html.

54. David Warren, "Two Solitudes," *Ottawa Citizen*.

55. Jeanne Sahadi, "47% will pay no federal income tax," CNNMoney.com, October 3, 2009; available online at http://money.cnn.com/2009/09/30/pf/taxes/who_pays_taxes/index.htm.

56. Benjamin Niolet, "Stimulus funds pay for monkey research in N.C." *The Raleigh News & Observer*, March 8, 2010; available online at http://www.mcclatchydc.com/2010/03/08/89974/stimulus-funds-pay-for-monkey.html.

57. Interview with WJR in Detroit, Michigan on October 7, 2009; facts available online at http://www.rushlimbaugh.com/home/daily/site_100809/content/01125107.guest.html.

58. Christopher Caldwell, "Islam on the Outskirts of the Welfare State," *New York Times*, February 5, 2006; available online at http://query.nytimes.com/gst/fullpage.html?res=9C01E1DA1E3FF936A35751C0A9609C8B63&pagewanted=1.

59. "The 'Shameless' generation of benefit addicts: Almost five million adults live in jobless homes," *UK Daily Mail*, August 26, 2009; available online at http://www.dailymail.co.uk/news/article-1209072/Five-million-job-Labour--raising-fears-Shameless-generation-benefit-addicts.html.

60. Remarks to the Oklahoma Council of Public Affairs in Oklahoma City, Oklahoma, March 31, 2010; available online at http://www.facebook.com/note.php?note_id=10150147642760012.

61. Pew Research Center, "A Balance Sheet at 30 Months: How the Great Recession Has Changed Life in America," June 30, 2010; available online at http://pewsocialtrends.org/files/2010/11/759-recession.pdf.

62. Interview with Robert Costa of *National Review* in New York, New York, September 2, 2010; available online at http://www.nationalreview.com/articles/245438/caddell-midterm-elections-robert-costa.

63. Remarks during first inaugural address in Washington, D.C., January 20, 1981; available online at http://www.reaganfoundation.org/pdf/Inaugural_Address_012081.pdf.

64. Dennis Cauchon, "For Feds, More Get 6-Figure Salaries," *USA Today*, December 11, 2009; available online at http://www.usatoday.com/news/washington/2009-12-10-federal-pay-salaries_N.htm.

65. Ibid.

66. Veronique de Rugy, "Interesting Data on Increasing Public Employment," *National Review*, July 22, 2010; available online at http://www.nationalreview.com/corner/233524/interesting-data-increasing-public-employment-veronique-de-rugy.

67. The Bureau of Public Debt, "Careers With Us," United States Department of the Treasury; available online at http://www.publicdebt.treas.gov/careers/careers_with_us.htm.

68. Dennis Cauchon, "Federal workers earning double their private counterparts," *USA Today*, August 13, 2010; available online at http://www.usatoday.com/money/economy/income/2010-08-10-1Afedpay10_ST_N.htm.

69. Ibid.

70.   "Charlie's Ways and Means," *New York Post*, September 19, 2008; available online at http://www.nypost.com/p/news/opinion/editorials/item_snml5IwUtfFmW-Wzs2g2BMK.

71.   Kerry Picket, "Rangel to TWT: I don't deal in average American citizens," *Washington Times*, December 3, 2010; available online at http://www.usatoday.com/money/economy/income/2010-08-10-1Afedpay10_ST_N.htm.

72.   Remarks at a town hall meeting in Hayward, California, August 2, 2010; available online at http://www.breitbart.tv/congressman-at-town-hall-the-federal-government-can-do-most-anything-in-this-country/.

73.   Remarks to the National Press Club at a luncheon, July 24, 2009; facts available online at http://www.cnsnews.com/node/51610 and http://press.org/speakers/speakers-press-club/luncheon-archive.

74.   Allahpundit, "Aw: John Conyers openly reading Playboy on airplanes now," HotAir.com, November 24, 2010; facts available online at http://hotair.com/archives/2010/11/24/aw-john-conyers-openly-reading-playboy-on-airplanes-now/.

75.   Charles Hurt and Yoav Gonen, "Teachers union gets a pass on ObamaCare rule," *New York Post*, October 8, 2010; available online at http://www.nypost.com/p/news/local/teachers_union_gets_pass_on_obamacare_dhoJQgXRKLwbYtp6Nam7LK.

76.   Todd J. Gillman, "Rep. Eddie Bernice Johnson repays Congressional Black Caucus Foundation for scholarships," *Dallas Morning News*, September 2, 2010; available online at http://www.dallasnews.com/news/politics/national-politics/20100901-Rep-Eddie-Bernice-Johnson-repays-6732.ece.

77.   Remarks at a press conference, July 4, 2005; facts available online at http://spectator.org/archives/2005/07/05/nullification-nancy and http://eminentdomain.blogspot.com/2005/07/pelosi-supreme-court-is-god.html.

78.   Remarks during first inaugural address, March 4, 1861; available online at http://www.nationalcenter.org/LincolnFirstInaugural.html.

79.   Theodore Lowi, *The End of Liberalism: The Second Republic of the United States* (New York: W. W. Norton, 1979).

80.   Remarks to the Legislative Conference for National Association of Counties, March 9, 2010; available online at http://washingtonexaminer.com/blogs/beltway-confidential/pelosi-health-care-039we-have-pass-bill-so-you-can-find-out-what-it039.

81.   Terence P. Jeffrey, "Obama Doesn't Rule Out Bypassing Congress and Using EPA Regulations to Cap Carbon Emissions," CNSNews.com, November 4, 2011; available online at http://www.cnsnews.com/news/article/obama-doesn-t-rule-bypassing-congress-an.

82. Robert Pear, "Obama Returns to End-of-Life Plan That Caused Stir," *New York Times*, December 26, 2010; available online at http://www.nytimes.com/2010/12/26/us/politics/26death.html; and Jay Solomon, "Medicare Will Pay for End-of-Life Talks," *Wall Street Journal*, December 27, 2010; available online at http://online.wsj.com/article/SB10001424052970203568004576043970989095748.html?mod=WSJ_topics_obama.

83. Philip Klein, "The Empress of ObamaCare," *American Spectator*, June 2010; available online at http://spectator.org/archives/2010/06/04/the-empress-of-obamacare.

84. Reuven Fenton and Jennifer Fermino, "Extra Tax for Slicing," *New York Post*, August 25, 2010; available online at http://www.nypost.com/p/news/local/ny_cut_of_bagel_dough_YEhNdwO7ZwlUO555GQ4rNN.

85. Cardwell, Diane, "A New Team Helps Steer Restaurateurs Through a Thicket of Red Tape," *New York Times*, December 27, 2010; available online at http://www.nytimes.com/2010/12/28/nyregion/28permits.html.

86. Danny Hakim, "Albany's Two Payrolls: One Is Anybody's Guess," *New York Times*, July 27, 2010; available online at http://www.nytimes.com/2010/07/28/nyregion/28payroll.html

87. Tom Cohen, "White House: $98 billion in bad payments," CNNMoney.com, November 18, 2009; available online at http://money.cnn.com/2009/11/18/news/improper_payments.cnnw/index.htm.

88. Jack Shafer, "Fannie Mae and the Vast Bipartisan Conspiracy," Slate.com, September 16, 2008; available online at http://www.slate.com/id/2200160/.

89. Clyde Wayne Crews, "Ten Thousand Commandments: An Annual Snapshot of the Regulatory State," Competitive Enterprise Institute report, June 28, 2006; available online at http://cei.org/studies-issue-analysis/ten-thousand-commandments-annual-snapshot-regulatory-state.

90. Joel Salatin, *Everything I Want To Do Is Illegal: War Stories From the Local Food Front*, Polyface, 2007; available online at http://acresusa.com/books/closeup.asp?prodid=1601&catid=13&pcid=2.

91. Interview during a Tea Party in Chicago, Illinois, April 15, 2009; available online at http://newsbusters.org/blogs/julia-seymour/2009/04/15/cnn-correspondent-claims-tea-parties-anti-government-anti-cnn.

92. Kris Maher, "Pennsylvania Pie Fight: State Cracks Down on Baked Goods," *Wall Street Journal*, April 10, 2009; available online at http://online.wsj.com/article/SB123932034907406927.html.

93. Helen Jung, "Portland lemonade stand runs into health inspectors, needs $120 license to operate," *The Oregonian*, August 4, 2010; available online at http://

www.oregonlive.com/portland/index.ssf/2010/08/portland_lemonade_stand_runs_i.html.

94.   State of the Union address in Washington, D.C., January 23, 1996; available online at http://clinton2.nara.gov/WH/New/other/sotu.html.

95.   Mark Storer, "County pulls plug on free coffee, doughnuts at Camarillo store," *Ventura County Star*, February 24, 2010; available online at http://www.vcstar.com/news/2010/feb/24/county-pulls-plug-on-free-coffee-doughnuts-at/?print=1.

96.   Bureau of Economic Analysis, Gross-Domestic-Product-by-Industry Accounts, 1947-2010, "Value Added by Industry as a Percentage of Gross Domestic Product," (Historical table); available online at http://www.bea.gov.

97.   David Streitfeld, "Housing Fades as a Means to Build Wealth, Analysts Say," (alternate headline online) *New York Times*, August 22, 2010; available online at http://www.nytimes.com/2010/08/23/business/economy/23decline.html.

98.   Ibid.

99.   David P. Goldman, "Demographics & Depression," *First Things*, May 2009; available online at http://www.firstthings.com/article/2009/05/demographics--depression-1243457089.

100. David Streitfeld, "Housing Fades as a Means to Build Wealth, Analysts Say," *New York Times*.

101. Simon Johnson, "The Quiet Coup," the *Atlantic Monthly*, May, 2009; available online at http://www.theatlantic.com/magazine/archive/2009/05/the-quiet-coup/7364/.

102. Office of the Comptroller of the Currency, "OCC's Quarterly Report on Bank Trading and Derivatives Activities Fourth Quarter 2010," 2011; available online at http://www.occ.treas.gov/topics/capital-markets/financial-markets/trading/derivatives/dq410.pdf.

103. "Taleb's 'Black Swan' Investors Post Gains as Markets Take Dive," *Bloomberg News*, October 14, 2008; available online at http://marketpipeline.blogspot.com/2008/10/talebs-black-swan-investors-post-gains.html.

104. Jay Currie, "2008 Adieu," JayCurrie.info-syn.com, December 31, 2008; available online at http://jaycurrie.info-syn.com/2008-adieu/.

105. Bureau of Economic Analysis, National Income and Products Accounts Table, 1982-2010, "Table 2.1: Personal Income and Its Disposition," (Historical table); available online at http://www.bea.gov.

106. Justin Lahart and Mark Whitehouse, "Families Slice Debt to Lowest in 6 Years," *Wall Street Journal*, March 11, 2011; available online at http://online.wsj.com/article/SB10001424052748704823004576192602754071800.html.

107. Ann Zimmerman, Jennifer Saranow and Miguel Bustillo, "Retail Sales Plummet," *Wall Street Journal*, December 26, 2008; available online at http://online.wsj.com/article/SB123025036865134309.html.

108. Remarks at a campaign stop in Roseburg, Oregon, May 16, 2008; facts available online at http://afp.google.com/article/ALeqM5h-wpxs1Re-8vx2Zk5xnYygW1W67w.

109. Martin Wolf, "Keynes offers us the best way to think about the financial crisis," *Financial Times*, December 23, 2008; available online at http://www.ft.com/cms/s/0/be2dbf2c-d113-11dd-8cc3-000077b07658.html#axzz1MYZ4Ba8m.

110. US Census Bureau, "International Data Base (IDB): Country Rankings," 2011; available online at http://www.census.gov/ipc/www/idb/rank.php.

111. Federal Reserve Bank of New York, "Quarterly Report on Household Debt and Credit," (page 27) February, 2011; available online at http://www.newyorkfed.org/research/national_economy/householdcredit/DistrictReport_Q42010.pdf.

112. *Fortune*, "Global 500," CNNMoney.com, July 26, 2010; available online at http://money.cnn.com/magazines/fortune/global500/2010/snapshots/11384.html.

113. Ibid.

114. Press release, "Minmetals & Jiangxi Copper Successfully Acquire Northern Peru Copper," China Minmetals Corporation, January 29, 2008; available online at http://www.minmetals.com/english/detail.jsp?article_millseconds=1201592566219.

115. Press release, "Minmetals Succeeds in OZ Minerals Deal," Minmetals Australia Pty. Ltd., June 11, 2008; available online at http://australia.minmetals.com.cn/news_1.jsp?article_millseconds=1248748749312.

116. Press release, "Minmetals Seals Bauxite Agreement with Jamaica.Premier Wen and Jamaican Prime Minister Attend the Ceremony," China Minmetals Corporation, June 23, 2005; available online at http://www.minmetals.com/english/detail.jsp?article_millseconds=200512150159.

117. Chris Nicholson, "Sinopec to Buy Addax Petroleum for $7.2 Billion," *New York Times*, June 24, 2009; available online at http://dealbook.nytimes.com/2009/06/24/sinopec-to-buy-addax-for-7-billion/.

118. Shawn McCarthy, "China's big move into Alberta," *Globe and Mail*, April 12, 2010; available online at http://www.theglobeandmail.com/globe-investor/chinas-big-move-into-alberta/article1532062/.

119. Press release, "Sinochem Completed the Acquisition of Emerald," Sinochem Group, November 13, 2009; available online at http://www.sinochem.com/tabid/696/InfoID/10994/Default.aspx.

120. Ahmed Rasheed, "Iraq inaugurates oil deal with China's CNPC," Reuters, March 11, 2009; available online at http://www.reuters.com/article/2009/03/11/iraq-oil-ahdab-idUSLB36965920090311.

121. Ezra Levant, "Collecting the weak," *Calgary Sun*, November 28, 2010; available at http://www.calgarysun.com/comment/columnists/ezra_levant/2010/11/26/16332861.html; and Shrikesh Laxmidas and Kevin Yao, "China offers to help Portugal, but silent on debt," Reuters, November 7, 2010; available at http://www.reuters.com/article/2010/11/07/us-china-portugal-hu-idUS-TRE6A616R20101107.

122. "GM's IPO Included Selling Holding of $500 Million to Chinese Partner SAIC," *Bloomberg News*, November 18, 2010; available at http://www.bloomberg.com/news/2010-11-18/gm-sells-500-million-stake-to-chinese-partner-saic-as-part-of-stock-offer.html; and "China's SAIC close to GM IPO stake buy-sources," Reuters, November 10, 2010; available at http://www.reuters.com/article/2010/11/10/gm-saic-idUSWEN287720101110.

123. Remarks at a conference in Montreal, Quebec, February 7, 2008; available online at http://www.nationalpost.com/news/story.html?id=290513.

124. Quoted by *Local Transport Today*, December 2007; available online at http://www.smalldeadanimals.com/archives/007646.html.

125. James Hansen, "The Price of Change," *South China Morning Post*, November 3, 2010; available online at http://www.columbia.edu/~jeh1/mailings/2010/20101122_ChinaOpEd.pdf.

126. Remarks on NBC's "Meet the Press," May 23, 2010; available online at http://www.msnbc.msn.com/id/37279599/ns/meet_the_press/.

127. Thomas L. Friedman, "Our One-Party Democracy," *New York Times*, September 8, 2009; available online at http://www.nytimes.com/2009/09/09/opinion/09friedman.html.

Chapter Three

1. Philip Pangalos, "Greece on brink of abyss as three bank workers killed in riots," *The Times*, May 6, 2010; available online at http://www.timesonline.co.uk/tol/news/world/europe/article7117546.ece.

2. Emily Ford and David Charter, "Q&A: The Greek Crisis," *The Times*, May 4, 2010; available online at http://business.timesonline.co.uk/tol/business/economics/article7115701.ece.

3. Interview with Thames TV, London, England, February 5, 1976; available online at http://www.margaretthatcher.org/document/102953.

4. United Nations, "Total Fertility Rate (children per woman)," UNData; available online at http://data.un.org/Data.aspx?d=PopDiv&f=variableID%3A54.

5. Alan S. Blinder, "The Concise Encyclopedia of Economics: Keynesian Economics," Library of Economics and Liberty; available online at http://www.econlib.org/library/Enc/KeynesianEconomics.html.

6. Remarks during state of the state address in Sacramento, California, January 9, 2007; available online at http://www.washingtonpost.com/wp-dyn/content/article/2007/01/09/AR2007010901427.html.

7. Jeff Gottlieb and Ruben Vives, "Benefits push Bell ex-manager's compensation to more than $1.5 million," *Los Angeles Times*, August 8, 2010; available online at http://articles.latimes.com/2010/aug/08/local/la-me-bell-benefits-20100808.

8. Christopher Palmeri, "California Official's $800,000 Salary in City of 38,000 Triggers Protests," Bloomberg, July 20, 2010; available online at http://www.bloomberg.com/news/2010-07-20/california-official-s-800-000-salary-in-city-of-38-000-triggers-protests.html.

9. Nicole Gelinas, "Bell's Debt Tolls," *City Journal*, August 6, 2010; available online at http://www.city-journal.org/2010/eon0806ng.html.

10. Peter S. Green and Martin Z. Braun, "NYC Snow 'Overwhelmed' Emergency System, Mayor Says," Bloomberg, December 31, 2010; available online at http://www.bloomberg.com/news/2010-12-29/new-york-city-s-emergency-response-overwhelmed-by-blizzard-mayor-says.html.

11. Ibid.

12. Sally Goldenberg, Larry Celona and Josh Margolin, "Sanitation Department's slow snow cleanup was a budget protest," *New York Post*, December 30, 2010; available online at http://www.nypost.com/p/news/local/sanit_filthy_snow_slow_mo_qH57MZwC53QKOJlekSSDJK.

13. Edgar Sandoval and Larry McShane, "Sanitation boss John Doherty's street plowed clean, but nearby streets remain winter blunderland," *New York Daily News*, December 29, 2010; available online at http://articles.nydailynews.com/2010-12-29/local/27085710_1_clean-street-winter-blunderland-east-side.

14. Ray Long and Michelle Manchir, "Thousands rally at Illinois Capitol—for a tax increase," *Chicago Tribune*, April 21, 2010; available online at http://articles.chicagotribune.com/2010-04-21/news/ct-met-state-capitol-rally-tax-increase-020100421_1_sales-tax-tax-increase-income-tax.

15. Landon Thomas Jr., "Patchwork Pension Plan Adds to Greek Debt Woes," *New York Times*, Mary 11, 2010; available online at http://www.nytimes.com/2010/03/12/business/global/12pension.html.

16. Ibid.

17. BBC, "Greek Officials Strike Over Cuts," February 4, 2010; available online at http://news.bbc.co.uk/2/hi/europe/8497912.stm.

18. CNN, "Greek PM slams European Union amid crisis," February 14, 2010; available online at http://articles.cnn.com/2010-02-14/world/greece.eu.crisis_1_european-union-van-rompuy-greece?_s=PM:WORLD.

19. Ian Traynor and Katie Allen, "Austerity Europe: Who Faces the Cuts," *The Guardian*, June 11, 2010; available online at http://www.guardian.co.uk/business/2010/jun/11/europe-deficit-crisis-austerity-budgets.

20. Ibid.

21. Robert Samuelson, "The Welfare State's Death Spiral," syndicated column, May 10, 2010; available online at http://www.realclearpolitics.com/articles/2010/05/10/the_welfare_states_death_spiral_105503.html.

22. Remarks to the *New York Times*, Berlin, Germany, March 29, 2009; available online at http://www.nytimes.com/2009/03/30/world/europe/30merkel.html?hp.

23. Luke Harding, "Germany agonises over 30% childless women," *The Guardian*, January 27, 2006; available online at http://www.guardian.co.uk/world/2006/jan/27/germany.lukeharding.

24. Tristana Moore, "Baby Gap: Germany's Birth Rate Hits Historic Low," *Time*, May 23, 2010; available online at http://www.time.com/time/world/article/0,8599,1991216,00.html.

25. Sacha Molitorisz, "Mama Mia: Won't You Leave Home, Big Baby?" *The Age*, January 23, 2010; available online at http://www.theage.com.au/opinion/society-and-culture/mama-mia-wont-you-leave-home-big-baby-20100122-mqqa.html.

26. Ibid.

27. Statistics Canada, "2006 Census," September 12, 2007; links to purchase report available online at http://www.statcan.gc.ca/daily-quotidien/070912/dq070912a-eng.htm.

28. Rachel Donadio, "Europe's Young Grow Agitated Over Future Prospects," *New York Times*, January 1, 2011; available online at http://www.nytimes.com/2011/01/02/world/europe/02youth.html.

29. Carl Mortished, "What do cars and cows have in common? No, not horns," *The Times*, March 10, 2009; available online at http://www.timesonline.co.uk/tol/news/environment/article5877416.ece.

30. Ibid.

31. Theodore Dalrymple, "Know Thyself," *City Journal*, May 7, 2010; available online at http://www.city-journal.org/2010/eon0507td.html.

32. "G20 summit: Nicolas Sarkozy and Angela Merkel demand tough market regulations," *The Telegraph*, May 17, 2011; available online at http://www.telegraph.

co.uk/finance/g20-summit/5090442/G20-summit-Nicolas-Sarkozy-and-Angela-Merkel-demand-tough-market-regulations.html.

33. Organization for Economic Co-operation and Development, "OECD Family database," 2010; available online at http://www.oecd.org/dataoecd/50/61/42294015.xls.

34. Ibid.

35. Organization for Economic Co-operation and Development, "OECD Family database," 2010; facts available line at http://www.oecd.org/dataoecd/52/26/41920005.pdf.

36. Russell Shorto, "No Babies?" *New York Times*, June 29, 2008; available online at http://www.nytimes.com/2008/06/29/magazine/29Birth-t.html?pagewanted=all.

37. Douglas A. McIntyre, "Memo To Congress: 'Buy Land, They Ain't Making Any More Of It,'" *Time*, January 28, 2009; available online at http://www.time.com/time/business/article/0,8599,1874407,00.html.

38. International Monetary Fund, "World Economic Outlook," (Chapter IV: Unemployment and Labor Market Institutions: Why Reforms Pay Off) April 2003; available online at http://www.imf.org/external/pubs/ft/weo/2003/01/pdf/chapter4.pdf.

39. Organization for Economic Co-operation and Development, "OECD Economic Outlook No. 88 Annex Tables," 2011; available online at http://www.oecd.org/dataoecd/5/51/2483816.xls.

40. Abul Taher, " 'Soviet' Britain Swells Amid the Recession," *Sunday Times*, January 25, 2009; available online at http://business.timesonline.co.uk/tol/business/economics/article5581225.ece.

41. "Islam and Phobias," *The Economist*, January 10, 2008; available online at http://www.economist.com/node/10499144?story_id=10499144.

42. Steven Erlanger, "Europeans Fear Crisis Threatens Liberal Benefits," *New York Times*, May 22, 2010; available online at http://www.nytimes.com/2010/05/23/world/europe/23europe.html.

43. Dan Bilefsky and Landon Thomas Jr., "The Bitter Pills in the Plan to Rescue Greece," *New York Times*, April 30, 2010; available online at http://www.nytimes.com/2010/05/01/business/global/01euro.html.

44. Paul Krugman, "The Comeback Continent," *New York Times*, January 11, 2008; available online at http://www.nytimes.com/2008/01/11/opinion/11krugman.html.

45. Post-election panel at the University of Calgary, Calgary, Alberta, November 3, 2008; available online at http://strictlyright.com/2010/11/video-post-election-panel-with-mark-steyn-howard-dean-fred-thompson/.

46.   Remarks during a press conference in Brussels, Belgium, November 21, 2009; available online at http://blogs.telegraph.co.uk/news/danielhannan/100017487/herman-van-rompuy-today-the-eu-tomorrow-the-world/.

47.   Vicki Needham, "Obama adviser Volcker says record deficits could lead to new VAT tax," *The Hill*, April 7, 2010; available online at http://thehill.com/blogs/on-the-money/domestic-taxes/90991-volcker-suggests-raising-taxes-possibly-adding-a-value-added-tax.

48.   Panel Study of Income Dynamics, University of Michigan, 2001.

49.   Remarks during the 2009 Irving Kristol Lecture at the annual AEI Annual Dinner in Washington, D.C., March 11, 2009; available online at http://www.aei.org/speech/100023.

50.   Tom Wolfe, "The 'Me' Decade and the Third Great Awakening," *New York Magazine*, August 23, 1976; available online at http://nymag.com/news/features/45938/.

51.   Remarks at the Munich Security Conference in Munich, Germany, February 7, 2009; available online at http://www.securityconference.de/index.php?id=242&zic=1117_1.

52.   Andreas Tzortzis, "One Wall Down, Thousands to Paint," *New York Times*, March 2, 2008; available online at http://travel.nytimes.com/2008/03/02/travel/02headsup.html.

Chapter Four

1.   Richard Wolffe, *Revival: The Struggle for Survival Inside the Obama White House* (New York: Crown, 2010); facts available online at http://www.nypost.com/p/news/opinion/opedcolumnists/how_the_nanny_president_sees_himself_Rz5QE1GoCFaiwCJvR9mrdP.

2.   Dan Jones, "A WEIRD View of Human Nature Skews Psychologists' Studies," *Science*, June 24, 2010; available online at http://www2.psych.ubc.ca/~henrich/pdfs/WEIRD%20in%20Science.pdf.

3.   Andrew Malcolm, "Michelle Obama serves food to D.C. poor and homeless, but…" *Los Angeles Times*, March 6, 2009; available online at http://latimesblogs.latimes.com/washington/2009/03/michelle-obama.html.

4.   Nicholas Timmins, "No worker in one-sixth of UK households," *Financial Times*, August 26, 2009; available online at http://www.ft.com/cms/s/0/0e1abd04-9221-11de-b63b-00144feabdc0.html#axzz1MqD08fIT.

5. Victor Davis Hanson, "Dronism," PajamasMedia.com, March 3, 2010; available online at http://pajamasmedia.com/victordavishanson/dronism/.

6. Remarks made on Al-Rahma TV, June 6, 2010; available online at http://www.memritv.org/clip_transcript/en/2503.htm.

7. Associated Press, "Israel pounds Luxembourg in World Cup qualifier," September 9, 2009; facts available online at http://www.usatoday.com/sports/soccer/2009-09-09-1359674765_x.htm.

8. Charles Murray, *In Our Hands* (AEI Press, 2006).

9. *New Threats to Freedom*, ed. Adam Bellow (Templeton Press, 2010).

10. John F. Burns, "Bill Millin, Scottish D-Day Piper, Dies at 88," *New York Times*, August 19, 2010; available online at http://www.nytimes.com/2010/08/20/world/europe/20millin.html.

11. Bruce Bawer, "A Plague of Poets," *The Hudson Review*, Winter 2004; available online at http://www.hudsonreview.com/BawerWi04.html.

12. Remarks made on MSNBC's *Hardball with Chris Matthews*, July 27, 2004; available online at http://www.msnbc.msn.com/id/5537671/42928946.

13. Remarks made during a Q&A at the University of Denver in Denver, Colorado, May 23, 2010; available online at http://lukeford.net/blog/?page_id=24561.

14. Bill Minutaglio, "School For Homosexuals An Ongoing Controversy," The *Dallas Morning News*, October 22, 1985; available online at http://articles.sunsentinel.com/1985-10-22/features/8502160307_1_harvey-milk-school-school-system-school-officials/3.

15. Rick Salutin, "Here's the Real Obama Question," *The Globe and Mail*, January 16, 2009; available online at http://v1.theglobeandmail.com/servlet/GIS.Servlets.HTMLTemplate?current_row=89&tf=tgam/columnists/FullColumn.html&cf=tgam/columnists/FullColumn.cfg&configFileLoc=tgam/config&date=&dateOffset=&hub=rickSalutin&title=Rick_Salutin&cache_key=rickSalutin&start_row=89&num_rows=1.

16. John Wildermuth, "Many Obama supporters also backed Prop. 8," *San Francisco Chronicle*, November 6, 2008; available online at http://articles.sfgate.com/2008-11-06/news/17128024_1_uncounted-field-poll-same-sex-marriage.

17. Iain Murray, "Boris Hacking Again," National Review Online, January 20, 2009; available online http://www.nationalreview.com/corner/176006/boris-hacking-again/iain-murray.

18. Remarks made during a speech in Berlin, Germany, July 24, 2008; available online at http://www.nytimes.com/2008/07/24/us/politics/24text-obama.html.

19. Michael Ignatieff, *The Rights Revolution* (Toronto: House of Anansi Press, 2007).

20. John Robson, "Media insult us with leadership coverage overkill," *The Ottawa Citizen*, October 6, 2006; available online at http://www.thejohnrobson.com/2006/10/06/media-insult-us-with-leadership-coverage-overkill/.

21. Remarks to National Review Online, September 23, 2009; available online at http://www.nationalreview.com/corner/187591/bolton-post-american-speech-our-first-post-american-president/robert-costa.

22. Dinesh D'Souza, *The Roots of Obama's Rage* (Washington, D.C.: Regnery, 2010).

23. James Gordon Meek, "America is strong enough to withstand another 9/11, President Obama tells author Bob Woodward," *New York Daily News*, September 22, 2010; available online at http://articles.nydailynews.com/2010-09-22/news/27076084_1_president-obama-terror-threat-terrorist-attack.

24. "Northern Ireland: Acceptable Violence?" *Time*, December 27, 1971; available online at http://www.time.com/time/magazine/article/0,9171,905596-2,00.html.

25. Board of Election Commissioners for the City of Chicago, "Election Results, November 2004 General"; facts available online at http://www.chicagoelections.com/.

26. Remarks during a Liberal Party fundraiser in Toronto, Ontario, May 17, 2010; facts available online at http://network.nationalpost.com/NP/blogs/fullcomment/archive/2010/05/18/matt-gurney-untitled-ignatieff.aspx.

27. Remarks made on FOX News' *The O'Reilly Factor*, September 22, 2010; available online at http://politicalticker.blogs.cnn.com/2010/09/23/stewart-saddened-by-obama/.

28. Glenn Reynolds, "Jon Stewart on Obama," Instapundit.com, September 23, 2010; available online at http://pajamasmedia.com/instapundit/106718/.

29. National Center for Education Statistics, National Assessment of Adult Literacy; available online at http://nces.ed.gov/naal/lit_history.asp#enrollment.

30. National Center for Education Statistics, "Digest of Education Statistics 2009," page 269, April 2010; available online at http://nces.ed.gov/pubs2010/2010013.pdf.

31. National Center for Education Statistics, "Digest of Education Statistics 2009," Table 64, April 2010; http://nces.ed.gov/pubs2010/2010013.pdf.

32. National Center for Education Statistics, "Digest of Education Statistics 2009," Tables 33, 34 and 80, April 2010; facts available online at http://www.cato-at-liberty.org/grigori-rasputin-bailout/.

33. Howard Blume, "Annual test scores rise in L.A. Unified schools," *Los Angeles Times*, August 17, 2010; available online at http://articles.latimes.com/2010/aug/17/local/la-me-0817-star-tests-20100817.

34. National Center for Education Statistics, National Assessment of Adult Literacy"; available online at http://nces.ed.gov/naal/lit_history.asp#illiteracy.

35. Jim Hoft, "Photo of the Day: Commie Students Protest Campus Budget Cuts," GatewayPundit.com, March 4, 2010; available online at http://gatewaypundit. rightnetwork.com/2010/03/photo-of-the-day-commie-students-protest-campus-budget-cuts/.

36. Keith O'Brien, "The Test Has Been Cancelled," *The Boston Globe*, October 3, 2010; facts available online http://taxprof.typepad.com/taxprof_blog/2010/10/only-23-of-.html.

37. Esther Rothblum and Sondra Solovay, eds., *The Fat Studies Reader* (NYU Press, November 2009); available online at http://nyupress.org/books/book-details. aspx?bookId=4528.

38. National Science Foundation, "First-Time, Full-Time Graduate Student Enrollment in Science and Engineering Increases in 2006, Especially Among Foreign Students," December, 2007; available online at http://www.nsf.gov/statistics/ infbrief/nsf08302/.

39. Remarks at a campaign stop in Madison, Wisconsin, February 17, 2008; facts available online at http://www.weeklystandard.com/Content/Public/ Articles/000/000/014/764fosie.asp and http://www.dailymotion.com/video/ x4f9af_obama_news.

40. Remarks made on MSNBC's Morning Joe, November 12, 2007; available online at http://newsbusters.org/blogs/mark-finkelstein/2007/11/12/michelle-obama-inferiority-complex-blocks-blacks-backing-barack.

41. Michelle LaVaugh Robinson, "Princeton-Educated Blacks and The Community: A Thesis," Princeton University, Department of Sociology, 1985; available online at http://www.politico.com/pdf/080222_MOPrincetonThesis_1-251.pdf.

42. Thomas J. Espenshade and Alexandria Walton Radford, *No Longer Separate, Not Yet Equal: Race and Class in Elite College Admission and Campus Life* (Princeton University Press, 2009).

43. Kate McMillan, "What's The Opposite Of Diversity?" SmallDeadAnimals.com, June 23, 2009; available online at http://www.smalldeadanimals.com/ archives/011678.html.

44. Angelo M. Codevilla, "America's Ruling Class— And the Perils of Revolution," *The American Spectator*, July-August, 2010; available online at http://spectator. org/archives/2010/07/16/americas-ruling-class-and-the/print#.

45. Remarks at a campaign stop in Powder Springs, Georgia, July 8, 2008; available online at http://www.washingtontimes.com/weblogs/bellantoni/2008/Jul/08/ que-obama-says-nations-kids-should-be-bilingual/.

46.   National Center for Education Statistics, "Digest of Education Statistics 2009," Table 29, page 59, April 2010; available online at http://nces.ed.gov/pubs2010/2010013.pdf.

47.   David Wright, "Los Angeles Public School Named After Robert Kennedy Costs $578 Million," ABCNews.com, August 23, 2010; available online at http://abcnews.go.com/WN/public-school-los-angeles-named-robert-kennedy-expensive/story?id=11462095.

48.   Remarks at a campaign stop in Zanesville, Ohio, February 28, 2008; facts available online at http://www.nationalreview.com/corner/159678/michelle-obama-dont-go-corporate-america/byron-york.

49.   The University of Chicago Medical Center, "Press Release: Michelle Obama appointed vice president for community and external affairs at the University of Chicago Hospitals," May 9, 2005; available online at http://www.uchospitals.edu/news/2005/20050509-obama.html.

50.   Remarks made to *The New Yorker*, March 10, 2008; available online at http://www.newyorker.com/reporting/2008/03/10/080310fa_fact_collins?currentPage=all.

51.   Byron York, "Michelle's Struggle," National Review Online, February 29, 2008; available online at http://www.nationalreview.com/articles/223808/michelles-struggle/byron-york.

52.   Peter Baker and David M. Herszenhorn, "Obama Signs Overhaul of Student Loan Program," *New York Times*, March 30, 2010; available online at http://www.nytimes.com/2010/03/31/us/politics/31obama.html.

53.   U.S. Census Bureau Annual Survey of Government Employment.

54.   Organisation for Economic Co-operation and Development, "Education at a Glance 2009: OECD Indicators," (Indicator B1 How much is spent per student?), 2009; available online at http://www.oecd.org/document/24/0,3343,en_2649_39263238_43586328_1_1_1_37455,00.html.

55.   National Governor's Association, "Return on Investment: Strategies for Improving Remedial Education," 2011; available online at http://www.nga.org/Files/pdf/C2CBriefingPaperRemedialEd.pdf.

56.   Scott Waldman, "State standards tweaks target early learners," *The Albany Times Union*, January 13, 2011; available online at http://www.timesunion.com/local/article/State-standards-tweaks-target-early-learners-953033.php.

57.   Lillian G. Katz, "Reading, Writing and Narcissism," *The American Educator*, Summer, 1993; available online at http://articles.baltimoresun.com/1993-07-16/news/1993197146_1_self-esteem-i-am-special-children.

58. Organisation for Economic Co-operation and Development, "Student Learning: Attitudes, Engagement and Strategies," Figure 3.6, p. 134, 2003; available online at http://www.oecd.org/dataoecd/58/37/33918006.pdf.

59. Organisation for Economic Co-operation and Development, "Education at a Glance 2009: OECD Indicators," Indicator A4, 2009; available online at http://www.oecd.org/document/24/0,3343,en_2649_39263238_43586328_1_1_1_37455,00.html.

60. Charles Savage, "Scouring Obama's Past for Clues on Judiciary," *New York Times*, May 9, 2009; available online at http://www.nytimes.com/2009/05/10/us/politics/10court.html.

61. Obama for America, "American Stories, American Solutions," October 29, 2008; available online at http://www.youtube.com/watch?v=GtREqAmLsoA.

62. Paul Bedard, "Help for Obama's Shack-Living Brother," *US News & World Report*, September 10, 2008; available online at http://www.usnews.com/news/blogs/washington-whispers/2008/09/10/help-for-obamas-shack-living-brother.

63. Remarks made during interview with Cathleen Falsani in Chicago, Illinois, March 27, 2004; available online at http://blog.beliefnet.com/stevenwaldman/2008/11/obamas-interview-with-cathleen.html.

64. Remarks made in video address aired in Berlin, Germany, November 9, 2009; available online at http://news.bbc.co.uk/2/hi/8351471.stm.

65. Remarks to Planned Parenthood in Washington, D.C., July 17, 2007; available online at http://firstread.msnbc.msn.com/_news/2007/07/17/4439758-obama-on-judges-supreme-court.

66. Interview with Paula Zahn, "People in the News," CNN, April 17, 2004; transcript available online at http://edition.cnn.com/TRANSCRIPTS/0404/17/pitn.00.html.

67. Andrew Sullivan, "Goodbye to All That: Why Obama Matters," *The Atlantic Monthly*, December, 2007; available online at http://www.theatlantic.com/magazine/archive/2007/12/goodbye-to-all-that-why-obama-matters/6445/1/.

68. "Al Qaeda leader mocks Obama in Web posting," CNN, November 19, 2008; available online at http://articles.cnn.com/2008-11-19/us/obama.alqaeda_1_al-zawahiri-barack-obama-obama-s-muslim?_s=PM:US.

69. Remarks during a Department of Defense news briefing in Washington, D.C., February 12, 2002; available online at http://www.youtube.com/watch?v=jtkUO8NpI84.

70. Remarks during 9/11 anniversary observance in Boston, Massachusetts, September 11, 2007; available online at http://hotair.com/archives/2007/09/11/video-911-was-a-failure-of-human-understanding-says-mass-governor/.

71.   Remarks made on *CBS Evening News*, May 3, 2010; available online at http://www.cbsnews.com/stories/2010/05/03/eveningnews/main6457014.shtml.

72.   Remarks at a press conference in New York, New York, May 4, 2010; available online at http://www.bloomberg.com/news/2010-05-03/new-york-city-plans-to-deploy-more-cameras-mayor-says.html.

73.   Bobby Cuza, "Bloomberg Repeatedly Defends Mosque By WTC Site," NY1 News, July 16, 2010; available online at http://manhattan.ny1.com/content/top_stories/122239/bloomberg-repeatedly-defends-mosque-by-wtc-site.

74.   Remarks made in New York, New York, August 3, 2010; available online at http://www.nytimes.com/2010/08/04/nyregion/04mosque.html.

75.   Hendrik Hertzberg, "Zero Grounds," *The New Yorker*, August 16, 2010; available online at http://www.newyorker.com/talk/comment/2010/08/16/100816taco_talk_hertzberg.

76.   Vince Veneziani, "Oh Please: CNN Anchors Wonder If Times Square Bombing Suspect Was Stressed From Being Foreclosed On," *Business Insider*, May 4, 2010; available online at http://www.businessinsider.com/faisal-shahzad-foreclosed-2010-5.

77.   James Gordon Meek, "Times Square bomb plotter Faisal Shahzad mumbles his way through 'suicide attack' video," *New York Daily News*, July 14, 2010; available online at http://articles.nydailynews.com/2010-07-14/news/27069966_1_bomb-plotter-pakistani-taliban-al-qaeda.

78.   Paul Berman, *The Flight of the Intellectuals: The Controversy Over Islamism and the Press* (Melville House, 2011).

79.   All headlines available online at http://www.navy.mil/swf/index.asp.

80.   Richard Esposito, Mary-Rose Abraham, and Rhonda Schwartz, "Major Hasan: Soldier of Allah; Many Ties to Jihad Web Sites," ABCNews.com, November 12, 2009; available online at http://abcnews.go.com/Blotter/hasan-multiple-mail-accounts-officials/story?id=9065692.

81.   Associated Press, "Clear warning signs, Hasan's colleagues say," November 7, 2009; available online at http://www.msnbc.msn.com/id/33753461/ns/us_news-tragedy_at_fort_hood/t/clear-warning-signs-hasans-colleagues-say/.

82.   Associated Press, "Some recognized Fort Hood Army psychiatrist was troubled," November 8, 2009; available online at http://www.tampabay.com/incoming/article1050288.ece.

83.   Barry Rubin, "Why I Murdered 13 American Soldiers at Ford Hood: Nidal Hassan Explains It All To You," *The Rubin Report*, November 14, 2009; available online at http://rubinreports.blogspot.com/2009/11/why-i-murdered-13-american-soldiers-at.html.

84. Daniel Zwerdling and Steve Inskeep, "Former Colleagues Say Hasan Was Detached," NPR, November 10, 2009; available online at http://www.npr.org/templates/story/story.php?storyId=120266836.

85. Philip Sherwell, "Fort Hood shooting: Nidal Malik Hasan 'said Muslims should rise up'," *The Telegraph*, November 6, 2009; available online at http://www.telegraph.co.uk/news/worldnews/northamerica/usa/6511591/Fort-Hood-shooting-Nidal-Malik-Hasan-said-Muslims-should-rise-up.html.

86. Remarks made during an interview with FOX News, November 5, 2009; available online at http://www.youtube.com/watch?v=cPrT0T3371Q.

87. Associated Press, "Napolitano Warns Against Anti-Muslim Backlash," FoxNews.com, November 8, 2009; available online at http://www.foxnews.com/politics/2009/11/08/napolitano-warns-anti-muslim-backlash/.

88. Andrew Bast, "Is Fort Hood a Harbinger? Nidal Malik Hasan May Be a Symptom of a Military on the Brink," *Newsweek*, November 6, 2009; available online at http://www.newsweek.com/blogs/the-human-condition/2009/11/06/is-fort-hood-a-harbinger-nidal-malik-hasan-may-be-a-symptom-of-a-military-on-the-brink.html.

89. Editorial, "In Plain Sight?" *Washington Post*, November 12, 2009; available online at http://www.washingtonpost.com/wp-dyn/content/article/2009/11/11/AR2009111123438.html.

90. Frank Gaffney, "Connect the Dots on CAIR's Foreign Funding and Lobbying at CAIRObservatory.org," BigGovernment.com, April 3, 2010; available online http://biggovernment.com/fgaffney/2010/04/03/connect-the-dots-on-cairs-foreign-funding-and-lobbying-at-cairobservatory-org/.

91. Chris Ayers, "Barack Obama 'insensitive' over his handling of Fort Hood shooting," *The Times*, November 9, 2009; available online at http://www.timesonline.co.uk/tol/news/world/us_and_americas/article6908849.ece.

92. Sharon Weinberger, "Fort Hood Shooting Puts Focus on 'Internal Threat'," AolNews.com, August 20, 2010; available online at http://www.aolnews.com/2010/08/20/fort-hood-shooting-prompts-focus-on-internal-threat/ and http://www.defense.gov/news/d20100820FortHoodFollowon.pdf.

93. Adam Sternbergh, "Up With Grups," *New York*, March 26, 2006; available online at http://nymag.com/news/features/16529/.

94. Remarks made during a town hall in Strongsville, Ohio, March 15, 2010; available online at http://www.whitehouse.gov/the-press-office/remarks-president-health-care-reform-strongsville-ohio.

95. Tim Craig, "D.C. to begin using more-expensive Trojan condoms in HIV prevention program," *Washington Post*, May 21, 2010; available online at http://www.

washingtonpost.com/wp-dyn/content/article/2010/05/20/AR2010052003980.
html.

96. April Gavaza, "Sweet Baby Jesus," *The Hyacinth Girl*, May 22, 2010; available
     online at http://thehyacinthgirl.wordpress.com/2010/05/22/sweet-baby-jesus/.

97. Kimi Yoshino, "For the 'funemployed,' unemployment is welcome," *Los Angeles
     Times*, June 4, 2009; available online at http://www.latimes.com/news/local/la-
     me-funemployment4-2009jun04,0,7581684.story.

98. Victor Davis Hanson, "Ten Random, Politically Incorrect Thoughts," Pajamas-
     Media.com, November 21, 2008; available online at http://pajamasmedia.com/
     victordavishanson/ten-random-politicially-incorrect-thoughts/.

99. Jessica Reaves, "Gore's Political 'Promiscuities," *Time*, November 1, 1999; avail-
     able online at http://www.time.com/time/nation/article/0,8599,33529,00.html.

100. Interview with Ross Robertson of Enlightenment, August-October 2008; avail-
     able online at http://www.enlightennext.org/magazine/j41/mansfield.
     asp?page=1.

101. Remarks at a press conference in Beverly Hills, California, August 8, 2010; avail-
     able online at http://www.people.com/people/article/0,,20408849,00.html.

102. Elizabeth Marquardt, Norval D. Glenn, and Karen Clark, "My Daddy's Name is
     Donor: New Study of Young Adults Conceived Through Sperm Donation,"
     Institute for American Values, 2010; available online at http://www.
     familyscholars.org/assets/Donor_FINAL.pdf.

103. Kristin Boehm, "Alexis Stewart Continues Fertility Treatments," *People*, October
     9, 2007; available online at http://www.people.com/people/article/0,,20151378,00.
     html.

104. Mark Dagostino, "My Struggle to Have a Baby," People, August 13, 2007; available
     online at http://www.people.com/people/archive/article/0,,20059186,00.html.

105. John F. Harris and Beth Frerking, "Clinton aides: Palin treatment sexist," *Politico*,
     September 3, 2008; available online at http://www.politico.com/news/
     stories/0908/13129.html.

106. Cherry Norton, "Maternal instinct 'is extinct for one woman in five'," *The Inde-
     pendent*, October 27, 1999; available online at http://www.independent.co.uk/
     news/uk/home-news/maternal-instinct-is-extinct-for-one-woman-in-
     five-743042.html.

107. Christina Hoff Summers, *The War Against Boys* (New York: Simon & Schuster,
     2001).

108. Interview with Ross Robertson of *Enlightenment*, August-October 2008; available
     online at http://www.enlightennext.org/magazine/j41/mansfield.asp?page=1.

109. Dennis Cauchon, "Women Gain as Men Lose Jobs," *USA Today*, September 3, 2009; available online at http://www.usatoday.com/news/nation/2009-09-02-womenwork_N.htm.

110. Sara Murray, "Grads Head to College In Record Numbers," *Wall Street Journal*, April 28, 2010; available online at http://online.wsj.com/article/SB1000142405 27487038322045752102442034 11342.html?mod=WSJ_hpp_ MIDDLENexttoWhatsNewsSecond.

111. National Center for Education Statistics, "Digest of Education Statistics 2009," Table 275, p. 400, April 2010; http://nces.ed.gov/pubs2010/2010013.pdf.

112. George F. Will, "The Basement Boys," *Newsweek*, March 8, 2010; available online at http://www.newsweek.com/2010/03/07/the-basement-boys.html.

113. Ibid.

114. Keturah Gray, "Quarterlife Crisis Hits Many in Late 20s," ABC News, April 21, 2005; available online at http://abcnews.go.com/Business/Careers /story?id=688240&page=1.

115. George F. Will, "The Basement Boys," *Newsweek*.

116. Kay Hymowitz, "Child-Man in the Promised Land," *City Journal*, Winter 2008; available online at http://www.city-journal.org/2008/18_1_single_young_men. html.

117. Ibid.

118. Ibid.

119. Peg Tyre, "Bringing Up Adultolescents," *Newsweek*, March 25, 2002; available online at http://www.newsweek.com/2002/03/24/bringing-up-adultolescents. html and http://www.hyper-parenting.com/newsweek5.htm.

120. Tom W. Smith, "The Emerging 21st Century American Family," National Opinion Research Center, University of Chicago, November 24, 1999; available online at http://cloud9.norc.uchicago.edu/dlib/sc-42.htm.

121. Gary Cross, *Men To Boys: The Making Of Modern Immaturity* (Columbia University Press, 2010).

122. Jenny Hope, "Concern as sperm count falls," *Daily Mail*, (no date given); available online at http://www.dailymail.co.uk/health/article-205209/Concern-sperm-count-falls.html.

123. Liz Hunt, "Sperm count drops 25% in younger men," *The Independent*, February 23, 1996; available online at http://www.independent.co.uk/news/sperm-count-drops-25-in-younger-men-1320456.html.

124. Lester Haines, "Swedish lesbians suck sperm banks dry," *The Register*, July 24, 2009; available online at http://www.theregister.co.uk/2009/07/24/swedish_ shortage/.

125. "Hero students leap into river to save drowning woman…as police officers refuse to help," *Daily Mail*, May 12, 2010; available online at http://www.dailymail.co.uk/news/article-1277480/3-students-leap-River-Clyde-save-drowning-woman-police-REFUSE.html.

126. Richard Savill and Andy Bloxham, "Police unable to save girl from icy river because of health and safety," *The Telegraph*, February 13, 2010; available online at http://www.telegraph.co.uk/news/uknews/crime/7224051/Police-unable-to-save-girl-from-icy-river-because-of-health-and-safety.html.

127. "Police defend drowning death case," BBC, September 21, 2007; available online at http://news.bbc.co.uk/2/hi/7006412.stm.

128. David Lister, "Fireman faces punishment for risking his life in rescue," *The Times*, March 26, 2007; available online at http://www.timesonline.co.uk/tol/news/uk/article1567322.ece.

129. Melanie Reid, "Firefighters left woman in mine shaft for six hours due to 'health and safety concerns,'" *The Times*, March 3, 2010; available online at http://www.timesonline.co.uk/tol/news/uk/scotland/article7047101.ece.

130. Edecio Martinez, "Seattle Bus Tunnel Beating: 15-Year-Old Girl Viciously Attacked, Guards Watched," Associated Press, February 12, 2010; available online at http://www.cbsnews.com/8301-504083_162-6197753-504083.html.

131. "Gunman massacres 14 women," CBC, December 6, 1989; available online at http://archives.cbc.ca/society/crime_justice/topics/398/.

132. Ingrid Peritz, "Are we ready to relive the Montreal massacre?" *The Globe and Mail*, January 30, 2009; available online at http://www.theglobeandmail.com/news/arts/are-we-ready-to-relive-the-montreal-massacre/article969167/singlepage/.

133. "Titanic hero apology cuts no ice," *The Herald*, April 16, 1998; available online at http://www.heraldscotland.com/sport/spl/aberdeen/titanic-hero-apology-cuts-no-ice-film-executive-s-visit-too-little-too-late-1.346954.

134. Accident Investigation Board of Finland, "MV Estonia," December 1997; available online at http://www.onnettomuustutkinta.fi/en/Etusivu/Tutkintaselostukset/Vesiliikenne/MVEstonia.

135. James O. Jackson, Ulla Plon, and Bruce van Voorst, "The Cruel Sea," *Time*, October 10, 1994; available online at http://www.time.com/time/magazine/article/0,9171,981585-2,00.html.

136. "Montreal Massacre movie depicts killer as non-bearded non-Muslim for some wacky reason," FiveFeetOfFury.com, February 15, 2009, http://www.fivefeetoffury.com/2009/02/7951/.

137. Paul Belien, "The Rape of Europe," *The Brussels Journal*, October 25, 2006; available online at http://www.brusselsjournal.com/node/1609.

Chapter Five

1.   Arnold J. Toynbee, *The Prospects of Western Civilization* (New York: Columbia University Press, 1949).

2.   "Britain makes final WW2 lend-lease payment," InTheNews.co.uk, December 29, 2006; available online at http://www.inthenews.co.uk/news/news/finance/britain-makes-final-ww2-lend-lease-payment-$1034891.htm.

3.   Remarks to the House of Commons, London, England, November 10, 1942; available online at http://www.churchill-society-london.org.uk/EndoBegn.html.

4.   Daniel Hannan, "Happy Independence Day to all my American readers: keep the torch of British liberty aflame!" *The Telegraph*, July 4, 2010; available online at http://blogs.telegraph.co.uk/news/danielhannan/100046044/happy-independence-day-to-all-my-american-readers-keep-the-torch-of-british-liberty-aflame/.

5.   "China 'will be the world's biggest economy by 2027,'" *The London Evening Standard* November 17, 2009; available online at http://www.thisislondon.co.uk/standard-business/article-23770626-china-will-be-the-worlds-biggest-economy-by-2027.do.

6.   Rich Miller and Simon Kennedy, "Lawrence SummersG-20 Plans to End 'Financial Balance of Terror' After Summit," Bloomberg News, September 27, 2009; available online at http://www.bloomberg.com/apps/news?pid=newsarchive&sid=aVpPMKLa50rc.

7.   Ben Arnoldy, "China warships dock in Burma, rattling rival naval power India," *The Christian-Science Monitor*, August 30, 2010; available online at http://www.csmonitor.com/World/Asia-South-Central/2010/0830/China-warships-dock-in-Burma-rattling-rival-naval-power-India.

8.   David Leonhardt, "The Real Problem With China," *New York Times*, January 11, 2011; available online at http://www.nytimes.com/2011/01/12/business/economy/12leonhardt.html.

9.   William Matthews, "Chinese Cyber Attacks On Rise: U.S. Report," Defense News, November 20, 2010; available online at http://www.defensenews.com/story.php?i=3830559.

10. Francis Harris, "Beijing secretly fires lasers to disable US satellites," *The Telegraph*, September 26, 2006; available online at http://www.telegraph.co.uk/news/worldnews/1529864/Beijing-secretly-fires-lasers-to-disable-US-satellites.html.

11. Paul Danahar, "Taliban 'getting Chinese arms,'" BBC, September 3, 2007; available online at http://news.bbc.co.uk/2/hi/6975934.stm.

12. Shaun Waterman, "China aids N. Korea, Iran with nuke advances," *The Washington Times*, May 17, 2011; available online at http://www.washingtontimes.com/news/2011/may/17/beijing-aiding-north-korea-and-iran-with-nuke-adva/.

13. Ibid.

14. Gordon G. Chang, "China's Illicit Nuclear Transfers to Iran," Hudson New York, April 12, 2010; available online at http://www.hudson-ny.org/1141/chinas-illicit-nuclear-transfers-to-iran.

15. Sam Jones, "Geert Wilders anti-Islam film gets House of Lords screening," *The Guardian*, March 5, 2010; available online at http://www.guardian.co.uk/world/2010/mar/05/geert-wilders-house-of-lords.

16. Remarks made to the House of Lords in London, England, March 5, 2010; available online at http://www.geertwilders.nl/index.php?option=com_content&task=view&id=1662&Itemid=1.

17. Tim Shipman, "Barack Obama sends bust of Winston Churchill on its way back to Britain," *The Telegraph*, February 14, 2009; available online at http://www.telegraph.co.uk/news/worldnews/barackobama/4623148/Barack-Obama-sends-bust-of-Winston-Churchill-on-its-way-back-to-Britain.html.

18. "Cambridge University college renames 'distasteful' Empire Ball," *The Telegraph*, February 12, 2009; available online at http://www.telegraph.co.uk/education/4604461/Cambridge-University-college-renames-distasteful-Empire-Ball.html.

19. "London bomber video aired on TV," BBC, September 2, 2005; available online at http://news.bbc.co.uk/2/hi/uk_news/4206708.stm.

20. Tim Shipman and Gerri Peev, "'They were lucky not to be shot': Police chief says armed officers showed 'enormous restraint' as mob attacked Charles and Camilla," *The Daily Mail*, December 10, 2010; available online at http://www.dailymail.co.uk/news/article-1337088/ROYAL-CAR-ATTACK-Mob-attacking-Charles-Camillas-car-lucky-shot.html.

21. "Charlie Gilmour pleads guilty to student protest disorder charges," *The Guardian*, May 6, 2011; available online at http://www.guardian.co.uk/education/2011/may/06/charlie-gilmour-pleads-guilty-protest.

22. Julie Burchill, "Spare us these pampered protesters who riot in defence of their privilege," *The Independent*, December 16, 2010; available online at http://www.independent.co.uk/opinion/columnists/julie-burchill/julie-burchill-spare-us-these-pampered-protesters-who-riot-in-defence-of-their-privilege-2161489.html.

23. Rebecca Atwood, "Brown Targets Work Skills," *The Higher Education*, July 6, 2007; available online at http://www.timeshighereducation.co.uk/story.asp?storyCode=209524&sectioncode=26.

24. All data available online via http://www.ukpublicspending.co.uk/charts.html.

25. Social Analysis & Reporting Division, National Statistics Quality Review Series, Report #31 (Office for National Statistics, London 2004).

26. James Tozer, "Christian preacher vows to fight after he's arrested for 'public order' offences after saying homosexuality is a sin," *The Daily Mail*, May 3, 2010; available online at http://www.dailymail.co.uk/news/article-1270650/Christian-preacher-trial-public-order-offences-saying-homosexuality-sin.html.

27. "Nursery alert for racist toddlers," BBC, July 7, 2008; available online at http://news.bbc.co.uk/2/hi/uk_news/7493654.stm.

28. Luke Salkeld, "Flipping madness! Police offer free flip-flops to binge drinkers who keep falling over in heels," *The Daily Mail*, November 27, 2008; available online at http://www.dailymail.co.uk/news/article-1089919/Flipping-madness-Police-offer-free-flip-flops-binge-drinkers-falling-heels.html.

29. Nick Allen, "Man escapes jail for punching war veteran, 96," *The Telegraph*, October 22, 2007; available online at http://www.telegraph.co.uk/news/uknews/1566972/Man-escapes-jail-for-punching-war-veteran-96.html.

30. George Jonas, "The Evil Men Do Lives After Them," *The National Post*, October 16, 2000; available online at http://jeanchretien.libertyca.net/html/0072.html.

31. David Millward, "Traffic wardens get head cameras," *The Telegraph*, December 21, 2009; available online at http://www.telegraph.co.uk/motoring/news/6840937/Traffic-wardens-get-head-cameras.html.

32. Maxine Frith, "How average Briton is caught on camera 300 times a day," *The Independent*, January 12, 2004; available online at http://www.independent.co.uk/news/uk/this-britain/how-average-briton-is-caught-on-camera-300-times-a-day-572781.html.

33. John Steele, "Britain has worst drug addiction rate in Europe," *The Telegraph*, April 19, 2007; available online at http://www.telegraph.co.uk/news/uknews/1549028/Britain-has-worst-drug-addiction-rate-in-Europe.html.

34. Steve Doughty, "Most teenage pregnancies now end with an abortion," *The Daily Mail*, May 11, 2009; available online at http://www.dailymail.co.uk/news/article-1180262/Most-teenage-pregnancies-end-abortion.html.

35. Steve Doughty, "Single mother Britain: U.K. has most lone parents of any major European nation," *The Daily Mail*, April 1, 2011; available online at http://www.dailymail.co.uk/news/article-1372533/Britain-lone-parents-major-Euro-nation.html.

36. Helen Weathers, "Why does Britain have record levels of abortion and an unprecedented need for IVF?," *The Daily Mail*, June 30, 2006; available online at http://

www.dailymail.co.uk/news/article-393236/Why-does-Britain-record-levels-abortion-unprecedented-need-IVF.html.

37. Jack Grimston, "Children wear body armour school uniform," *The Times*, September 9, 2007; available online at http://www.timesonline.co.uk/tol/news/uk/article2414704.ece

38. "The plan for social security: full outline," *The Guardian*, December 2, 1942; available online at http://century.guardian.co.uk/1940-1949/Story/0,,127564,00.html.

39. Patrick Wintour, "Brown: Remembrance Sunday should become 'British Day'," *The Guardian*, January 14, 2006; available online at http://www.guardian.co.uk/uk/2006/jan/14/britishidentity.labour.

40. John Carvel, "Brown urged to create holiday on birthday of health service," *The Guardian*, January 1, 2008; available online at http://www.guardian.co.uk/politics/2008/jan/01/uk.publicservices.

41. Jason Groves, "'Shameless' generation grows as seven million now live in households where no one works," *The Daily Mail*, September 14, 2010; available online at http://www.dailymail.co.uk/news/article-1310220/7-million-live-jobless-households-works.html.

42. Tim Shipman, "More than 900,000 have been off sick for a DECADE–costing taxpayer £4bn a year," *The Daily Mail*, August 16, 2010; available online at http://www.dailymail.co.uk/news/article-1303320/4bn-year-900-000-whove-decade-sick.html.

43. Paul Sims, "Councils pay for disabled to visit prostitutes and lap-dancing clubs from £520m taxpayer fund," *The Daily Mail*, August 16, 2010; available online at http://www.dailymail.co.uk/news/article-1303273/Councils-pay-disabled-visit-prostitutes-lap-dancing-clubs.html.

44. Abul Taher, "'Soviet' Britain swells amid the recession," *The Times*, January 25, 2009; available online at http://business.timesonline.co.uk/tol/business/economics/article5581225.ece.

45. House of Commons, "A Century of Change: Trends in UK statistics since 1900," December 21, 1999; available online at http://www.parliament.uk/documents/commons/lib/research/rp99/rp99-111.pdf.

46. Alison Little, "20,000 Families to be put under 24/7 CCTV surveillance in their own homes 'to change their bad behaviour'," *The Daily Express*, July 29, 2009; available online at http://justgetthere.us/blog/archives/20,000-Families-to-be-put-under-247-CCTV-surveillance-in-their-own-homes-to-change-their-bad-behaviour.html.

Chapter Six

1.   Michael Snyder, "The Middle Class in America Is Radically Shrinking. Here Are the Stats to Prove it," *The Business Insider*, July 15, 2010; available online at http://finance.yahoo.com/tech-ticker/the-u.s.-middle-class-is-being-wiped-out-here's-the-stats-to-prove-it-520657.html?tickers=%5EDJI,%5EGSPC,SPY,MCD,WMT,XRT,DIA.

2.   Bureau of Labor Statistics, "Data Retrieval: Labor Force Statistics (CPS)"; available online at http://www.bls.gov/webapps/legacy/cpsatab13.htm.

3.   Carolyn Dimitri, Anne Effland, and Neilson Conklin, "The 20th Century Transformation of U.S. Agriculture and Farm Policy," US Department of Agriculture, June 3, 2005; available online at http://www.ers.usda.gov/publications/eib3/eib3.htm#changes and http://www.agclassroom.org/gan/timeline/farmers_land.htm.

4.   Remarks by the Secretary of Agriculture Tom Vilsack before US House Committee on Agriculture in Washington, DC, May 12, 2011; available online at http://www.usda.gov/wps/portal/usda/usdahome?contentid=2011/05/0208.xml&contentidonly=true.

5.   Aaron E. Cobet and Gregory A. Wilson, "Comparing 50 years of labor productivity in U.S. and foreign manufacturing," Bureau of Labor Statistics, June 2002; available online at http://www.bls.gov/opub/mlr/2002/06/art4full.pdf.

6.   Bureau of Labor Statistics, "Employment Situation Summary," May 6, 2011; available online at http://www.bls.gov/news.release/empsit.nr0.htm.

7.   Dennis Cauchon, "Summer jobs hit all-time low for youths," *USA Today*, September 3, 2010; available online at http://www.usatoday.com/money/economy/employment/2010-09-03-youth-unemployment_N.htm.

8.   Susan Page, "Married? Single? Status affects how women vote," *USA Today*, August 25, 2004; available online at http://www.usatoday.com/news/politicselections/nation/polls/2004-08-25-female-vote_x.htm.

9.   US Department of Commerce, "Projections of the Number of Households and Families in the United States: 1995 to 2010," 2010; available online at http://www.census.gov/prod/1/pop/p25-1129.pdf.

10.   U.S. Census Bureau, Current Population Survey, 2008 Annual Social and Economic Supplement.

11.   "Busy Not Running GM," *Wall Street Journal*, June 3, 2009; available online at http://online.wsj.com/article/SB124389952143874411.html.

12.   John Tamny, "Memo To Washington: Let GM Fail," *Forbes*, July 10, 2008; available online at http://www.forbes.com/2008/07/09/gm-washington-detroit-oped-cx_jt_0710tamny.html.

13.   Robert W. Crandall and Clifford Winston, "Detroit Needs a Selloff, Not a Bailout," *Wall Street Journal*, November 28, 2008; available online at http://online.wsj.com/article/SB122783248646663009.html.

14.   Testimony of Rick Wagoner (CEO of the General Motors Corporation) to the United States Senate in Washington, D.C., November 18, 2008; available online at http://s.wsj.net/public/resources/documents/WSJ_WagonerTestimony-081118.pdf.

15.   Associated Press, "Detroit Three erasing productivity gap," June 5, 2008; available online at http://www.rrstar.com/archive/x142951738/Detroit-Three-erasing-productivity-gap.

16.   Jennifer Harper, "Kerry aims to rescue newspapers," *The Washington Times*, April 22, 2009; available online at http://www.washingtontimes.com/news/2009/apr/22/kerry-aims-to-rescue-newspaper-industry/.

17.   Yves Marchand and Romain Meffre, *The Ruins of Detroit* (London: Steidl, 2011).

18.   John Huey, "Assignment Detroit: Why Time Inc. Is in Motown," *Time*, September 24, 2009; available online at http://www.time.com/time/nation/article/0,8599,1925681,00.html.

19.   Jonathan Oosting, "Detroit school board president struggles to write a coherent sentence; does it matter?" MLive.com, March 4, 2010; available online at http://www.mlive.com/news/detroit/index.ssf/2010/03/detroit_school_board_president.html.

20.   Anthony Daniels, "Britain, benign & proud," Speech reprinted in *The New Criterion*, January 2011; available online at http://www.newcriterion.com/articles.cfm/Britain--benign---proud-6752.

21.   Laura Berman, "Does DPS leader's writing send wrong message?" *The Detroit News*, March 4, 2010; available online at http://detnews.com/article/20100304/OPINION03/3040437/Does-DPS-leader-s-writing-send-wrong-message.

22.   Michelle Malkin, "Diplomas Won't Make Jihadis Go Away, Barack," *Human Events*, July 16, 2008; available online at http://www.humanevents.com/article.php?id=27552.

23.   Laura Berman, "Does DPS leader's writing send wrong message?" *The Detroit News*.

24.   "Detroit: Now a Ghost Town," *Time*, 2009; available online at http://www.time.com/time/interactive/0,31813,1925735,00.html.

25.   Henry Payne, "Unions of Urban Decay," *National Review* Online, August 6, 2007; available online at http://www.nationalreview.com/articles/221777/unions-urban-decay/henry-payne.

26. Steven Gray, "In Detroit, Nearly 50% Unemployment Rate?" *Time*, December 16, 2009; available online at http://detroit.blogs.time.com/2009/12/16/in-detroit-nearly-50-unemployment-rate/.

27. Ibid.

28. John Huey, "Assignment Detroit: Why Time Inc. is in Motown," *Time*, September 24, 2009; available online at http://www.time.com/time/nation/article/0,8599,1925681,00.html.

29. Niall Ferguson, "Empire Falls," *Vanity Fair*, October 2006; available online at http://fnf.org.ph/downloadables/Empire_Falls_as_published_in_Vanity_Fair_Oct_06.pdf.

30. Centers for Disease Control, "Prevalence of overweight, obesity and extreme obesity among adults: United States, trends 1960-62 through 2005-2006"; available online at http://www.cdc.gov/nchs/data/hestat/overweight/overweight_adult.htm.

31. John G. Spangler, "Childhood Obesity: Attacking a Crushing Epidemic," ABCNews.com, May 13, 2010; available online at http://abcnews.go.com/Health/Wellness/childhood-obesity-white-house-task-force-childhood-obesity/story?id=10631915.

32. "Not grrrreat: After five decades, anti-obesity Bill could ban cartoon Tony the tiger from TV," *The Daily Mail*, May 19, 2008; available online at http://www.dailymail.co.uk/news/article-1015879/Not-grrrreat-After-50-years-anti-obesity-Bill-ban-Tony-tiger-TV.html.

33. Sharon Bernstein, "San Francisco bans Happy Meals," *Los Angeles Times*, November 2, 2010; available online at http://articles.latimes.com/2010/nov/02/business/la-fi-happy-meals-20101103.

34. Public Health Agency of Canada, "Preconception Health and Folic Acid," 2005; available online at http://www.phac-aspc.gc.ca/fa-af/backgrounder-eng.php.

35. Steven Reinberg, "Folic Acid Fortification Might Boost Cancer Risk," ABCNews.com, November 18, 2009; available online at http://abcnews.go.com/Health/Healthday/folic-acid-fortification-boost-cancer-risk/story?id=9109220.

36. Senator Richard Lugar, "Lugar praises passage of child nutrition bill," press release, August 5, 2010; available online at http://lugar.senate.gov/record.cfm?id=327017&.

37. Madison Park, "Ex-military leaders: Young adults 'too fat to fight,'" CNN, April 20, 2010; available online at http://www.cnn.com/2010/HEALTH/04/20/military.fat.fight/index.html.

38.   Viktoria Lapko, "Family Becomes Extinct, To Be Replaced with Feminism and Gender Equality," Pravda, August 19, 2010; available online at http://english.pravda.ru/history/19-08-2010/114665-family_feminism_gender_equality-0/.

39.   Ralph Waldo Emerson, "The American Scholar," August 31, 1837.

40.   "Follow the Leader," *The Economist*, July 8, 2010; available online at http://www.economist.com/node/16542808.

41.   Paul A. Rahe, *Soft Despotism, Democracy's Drift* (Yale University Press, 2010).

42.   Kenneth Minogue, "The New Epicureans," *The New Criterion*, September 2001; available online at http://www.newcriterion.com/articles.cfm/The-new-Epicureans-2131.

43.   "Millionaire gay fathers celebrate arrival of twins with triple christening ceremony," *The Daily Mail*, July 3, 2010; available online at http://www.dailymail.co.uk/news/article-1291664/Millionaire-gay-fathers-Barrie-Tony-Drewitt-Barlow-celebrate-arrival-twins-triple-christening-ceremony.html.

44.   James Bone, "'Pregnant man' Thomas Beatie gives birth to baby girl," *The Times*, July 4, 2008; available online at http://www.timesonline.co.uk/tol/news/world/us_and_americas/article4265368.ece.

45.   Julia Steinecke, "Border skirmishes," *The Toronto Star*, August 15, 2009; available online at http://www.thestar.com/travel/article/680107.

46.   Christopher Ryan and Cacilda Jetha, *Sex at Dawn: The Prehistoric Origins of Modern Sexuality* (New York: Harper, 2010).

47.   Jared Diamond, "The Worst Mistake in the History of the Human Race," *Discover*, May 1987; available online at http://www.scribd.com/doc/2100251/Jared-Diamond-The-Worst-Mistake-in-the-History-of-the-Human-Race.

48.   Roger Scruton, *The Uses of Pessimism: And the Danger of False Hope* (Oxford University Press, 2010).

49.   George F. Will, "Why Mike Pence catches conservatives' eyes," The *Washington Post*, December 8, 2010; available online at http://www.washingtonpost.com/wp-dyn/content/article/2010/12/08/AR2010120805110.html.

50.   Centers for Disease Control, "National Vital Statistics Report," August 9, 2010; available online at http://www.cdc.gov/nchs/data/nvsr/nvsr58/nvsr58_24.pdf.

51.   Milton and Rose Friedman, *Free to Choose: A Personal Statement* (New York: Harcourt, 1979).

52.   Gayle Fee and Laura Raposa, "Sen. John Kerry skips town on sails tax," *The Boston Herald*, July 23, 2010; available online at http://www.bostonherald.com/track/inside_track/view.bg?articleid=1269698.

53. International Court of Justice, "Accordance with International Law of the Unilateral Declaration of Independence in Respect of Kosovo," July 22, 2010; available online at http://www.icj-cij.org/docket/files/141/15987.pdf.

54. "Kosovo independence move not illegal, says UN court," BBC, July 22, 2010; available online at http://www.bbc.co.uk/news/world-europe-10730573.

55. Alberto Alesina and Enrico Spolaore, *The Size of Nations* (The MIT Press, 2005).

56. Remarks made before the United States Congress in Washington, D.C., November 7, 2007; available online at http://www.nysun.com/national/speech-by-president-sarkozy-before-congress/66054/.

57. Joe Klein, "Yes, It's Racism…but it's Complicated," *Time*, September 16, 2009; available online at http://swampland.time.com/2009/09/16/yes-its-racism-but-its-complicated/.

58. Jonah Goldberg, "Joe Klein Loves Diversity," National Review Online, September 17, 2009; available online at http://www.nationalreview.com/corner/187380/joe-klein-loves-diversity/jonah-goldberg.

59. Jared Taylor, "Jared Taylor Remembers Joe Sobran," VDare.com, October 1, 2010; available online at http://vdare.com/taylor/101001_sobran.htm.

60. Philippe Legrain, *Immigrants: Your Country Needs Them* (Princeton University Press, 2007).

61. Christopher Caldwell, *Reflections on the Revolution in Europe* (New York: Anchor, 2010).

62. Giovanni di Lorenzo, "Drinnen vor der Tür," *Die Zeit* No. 41, 2004.

63. Chistopher Caldwell, "Think Tank: New Ideas For The 21st Century: Immigration and welfare: a bad mix," *The Times*, April 26, 2009; available online at http://www.timesonline.co.uk/tol/news/uk/crime/article6168821.ece.

64. "Somali Refugees Settle in Maine Town," ABC News; available online at http://abcnews.go.com/WNT/story?id=130098&page=1.

65. Federation for American Immigration Reform, "Birthright Citizenship," August 2010; available online at http://www.fairus.org/site/News2?page=NewsArticle&id=16535&security=1601&news_iv_ctrl=1007.

66. "Stockton School Trustee Used District Credit Card For Personal Purchases," CBS Sacramento, February 10, 2011; available online at http://sacramento.cbslocal.com/2011/02/10/stockton-school-trustee-used-district-credit-card-for-personal-purchases/.

67. Sherry Jacobson, "Across Texas, 60,000 babies of noncitizens get U.S. birthright," *Dallas News*, August 8, 2010; available online at http://www.dallasnews.com/news/state/headlines/20100807-Across-Texas-60-000-babies-3859.ece.

68.   Ronald J. Hansen, "Arizona children becoming more diverse, census report says,"
      The Arizona Republic, April 7, 2011; available online at http://www.azcentral.
      com/news/articles/2011/04/07/20110407arizona-census-results-diverse-kids.
      html.

69.   Brian Montopoli, "Obama Criticizes 'Misguided' Arizona Immigration Bill," CBS
      News, April 23, 2010; available online at http://www.cbsnews.com/8301-
      503544_162-20003274-503544.html.

70.   RealityUncovered.net forum; comment available online at http://www.
      realityuncovered.net/forum/viewtopic.php?f=19&t=1088&start=45.

71.   Note to Marquis de Lafayette, May 1807; available online at http://www.
      napoleon-series.org/research/napoleon/jefferson/c_jefferson3.html.

72.   Tami Luhby, "Maywood, Calif., to city cops and employees: You're fired," CNN,
      July 1, 2010; available online at http://money.cnn.com/2010/06/29/news/
      economy/city_fires_employees/index.htm.

73.   "Town creates sanctuary for illegal immigrants," MSNBC, March 27, 2006; avail-
      able online at http://www.msnbc.msn.com/id/11964275/.

74.   Heather Scroope, "Suspect Pleads Not Guilty in New Jersey Students' Execution-
      Style Deaths," FOX News, August 10, 2007; available online at http://www.
      foxnews.com/story/0,2933,292717,00.html.

75.   George P. Hassett, "Feds raid local shop; arrest one, *The Somerville News,* August
      28, 2007; available online at http://www.thesomervillenews.com/archives/2934.

76.   Michelle Malkin, "Sanctuary Nation or Sovereign Nation?" MichelleMalkin.com,
      August 15, 2007; available online at http://michellemalkin.com/2007/08/15/
      sanctuary-nation-or-sovereign-nation-its-your-choice/.

77.   "Mexican Drugs, U.S. Markets," NPR, April 17, 2009; available online at http://
      www.npr.org/templates/story/story.php?storyId=103224933.

78.   Ken Ellingwood, "A side of Cancun not seen during spring break," *Los Angeles
      Times,* March 2, 2009; available online at http://www.latimes.com/news/nation-
      world/world/la-fg-mexico-cancun-drugs2-2009mar02,0,3441309.story.

79.   "6 bodies found in cave, 3 with hearts cut out," *Associated Press,* June 7, 2010;
      available online at http://www.chron.com/disp/story.mpl/world/7039966.html.

80.   Alfredo Corchado and Lauren Villagran, "Drug violence in Mexico hit new level
      of brutality in 2010," The *Dallas Morning News,* January 1, 2011; available online
      at http://www.dallasnews.com/news/nation-world/mexico/20110101-drug-
      violence-in-mexico-hit-new-level-of-brutality-in-2010.ece.

81.   "Ciudad Juárez Hits 3,000 Murders in 2010," FOX News, December 15, 2010;
      available online at http://latino.foxnews.com/latino/news/2010/12/15/border-
      city-hits-dead/.

82.   "Timeline: Toronto 18: Key events in the case," CBC, June 2, 2008; available online at http://www.cbc.ca/news/canada/story/2008/06/02/f-toronto-timeline.html.

83.   Jim Benning, "In Tijuana, the Real 'Nacho Libre,'" *Washington Post*, July 9, 2006; available online at http://www.washingtonpost.com/wp-dyn/content/article/2006/07/07/AR2006070700419.html.

84.   "Headless, mutilated bodies hung from Mexico bridge," Reuters, August 22, 2010; available online at http://www.reuters.com/article/2010/08/22/us-mexico-drugs-idUSTRE67L1Y620100822.

85.   "Mexico arrests 14-year-old 'drug hitman,'" BBC, December 3, 2010; available online at http://www.bbc.co.uk/news/world-latin-america-11913976.

86.   Gustavo Ruiz, "Small-Town Mayor Stoned to Death in Western Mexico," Associated Press, September 27, 2010; available online at http://abcnews.go.com/International/wireStory?id=11739050.

87.   David Frum, "Mexico drug war a nightmare scenario," CNN, January 3, 2011; available online at http://articles.cnn.com/2011-01-03/opinion/frum.mexico.risk_1_drug-violence-mexico-drug-war-mexican-born-people?_s=PM:OPINION

88.   Jason DeParle, "Struggling to Rise in Suburbs Where Failing Means Fitting In," *New York Times*, April 18, 2009; available online at http://www.nytimes.com/2009/04/19/us/19immig.html?_r=1&ref=us&pagewanted=all.

89.   Mickey Kaus, "JournoList Revealed! Inside the Secret Liberal Media Email Cabal," Slate.com, March 26, 2009; available online at http://www.slate.com/blogs/blogs/kausfiles/archive/2009/03/26/journolist-revealed-inside-the-liberal-media-email-cabal.aspx.

90.   Martin Peretz, "No Special Envoy, No Crisis," *The New Republic*, March 23, 2009; available online at http://www.tnr.com/blog/the-spine/no-special-envoy-no-crisis.

91.   NAACP Urges Hallmark to Pull 'Racist' Card From Shelves," FOX News, June 11, 2010; available online at http://www.foxnews.com/us/2010/06/11/naacp-urges-hallmark-pull-racist-card-shelves/.

92.   Jon Richards, editorial cartoon, *The Albuquerque Journal*, August 4, 2010; available online at http://web.mac.com/moviecritic1/Site/Cartoons.html.

93.   B.F. Skinner, *Beyond Freedom & Dignity* (Indianapolis, IN: Hackett Publishing Company, 2002).

94.   Graeme Wilson, "Tories face fury over air travel taxes," *The Telegraph*, March 12, 2007; available online at http://www.telegraph.co.uk/news/uknews/1545262/Tories-face-fury-over-air-travel-taxes.html.

95. Pew Hispanic Center, "Unauthorized Immigrant Population: National and State Trends, 2010," February 1, 2011; available online at http://pewhispanic.org/reports/report.php?ReportID=133.

96. Victor Davis Hanson, "Two Californias," *National Review* Online, December 16, 2010; available online at http://www.victorhanson.com/articles/hanson121610.html.

97. "Politicians narrate Peter and the Wolf," BBC, February 5, 2003; available online at http://news.bbc.co.uk/2/hi/entertainment/2730119.stm.

98. "Sharks in Shallow Water," *New York Times*, July 27, 2001; available online at http://www.nytimes.com/2001/07/27/opinion/sharks-in-shallow-water.html.

99. "Woman killed by cougar identified," CBC, January 3, 2001; available online at http://www.cbc.ca/news/story/2001/01/03/frost030101.html.

100. Cory Ruf, "Coyote in Nova Scotia attacks sleeping girl, bites her head," *The National Post*, August 10, 2010; available online at http://news.nationalpost.com/2010/08/10/coyote-in-nova-scotia-attacks-sleeping-girl-bites-her-on-head/.

101. Craig Medred, "Wildlife author killed, eaten by bears he loved," *Anchorage Daily News*, February 5, 2003; available online at http://www.alaska.net/~jlanders/Fatal/Treadwell%20Huguenard%2010-05-03.htm.

102. Ibid.

103. "Flashdance for Boycott of Israeli Hummus Hits West Philly Supermarket," PhillyIMC.org, October 26, 2010; available online at http://www.phillyimc.org/en/flashdance-boycott-israeli-hummus-hits-west-philly-supermarket.

104. Jonathan Kay, "War within Pride leaves anti-Israel group on the outside," *The National Post*, May 25, 2010; available online at http://fullcomment.nationalpost.com/2010/05/25/war-within-pride-leaves-quaia-on-the-outside/.

105. "Ahmadinejad Blasts Israel, Denies Existence of Iranian Gays During Columbia Speech," FOX News, September 24, 2007; available online at http://www.foxnews.com/story/0,2933,297823,00.html.

106. "Profile: Mullah Mohammed Omar," BBC, July 6, 2010; available online at http://news.bbc.co.uk/2/hi/south_asia/1550419.stm.

107. Stephanie Chen, "Pressure for female genital cutting lingers in the U.S," CNN, May 21, 2010; available online at http://articles.cnn.com/2010-05-21/health/america.female.genital.cutting_1_female-circumcision-cultural-beliefs-somali-immigrant/3?_s=PM:HEALTH.

108. Remarks during interview with lailatalqadr.com, October 4, 2001; available online at http://www.memri.org/report/en/0/0/0/0/0/0/533.htm.

109. Elisabetta Povoledo, "Performance Artist Killed on Peace Trip Is Mourned," *New York Times*, April 19, 2008; available online at http://www.nytimes.com/2008/04/19/theater/19peac.html.

Chapter Seven

1. "Benjamin Netanyahu's speech to the UN," *New York Post*, September 24, 2009; available online at http://www.nypost.com/p/news/international/item_ix2gXkzh5VFshJUxxcb5HJ.

2. Julian Borger, "Poll shows Muslims in Britain are the most anti-western in Europe," *The Guardian*, June 23, 2006; available online at http://www.guardian.co.uk/world/2006/jun/23/uk.religion.

3. Robert Mackey, "Is Ahmadinejad a 'Gift' for Israel?" *New York Times*, September 25, 2009; available online at http://thelede.blogs.nytimes.com/2009/09/25/is-ahmadinejad-a-gift-for-israel/.

4. Richard Ingrams, "Who will dare damn Israel?" *The Observer*, September 16, 2001; available online at http://www.guardian.co.uk/world/2001/sep/16/september11.usa19.

5. Nick Collins, "Shark 'sent to Egypt by Mossad,'" *The Telegraph*, December 7, 2010; available online at http://www.telegraph.co.uk/news/worldnews/africaandindianocean/egypt/8185915/Shark-sent-to-Egypt-by-Mossad.html.

6. Paul Schemm, "Bill Clinton: Mideast peace would undercut terror," October 5, 2010; available online at http://www.msnbc.msn.com/id/39522892/ns/world_news-mideast_n_africa/t/bill-clinton-mideast-peace-would-undercut-terror/.

7. Remarks made on the Nine Network in Australia, October 2002; available online at http://www.smh.com.au/articles/2002/10/14/1034222719974.html.

8. Ross Colvin, "'Cut off the head of the snake' Saudis told US on Iran," Reuters, November 28, 2010; available online at http://www.reuters.com/article/2010/11/28/wikileaks-iran-saudis-idUSN2862745120101128.

9. John Podhoretz, "The Danger of Normaliut," Commentary, January 2010; available online at http://www.commentarymagazine.com/article/the-danger-of-normaliut/.

10. "2010 Arab Public Opinion Poll," Zogby International, August 5, 2010; available online at http://www.brookings.edu/~/media/Files/rc/reports/2010/08_arab_opinion_poll_telhami/08_arab_opinion_poll_telhami.pdf.

11. "2008 Annual Arab Public Opinion Poll," Zogby International, March 2008; available online at http://www.brookings.edu/~/media/Files/events/2008/0414_middle_east/0414_middle_east_telhami.pdf.

12. Benjamin Weinthal, "'Die Welt': Iran building rocket bases in Venezuela," *Jerusalem Post*, May 17, 2011; available online at http://www.jpost.com/International/Article.aspx?id=220879.

13. Parisa Hafezi, "Turkey, Brazil seal deal on Iran nuclear fuel swap," Reuters, May 16, 2010; available online at http://www.reuters.com/article/2010/05/16/us-iran-nuclear-deal-idUSTRE64F29P20100516.

14. "Australia, China Conduct Live-Fire Naval Exercise in Yellow Sea," *The China Times*, September 25, 2010; available online at http://www.thechinatimes.com/online/2010/09/41.html.

15. "G20 to tackle US-China currency concerns," BBC, November 12, 2010; available online at http://www.bbc.co.uk/news/business-11739748.

Chapter Eight

1. Xavier Sala-i-Martin, "The World Distribution of Income," The National Bureau of Economic Research, May 2002; available online at http://www.nber.org/papers/w8933

2. Virginia Postrel, "Economic Scene; The rich get rich and poor get poorer. Right? Let's take another look," *New York Times*, August 15, 2002; available online at http://www.nytimes.com/2002/08/15/business/economic-scene-rich-get-rich-poor-get-poorer-right-let-s-take-another-look.html?src=pm

3. World Bank, "Gross national income per capita 2009," 2010; available online at http://siteresources.worldbank.org/DATASTATISTICS/Resources/GNIPC.pdf.

4. World Bank, "Country Eligibility for Borrowing from the World Bank," 2005; available online at http://web.worldbank.org/WBSITE/EXTERNAL/EXTABOUTUS/EXTANNREP/EXTANNREP2K5/0,,print:Y~isCURL:Y~contentMDK:20647778~menuPK:1606029~pagePK:64168445~piPK:64168309~theSitePK:1397343,00.html and http://www.freeworldacademy.com/globalleader/realworld.htm.

5. Celia W. Dugger, "Unicef Report Says Children in Deprivation Reach a Billion," *New York Times*, December 10, 2004; available online at http://www.nytimes.com/2004/12/10/international/10children.html.

6. Mark McDonald, "'Crisis Status' in South Korea After North Shells Island," *New York Times*, November 23, 2010; available online at http://www.nytimes.com/2010/11/24/world/asia/24korea.html.

7. World Bank, "GDP per capita (current US$)," 2011; available online at http://data.worldbank.org/indicator/NY.GDP.PCAP.CD.

8.   James Martin, *The Meaning of the 21st Century: A Vital Blueprint For Ensuring Our Future* (New York: Riverhead Trade, 2007).

9.   Fred Pearce, "When Britain's taps run dry," *The Guardian*, April 17, 2009; available online at http://www.guardian.co.uk/commentisfree/2009/apr/17/australia-murray-river-water

10.   Alastair Jamieson, "'Muslims want sharia law in Britain' claim," *The Telegraph*, October 15, 2009; available online at http://www.telegraph.co.uk/news/uknews/law-and-order/6334091/Muslims-want-sharia-law-in-Britain-claim.html.

11.   United Nations, "Cairo Declaration on Human Rights in Islam," August 5, 1990; available online at http://www.unhcr.org/refworld/publisher,ARAB,,,3ae6b3822c,0.html.

12.   Toby Harnden, "Barack Hussein Obama: US 'one of the largest Muslim countries in the world'," *The Telegraph*, June 3, 2009; available online at http://blogs.telegraph.co.uk/news/tobyharnden/9959057/Barack_Hussein_Obama_US_one_of_the_largest_Muslim_countries_in_the_world/.

13.   Stephen Schwartz, "Meet Sada Cumber," *The Weekly Standard*, March 5, 2008; available online at http://www.weeklystandard.com/Content/Public/Articles/000/000/014/835mgwfz.asp.

14.   Christopher Caldwell, *Reflections on the Revolution in Europe* (New York: Anchor, 2010).

15.   Comment in the *Vancouver Sun*, March 18, 1965.

16.   Lewis Page, "Royal Navy won't fight pirates 'in case they claim asylum'," *The Register*, September 25, 2008; available online at http://www.theregister.co.uk/2008/09/25/royal_navy_pirate_asylum_seekers/.

17.   Associated Press, "Pirates 'Have All Died,' Russia Says, After Decrying 'Imperfections' In International Law," May 11, 2010; available online at http://www.cleveland.com/world/index.ssf/2010/05/pirates_have_all_died_russia_s.html.

18.   Pew Research Center, "The Future of the Global Muslim Population," January 27, 2011; available online at http://pewresearch.org/pubs/1872/muslim-population-projections-worldwide-fast-growth.

19.   CNN, "U.N.: Earth's population to hit 9 billion by 2050, 10 billion by 2100," May 3, 2011; available online at http://articles.cnn.com/2011-05-03/us/united.nations.population.forecast_1_population-forecast-population-growth-fertility?_s=PM:US.

20.   Reuters, "Niger averts food crisis but faces population boom," October 18, 2010; available online at http://www.reuters.com/article/2010/10/18/us-niger-food-idUSTRE69H22J20101018.

21. "Niger's starving children are dying as we speak, UN humanitarian chief tells world," *The Times*, July 21, 2005; available online at http://www.timesonline. co.uk/tol/news/world/article546355.ece.

22. Samuel P. Huntington, *The Clash of Civilizations and the Remaking of World Order* (New York: Simon & Schuster, 1998).

23. BBC, "One in four is Muslim, study says," October 8, 2009; available online at http://news.bbc.co.uk/2/hi/8296200.stm.

24. Francis Gibb, "Rise in marriages between cousins 'is putting children's health at risk'," *The Times*, March 20, 2010; available online at http://www.timesonline. co.uk/tol/news/uk/health/article7069255.ece.

25. Mark Bulstrode, "Muslim Peer in Marriage Attack," *The Express*, January 30, 2011; available online at http://www.express.co.uk/posts/view/226148/Muslim-peer-in-marriage-attack-.

26. Martin Amis, "No, I am not a racist," *The Guardian*, December 1, 2007; available online at http://www.guardian.co.uk/books/2007/dec/01/race.islam.

27. Dipesh Gadher, Christopher Morgan and Jonathan Oliver, "Minister warns of 'inbred' Muslims," *The Times*, February 10, 2008; available online at http://www. timesonline.co.uk/tol/news/politics/article3342040.ece.

28. TED.com, "Hans Rosling's new insights on poverty," June 2007; available online at http://www.ted.com/talks/hans_rosling_reveals_new_insights_on_poverty. html.

29. Ezra Levant, "Ezra Levant's opening remarks to the Alberta Human Rights Commission," *The National Post*, January 14, 2008; available online at http://network. nationalpost.com/np/blogs/fullcomment/archive/2008/01/14/ezra-levant-s-opening-remarks-to-the-alberta-human-rights-commission.aspx.

30. *The Brussels Journal*, "Jihad and the Collapse of the Swedish Model," April 19, 2007; available online at http://www.brusselsjournal.com/node/2065.

31. JihadWatch.org, "Dutch Justice Minister: 'If two-thirds of the Dutch population should want to introduce the Sharia tomorrow, then the possibility should exist'," September 13, 2006; available online at http://www.jihadwatch.org/2006/09/dutch-justice-minister-if-two-thirds-of-the-dutch-population-should-want-to-introduce-the-sharia-tom.html.

32. Bruno Waterfield, "Geert Wilders trial suspended after he attacks judge," *The Telegraph*, October 4, 2010; available online at http://www.telegraph.co.uk/news/worldnews/europe/netherlands/8041998/Geert-Wilders-trial-suspended-after-he-attacks-judge.html.

33. Lilit Wagner, "The escape from Holland," YNetNews.com, December 17, 2010; available online at http://www.ynetnews.com/articles/0,7340,L-3998968,00.html.

34. Allah.eu, "Amsterdam: Gay Hotel Turns Muslim," October 2, 2009; available online at http://www.allah.eu/about-islam/amsterdam-gay-hotel-turns-muslim.html.

35. Bruce Crumley and Adam Smith, "Sisters in Hell," *Time*, November 24, 2002; available online at http://www.time.com/time/europe/magazine/2002/1202/crime/bellil.htm.

36. Samira Bellil, *Dans L'enfer Des Tournantes* (Quebec: Editions Flammarion, 2003).

37. James Chapman, "Women get 'virginity fix' NHS operations in Muslim-driven trend," *The Daily Mail*, November 15, 2007; available online at http://www.dailymail.co.uk/news/article-494118/Women-virginity-fix-NHS-operations-Muslim-driven-trend.html.

38. Martha Nussbaum, "Beyond the Veil: A Response," *New York Times*, July 15, 2010; available online at http://opinionator.blogs.nytimes.com/2010/07/15/beyond-the-veil-a-response/.

39. Claire Berlinski, "Ban the Burqa," *National Review*, August 16, 2010; available online at http://www.nationalreview.com/articles/243587/ban-burqa-claire-berlinski?page=1.

40. Robert Spencer, "The erosion of women's rights in Egypt, illustrated," Jihad-Watch.org, February 1, 2010; available online at http://www.jihadwatch.org/2010/02/the-erosion-of-womens-rights-in-egypt-illustrated.html.

41. Phyllis Chesler, "The Steady Erosion of Women's Rights in Egypt: A Photographic Story," ChelserChronicles.com, January 28, 2010; available online at http://pajamasmedia.com/phyllischesler/2010/01/28/the-steady-erosion-of-womens-rights-in-egypt-a-photographic-story/.

42. BBC, "MPs attack Greer on female circumcision," November 25, 1999; available online at http://news.bbc.co.uk/2/hi/uk_news/politics/535488.stm.

43. Paul Richter, "U.S. wants no more Jewish settlement growth, Clinton says," *Los Angeles Times*, May 28, 2009; available online at http://articles.latimes.com/2009/may/28/world/fg-us-israel28.

44. Julia Magnet, "The terror behind Iraq's Jewish exodus," *The Telegraph*, April 15, 2003; available online at http://www.telegraph.co.uk/news/1427599/The-terror-behind-Iraqs-Jewish-exodus.html.

45. PBS, "Disappearing Christians of Iraq," July 23, 2010; available online at http://www.pbs.org/wnet/religionandethics/episodes/july-23-2010/disappearing-christians-of-iraq/6701/.

46. Reuters, "Iraq church raid ends with 52 dead," November 1, 2010; available online at http://www.reuters.com/article/2010/11/01/us-iraq-violence-idUSTRE69U1YE20101101.

47.   Lindsey Hilsum, "Iraq's Christians plan a simple Christmas in the shadow of
        violence," *The Telegraph*, December 21, 2010; available online at http://www.
        telegraph.co.uk/news/worldnews/middleeast/iraq/8216416/Iraqs-Christians-
        plan-a-simple-Christmas-in-the-shadow-of-violence.html.

48.   Tim Graham, "Katie Couric: 'Maybe We Need a Muslim Version of The Cosby
        Show'," NewsBusters.org, December 30, 2010; available online at http://
        newsbusters.org/blogs/tim-graham/2010/12/30/katie-couric-maybe-we-need-
        muslim-version-cosby-show.

49.   Remarks made during speech in Cairo, Egypt, June 4, 2009; available online at
        http://www.nytimes.com/2009/06/04/us/politics/04obama.text.html.

50.   Nadya Labi, "An American Honor Killing: One Victim's Story," *Time*, February
        25, 2011; available online at http://www.time.com/time/nation/
        article/0,8599,2055445,00.html.

51.   Joshua Rhett Miller, "Beheading in New York Appears to Be Honor Killing,
        Experts Say," FOX News, February 17, 2009; available online at http://www.
        foxnews.com/story/0,2933,494785,00.html.

52.   CBC, "Canal victims killed by family: police," July 23, 2009; available online at
        http://www.cbc.ca/news/canada/story/2009/07/23/canal-arrests023.html.

53.   Güner Balci, "Taboos and Fear among Muslim Girls," *Der Spiegel*, January 6,
        2011; available online at http://www.spiegel.de/international/
        germany/0,1518,737683,00.html.

54.   Lee Harris, *Civilization and Its Enemies: The Next Stage of History* (Free Press,
        2004); available online at http://books.simonandschuster.com/Civilization-and-
        Its-Enemies/Lee-Harris/9780743267007/print.

55.   Nick Foulke, "The king's in town," *The London Evening Standard*, August 21,
        2002; available online at http://www.thisislondon.co.uk/promotions/article-
        1263358-the-kings-in-town.do.

56.   *Der Spiegel*, "How Much Allah Can the Old Continent Bear?" December 11, 2009;
        available online at http://www.spiegel.de/international/europe/0,
        1518,666448-2,00.html.

57.   Andrew C. McCarthy, "AG Eric Holder Refuses to Say 'Radical Islam' Is a Cause
        of Terrorism Committed by Muslims," National Review Online, May 13, 2010;
        available online at http://www.nationalreview.com/corner/199355/ag-eric-
        holder-refuses-say-radical-islam-cause-terrorism-committed-muslims-andrew-
        c-mc.

58.   Ian Rowley, "Japan's population decline is gathering momentum," *Businessweek*,
        August 11, 2009; available online at http://www.businessweek.com/blogs/
        eyeonasia/archives/2009/08/japans_population_decline_is_gathering_
        momentum.html.

59. Donald Melanson, "Yurina health care robot promises to help lift, terrify patients," Engadget.com, August 13, 2010; available online at http://www. engadget.com/2010/08/13/yurina-health-care-robot-promises-to-help-lift-terrify-patients/.

60. AFP, "'Welfare robots' to ease burden in greying Japan," July 29, 2010; available online at http://www.france24.com/en/20100729-welfare-robots-ease-burden-greying-japan.

61. Gary Wolf, "Futurist Ray Kurzweil Pulls Out All the Stops (and Pills) to Live to Witness the Singularity," Wired.com, March 24, 2008; available online at http://www.wired.com/medtech/drugs/magazine/16-04/ff_kurzweil.

62. Samuel P. Huntington, *The Clash of Civilizations and the Remaking of World Order* (New York: Simon & Schuster, 1998).

63. Thomas L. Friedman, "Time to Reboot America," *New York Times*, December 23, 2008; available online at http://www.nytimes.com/2008/12/24/opinion/24friedman.html.

64. Thomas L. Friedman, "Who will tell the people?" *New York Times*, May 4, 2008; available online at http://www.nytimes.com/2008/05/04/opinion/04friedman.html?_r=1&scp=1&sq=Thomas%20L.%20Friedman%20sigapore%20airport&st=cse&oref=slogin.

65. Thomas L. Friedman, "We don't need another 9/11 president," *New York Times*, October 2, 2007; available online at http://www.signonsandiego.com/union-trib/20071002/news_lz1e2friedman.html.

66. Thomas L. Friedman, "A word from the wise," *New York Times*, March 2, 2010; available online at http://www.nytimes.com/2010/03/03/opinion/03friedman.html.

67. Thomas L. Friedman, "Cracks in the rubble," *New York Times*, January 16, 2002; available online at http://www.nytimes.com/2002/01/16/opinion/cracks-in-the-rubble.html.

68. Andrew Johnson, "Taliban make 'undetectable' bombs out of wood," *The Independent*, January 10, 2010; available online at http://www.independent.co.uk/news/world/asia/taliban-make-undetectable-bombs-out-of-wood-1863353.html.

69. The Blog Prof, "Gunnar Heinsohn on Germay's cultural suicide: 1,000 German men get 480 sons–1,000 Afghans get 4,000," January 18, 2011; available online at http://theblogprof.blogspot.com/2011/01/gunnar-heinsohn-on-germays-cultural.html.

70. Charles Onyango-Obbo, "Stop the War, And Maybe I Won't Eat You," *The East African*, January 20, 2003; available online at http://allafrica.com/stories/200301220129.html.

71. Michael Dynes, "Pygmies beg UN for aid to save them from Congo cannibals," *The Times*, May 23, 2003; available online at http://www.timesonline.co.uk/tol/news/world/article1135111.ece.

72. Thomas P. M. Barnett, *Blueprint for Action: A Future Worth Creating* (Berkley Trade, 2006).

73. Robert D. Kaplan, "The Coming Anarchy," The Atlantic, February 1994; available online at http://www.theatlantic.com/ideastour/archive/kaplan.html.

74. Andrew C. McCarthy, "Pirates Test the 'Rule of Law'," National Review Online, April 10, 2009; available online at http://www.nationalreview.com/articles/227281/pirates-test-rule-law/andrew-c-mccarthy.

75. Nazila Fathi, "Iran Says It Will Share Nuclear Skills," *New York Times*, April 25, 2006; available online at http://www.nytimes.com/2006/04/25/world/middleeast/25cnd-iran.html.

76. André Glucksmann, "From the H-Bomb to the Human Bomb," *City Journal*, Autumn 2007; available online at http://www.city-journal.org/html/17_4_modern_terrorism.html.

77. Tom Wolfe, "Sorry, but your soul just died," *The Independent*, February 2, 1997; available online at http://www.independent.co.uk/arts-entertainment/sorry-but-your-soul-just-died-1276509.html.

78. Carl Haub, "Birth Rate Trends in Low-Fertility Countries," Population Reference Bureau, March 2011; available online at http://www.prb.org/Articles/2011/low-fertility-countries-tfr.aspx.

Epilogue

1. Remarks during address to joint session of Congress in Washington, DC, February 24, 2009; available online at http://www.whitehouse.gov/the_press_office/Remarks-of-President-Barack-Obama-Address-to-Joint-Session-of-Congress/.

2. John Derbyshire, "February Diary," National Review Online, March 4, 2009; available online at http://www.nationalreview.com/articles/227002/february-diary/john-derbyshire.

3. Dillon County Economic Development Partnership, "Demographics," 2011; available online at http://www.dilloncounty.org/site_consultant/demographics/.

4. Michael Muskal, "'I am not king': Obama tells Latino voters he can't conjure immigration reform alone," *Los Angeles Times*, October 25, 2010; available online at http://articles.latimes.com/2010/oct/25/news/la-pn-obama-immigration-reform-20101026.

5. FOX News, "Goodbye to Bake Sales? Nutrition Bill Subjects School Fundraisers to New Regs," December 8, 2010; available online at http://www.foxnews.com/politics/2010/12/08/goodbye-bake-sales-nutrition-subjects-school-fundraisers-new-regs/.

6. Andrew G. Biggs, "Entitlement Apocalypse," *National Review*, March 22, 2010; available online at http://www.nationalreview.com/articles/229431/entitlement-apocalypse/andrew-g-biggs.

7. N. Gordon and B. Knight, "Spatial Merger Estimator with an Application to School District Consolidation," *Journal of Public Economics*, 2009; facts available online at http://www.mpa.unc.edu/students/documents/KevinBryant.pdf.

8. Executive order, 1987; facts available online at http://www.cato.org/pubs/handbook/hb111/hb111-5.pdf.

9. Paul Krugman, "Runaway health care costs — we're #1!," *New York Times*, March 28, 2008; available online at http://krugman.blogs.nytimes.com/2008/03/28/runaway-health-care-costs-were-1/.

10. Organisation for Economic Co-operation and Development, "Education at a Glance 2009: OECD Indicators," Indicator B1, 2009; available online at http://www.oecd.org/document/24/0,3343,en_2649_39263238_43586328_1_1_1_37455,00.html.

11. Richard Arum and Josipa Roksa, *Academically Adrift: Limited Learning on College Campuses* (University of Chicago Press, 2011).

12. Paul A. Rahe, *Soft Despotism, Democracy's Drift: Montesquieu, Rousseau, Tocqueville, and the Modern Prospect* (Yale University Press, 2010).

13. Kathryn Jean Lopez, "That Other Hollywood: Cheers!" National Review Online, January 17, 2009; available online at http://www.nationalreview.com/corner/192973/other-hollywood-cheers/kathryn-jean-lopez.

14. Nuts, Bolts & Thingamajigs Foundation, "A Word from John Ratzenberger"; available online at http://www.nutsandboltsfoundation.org/word-from-john.cfm.

15. John Derbyshire, "Tinker, Tailor, Bureaucrat, Diversity Consultant," National Review Online, May 13, 2008; available online at http://www.nationalreview.com/corner/163046/tinker-tailor-bureaucrat-diversity-consultant/john-derbyshire.

16. J. R. McNeill an Paul Kennedy, *Something New Under the Sun: An Environmental History of the Twentieth-Century World* (New York: W. W. Norton & Company, 2001).

17. Nuts, Bolts & Thingamajigs Foundation, "A Word from John Ratzenberger"; available online at http://www.nutsandboltsfoundation.org/word-from-john.cfm.

18. Elisabeth Rosenthal, "Biggest Obstacle to Global Climate Deal May Be How to Pay for It," *New York Times*, October 14, 2009; available online at http://www.nytimes.com/2009/10/15/science/earth/15climate.html.

INDEX

A

ABC, 64

Abdulla, King, 273

abortion, 80, 161, 177, 178, 180, 204, 304, 309

Acheson, Dean, 199

Acres, 85

Adams, Sam, 201

addiction, 20, 22, 36, 256

Addonizio, Kim, 140

Adkins, Lucy, 140

adolescence, 129, 172, 181

"adultescence" phenomenon, 181

"affirmative action," 151–53, 165, 238

Affleck, Ben, 141

"after man," 306–10

"age of chivalry," 186

"age of empathy," 158,160

Agodon, Kelli Russell, 140

agricultural labor, 211–12

Ahmadinejad, Mahmoud, 264, 270, 275–76

al-Assad, Bashar, 275

al-Awlaki, Anwar, 169-70

al-Din, Taqi, 32

al-Gamei'a, Muhammad, 265

al-Khwarizmi, Muhammad, 32

al-Qaeda, 42–43, 162, 263

al-Zawahiri, Ayman, 162

Albuquerque Journal, 254

Aldrin, Buzz, 28–29

Alesina, Alberto, 237–38

Ali, Ayaan Hirsi, 297

Almaleki, Noor, 303–4

"Alpha male," 176

Alterman, Eric, 67

Amazing Stories, 38–39

America

    chance for, 22–23, 279–324

    cushion for, 16

    debt of, 2–23

decay of, 21–22
decline of, 12–13, 17-18, 32, 43, 127–87
Europeanization of, 120–22
fall of, 13–14, 211–67
hope for, 279–324
post-American world, 279–324
undreaming, 45–102
vulnerability of, 19–20, 230, 259, 281
world after, 279–324
America Alone: The End of the World as We Know It, 1–2, 15, 19, 28, 105, 118, 129, 189
"America the Beautiful," 40
American Dream
  beneficiaries of, 131
  desire for, 244–45, 253–54, 331–32
  loss of, 15, 22–23, 326, 331–32
  requirement of, 35
American Educator, The, 157
American idea, 16, 21, 38, 70, 102, 267, 306, 326, 342, 348–49
American Idol, 45
American idyll, 127–87
American Journal of Medicine, The, 226
American, meaning of, 141–42
American Nightmare, 22
American Prospect, The, 63
"American Recovery and Reinvestment Plan," 33
American Spectator, The, 82

Amis, Martin, 293
Aniston, Jennifer, 176–78
Annie, 1
Antitrust Division, 46–47, 49
Anwar, Mus'id, 135–36
apartheid, 152, 245, 263–65
apocalypse, 1–2
Apple, 32
Arbogast, Jessie, 260
Archuleta, Deanna, 34
Armageddon, 20–22
Armstrong, Neil, 28
arteriosclerosis, 20, 22
Arum, Richard, 340
Associated Press, 165, 167, 290
Astaire, Fred, 41, 166
Astor, Mary, 65
Astounding Science Fiction, 38–39
atheists, 321
Athens, drowning of, 103–25
Atlantic Monthly, 93, 161–62, 319
Atta, Mohammed, 283
audacity, hope of, 325–49
Austin Powers, 242
automobile industry, 47, 101, 217–20
Ayers, William, 42, 145, 147

B

Babylon, 7, 14
Bacca, Pippa, 265–66
bailouts, 64, 109, 218, 346
Baker, Dean, 93
Balls, Ed, 192
Banting, Frederick, 27–28

Barnett, Thomas P. M., 318

Bast, Andrew, 168

Bastiat, Frédéric, 45

Bates, Katharine Lee, 40, 41

Baucus, Max, 63

Bawer, Bruce, 141

Bayer, Henry, 108

Beamer, Todd, 296

Beecham, Thomas, 39

Bellil, Samira, 299, 300, 302

Belshazzar, King, 7, 14–15, 18–19, 124–25

Bennet, Michael, 2

Bentham, Jeremy, 257

Berg, Nick, 321

Berger, David, 161

Berkowitz, Peter, 63

Berle, Milton, 26–27

Berlin, Irving, 166

Berlin Wall, 159, 237

Berlinski, Claire, 300

Berman, Paul, 165

Bernanke, Ben, 97–98, 326

Beschloss, Michael, 55

Bethea, Ty'Sheoma, 325–26, 329–30

Beveridge, William, 204

Bevin, Ernie, 58

Bharuchi, Shayna, 319

Biden, Joe, 147

Bieber, Justin, 35

Big Government

 "Brains Trust," 53–54, 57

 controlling price, 48–49

 curse of, 47–49

 father of, 33–34

 funding, 72, 109, 129

 future of, 75, 329, 333

 growth of, 9–10, 15, 21–22

 ineptitude of, 34, 56, 63–64, 85–86, 92, 102–3, 204–6, 213–14, 217–18, 230–36, 255–56

 monopoly by, 20, 22, 48–53, 236, 337–38

 results of, 75, 106, 204–6, 213–14, 217–18, 230–36, 244, 255–56

 rolling back, 333–47

 secularism of, 305–6

 seduction by, 70–72

 small government and, 90–91, 335, 346–48

 as technocracy, 53–55, 67–68

 unemployment and, 48

 vote for, 214, 228

Biggs, Andrew, 332

bin Laden, Osama, 39, 41, 162, 164, 275

bin Rashid, Maktoum, 275

bin Zayed, Mohammed, 275

Bing, Dave, 222

Black-Eyed Peas, 30

Black Hawk Down, 315

Blair, Tony, 57–58, 63, 182, 203

Bloomberg, Michael, 40, 59–60, 80, 164–65, 168, 208

Bobb, Robert, 220

Bogart, Humphrey, 65

Bokassa, Emperor, 222

Bolden, Charles, 31–32

Bolkestein, Frits, 298

Bolkestein, Minheer, 298

Bolton, John, 145

Bolton, Judge, 80

bond markets, 9–10

Bono, 131, 146

bonobos, 230–34

Border Patrol, 324

Boston Tea Party, 91

Bradbury, Ray, 133

"Brains Trust," 53–54, 57

Brandeis, Louis, 47–48

Brann, Ty, 90–91

Brave New World, 36, 137

Brecht, Bertolt, 180, 241

Britannia, depravity of, 189–209

British elites, 197, 208. *See also* elites

Brokaw, Tom, 187

broke, stupidity of, 1–23

Brooks, David, 55

Brooks, Mel, 4

Brother Bear, 261–62

Brown, Gordon, 199, 204

Brown, Scott, 61, 342

Brown, Tam, 183

Bruni, Carla, 118

"bubble," 16, 96

Buckingham Palace, 39

budget

    Big Government and, 346

    Contract with America and, 9

    cuts in, 108, 148–49

    defense budget, 119

    deficits, 3–16, 110–11, 117–18, 228–29, 245, 345–46

    health-care budget, 294

    military budget, 5–6

    outlook on, 4–5

    school budgets, 148–49

    welfare state and, 228–30

Burchill, Julie, 199

Bureau of Compliance, 80–87, 93–94, 336–37

Bureau of the Public Debt (BPD), 75

Bureaucratic Expeditiousness Regulation, 83–84

Burgess, Anthony, 206, 207

Bush, George H., 58

Bush, George W., 38, 56, 58, 101, 197, 257, 302, 314, 317

"businessmen," 2, 272, 280–81

Byrd, Robert C., 79

Byron, Lord, 1

Byron, Robert C., 76

C

Cabaret, 292

Cadell, Pat, 73

Caldwell, Christopher, 242, 287

Caliphate, 19, 21, 72, 277, 286, 296, 299, 323–24

Callaghan, Jim, 200

Cameron, James, 185

can-do spirit, 31, 40, 108, 328

capitalism, 23, 35, 72, 115, 119, 192

Casagrande, Marina, 112–13

Casey, George W., Jr., 169–70

CBS, 64, 303

centralization, 71, 156, 333–35

certification fees, 48–49

Chamberlain, Neville, 270

Charlton, Bruce, 30, 31

Charnin, Martin, 1

Chaudhury, Shah, 202, 203

Chavez, Hugo, 275, 276

Cheney, Dick, 69

Chicago Sun-Times, 159

Childe Harold's Pilgrimage, 1

children, education of, 148–57

children, future of, 171–75

children, war on, 346

Chinese, and globalization, 97–102, 194–95, 312

Chinn, Menzie, 10

Chirac, Jacques, 192, 275

chivalry, 186

"choice mothers," 176

Chrysler Building, 41

Churchill, Winston, 59, 191-92, 197, 199, 203

Cicero, Marcus Tullius, 144, 211

City Journal, 181

civic participation, 87–92

Civilization and Its Enemies, 135

Clash of Civilizations, The, 18, 292

Cleveland, Grover, 58

Clinton, Bill, 58, 62, 90, 147, 159, 161, 259–60, 272, 318

Clinton, Hillary, 302

Clockwork Orange, A, 206–7

Clooney, George, 64, 320

Cloverfield, 37

CNN, 64, 86, 165, 280, 317

Coakley, Martha, 60–61

Code Orange alert, 138, 258, 296

code words, 61–62, 66

Codevilla, Angelo, 153

coexisting, 131, 133, 143, 240

college, 35, 56, 58, 149–57, 173–74, 180, 197

college loans, 47, 156

Collins, Randy, 91–92

Columbia, 32

Communism, 206

Compliance Bureau, 80–87, 93–94, 336–37

computer age, 32–33, 36

conformicrats, 20, 57, 63–64, 67–72, 81, 92, 254–55

conformocracy, 58, 101–2, 128

Congressional Budget Office (CBO), 4–5, 8–9

Constitution, 63, 73, 77–78, 80, 147, 192, 290

Consumer Product Safety Commission (CPSC), 82

consumer spending, 97, 224–25

consumerism, 35

Contract with America, 9

Contrast, The, 103

control of price, 48–49

Conyers, John, 78, 83

Coolidge, Calvin, 62

corrupt elites, 223, 227–28. *See also* elites

Count Basie, 29, 30
Coyote, Ivan E., 231–32
credentialization, 150–51, 154, 156–57, 339–40
credit boom, 14–16, 92–96
credit "bubble," 16, 96
credit cards, 9, 96, 105, 218, 310, 345
"credit crunch," 96
"credit default swap," 94–96
Crosby, Bing, 53
Cross, Gary, 181
Cultural Revolution, 100
Culture of Pleasure, 136–37
culture wars, 73
cures, races for, 27–28
Currie, Jay, 95
Curse of Bigness, 47–49

D

Daily Express, 207
Daily Mail, 182, 205
Daily Star, The, 54
Daily Telegraph, 197
Dalrymple, Theodore, 115
Dancing with the Stars, 45
Daniels, Anthony, 220
Dawkins, Richard, 321
Day, Doris, 3
de-centralization, 238, 333–35
de-complicating, 339
de-credentializing, 339–40
de-governmentalization, 335
de-monopolizing, 337–38
de-normalizing, 341–42

de-regulation, 336–37
De Standaard, 187
Dean, Howard, 120
debt, 2–23, 96–97, 114–15, 346
debt interest, 5, 228
decay of America, 21, 22
decay of Rome, 25–43
Declaration of Independence, 193, 247
Decline and Fall of the Roman Empire, 12–13, 25
decline of America, 13–14, 32, 43, 127–87
decline of Greece, 103–7
Deemer, Andy, 174
defense budget, 119
deficit, 3–16, 110–11, 117–18, 228–29, 245, 345–46
DeParle, Jason, 252
Dependistan, 225, 228–30
depravity of Britannia, 189–209
Depression, 34, 69, 115, 135
Der Spiegel, 304–5
Derbyshire, John, 344
despotism, 45–46, 235
Detroit News, 222
Diamond, Jared, 233
Diary of Anne Frank, The, 297
Diaz, Porfirio, 254
dictatorships, 101–2, 192–93, 241, 281, 311, 323
Die Welt, 276
Dingell, John, Jr., 76
Dingell, John, Sr., 76

dis-entitle, 340–41

disintegration, 21, 22, 206, 256

diversity, 63–64, 131, 146, 153

diversity outreach, 31–32

diversity training, 68

"do something" attitude, 61, 342–45

Doherty, John, 108

Dohrn, Bernardine, 145

Dole, Bob, 70

Domville, William, 189

Douglas, William, 47

Douglass, Frederick, 182

drowning of Athens, 103–25

D'Souza, Dinesh, 145

Duranty, Walter, 102

dystopian future, 38, 182–83

E

East African, The, 316

eco-totalitarianism, 101

economic downturn, 16, 74–75, 92, 97–98, 105, 179, 181, 289

economic growth, 6, 55, 94, 117, 243, 284

Economic Sophisms, 45

Economist, The, 118, 228

Eden, Anthony, 195–96

Edison, Thomas, 344

education, 148–57, 198–99. *See also* college

education "reform," 156

Edwards, Elizabeth, 151

Edwards, John, 69, 213, 326, 338

Eighties (1980s), 180, 221, 222, 300

Eisenhower, Dwight, 195–96

elites
  belief of, 16, 21
  British elites, 197, 208
  contempt of, 68, 102
  corrupt elites, 223, 227–28
  education of, 13, 152–53
  new elites, 59, 63, 135, 208, 246, 266–67, 318–19
  vegetarian elites, 127–28
  western elites, 59, 101, 143, 287, 293

Elmendorf, Douglas, 4, 8, 11

Emerson, Ralph Waldo, 228

empathy, 158–61, 163

Empire State Building, 41

End of History, The, 18

engineering, 21, 22, 344

"enhanced patdowns," 32, 68, 223, 263

entitlement, 19, 104–11, 117–19, 200, 209, 242, 294, 332–33, 340–41

Environmental Protection Agency (EPA), 82, 134

Erdogan, Prime Minister, 275

Espenshade, Thomas, 152

Esposito, Francesca, 113

Estonia, 186

European Union (EU), 11, 98–99, 109–23

Europeanization of America, 120–22

Evers, Benzion, 298

exceptionalism, 16, 148, 204, 326

F

Fahrenheit 451, 133

Fake's Progress, 62

fall of America, 13–14, 211–67

Falsani, Cathleen, 159

Fannie Mae, 47, 85

Farrakhan, Louis, 42

Fascism, 57, 197–98, 206

Faulks, Sebastian, 94

federal aid "giveaway," 71

federal budget. *See* budget

Federal Communications Commission (FCC), 33

Federal Emergency Management Agency (FEMA), 68

Federal Reserve, 98, 224, 326

federalism, 235–36, 306

"feelies," 36, 157–60

Ferdinand, Franz, 159

Ferguson, Niall, 225

fertility rates, 105

fertility treatments, 176–78

Fifties (1950s), 25–27, 35, 212–17, 224, 249, 283, 345–46

final frontier, 31–33

"Final Solution," 269–70

financial sector, 49–50, 93–95

Financial Times, 98

Financing U.S. Debt: Is There Enough Money in the World—and At What Cost?, 10

Fineman, Howard, 61

First Amendment, 23, 297, 306

Fleischer, Michael, 48

Follow the Fleet, 166

following orders, 182–87

Food and Drug Administration (FDA), 28

Ford, Henry, 218, 344

Fort Hood shooting, 167–69, 306

Forties (1940s), 148, 249, 312

Fortuyn, Pim, 297

Foster, Jodie, 232

Frank, Barney, 65

Franklin, Benjamin, 344

Freddie Mac, 47, 85

free trade, 54, 97

freedom, 38, 347–49. *See also* liberty

Freeman, Yvonne, 107–8

Friedman, Milton, 235, 325

Friedman, Thomas L., 17, 18, 102, 313–15, 318, 342, 348

Frost, Frances, 260, 263

Fukuyama, Francis, 18

Furstenberg, Frank, 181

future, after America, 279–324

future, giving up on, 37–38

G

G7 members, 10, 12, 99, 190, 289, 345

Gaddafi, Colonel, 76

Gates, Bill, 15

Gates, Robert, 170

Gavaza, April, 173

gay community, 202

gay marriage, 66, 73, 80, 106, 132, 143, 179

GDP
    growth of, 8–10, 16, 95, 99, 110
    percentage of, 2, 4, 85, 110–11,
        118–20
    proportion of, 285, 337
Geithner, Timothy, 49
Gelb, Leslie, 43
"gender-neutral society," 179, 185
George III, King, 91
George VI, King, 191
German economy, 116–20
Germany, bailouts, 111–12
Gharbi, Gamil, 184
Gibbon, Edward, 12, 25
Gilmour, Charlie, 199
Gilmour, David, 199
Gingrich, Newt, 8, 10
global currency, 99–100, 194, 256,
    266, 281
global economy, 85, 97–98, 120
global retreat, 21–22, 206
globalization
    China and, 97–102, 194–95, 312
    complexity of, 51, 317–18
    crisis of, 115
    ideology of, 97–100
    networks of, 280
    prototype of, 13
    roles in, 17–18
    terrorist plots, 250–51
Globe and Mail, 142
Goethe, 123
Goldberg, Jonah, 345–46
Goodwin, Doris Kearns, 53

Google, 32
Gorbachev, Mikhail, 259–60
Gore, Al, 34, 40, 57, 61, 176, 214, 257,
    286
Gorelick, Jamie, 85
government
    accounting abilities of, 84–85
    bailouts by, 64, 109, 218, 346
    de-governmentalization, 335
    de-monopolizing, 337–38
    growth of, 55
    monopoly by, 20, 46–51, 89, 337–38
Gracchus, Gaius, 211
graffiti, 124–25
Graham, Donald, 173
Great Depression, 34, 69, 115, 135
Great Fire, 43
Great Recession, 33. See also recession
"Greatest Generation," 187
Greece, debt in, 110–11
Greece, decline of, 103–7
Greek riots, 103–4
Green Day, 64
"green jobs," 33
green zone, 211–67
Greer, Germaine, 302
Ground Zero, 39–43, 80, 164, 297, 314
Grunwald, Michael, 59
Guardian, The, 286
Guys and Dolls, 343

H

Hamilton, Alexander, 15
Hamza, Abu, 32

Handel, 125

Hansen, James, 101

Hanson, Victor Davis, 133–35, 175, 181, 258

Hargreaves, James, 344

Harris-Lacewell, Melissa, 66

Harris, Lee, 135

Harris, Sam, 321

Harrison, George, 46–48, 51, 54

Harstedt, Kent, 186

Harvard Law Review, 62

Hasan, Nidal, 167–70

Hassan, Aasiya, 303–4

Hayek, Friedrich, 198, 200

Hayes, Stephen, 61

hazardous professions, 109–10

health care, 47, 52–55

health-care bill, 78, 164, 173

health-care budget, 294

health-care system, 33, 65–66, 337

Heartbreak House, 209

Heinsohn, Gunnar, 315

"helicopter parents," 179

Heston, Charlton, 37, 38, 245

Hillman, Mayer, 101

Hilton, Paris, 233, 300

Himmler, Heinrich, 269

History of the English-Speaking Peoples, 191, 203

Hitler, Adolf, 257, 270, 305

Hoffer, Eric, 269

Hogarth, 62

Hollywood, 36, 39, 57, 272, 341, 343

Holocaust, 269–71, 299

homophobes, 65–68, 217, 303, 305

homosexuals, 132, 202, 263–65, 299

homosexuals, and marriage, 66, 73, 80, 106, 132, 143, 179

Hoover Dam, 33–34

Hope, Bob, 53

hope of audacity, 325–49

household debt, 96–97

housing market, 16, 47–49, 92–93, 165, 212, 218–19, 253. *See also* mortgage crisis

Houston, Sam, 247

Huff, Elizabeth, 91–92

Hughes, Elizabeth, 28

Hughes, Henrietta, 53, 68, 235

human capability, decline of, 30–31, 219–20, 285

human capital, 35, 101, 156, 204, 211–12, 219, 254, 285

Humbert, Louise, 88

Hume, Alison, 183

Huntington, Samuel, 11, 12, 18, 292

Hussein, Saddam, 140–41, 275, 302

Huxley, Aldous, 36, 137, 207

Hymowitz, Kay, 181

I

I, Rigoberta Menchu, 57

Ignatieff, Michael, 144, 146

illegal immigration, 60, 66–67, 80, 132–33, 241–49, 257–59, 284, 324

Immigrants: Your Country Needs Them, 242

Independence Day, 37, 38

Independent, The, 182
Industrial Revolution, 344
Ingrams, Richard, 271
Inouye, Daniel, 76
Invasion of the Body Snatchers, 128
inventions, 25–28, 32–33, 344
Iron Curtain, 289, 318
Islam, 18, 31–32, 36–37, 42, 72, 129–32
"Islamophobia," 32, 66, 169, 196, 286, 297–98, 303–4
It Can't Happen Here, 57
It Takes a Village, 319

J

Jackson, Jesse, 143
Jagger, Dean, 175
Jefferson, Thomas, 56, 57, 87, 193
Jerusalem besieged, 269–78
Jethá, Cacilda, 232
jobs
    federal workers, 75–76
    high-income regions, 50–51
    illegal immigrants and, 246
    loss of, 74–75, 213, 246
    low-paying jobs, 211–12
    in private sector, 75–76
    unemployment, 74–75, 213, 246
jobs bill, 23
Johnson, Barbara, 161
Johnson, Boris, 144
Johnson, Eddie Bernice, 79
Johnson, Simon, 93
Jonas, George, 203

Jones, Quincy, 29
Jones, Van, 145
Jong-Il, Kim, 336
Julius Caesar, 57
Jyllands-Posten, 296

K

Kael, Pauline, 54
Kanjorski, Paul, 62
Kaplan, Robert D., 319
Katz, Lillian, 157
Kennedy, John F., 29
Kennedy, Ted, 56, 60–61
Kerry, John, 56, 58, 61, 141, 163, 214, 338
Kerry, Teresa Heinz, 151
Keynes, John Maynard, 106, 111–12, 123
Keynesians, 106
King, Martin Luther, 56
Kitchen, John, 10
Klein, Joe, 239–40
Klein, Philip, 82
Kobayashi, Yoshinori, 308
Kodak, 47–48
Kohen, Roger, 186
Kröhnert, Steffen, 112
Krugman, Paul, 16, 119
Kurzweil, Ray, 309–10

L

labor force, 211–12
Lady Gaga, 30
Lady Liberty, 37–39, 164, 245

Lardner, Ring, 67
Last American, The, 37, 279
Lauper, Cyndi, 327
Lee, Terry, 167
Legrain, Philippe, 242
Lehman Brothers collapse, 74, 129
Lépine, Marc, 184
letter from post-American world, 279–324, 345
Levant, Ezra, 295–96
Lewis, Sinclair, 57
liberalism, 21, 57, 62, 67, 82, 121, 131, 234–35
liberty
    fall of, 38–39
    last sigh of, 189, 207–8
    price of, 15, 347–49
Life, 37
Lileks, James, 42
Lincoln, Abraham, 58, 62, 80, 86, 155
"live free or die," 347–49
Loesser, Frank, 343
Los Angeles Times, 174, 269
"lottery of life," 208–9
Louis XVI, 5
Lowi, Theodore, 82
Lyon, Jordon, 183

M
Machiavelli, Niccolò, 205
Mackey, Robert, 271
MacLennan, Hugh, 68
Macmillan, Harold, 195
Madame Cornuel, 59

Maidre, Andrus, 186
Major, John, 182
Malkin, Michelle, 221, 250
Maltese Falcon, The, 65
Man for All Seasons, A, 86
man, world after, 306–10
"managed capitalism," 23
Manliness, 176, 184
Mansfield, Harvey, 176, 179, 184–85
manufacturing jobs, 211–12
Mao, 100, 247, 333
Marchand, Yves, 219
marriage, gay, 66, 73, 80, 106, 132, 143, 179
marriage, traditional, 179
Marshall, Justice, 48, 50
Martin, Dean, 280
Martin, James, 285
marvels, 25–28
Marx, Groucho, 3
Mathis, Otis, 220, 221
Maude, General, 302
McAlpine, Dale, 201
McCain, John, 70
McCarthy, Andrew, 319
McKinley, William, 58
McMillan, Kate, 153
McNeill, J. R., 344
Meaning of the 21st Century: A Vital Blueprint for Ensuring Our Future, 285
Medes, 18–19
medical advancements, 27–28
"mediocrity of spirit," 43

Meffre, Romain, 219

Men to Boys: The Making of Modern Immaturity, 181

meritocracy, 20, 57–58, 63, 153

Merkel, Angela, 111, 192

metaphors, 61–62

Mexico, 247–54

micro-tyrannies, 90, 336–37

military budget, 5–6, 19–20

Mill, John Stuart, 97

Millin, Bill, 139

Minogue, Kenneth, 230

Mitchell, J. A., 37, 279

Mitchell, Taylor, 261

mobs, 22–23

modernity, 40, 314

Mohammed, Khalid Sheikh, 221

monopolies, 20, 46–51, 89, 337–38

Monopolies Commission, 46–47, 54

Montesquieu, 189, 207

moon landings, 28–30

More, Thomas, 86

Morrison, Herbert, 58

mortgage crisis, 47, 85, 107, 165, 168, 212, 253

motivational speech, 330–32

movies, 36, 39, 272. *See also* Hollywood

Mrs. Lovett, 88

MSNBC, 61, 128

Mubarak, Hosni, 275

multiculturalism, 139, 191–92, 298–99, 302, 322

Murdoch, William, 185

Murphy, Julie, 89

Murray, Charles, 122, 137, 230

Murtha, Marge, 88, 90

Muslim world, 18, 31–32, 72, 162, 270–75, 283, 287–88, 291–302, 307

myopia, 133–41

N

nanny state, 23, 69–70, 124, 200, 205–7, 214, 225, 258

Napoleon, 159, 247

NASA, 28–32, 101

Nasrallah, Hassan, 275

nation-states, 2, 12, 190, 286

national landmarks, 38–39

National Public Radio (NPR), 54, 66–67, 118, 133, 169

National Review, 344

nativists, 239–40, 253

NBC, 64

nepotism, 63

Netanyahu, Benjamin, 269–71, 278

"New Action Heroes, The," 59–60

New Athens, 103–25

New Britannia, 189–209

"New Deal," 53

new elites, 59, 63, 208, 318–19. *See also* elites

New England Primer, The, 328

"New Foundation," 53

"new freedoms," 38

New Jerusalem, 269–78

New Republic, 33, 252

New Rome, 25–43

New York magazine, 171

New York Times, 16–17, 54–56, 64, 66, 84, 92, 102, 109, 113, 118–19, 124, 219, 252–54, 260, 270, 283, 287, 300, 303, 313, 317

New Yorker, 54

newspaper industry, 33

Newsweek, 61, 168

"Next Morning, The," 37

Nichols, Mary Anne, 220–21

Nietzsche, Friedrich, 321–22

Nineties (1890s), 25, 35, 214–15, 217, 224

Nineties (1990s), 27–28, 73, 212, 219, 261, 273–74, 335

Nixon, Richard, 29, 54

"no man's land," 182–87

"no two sides," 132–33

North Korea, 18–19, 22–23, 195, 285, 319–20, 323, 338

nuclear weapons, 18–19, 22–23

Nussbaum, Martha, 300

O

Obama, Barack. *See also* ObamaCare; "stimulus"
   "apology tour" of, 275
   Berlin speech and, 159
   on children, 172
   college and, 56–59, 154
   debt and, 10
   on exceptionalism, 16
   friends of, 41–42

   health-care system and, 33, 65–66
   indifference of, 145–46
   no experience, 49, 344
   Oval Office and, 56–59, 197
   props and, 61–62
   on space exploration, 31–32
   speeches by, 144, 325–26, 329–30
   tax credits and, 86–87
   unemployment and, 213
   voting for, 141–43, 158–59
   weirdness of, 147–48

Obama, Michelle, 13, 61, 131, 151–55, 213

ObamaCare, 3, 55, 65–66, 77–79, 337, 339

"Obamafication of economy," 97–98

Occupational Safety and Health Administration (OSHA), 82, 336

Olbermann, Keith, 61

Omar, Mullah, 264

One-Child Policy, 19, 305

Onyango-Obbo, Charles, 316, 317

open season, 21–22

Orback, Jens, 297

orders, following, 182–87

Orwell, George, 207, 320

Ottawa Citizen, The, 69, 144

Oughts (2000s), 261, 288

P

Palin, Sarah, 57, 58, 59, 147, 161, 177, 239

Palmerston, Lord, 199

Palovak, Jewel, 262

Parasite Eve, 113

patdowns, 32, 68, 223, 263

Paterson, David A., 84

Patrick, Deval, 163

"Patriot Act," 101

Pearce, Fred, 286

Pearl, Daniel, 221

Pearson, Lester, 289

Peck, Gregory, 175

Pelosi, Nancy, 10, 65, 80

Pence, Mike, 234

Pentagon's New Map: War and Peace in the Twenty-First Century and Blueprint for Action, 318

People magazine, 177

Peretz, Martin, 252, 254

permits, 83–84, 88–92

Peter and the Wolf, 259–60

Picket, Kerry, 77

Pink Floyd, 198–99

Pinsky, Mark, 33

Pirates of the Caribbean, 202, 290

Planet of the Apes, 37

Plato, 176, 184

pleasure, culture of, 136–37

Podhoretz, John, 273

Poems Against the War, 140

Politburo, 2, 64, 71

political correctness, 166–69, 171, 240

Political Economy, 87

Polonius, 95, 96

Polytechnique, 185

population statistics, 105, 116, 237, 239–40

post-American world, 279–324

post-traumatic stress disorder (PTSD), 168–69

Postrel, Virginia, 283

Prager, Dennis, 141

Pratte, Mary, 88

Pravda, 227

"President of Europe," 120–21

price, control of, 48–49

production, 224–25

"progressives," 14–16, 34, 63, 86, 105, 141, 305. *See also* elites

property market, 16, 47–49, 92–93, 165, 212, 218–19, 253. *See also* mortgage crisis

props, 61–62

protests, 22–23, 64

Protocols of the Elders of Zion, The, 136

"public service" incentive, 156

Putin, Vladimir, 289

Q

Quann, Derek, 261

R

racism, 61–67, 151, 160, 162

racists, 64–67, 133, 202, 239–40, 245, 252–53, 292, 297

Radford, Alexandria, 152

Rahe, Paul, 230, 341

Raines, Franklin, 85

Rangel, Charlie, 77, 79–80

Ratzenberger, John, 342–44

Reagan administration, 3, 96

Reagan, Ronald, 58, 62, 74, 333

real-estate market, 16, 47–49, 92–93, 165, 212, 218–19, 253. *See also* mortgage crisis

recession, 33, 52, 117, 174, 179–80, 212–16

"red tape," 83–85

redistribution, 20, 22, 87, 332–33

Reed, Josie, 88

Reeve, Christopher, 161

Reflections on the Revolution in Europe, 242

Reid, Harry, 10

relativism, 146, 165, 254, 293

Rembrandt, 125

"Retail Sales Plummet," 97

Reuters, 50–51

Reynolds, Glenn, 147

Rice, Condi, 151

Rich, Frank, 64, 303

Richards, Jon, 254

Right Ho, Jeeves, 6

riots, 22–23, 103–4

Rizzo, Robert, 107

Road to Serfdom, The, 200

Road to Utopia, The, 53

Roberts, Andrew, 191, 192

robotics, 306–10

Robson, John, 144

Rockefeller, John D., 143

Rockwell, Norman, 328

Roesgen, Susan, 86–87

Rogers, Ginger, 41

Rogulski, Ken, 71

Roksa, Josipa, 340

Roman Empire, 12–13, 25, 34, 191

Rome, decay of, 25–43

Romney, Mitt, 339

Roosevelt, Franklin D., 33–34, 53, 192, 194

Rosling, Hans, 294

Rounsaville, Amanda, 174

Rowling, J. K., 110

Rubin, Barry, 167

Rumsfeld, Donald, 162

"Run Upon the Bankers, The," 2

Rush, Geoffrey, 290

Rushdie, Salman, 311

Russian "businessmen," 2, 280–81

Ryan, Christopher, 232

Ryan, Paul, 72–73

S

"safety net," 229–30

Safire, William, 29

Sala-i-Martin, Xavier, 283

Salutin, Rick, 143

Sanchez, Gustavo, 251

Sarkozy, Nicolas, 115, 124, 238, 275

Saudi Arabia, 5, 249–50, 272–79, 306, 312, 338

Saudi *mutaween*, 89

Saudi princes, 292, 299, 305–6

Saudi sheiks, 2, 117, 163–64, 169, 280–81

Saudi Wahhabists, 249–50, 306

Schiller, Vivian, 67

Schindler's List, 272

school budgets, 148–49. *See also* student education
Schwarzenegger, Arnold, 59, 234
scientific advancements, 25–28
Scruton, Roger, 233–34
Sebelius, Kathleen, 78, 82
Second Amendment, 23, 240
Secondat, Charles-Louis de, 189
Securities and Exchange Commission (SEC), 9, 85
sedentary lifestyles, 224–25
segregation, 151, 239, 241, 294, 305
sensory distraction, 36–37
September 11, 39–43, 163–64, 169, 193, 221, 270, 296
serfdom, 45–102, 104, 200
Sestius, Publius, 211
Seventies (1970s), 30–31, 82, 93, 118, 219, 222, 300
Sex at Dawn: The Prehistoric Origins of Modern Sexuality, 232
sexists, 65–67
sexual-harassment training, 68
sexual identity, 230–32
sexual license, 232, 304–5, 322
Sexual Revolution, 233–34
shadowlands, 254–59
Shafia family, 303–4
Shahzad, Faisal, 164–65
Shaidle, Kathy, 186
Shakespeare, William, 56–57
Sharpton, Al, 143
Shaw, Bernard, 209
Shepard, Matthew, 303–4

Shore, Dinah, 101
Shousha, Abdel Fadil, 271–72
Sinatra, Frank, 29, 30
single parents, 214, 228, 234
Singularity, 309–10, 319
Sixties (1960s), 28–29, 64, 118, 137, 171, 174, 249, 300, 332, 342–43
Size of Nations, The, 237
Skinner, B. F., 255
skyscrapers, 39–43
small business, 90–93, 156, 224, 244
small government, 8–9, 52, 90–91, 243, 335, 346–48
Smith, Adam, 11, 12, 97
Sobran, Joseph, 240
social engineering, 21–22, 81, 86, 340, 348–49
social media, 36–37, 46
social spending, 17–20
Soft Despotism, Democracy's Drift, 230
solitudes, 68–69
Sondheim, Stephen, 64
Sotormayor, Sonia, 153
South China Morning Post, 101
space exploration, 28–32
Spaceballs, 4
Spendballs, 4
spirit, can-do, 31, 40, 108, 328
spirit, mediocrity of, 43
Spolaore, Enrico, 237–38
Squalls, T., 173
Stalin, Joseph, 257
Stark, General, 347
Stark, Pete, 77

statism, 28, 52–68, 71–75, 90, 232–44, 255–59, 326, 336–38, 347
Statue of Liberty, 37–39, 164, 245
Stein, Herbert, 3
Steinem, Gloria, 181, 184
Sternbergh, Adam, 174
Stewart, Alexis, 177–78
Stewart, Jon, 147
Stewart, Martha, 177–79
Steyn, Mark, 143, 149
"stimulus," 3, 23, 74–75, 96, 98, 213, 334
Stockhausen, Karlheinz, 39, 41
Streisand, Barbra, 1, 56–57
Strouse, Charles, 1
student education, 148–57, 198–99
student loans, 47, 156
stupidity of broke, 1–23
success stories, 28–33
Sullivan, Andrew, 161–62
Summers, Christina Hoff, 179
Summers, Lawrence, 194
"sustainable" consumerism, 35
Suzuki, David, 101
Swift, Jonathan, 2, 95, 124

T

Taleb, Nassim, 95
Taliban, 36, 195, 198, 314
"talkies," 36. See also movies
"tax credit," 72, 86–87
"tax cuts," 8, 72–73, 83
taxes, raising, 108–9, 114–15
Taylor, Zachary, 58

Tea Parties, 64, 86–87, 239
"teabaggers," 239
technocracy, 53–55, 67–68
technology, 25–28, 51
Tennyson, Lord, 270
terror, war on, 76, 102, 138
terrorist attacks, 39–43, 164–65, 169–70, 194, 221, 270, 272, 296
Thatcher, Margaret, 51, 335
Thirties (1930s), 41, 96
"thumos," 176, 184
Time Machine, The, 127
Time magazine, 59, 220, 239
Times, 85, 103, 114
tinkering, 344
Titanic, 185–86
Tocqueville, Alexis de, 37, 45–46, 89, 235, 328, 334
Todd, Sweeney, 88
Tomasky, Michael, 63, 64
totalitarianism, 101–2, 207
town hall meetings, 53, 64, 68, 172
Toynbee, Arnold, 190
traditional family, 177–78, 234
traditional marriage, 179
transnationalism, 17, 121, 283, 287, 289, 306
Transportation Security Administration (TSA), 33, 68, 223, 258
Treadwell, Timothy, 261–63, 266
Treasury bonds, 9–10
"trinity of evil," 32
Trudeau, Pierre, 203
Truman, Harry S., 58, 345

Tucson shootings, 57, 62
Twain, Mark, 116, 220
Twelve O-Clock High, 175
Twenties (1920s), 27–28, 137
twentieth century, 27, 33–35, 104–6, 130, 186–90, 195, 217–19, 235, 283–86, 302, 313–22
twenty-first century, 15–17, 27–30, 128–30, 183, 191, 214–15, 287–99, 301–24
"two Americas," 68–69
Two Solitudes, 68–69
Tyler, Royall, 103
tyranny, 87–92, 284, 336–37

U
U. S. Constitution, 63, 73, 77–78, 80, 192, 290
undreaming America, 45–102
unemployment, 74–75, 213, 246. *See also* jobs
unionization, 120–21, 156
United Nations (UN), 12, 105, 146–47, 270–73, 277, 282–83, 289
United States, hope for, 22–23, 279–324. *See also* America
United States vs. Columbia Steel Co., 47–48
universities, 35, 56, 58, 148–57, 180
Urban II, Pope, 314
USS *Cole*, 221
ut-Tahrir, Hizb, 286
utopianism, 233–34, 341

V
Van Buren, Martin, 58
van den Boogaard, Oscar, 187
van Gogh, Theo, 297
van Rompuy, Herman, 120
Ventura County Star, 90
Veremi, Vasia, 109
Villeneuve, Denis, 185
virtual reality, 33, 36

W
Walker, Judge, 80, 179
Wall Street Journal, 48, 88
Walton, William, 125
war on children, 346
war on terror, 76, 102, 138
War Room, The, 62
Warren, David, 69
Washington Post, 55, 64, 165, 173
Washington Times, 77
Waters, Maxine, 63
Waziristan, 38–39, 43, 257, 259, 274, 303
Webb, Jimmy, 29
Week in December, A, 94
Weekly Standard, 61
welfare state, 104–5, 130–31, 204, 223–24, 229–30, 319
Wells, H. G., 25, 100, 127–28, 131–37, 175, 182–83, 187, 213, 217, 266, 316
western elites, 59, 101, 143, 287, 293. *See also* elites
western world, 2, 15, 19, 38, 52, 66, 105, 110

What's the Matter with Kansas?, 86

"White City," 40, 41

Whitelaw, Willie, 51

Who Are We?, 11

Wilberforce, William, 198

Wilders, Geert, 196

wildlife, 260–63

Will, George, 181

Williams, Juan, 67

Wodehouse, P. G., 6

Wolf, Martin, 98, 117

Wolfe, Tom, 123

Wolffe, Richard, 128

Wood, May, 249

Woodstock, 342–43

Woodward, Bob, 145

world after America, 279–324

world after man, 306–10

World Distribution of Income, The, 283

World Trade Center, 39–43, 221

Wren, Christopher, 43

Wright, Jeremiah, 42, 145

Wright, Orville, 27, 33

Wright, Wilbur, 27, 33

"writing on the wall," 2, 7, 14, 18, 124–25

X

xenophobe, 66, 239

Y

Young, Coleman, 222

Young Immigrunts, The, 67

Young, Michael, 57–58, 63

Yufzai, Mushtaq, 36